The
ENCLOSURE
of
OCEAN RESOURCES

The ENCLOSURE of OCEAN RESOURCES

Economics and the Law of the Sea

ROSS D. ECKERT

HOOVER INSTITUTION PRESS
Stanford University, Stanford, California

Acknowledgment is hereby gratefully made to the following sources for permission to use material from various publications, as cited fully on the specific pages in the text: *American Economic Review* (American Economic Association); American Petroleum Institute; *Engineering and Mining Journal* (© McGraw-Hill, Inc.); Environment Canada, Fisheries and Marine, Pacific Region; Geological Society of America; *Journal of Economic History* (Economic History Association); *Journal of Law and Economics*; *Journal of Maritime Law and Commerce*; *Journal of Navigation* (Royal Institute of Navigation); Law of the Sea Institute, Kingston, R.I.; National Academy of Sciences; National Petroleum Council; National Science Foundation; *Ocean Industry*; *Oceanus*; *Offshore*; *Oil and Gas Journal*; *San Diego Law Review*; *Scientific American*; Sun Shipbuilding and Dry Dock Company; University of Wisconsin Press (© by the Board of Regents of the University of Wisconsin System); Woods Hole Oceanographic Institution.

Hoover Institution Publication 210

This is dedicated to my Dad. He too wanted this book.

CHESTER HAROLD ECKERT
1911−1978

Contents

Illustrations

Tables

Acknowledgments

This book began with a year's leave of absence at the Hoover Institution at Stanford, but did not end until well after I had returned to the University of Southern California. For their keen interest and support during this period, and for their patience, I must thank Dr. W. Glenn Campbell, director of the Hoover Institution, and Professor Thomas Gale Moore, director of its Domestic Studies Program.

I have tried to keep a list of all those who assisted, and will give credit here at the risk of missing a name or two. In the United States government, James L. Johnston and Gregory C. Christopoulos at the Treasury Department were very helpful in providing me with copies of United Nations publications on the Law of the Sea Conference and of the reports of the U.S. delegation to UNCLOS. In the U.S. Senate, D. Michael Harvey of the Committee on Energy and Natural Resources kept me abreast of happenings in the U.S. legislative process. Much of the book would have been impossible without the public record on U.S. participation in UNCLOS which was compiled by the late Senator Lee Metcalf (D.-Mont.) and his administrative assistant, the late Britt Englund. At the U.S. Department of State, Dr. Robert D. Hodgson, Office of the Geographer, supplied me with a set of useful maps.

At universities, I must thank Professor Robert L. Friedheim of the Institute for Marine and Coastal Studies of the University of Southern California for giving me access to his clipping file on the law of the sea, some of his unpublished work on voting procedures at the United Nations Conference on the Law of the Sea, and a number of UN documents from his own collection. At U.S.C.'s libraries Mrs. Fannie L. Fishlyn at the Law Center and Mr. Lynn Sipe at the VonKlein-Smid Center for Public Affairs were most helpful on many occasions. Professor Ann L. Hollick of the School of Advanced International Studies of The Johns Hopkins University (Washington, D.C.) allowed me to review the collection of UN documents on file at the SAIS Ocean Policy Project. Dr. J. Paul Dauphin of the Graduate School of Oceanography at the University of Rhode Island supplied the original graphic materials from several documents published by the National Science Foundation. Dr. Michael Canes of the American Petroleum Institute provided the data for several tables. Robert Burke of *Offshore* kindly allowed me the use of a number of illustrations. (I should add that, for the most part, the study reflects data that were available, or events that had occurred, by June 1978.)

I was first introduced to the topic of the law of the sea in 1973 by R. David Ranson and the late Stephen Enke. Since then I have benefited from the comments and criticisms of many. In particular, I am indebted to Kenneth W. Clarkson, Robert L. Friedheim, George W. Hilton, Michael E. Levine, and James L. Johnston for reviewing the entire manuscript and some parts of it more than once. Those who read individual chapters or made helpful comments were Yoram Barzel, R. H. Coase, Harold Demsetz, Jack Hirshleifer, Donald L. Martin, Charles J. Meyers, Donald J. O'Hara, Guilio Pontecorvo, and Leigh Tesfatsion. Only with great reluctance do I absolve all the foregoing persons from any responsibility for errors that may remain. I thank Carol Albrigo for redrawing several of the illustrations, and Patricia Caldwell for the cartography. My research assistants were Diane Richey and Stephen Scharf. The overworked but still cheerful typists were Susan Anderson, Paula Browne, Ida Abe, and Vivian Smith. Although the great preponderance of the financial support I received came from the Hoover Institution at Stanford, I must also thank the University of Southern California for making additional typing and research-assistant services available to me, for help in preparing the final manuscript, and for granting a full year's leave of absence in 1974–75 and a sabbatical in Spring 1977.

The last thanks are personal: to my parents who helped in at least a thousand ways on this effort just as they have on all the others; and to Enid, who has carried the burden of "the book" throughout our marriage—occasionally with her own labor and always with loyalty and patience and understanding.

University of Southern California   Ross D. Eckert

PART ONE
The Economic Problems

CHAPTER 1

The Changing Economics of Ocean Uses

In the era between the Tudors and Harry Truman, the principle of freedom of the high seas generally governed the access of states and their nationals to use of most of the world's oceans. This principle, established by the major maritime powers and reflecting mainly their interests, allowed states equal and unfettered access rights during peacetime to all seas save a narrow band adjacent to coastlines. The breadth of this band, called the territorial sea, was set in the eighteenth century at three miles and was apparently based on the range of a shore battery. A state could control navigation within its territorial sea, although these controls were by general acceptance somewhat weaker than the restrictions placed on use in such internal waters as lakes, rivers, harbors, and some bays. High seas freedoms often were modified by bilateral agreements concerning the use of certain fisheries and occasionally by limitations on navigation. But the general rule was that states, their navies, and their nationals could freely travel, extract, and keep the ocean resources that they found as long as they did not occupy or claim permanent and sovereign rights to any part of either the ocean floor beyond the territorial sea or the water column lying above it.[1]

The erosion of this historic principle, which survived nearly intact for almost 400 years, began in 1945 with a United States presidential proclamation.[2] President Truman asserted that the United States had exclusive rights to exploit the mineral and hydrocarbon resources lying on or under its continental shelf, the submerged land mass that extended seaward from the U.S. coastline. Truman carefully avoided making new claims of sovereignty: he did not extend the U.S. territorial sea beyond its three-mile limit and did not challenge the high seas rights of other nations freely to navigate in the waters superjacent to the U.S. shelf. Virtually no opposition was registered against this proclamation, perhaps because the U.S. then led in the development of recovery technologies and would in any event probably have been the first nation to exploit these resources.

The erosion accelerated rapidly after 1945. More coastal nations followed Truman's suit by enclosing the resources of their adjacent continental shelf areas. Others extended also the limits of sovereign internal waters and of territorial seas, usually from three to twelve nautical miles, and therefore pushed further seaward the limits from which their continental shelf claims (or even broader claims) would be measured. Some claimed rights to the fish swimming above the shelf as well as to the minerals on or under it. Initially a few and later many countries claimed resource rights according to distance from shore, usually 200 miles, without regard to the geographical extent of the submerged land mass. Eventually some nations made claims on the basis of submerged land masses beyond the recognized continental shelf even where they extended beyond 200 miles. Some claims were stated vaguely when this served national economic purposes, as did Truman's claim, but other nations made unmistakable claims to specific ocean areas when this would advance different interests. Within thirty years of Truman's proclamation, authority over coastal areas—the most valuable one-third of all ocean space—had been converted from a regime of largely open access and high seas freedoms to one with significant national controls over resource uses.

The steady procession of enclosures in the late 1940s and early-to-mid-1950s produced concerns among a variety of countries. Nations that were landlocked or that lacked significant coastal areas initially feared that the process of enclosure would twist the distribution of world oceanic wealth against their interests and would exacerbate ocean rivalries among the major powers. Many maritime nations favored internationally imposed limits on enclosure to maintain unrestricted transit rights for their naval and commercial fleets, especially in international straits. These nations were instrumental in convening the first United Nations Conference on the Law of the Sea (UNCLOS) in 1958, but the resulting agreements were ineffectual in halting enclosures. A second UNCLOS, convened in 1960, met a similar fate, and a third UNCLOS, begun in 1973, has had even less success than the first two. After six years of preparatory work and another five years of annual meetings, this UNCLOS, at least to this writing, has moved at almost a snail's pace toward agreement on a draft treaty text.

Ironically, these conferences may have accelerated enclosures more than halted them. The prospect of a universal limitation on national ocean jurisdiction appears to have given individual countries strong incentives to make broader enclosures in advance of the international meetings just as if they were establishing "squatters' rights" on land. Moreover, nations benefiting from territorial extensions have banded together and insisted upon treaty articles that anoint rather than reverse preexisting national claims. Controversies between blocks of countries with different interests in the limits of enclosure usually have been resolved in favor of those seeking more rather than less.

My purpose is to analyze the consequences of the conversion from high seas or communal ownership of ocean resources to a regime of somewhat more exclusive rights, and to show that this conversion has been an economic response to fundamental changes in world population growth, demands for goods and services from the sea, and the technologies for extracting these goods and services. In this sense there are interesting parallels between "the enclosure movement of the oceans" that has occurred since 1945 and the process of fencing off land and allied resources that has occurred numerous times in history.[3] In most of these cases, resource rights have been converted to more exclusive forms—titles held by individuals in the case of land and rights to control resource uses (but usually not to own territory) which are held mainly by coastal states for resources at sea. In addition, I propose to show that the theory of the conversion process for land resources which has been developed by economists is equally applicable to enclosures of ocean resources. Economic analysis suggests that the property arrangements associated with enclosure by coastal nations would reduce the likelihood that ocean resources would be exploited wastefully. Therefore, enclosures, according to economic criteria, will usually be superior either to the preexisting regime based entirely on high seas freedoms or to the international controls for certain resources which may evolve from the treaty negotiations that have been under way since 1974 at UNCLOS.

1. NEW DEMANDS AND TECHNOLOGIES

Traditionally, mankind has extracted wealth and services from the oceans in several forms: (1) sources of food from animals, plants, and fish; (2) means of transportation and communication by shipping and cables for both commerce and security; (3) an area for implanting fixed navigational installations such as lighthouses and piers; (4) places for recreation; (5) an ultimate "sink" for waste materials; (6) a field for scientific research on the planet's basic physical and biological processes; and (7) a battlefield.

Man's perceptions and uses of the oceans began to change drastically in both their nature and their extent after the close of World War II. Increased world population led to greater demand for foods, energy, minerals and other materials, and information. The rate at which mankind learned about the oceans and how to extract wealth from them surged as a result of wartime technological developments. Fresh scientific information revealed the extent of ocean resource supplies, and the higher extraction costs of land-based substitutes made harvesting of marine resources appear even more attractive. The result was to increase the demand for oceans goods and services in both traditional uses and in entirely new categories of use. The several following examples illustrate the point.[4]

The rising volume of international trade caused shipping to rise, and containerization has lowered transport costs by reducing turnaround times. Weather satellites have helped to modify the routings of some ships and to reduce their losses caused by wrecks and breakage. Such recent innovations as inertial guidance systems, shipboard computers, and navigation satellites will enable ships increasingly to pinpoint their locations in mid-ocean and to sail more safely in confined waters, even while carrying dangerous cargoes.

Increased energy demands led to intensified exploration on both land and sea. New drilling technologies enabled exploration wells to be set in deeper water either from floating platforms or from ships that held their positions without the aid of anchors. The world's total offshore hydrocarbon resources are evidently on a par with the known reserves of Saudi Arabia, and by 1976 offshore production amounted to almost 20 percent of the world production of hydrocarbons. Creating supertankers and the port facilities to handle them lowered the cost of moving oil, often halfway around the globe.

Greater demands for food have led to a surge in fishing. Technology has provided ships of greater range to reach the preferred species, sonars to locate particular schools, seine nets and better trawling methods to catch a greater percentage of the school, and quick freezing to store and preserve the larger catch. Harvesting has increased so fast that some species are now overfished. Competition between nations for access to prime fisheries has become commonplace and has occasionally led to diplomatic friction.

Greater and greater amounts of wastes and obsolete materials have been deliberately cast into the seas, and other forms of pollution have been drawn there by the natural action of weather and rivers. Rates of pollution appear to be rising fastest in populated coastal areas where the oceans also provide multiple recreational and sporting uses.

In deep sea areas, the demand of navies for use of the water column has increased owing to the advantages—in terms of both mobility and concealment—of submarine-based strategic systems. The development of technologies designed to locate submersibles and other objects, to map the bottom terrain, to withstand the pressures of enormous depths, and to resist corrosion have all had important incidental (spillover) benefits for the civilian sector. These advances have included such devices as sonars, hydrophones, and underwater television, and stronger new materials made of alloys, plastics, and glass.

The extraction of hard minerals is one of the most attractive of the class of potential uses. In coastal areas, scientists have found deposits of bromine, coal, magnesium, phosphorite, sulfur, and tin. Copper, gold, lead, silver, and zinc have been located in the hot brines beneath the Red Sea. Sand and gravel, oyster shells for lime, clays and oozes for the manufacture of cement, diatomaceous earth, silica, and other construction materials have been found at shallow depths where they can be dredged at relatively low cost. The deep seabeds contain the largest deposit of minerals on the planet. Vast areas of the ocean floor are littered with rocklike nodules that are rich in cobalt, copper, manganese, and nickel plus trace elements of silver, zinc, and a dozen other metals. Falling assays and higher production costs of land-based ores are making ocean supplies of minerals more economical to extract, and the technologies to accomplish the job are under development.

Certain engineering innovations remain uneconomic. Airports and storage facilities are still less expensive to build on land than on water. Salmon, oysters, clams, and scallops can be cultivated on land with piped-in seawater, but ocean supplies remain cheaper in spite of overfishing some species and the susceptibility of others to pollution. Electric power plants have been constructed at several locations to take advantage of powerful currents and tides, but plans to use the oceans as a source of solar heat or as a site for nuclear or thermal power are still being worked on. Although the oceans continue to offer a relatively cheap source of salt, there are less expensive ways of finding fresh water than by desalinizing, tapping subsea aquifers, or towing icebergs, at least for the present.

For several centuries, the bounty of the oceans was so vast that it was believed to be limitless. But this was only because the demand for ocean uses was small relative to supply. The availability of ocean space for navigation or fishing was so vast in proportion to these demands that it was essentially a free good: individuals were rarely willing to pay for the rights to use a particular ocean area since equivalent areas were commonly available at zero price. Even in valuable fisheries or narrow straits, congestion costs were generally trivial, making it unnecessary to ration access by means other than queuing—first come, first served. Where fisheries were extraordinarily valuable, rationing usually took place by nations reaching bilateral agreements to divide the resource. But most ocean values were relatively small and enforcement costs were high, so the expansion of jurisdiction by coastal states was unattractive.[5]

As time passed, however, it became clear that scarcity—the general economic fact of life—applies even to the oceans. As with land, resources cannot be extracted from the ocean without a cost that varies with location; the greater the extraction cost, the greater the scarcity of the resource in question. With the greater variety of ocean uses and the rising number of users within both traditional and new categories of use, certain ocean areas became increasingly areas of scarcity. At the nub of the problem is choosing to which use or uses these areas should be put.

2. PROBLEMS OF COMMUNAL OWNERSHIP

Rising demands relative to supplies occur often in society and usually present no special economic problems. As long as the right of access to available supplies is owned or controlled by some entity, the scarcer supplies can be allocated among demanders according to either prices or administrative criteria depending upon society's preferences between market-oriented versus centralized rationing processes. In the case of the oceans, however, the property rights that serve as a necessary precondition for rationing by either process have rarely been established on a large scale.

Historically, the oceans have been organized according to two basic principles: first, they should be used to generate wealth; second, access for this purpose should be essentially free beyond narrow territorial seas. Now we find that in this era of rising demands, changing technologies, and the introduction of new ocean uses and users which are sometimes wholly incompatible with other new uses or traditional uses, these two principles have become contradictory. For example, offshore drilling can limit the effective "freedom" of navigation. Using oceans as a sink often harms ground fisheries or recreation. Maintaining beaches as recreation spots may preclude offshore oil exploration and raise petroleum prices, and may additionally require that supertankers be diverted from coastal areas to avoid groundings and spills. Unless new institutions can generate new principles that are appropriate to the changed economic and technological conditions, unrestricted competition among these conflicting uses will limit the new wealth that the oceans are capable of producing.

Up to now, most ocean space has been "owned" either communally or not at all. Individual persons or nations have usually had no responsibility to make sure that the value of ocean resources is maintained rather than depleted, that the seas are kept clean rather than polluted, or that areas of particular scarcity are allocated to society's highest valued purpose. As a result, the oceans, much like communal resources and facilities on land, tend to be inefficiently dirty and overcongested. Buildings, roads, water, land, and other natural resources that are owned privately tend to be better maintained than public facilities of the same sort simply because a single owner can capture the resulting increase in value. Although the value of public facilities and resources rarely goes absolutely to zero as long as fines and rules are established for their misuse and are enforced regularly, enforcement by police and other territorial authorities is often so expensive that there are still sharp differences between the ways in which public and private facilities are used. Such differences would vanish if the right of access to the private facilities became free of charge and therefore was rationed in the same manner as with public facilities.

Oceans, being communally owned, are especially vulnerable to despoliation since particular uses and users can create inefficient side effects which can alter the physical characteristics of the sea and thus the values of resources that are used by others, though not at all entering into the concerns of the first user. Since these positive (beneficial) or negative (costly) impacts are external to the decision maker, they are assigned a low weight as he contemplates alternative resource uses. For example, owners of oil tankers who insist upon unrestricted navigation in confined areas may not take into account the opportunity cost of requiring offshore oil drilling rigs to locate on less productive sites. The opportunity costs of creating unobstructed shipping lanes will be even larger if oil leaks from groundings or tank washings diminish the values of local wildlife or recreational beaches. Unless ship owners are given incentives to internalize spillovers and take them into account in their overall considerations, the value of resources devoted to oil shipping will be inefficiently large and the output of oil will be greater than it would be if all the costs of tanker voyages were recognized by the parties involved; furthermore, the ocean space available for recreational and fishing activities will be too small, and the prices of such activities will be too high.

Other ocean uses produce spillovers that are beneficial. Salmon and other anadromous species are born in fresh water rivers, migrate through the world oceans, and eventually return to their home streams to spawn. The productivity of these fisheries will be increased if the home country invests in "fish ladders" to facilitate upstream migration or in pollution controls around breeding grounds. But the incentives for these actions are weak since many of the resulting benefits accrue to countries that catch salmon on the high seas. As a rule, the costs of high seas enforcement by the home country exceed the extra value of its catch that more husbandry yields. Unless more of the spillover benefits are internalized to (captured by) the home country—such as by other nations sharing in the investment costs of the ladders—the stock of anadromous species and the value of catches will be inefficiently small. There will be too few resources in salmon production relative to other activities, and fish prices will therefore be higher than otherwise.

When spillovers are large in comparison with the gains and costs of resource use that fall exclusively on the decision maker, he may favor options that provide higher returns for him and ignore options that provide greater returns for society at large. Thus, when the exclusivity of resource rights is relatively weak, the cost to the resource user of avoiding economically wasteful activities is lower. A first step toward making resource rights more exclusive is to replace communal patterns of ownership with express rights to control, regulate, or exchange that are vested in particular persons, firms, or other entities. In the case of the oceans, the right to determine resource outcomes has itself risen in value, and queuing, the process of rationing that is employed in communal situations, has been replaced in large measure by the fiat of coastal nations. The process of enclosure not only gives to coastal states a larger share of rising ocean use values but also creates new opportunities for avoiding inefficiencies. This suggests that economic forces will figure prominently in explaining the dramatic change in the structure of ocean institutions that has occurred so rapidly yet peacefully since 1945.

3. A THEORY OF EMERGING PROPERTY ARRANGEMENTS

Economists have recognized that ownership structures tend to change when the value of better defined property rights exceeds the cost of bringing them about. Harold Demsetz has argued that the main reason for conversion from communal ownership of resources to increasingly private property rights is the incentive to achieve a greater internalization of spillovers.[6] Property rights tend to remain static when the cost of removing certain inefficiencies exceeds the potential economic gains. As changes in market prices and technologies lower these costs, it becomes more rewarding to the community to eliminate or reduce the efficiency losses that stem from less exclusive structures of ownership.

Demsetz states his theory, and an important qualification to it, in the following way:

> . . . property rights develop to internalize externalities when the gains of internalization become larger than the cost of internalization. Increased internalization, in the main, results from changes in economic values, changes which stem from the development of new technology and the opening of new markets, changes to which old property rights are poorly attuned. A proper interpretation of this assertion requires that account be taken of a community's preferences for private ownership. Some communities will have less well-developed private ownership systems and more highly developed state ownership systems. But, given a community's tastes in this regard, the emergence of new private or state-owned property rights will be in response to changes in technology and relative prices.
>
> I do not mean to assert or to deny that the adjustments in property rights which take place need be the result of a conscious endeavor to cope with new externality problems. These adjustments have arisen in Western societies largely as a result of gradual changes in social mores and in common law precedents. At each step of this adjustment process, it is unlikely that externalities per se were consciously related to the issue being resolved. These legal and moral experiments may be hit-and-miss procedures to some extent but in a society that weights the achievement of efficiency heavily, their viability in the long run will depend on how well they modify behavior to accommodate to the externalities associated with important changes in technology or market values.[7]

Demsetz supported his theory with the widely known anthropological studies of the development of hunting territories among North American Indians following the introduction of the fur trade in the seventeenth century. Before the fur trade was established, Indians hunted game chiefly to obtain food and clothing. Property rights in particular kinds of game could be established only by capture since the rights to hunt this migratory resource were communally owned. There being thus few incentives for husbandry—as in the underinvestment and overfishing of anadromous species mentioned earlier—the stock of living fur animals declined excessively. But because furs were used for strictly family purposes, "these external effects were of such small significance that it did not pay for anyone to take them into account."[8] The advent of the fur trade changed the situation dramatically: "First, the value of furs to the Indians was increased considerably. Second, and as a result, the scale of hunting activity rose sharply. Both consequences must have increased considerably the importance of the externalities associated with free hunting. The property right system began to change, and it changed specifically in the direction required to take account of the economic effects made important by the fur trade."[9] Quasi-territorial arrangements were established either by seasonal quotas or by marking trees with symbols to identify certain areas with particular tribes or individuals. Over a period of about fifty years, the relatively private rights internalized enough of the spillovers of the previous structure of communal rights to turn fur animal husbandry into an economic activity. Demsetz also tested the theory by comparing the behavior of the Northwestern Indians with that of the Southwestern Plains Indians who did not establish property arrangements. The Plains animals wandered over such a large land area that the cost of creating and enforcing territories would have been relatively high. Moreover, a trade did not develop in either their skins or other products. As Demsetz says of the Plains animals, the externality continued to exist but it "was just not worth taking into account."[10]

In a later paper Demsetz and Armen A. Alchian stressed the inherent instability of communal rights structures:

> Under a communal right system each person has the *private* right to the use of a resource once it is captured or taken, but only a communal right to the same resource before it is taken. This incongruity between ownership opportunities prompts men to convert their rights into the most valuable form; they will convert the resources owned under communal arrangements into resources owned privately, that is, they will hunt in order to establish private rights over the animals. The problem can be resolved either by converting the communal right to a private right, in which case there will be no overriding need to hunt the animals in order to establish a private claim, or the incentive to convert communal rights to private rights can be restrained through regulation.
>
> There is a basic instability in an arrangement which provides for communal rights over a resource when that resource takes one form and private rights when it takes another form. The private right form will displace the communal right form. . . .
>
> The instability inherent in a communal right system will become especially acute when changes in technology or demands make the resource which is owned communally more valuable than it has been. Such changes are likely to bring with them harmful and beneficial effects which can be measured and taken account of

only by incurring large transaction costs under the existing property rights structure. In such situations, we expect to observe modifications in the structure of
rights which allow persons to respond more fully and appropriately to these new
costs and benefits.[11]

The wastes generated by communal rights structures can be reduced by
converting to either an increasingly private structure of property rights or an
increasingly centralized structure which regulates the share of the resources that
each member of the community can appropriate. Whichever variant survives, the
process of converting from one structure to the other occurs quickly as soon as
technologies and economics begin a rapid alteration, simply because a failure to
abandon the communal rights structure will result in the destruction of the
resources in question. Thus, Demsetz's theory also helps to explain the speed at
which the rearrangement of rights to fur animals took place among the Indians.
This conversion required only fifty years or so, a relatively short time in spite of
the large geographical areas and high costs of communicating that were involved.
    Demsetz believed that "a rigorous test" of his theory would require
"extensive and detailed empirical work" to illustrate the manner in which
privatization occurred in several different eras for different resources.[12] Three
examples of changes in land rights and a fourth involving radio frequencies
illustrate the richness and possibly the wide applicability of this theory.
    The conversion of English agriculture from a system of communal open-field
cultivation to separate compact estates took place gradually over several
centuries.[13] In the manorial village of the Middle Ages, land was divided into a
multitude of strips, each about the size that a peasant could till in one day, and
each peasant's strips were, for a variety of reasons, scattered piecemeal over
different parts of the manor instead of being all in one convenient block. Use was
private during the growing season, but after harvests the strips were consolidated
into fields for common grazing by all villagers. This system contained a host of
inefficiencies. Time was wasted in getting to and from the strips; land was wasted
because there had to be access to the strips and because individual peasants often
left a furrow untilled as a marker; the presence of weeds in a poorly farmed strip
could affect the crop of a neighbor. Cross-plowing, systematic crop rotation, and
careful drainage were infrequent since they required the consent of so many field
participants. The commons was overgrazed for the same reason that game was
overhunted in Demsetz's example. Livestock were underfed and susceptible to
disease and theft, and there was too little fertilizer to increase crop yields. As
these external effects mounted, there were more incentives to consolidate fields
and to enclose uncultivated lands by surveying, fencing, and hedging. Enclosure
had its costs, but these were smaller than the communal inefficiencies. Enclosure
advanced gradually until technologies and market conditions began to change
rapidly and in reinforcing ways. An agricultural "revolution" occurred in the

seventeenth and eighteenth centuries. This involved better crop rotation, the widespread use of root crops (which no open-field farmer would introduce out of a fear that the clover or turnips would be eaten by his neighbor's sheep), and marked improvements in animal husbandry. With population growth, urbanization, better roads and improved forms of transport, and rising trade and prices, the demand for grains, wool, and other animal products increased. More specialized use of land was impossible without privatization, and accordingly English public policy encouraged enclosure through numerous acts of Parliament after 1700. In the ensuing century and a half, nearly one-fifth of the country was enclosed.

The process of conversion to private property rights in range land on most of the Great Plains in the United States was even more rapid than the process in England. During the 1860s most range lands were communally owned in spite of rising populations owing to the lack of such fencing materials as rocks and trees, or water in sufficient supply to grow hedgerows. But the introduction of barbed wire in the 1870s lowered the cost of establishing boundaries between particular cattle ranches as well as between cattle ranches and farms. The gains from purchasing land rose sharply, and by the 1890s a realignment of relatively exclusive and transferable property rights had occurred.[14]

The transition from communal to exclusive mining rights during the California Gold Rush also fits Demsetz's model. Communal rights to mine in 500 or so large districts varying in size between 4,000 to 8,000 people each were economical before 1849. The dominant technology was to pan gold by hand, and districts of this size made it possible for individual miners to take advantage of scale economies in food, shelter, and medical care. After new technologies were introduced, it became more efficient for miners to work in small groups, of no more than eight. The sharp influx of population during 1849 caused streams that had formerly been worked by a half-dozen miners to have thousands. Thus by the end of 1849, all the mining districts had been replaced by a system of exclusive rights for individual miners, usually of fifteen feet along a river bank or a thirty-foot square in a ravine. Within the space of one year, all communal arrangements had disappeared. The new exclusive mining rights were so successful that the federal mining law of 1866 was patterned after them.[15]

The fourth example of the instability of communal structures of ownership involves the development of radio in the United States during the 1920s.[16] The invention of wireless communication had broad application to shipping and prompted the creation of entirely new industries such as commercial broadcasting. But the incentives of almost all broadcasters to use frequencies at the lower end of the electromagnetic spectrum produced so much interference that few messages could be received intelligibly. As in the case of other communal rights structures, there were strong incentives for public policy to realign rights into more valuable configurations. Unlike the previous examples, however, greater exclusivity was established by converting from communal rights to centralized regulations—the second of the two conversion processes that were described by Alchian and Demsetz. This was accomplished by the creation in 1927 of the Federal Radio Commission, succeeded in 1934 by the Federal Communications Commission, both of which were empowered to grant licenses that amounted to exclusive but largely nontransferable rights to use given frequencies at certain times of the day and in certain locations. This highly centralized system of regulation constituted a more valuable alignment of rights than the communal system that had preceded it, but it is doubtful that it would be superior now to a decentralized market-oriented system based on private and exchangeable rights.[17]

4. APPLICATION TO THE OCEANS

The realignment of resource rights in the oceans from more communal to more exclusive forms between 1945 and 1978 appears to fit the main elements of Demsetz's theory.[18] In the remaining chapters of Part One, I shall describe some of the characteristics of several ocean resources and present evidence suggesting that demands began to change more rapidly following the end of World War II. This process probably changed the values of the goods and services that the seas can produce—shipping transport, petroleum, food, environmental quality and recreational services, new data from scientific research, and hard minerals from the deep seabeds. These changes, in turn, appear to have presented new market opportunities to which "the old property rights [based strictly on freedom of the seas] are poorly attuned."[19]

At the same time, the cost to coastal nations of enforcing claims to broader ocean areas fell sharply owing to changes in military and civilian technologies. The speed and range of aircraft and naval vessels rose. Radar, transponders, and other navigational aids were introduced. In addition, there was a large surplus of unused military equipment left from the war. Eventually, the use of satellites for surveillance purposes would drastically reduce the cost of monitoring ship movements and other activities over extensive areas. Remote-sensing satellites can now be used not only for natural phenomena, such as water temperatures (day and night), seismic faults, weather, and resource deposits, but also for oil spills from ships and other installations. Although satellites, unlike barbed wire, were introduced for reasons other than internalizing spillovers and reducing inefficiencies, they have had a clear and useful application in this area. Whether the changes in demands on the oceans caused an acceleration in the rate at which ocean technologies changed or whether the chain of causation was the other way around is a "chicken-egg" problem beyond the range of this study. It is sufficient for my purposes to note that changes in technologies that occurred were complementary to changes in ocean demands. Changes of both types spurred the incentives for enclosure in a way that corresponds to other historical episodes in which new property arrangements that reduced inefficiencies were introduced.

Whether or not the change in ocean property arrangements has been a conscious effort to internalize spillovers (and thus raise the total gains of ocean use) is difficult to say. The simultaneous shifts away from communal arrangements either toward decentralized ownership of resources via coastal state enclosures or toward centralized allocation via parliamentary-like procedures may be good examples of the hit-and-miss procedures that Demsetz referred to. Many of these actions could have been motivated more by distributional national self-interests than by attempts to avoid economic waste. As Demsetz points out, however, whatever the motivations for realignment may have been, "their viability in the long run will depend [at least in part] on how well they modify behavior to accommodate to the [spillovers] associated with important changes in technology or market values."[20] My economic analyses of the consequences of the enclosure movement (in Part One) versus the consequences of the UNCLOS process (in Part Two) strongly suggest that the enclosure movement will reduce more of the major sources of ocean inefficiencies. In the terms that Demsetz suggested, this accounts for the greater workability of the enclosure movement as compared with UNCLOS as a device for creating new international law that is attuned to new values of the oceans.

For several reasons, these changes in property arrangements of oceans are not as vivid an example of Demsetz's theory as is his own example of North American game or the other case studies of enclosures on land that I described. For one thing, the process of conversion from a communal alignment of rights is not yet complete. The right of coastal states to certain offshore resources, such as continental shelf minerals, has now been established. But realignments for fisheries and environmental quality remain uncertain in different degrees, and the question of ownership of the deep seabeds is still quite unsettled. On the other hand, even if the conversion to enclosure requires another quarter-century to complete, it will have begun and ended within the span of about sixty years—which, given the large number of countries and the size of the oceans involved, strikes me as a relatively rapid movement. This underscores the instability of communal rights structures that Alchian and Demsetz stressed.

Second, the enclosure movement and UNCLOS are competitive processes for changing ocean property arrangements. It is a bit too early to predict which process will determine the future law of the sea, but the enclosure movement has been dominant so far. UNCLOS, if it produces a treaty, is likely to parallel the outcomes of enclosure for certain coastal resources while creating a relatively centralized international regime (the second conversion process described by Alchian and Demsetz) for the deep seabeds and possibly for certain sources of pollution.[21]

Third, the process of conversion to more exclusive ocean resource rights, either through enclosure or UNCLOS, is only a first step for removing the inefficiencies that result from communal rights. The second step is for authorities to assign exclusive and transferable private property rights to individuals, firms, or other entities that will ultimately exploit the resources. Obviously, this step would essentially complete the process of "privatization" in ocean resources, simply because the holder of these relatively exclusive rights would have stronger wealth incentives to reduce the inefficiencies associated with communal situations. Unless this step is taken, economic wastes will continue in spite of the appearance of restrictions on open access. Thus the conversion from a strictly freedom-of-the-seas regime to enclosure does not guarantee the improved allocation of ocean resources. But it does offer greater opportunities for such improvements, and makes them more likely where efficiency losses are large and the cost of eradicating them is relatively low.

5. PLAN OF THE BOOK

The remaining chapters of Part One will describe some of the new property arrangements for important ocean resources that have been developed either by coastal state enclosures or by new international agreements, and attempt to trace out the implications for efficient resource use of institutions of each type, as follows:

1. The nature of coastal state enclosures, a brief history of the enclosure movement and the international reaction to it, and the economic paradigm for comparing the outcomes of coastal versus international mechanisms for resource allocation (Chap. 2).

2. The economic consequences upon navigation of coastal states' extending their territorial seas to twelve miles, and the rights of such states to interfere with the transit of ships through international waterways that would be overlapped (Chap. 3).

3. The economic consequences of exclusive coastal control over hydrocarbon exploitation and of mechanisms for sharing some of the revenues of exploitation with the international community (Chap. 4).

4. The economic consequences of increased coastal state controls over fish and other living resources of coastal areas, and the problem of dividing access rights between coastal nations and other countries that have traditionally fished coastal waters (Chap. 5).

5. The economic consequences of increased coastal state control over activities that cause marine pollution, especially pollution of petroleum by ships,

and the division of this authority between coastal states versus extant or hypothetical international institutions (Chap. 6).

6. The economic and other consequences of coastal states demanding prior consent before authorizing bona fide civilian organizations to conduct basic scientific inquiries within adjacent coastal areas (Chap. 7).

7. The economic consequences of creating an international regime to control access to the deep seabed areas beyond the present boundaries of national resource jurisdiction, the entities that this regime may authorize to exploit minerals that the seabed contains, and the division of revenues from such exploitation between these entities and the international regime (Chap. 8).

Part Two will then be devoted to an evaluation of the policies of the treaty negotiations under way at UNCLOS and of the development of the U.S. policy toward this conference.

Notes

1. See Louis Henkin, "The Changing Law of Sea-Mining," in *Inter-University Program of Research on Ferromanganese Deposits of the Ocean Floor, Phase I Report* (Washington, D.C.: National Science Foundation, International Decade of Ocean Exploration, Seabed Assessment Program, April 1973), pp. 338–40. The historical development of the principle is documented by T. W. Fulton, *The Sovereignty of the Sea* (Edinburgh and London: William Blackwood and Sons, 1911), chaps. 1–7; and is summarized by Kenneth W. Clarkson, "International Law, U.S. Seabeds Policy and Ocean Resource Development," *Journal of Law and Economics* 17 (1974):118–25.

2. U.S. Presidential Proclamation No. 2667, Natural Resources of the Subsoil and Sea Bed of the Continental Shelf, *Federal Register*, vol. 10, p. 12303 (September 28, 1945); reprinted in U.S. Department of State, *Bulletin*, vol. 13, no. 327, September 30, 1945, p. 485. See Appendix for the full text.

3. Robert L. Friedheim, "Enclosure Movement of the Oceans," paper presented at the University of Southern California, October 30, 1975. See also R. D. Eckert, "On the International Assignment of Property Rights in Ocean Resources," paper presented at the American Economic Association Annual Meetings, San Francisco, December 28, 1974, reprinted in *Congressional Record*, vol. 121, pt. 1, 94th Cong., 1st Sess. (January 23, 1975), pp. 1093–1103.

4. For a more complete discussion of these issues, see Edward Wenk, Jr., "The Physical Resources of the Ocean," *Scientific American*, September 1969, pp. 166–76;

S. J. Holt, "The Food Resources of the Ocean," ibid., pp. 178−94; Willard Bascom, "Technology and the Ocean," ibid., pp. 198−217.

5. This is emphasized in Clarkson, pp. 118−25.

6. Harold Demsetz, "Toward a Theory of Property Rights," *American Economic Review, Papers and Proceedings* 57 (1967):347−59.

7. Ibid., p. 350. Demsetz uses the term "externality" as a synonym for various side effects or spillovers.

8. Ibid., pp. 351−52.

9. Ibid., p. 352.

10. Ibid., p. 353.

11. Armen A. Alchian and Harold Demsetz, "The Property Rights Paradigm," *Journal of Economic History* 33 (1973):22−24.

12. Demsetz, p. 350.

13. In general, see W. H. R. Curtler, *The Enclosure and Redistribution of Our Land* (Oxford: Clarendon Press, 1920); E. C. K. Gonner, *Common Land and Inclosure* (London: Macmillan and Co., Ltd., 1912); Harriet Bradley, *The Enclosures in England: An Economic Reconstruction* (New York: AMS Press, 1968, from the 1918 ed.); Warren C. Scoville and J. Clayburn La Force, *The Economic Development of Western Europe*, I, *The Middle Ages and the Renaissance* (Lexington, Mass.: D. C. Heath and Co., 1969), 1−18; III, *The Eighteenth and Early Nineteenth Centuries*, 1−16; Witt Bowden, Michael Karpovich, and Abbott Payson Usher, "Agrarian Reorganization and Reform in the Eighteenth Century," reprinted in Scoville and La Force, III, 66−89, from *An Economic History of Europe Since 1750* (New York: American Book Company, 1937), pp. 146−70; G. E. Mingay, "The 'Agricultural Revolution' in English History: A Reconsideration," reprinted in Scoville and La Force, III, 118−34, from *Agricultural History*, vol. 37 (1963).

14. Terry L. Anderson and P. J. Hill, "The Evolution of Property Rights: A Study of the American West," *Journal of Law and Economics* 18 (1975):163−79.

15. John C. Umbeck, "A Theory of Contract Choice and the California Gold Rush," ibid. 20 (1977):421−37.

16. R. H. Coase, "The Federal Communications Commission," ibid. 2 (1959):1−40.

17. A. S. De Vany, R. D. Eckert, C. J. Meyers, D. J. O'Hara, and R. C. Scott, "A Property System for Market Allocation of the Electromagnetic Spectrum: A Legal-Economic-Engineering Study," *Stanford Law Review* 21 (1969):1499−1561; J. R. Minasian, "Property Rights in Radiation: An Alternative Approach to Radio Frequency Allocation," *Journal of Law and Economics* 18 (1975):221−72.

18. This was first recognized by Charles S. Pearson, *International Marine Environment Policy: The Economic Dimension* (Baltimore and London: Johns Hopkins University Press, 1975), pp. 18−23.

19. Demsetz, p. 350.

20. Ibid.

21. Pearson appears to give almost equal emphasis to the potential efficiency gains from moving toward a more centralized structure of ocean rights via the UNCLOS process (and other international agreements) versus the more decentralized process of enclosures by coastal states; see pp. 18–23, 38–49, 62–63. It is my argument that the enclosure movement offers a far greater potential for reducing inefficiencies relative to most international processes.

CHAPTER 2

The Continental Margin: From High Seas to Enclosure

The most valuable ocean areas generally lie along coasts. Coastal waters, shallow and close to concentrations of populations, are the focus of all but a few of the traditional and the new ocean activities. Ship traffic naturally concentrates around straits and ports, and these are where most of the collisions, groundings, and oil spills occur. The cost of drilling exploratory and production wells and of installing pipelines increases so rapidly with water depth and distance from shore that offshore hydrocarbon production now is largely a coastal activity. The best fisheries lie within two or three hundred miles of land since shallower areas collect the necessary food supplies. Coastal areas are usually the first to be polluted as gravity, rivers, and weather haul pollutants to the sea and as man for the sake of convenience dumps other materials there. A great deal of the scientific research of the oceans takes place in shelf areas that are rich in biota and most accessible. Also, coasts that are high in population tend to be most in demand for recreational uses, for mariculture, for open space areas to be preserved for scenic beauty, and for probably other uses yet to be dreamed of. And though ocean mining and national security missions make greater use of deeper areas, naval activities, too, cluster around ports.

1. THE CONTINENTAL MARGIN: DEFINITION

Jutting out from the shores of all continents and islands is a relatively narrow and shallow platform of submerged land that is called the continental shelf. Beginning at the low-water mark, the continental shelf slopes gently at a grade of less than one degree to a maximum depth that averages less than 600 feet (200 meters) and rarely exceeds 1,500 feet. The slope is so gentle in most areas that it would not be apparent to the human eye even without its water cover.[1] The average width of the shelf is between 30 and 40 nautical miles, but its actual width varies between two and 700 miles depending upon its slope at different locations. "Because of their proximity to shore, their shallow depth, and their importance in navigation the continental shelves are now the best-known part of the oceans."[2] Shelves constitute 7.5 percent of the total area of the world and 18 percent of its land area.[3]

Past the edge of the shelf and across the very narrow continental slope, the sea floor falls more rapidly at gradients of between 3 and 4 degrees to depths of 4,500 to 10,000 feet. Forming the base of the continental slope is the continental rise, an area variable in width but usually broader than either the shelf or the slope. The rise, where it exists, has gradients that are steeper than the shelf but much less steep than the relatively precipitous slope. The depth of the rise varies between 1,500 and 17,000 feet.

Together, the shelf, slope, and rise constitute the entire continental margin, that is, the full extent of the continental elevation lying landward of the abyssal plains on the deep ocean floor (see Fig. 1).[4] There are striking differences in the relative dimensions of the shelf, slope, and rise in various parts of the world. At Martha's Vineyard, for example, the shelf is much broader than it is at Gibraltar on the opposite side of the Atlantic. In the South Atlantic, however, the shelves at both Recife and Freetown are relatively narrow, and the continental slopes are very steep (see Fig. 2). At roughly the center point of the Atlantic is a chain of mountains known as the Mid-Atlantic Ridge. This is dramatically gashed by a wide and continuous fracture which runs through the North and South Atlantic and continues in the Indian and South Pacific oceans, for a total distance of 40,000 miles, skirted on both sides by abyssal plains.[5] Recent geological research has revealed that this rift-valley crest is the seam along which the oceans spread. As molten materials are forced up from the earth's mantle below the ocean basins, they cool, harden, and eventually form new ocean bottom. Thus, hard minerals are likely to be found along such seams. The mineral-rich, hot brines found beneath the ridge of the Red Sea are one example, and small veins of pure copper have been found beneath the Mid-Indian Ocean ridge.[6] In contrast, petroleum resources are more likely to be found in shallower areas beneath the continental shelves. A hypothetical distribution of minerals according to a cross-sectional view of an ocean basin is shown in Figure 3.

2. NATURE OF ENCLOSURES

Coastal states have employed two principal techniques for extending the seaward boundary of the continental margin over which they control resources. First, they stretch their sovereignty to immediately adjacent areas by adopting broad interpretations of both inland waters and territorial seas (foreign countries

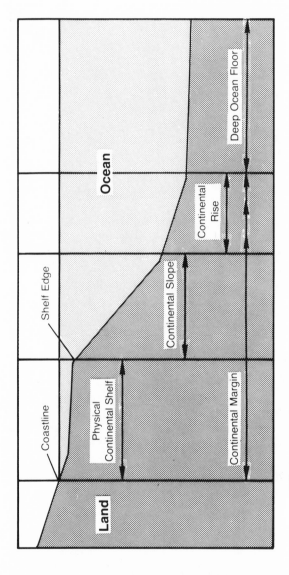

FIG. 1. Schematic representation of the seabeds and ocean floor (vertical scale exaggerated).

Source: U.S. Council on International Economic Policy, *International Economic Report of the President*, February 1974, p. 82.

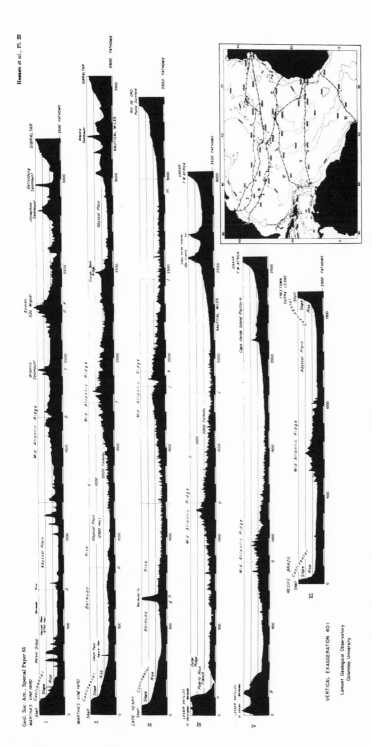

FIG. 2.   Six trans-Atlantic topographic profiles. Soundings in fathoms continuously recorded by an NMC echo sounder on the R. V. ATLANTIS. The letters a–q indicate where soundings from different cruises were joined.

SOURCE: Bruce C. Heezen, Marie Tharp, and Maurice Ewing, *The Floors of the Oceans: I. The North Atlantic*, Geological Society of America Special Paper No. 65 (April 1959), Plate No. 22.

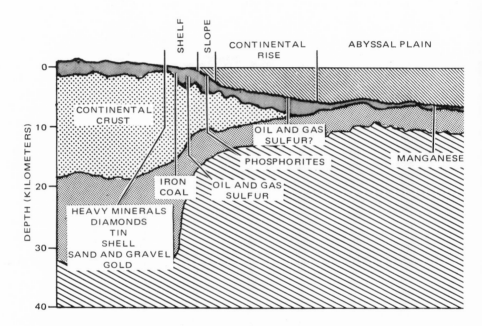

FIG. 3. Schematic cross section of the ocean basin (vertical scale exaggerated) extending from a continent out to a mid-ocean ridge, indicating ocean-floor resources known or believed to exist in various physiographic provinces and depths.

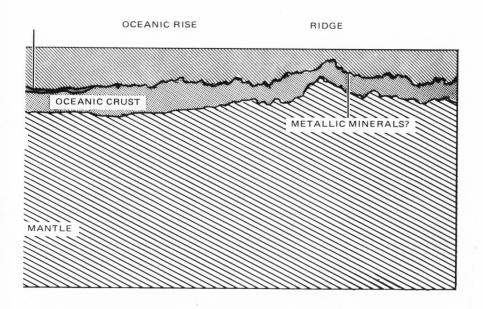

have no transit or exploitation rights in the former and only limited rights in the latter). Second, beyond sovereign areas, coastal states claim jurisdiction over resources in what are usually called Economic Zones.

Historically, the outer boundary of the territorial sea has been governed by the natural indentation of the coastline; the boundary was everywhere a fixed distance from the closest low-water mark along the littoral. This procedure yielded a well-defined boundary when the coastline was smooth, but it produced an irregular curve if the coast was deeply indented or fringed with islands, or if the nation consisted entirely of islands (that is, an archipelago). Recently, certain nations with irregular coastlines have adopted a different method of measuring, using a series of segmented straight ''base lines'' which create an artificial coastline by connecting the outermost points of islands or other geographic features. If the base lines are drawn generously and the individual segments are relatively long, the extra area enclosed can be substantial. Since the use of straight base lines extends the coastal state's internal waters, it also increases the ''base'' from which other claims are measured. This pushes seaward the boundary of the territorial sea as well as the delimitation of additional claims to resource jurisdiction that are measured from the boundary of the territorial sea. A hypothetical application of straight base lines to a coastline that is deeply indented or fringed with islands is depicted in Figure 4.

Enclosures of this type have generally been accepted at international law. For example, the Geneva Convention on the Territorial Sea permits bays and fjords to be enclosed as internal waters by joining the outermost low-tide promontories of the indentation with closing base lines of not more than 24 nautical miles in length,[7] although some nations have enclosed bays regardless of width. Norway constructed a system of straight base lines to enclose 645.9 miles of its Arctic and Atlantic coasts that are fringed by islands, islets, and ramparts of rocks. This base-line system was accepted by the International Court of Justice in 1951 in spite of several possibly extravagant features.[8] Norway used straight base lines to enclose ''fjords'' where one shore was constituted not by land itself but by a group of flanking islands sufficiently linked in the court's view to give the appearance of unbroken land.[9] The court also agreed to Norway's use of straight base lines to enclose all of both coasts although fringed islands were characteristic of as little as 60−70 percent of each area. Some of the Norwegian baseline segments exceeded 40 nautical miles in length and diverted from the general direction of the coastline by as much as 15 degrees. Base points on the outermost fringe often consisted of insignificant islets or rock clusters, one of which was visible only at low tide.[10]

Norway's practice of delimiting its internal waters and territorial sea according to the outermost points of offshore islands has been followed by Canada, and it carries obvious implications for Denmark, Greece, India, Ireland, the United Kingdom (particularly Scotland), and Yugoslavia.[11] In 1974, Canada

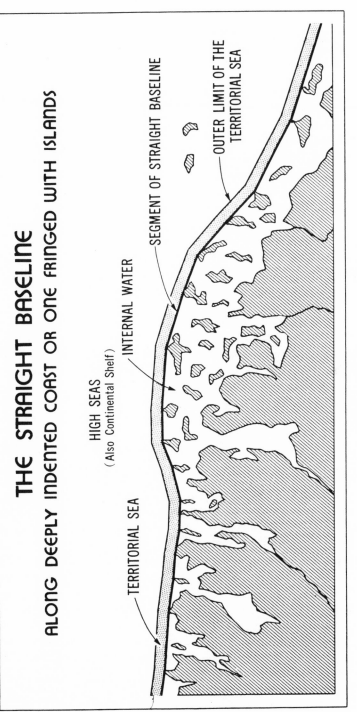

THE STRAIGHT BASELINE
ALONG DEEPLY INDENTED COAST OR ONE FRINGED WITH ISLANDS

HIGH SEAS
(Also Continental Shelf)

INTERNAL WATER

SEGMENT OF STRAIGHT BASELINE

OUTER LIMIT OF THE
TERRITORIAL SEA

TERRITORIAL SEA

FIG. 4.   Territorial consequences of the straight base line.

SOURCE: U.S. Department of State, Bureau of Public Affairs, *U.N. Law of the Sea Conference 1975*, Department of State Publication 8764, February 1975, p. 10.

drew straight base lines to replace the sinuosities of the coast of Labrador, the south and east coasts of Newfoundland, the east coast of Nova Scotia, and the west coasts of Vancouver and the Queen Charlotte Islands. This combined area of enclosure exceeded 100,000 square miles. Canada's proposal to enclose the Gulf of St. Lawrence was withdrawn only after strong objections by the United States.[12]

The enclosures of offshore archipelagoes by mainland states has served as a precedent for vaster enclosures by such archipelagic states as Fiji, Ecuador (the Galapagos), Indonesia, the Maldive Islands, Mauritius, the Philippines, and Tonga. The possibilities for enclosure by a hypothetical archipelagic state are shown in Figure 5. For example, Indonesia's base-line system is 8,167 miles long, creates 660,000 square miles of internal waters in an area roughly 3,000 miles long by 1,300 miles wide, and contains about 14,000 islands (of which 13,000 are uninhabited and 6,000 are unnamed). Segments of Indonesia's base lines are over 120 miles long, and the Philippines has enclosed areas that lie 285 miles from the nearest land.[13]

Enthusiasm for enclosure has led a few states to draw base lines that ignore land altogether: Bangladesh, for example, has delimited straight base lines according to the criterion of water depth, and the Maldive Islands have defined their internal waters according to geographical coordinates rather than to points on land. By December 23, 1975, about 50 of the 128 independent coastal states in the United Nations had drawn straight base lines to enclose bays, river mouths, or other coastal areas.[14]

Another common device for extending coastal state sovereignty is to claim territorial seas of twelve rather than three nautical miles in breadth, measured from shore lines or base lines depending upon the character of the coast. Table 1 indicates that only 26 states still retain the historic three-mile limit. Another 73 extend their territorial seas out to twelve miles, and another 27 claim between fifteen and 200 miles. A universal application of the twelve-mile territorial seas, assuming that such seas were measured from shore lines, would overlap 121 international straits of less than 24 miles in breadth of which about a dozen have naval or commercial significance. Converting international waterways to territorial seas raises to maritime states the specter of coastal states restricting commercial shipping by charging tolls or requiring rigid sea-lanes, forcing circuitous passages, or blocking naval transit. Such results would be magnified where base lines were drawn to convert international waterways to internal waters rather than territorial seas.

The second principal technique for enclosure is to claim exclusive jurisdiction to exploit one or more resources beyond the territorial sea. Most of these "functional" claims limit jurisdiction to a single economic purpose. Examples would be the United States' claim to continental shelf minerals, Canada's "pollution control zone" extending 100 miles into the Arctic Ocean, and the

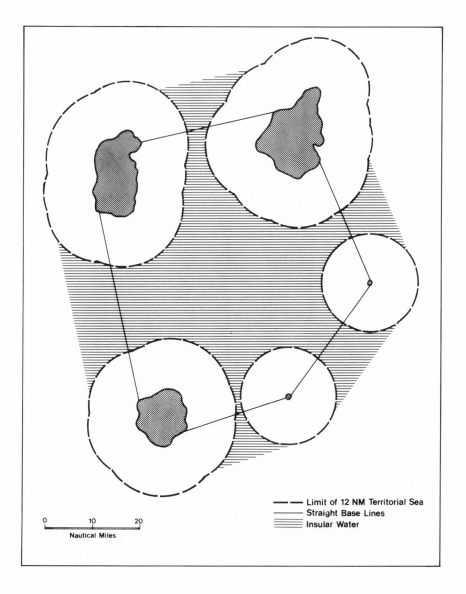

FIG. 5. Hypothetical enclosures of an archipelagic nation employing
a system of straight base lines.

Source: Robert D. Hodgson and Lewis M. Alexander, *Towards an Objective Analysis of Special Circumstances* (Kingston, R.I.: Law of the Sea Institute, Occasional Paper No. 13, 1972), p. 51.

TABLE 1

NATIONAL CLAIMS TO TERRITORIAL SEAS AS OF SEPTEMBER 1, 1977

Breadth (Nautical Miles)	Number of States
3	26
4	4
6	8
10	1
12	60
15	1
20	1
30	3
50	4
100	2
150	2
200	14
Modified archipelago	3
No legislation	1

claims to various fishing limits that are listed in Table 2, 51 of which go out to 200 nautical miles. However, there is a strong trend for coastal states to claim exclusive rights to exploit all living and nonliving resources within a zone having a seaward limit of 200 nautical miles from the base lines used to measure the territorial sea. This area is generally called an Exclusive Economic Zone (EEZ).[15] Thus, a nation that claims a 200-mile EEZ and a twelve-mile territorial sea would effectively have a 188-mile EEZ if the same base lines were used to draw the boundaries of both, as is the custom. Within its EEZ a coastal state usually asserts rights to control minerals, fisheries, scientific research activities by foreign countries, and in some cases navigation that is prone to pollution. By September 1, 1977, twenty countries, most of which also assert 200-mile special-purpose fisheries zones, asserted claims to 200-mile general purpose zones (see Table 3). The degree of exclusivity that is claimed varies between coastal states, but some are so stringent as to cloud the distinction between the EEZ and the territorial sea. Such claims arouse concern among maritime countries that their historic rights to fish or navigate freely in what once were high seas could be limited.

One of the most important issues under consideration at UNCLOS is the extent to which EEZs will be recognized for islands of varying sizes. It is certain that UNCLOS will recognize full 200-mile EEZs for such island nations as Iceland, Jamaica, Japan, Madagascar, and the United Kingdom, and it will probably recognize those of inhabited island possessions, such as Greenland and Spitsbergen. Somewhat more problematical is the creation of full EEZs around European island possessions, such as the Faeroes and French Polynesia, that do not wash also against the metropolitan territory. Most controversial of all,

TABLE 2

National Claims to Fishing Limits as of September 1, 1977

Breadth (Nautical Miles)	Number of States
3	8
6	3
12	51
15	1
20	1
30	2
36	1
50	5
70	1
100	1
150	2
200	51
Modified archipelago	3

Note: Tables based on 129 independent coastal states (plus Ukrainian S.S.R.).

Source: U.S. Department of State, Bureau of Intelligence and Research, Office of the Geographer, *Limits in the Seas, No. 36: National Claims to Maritime Jurisdictions* (3d rev.; Washington, D.C.; suppl. dated September 1, 1977), mimeo.

TABLE 3

National Claims to 200-Nautical-Mile Economic or General Purpose Zones

Bangladesh	Haiti	Pakistan
Burma	India	Portugal
Comoros	Korea, North[*]	Senegal
Cuba	Maldive Islands[†]	Seychelles
Dominican Republic	Mauritius	Sri Lanka
Guatemala	Mexico	Vietnam
Guyana	Mozambique	

[*]North Korea has also claimed a 50-mile "military line" in which all foreign vessels and aircraft are banned without permission.

[†]Maldives' economic zone is defined by geographical coordinates. The zone is in part a rectangle and in part a boundary with India and Sri Lanka. The breadth of the zone varies from approximately 35 nautical miles to 300 nautical miles.

Source: U.S. Department of State, Bureau of Intelligence and Research, Office of the Geographer, *Limits in the Seas, No. 36: National Claims to Maritime Jurisdictions*, (3d. rev.; Washington, D.C.; suppl. dated September 1, 1977), mimeo.

however, is to grant full EEZs for such uninhabited possessions as islets, banks, drying reefs, and mid-ocean rocks. International law already recognizes that inhabited artificial islands, oil rigs, and fixed installations are entitled to "safety zones" of 500 meters in radius.[16] But creating a twelve-mile territorial sea plus an additional 188-mile EEZ for a mid-ocean rock encloses in each case a little more than 125,000 square miles of additional ocean space. An EEZ of approximately this size would accrue to the mid-Pacific island nation of Nauru, with nine miles of coastline and a population of about 6,500, since no other land is located nearby.[17]

The potential wealth from EEZs around mid-ocean rocks or other geographical "flyspecks" has led to competition for their ownership. Recently the United Kingdom asserted sovereignty over tiny Rockall Island, roughly 100 meters in circumference, which lies some 200 miles west of Scotland. In the South China Sea, four nations—China, the Philippines, Taiwan, and Vietnam—are asserting ownership to the 200-odd islets and reefs that form the Paracel and Spratly archipelagoes. In one of the few instances in which competition over enclosures has led to violence, China in 1974 seized the Paracel Group from South Vietnam during its waning days.[18] These small island groups have not only economic but strategic significance. The Philippines has begun oil drilling on one reef, and the sea-lane between the two groups is the only major route linking East Asia with Africa and Europe.

3. A BRIEF HISTORY OF RECENT ENCLOSURES

The Economics of Alternative Boundaries

National economic interests in obtaining favorable distributions of oceanic wealth in the face of substantial uncertainty over resource locations appear to be the strongest explanation both for the extent of recent enclosures and for the criteria by which they were justified. As long as the extent and location of ocean resource supplies were uncertain—as was the case after World War II for almost every category of resources except fisheries—nations tended to couch their claims in vague generalities and to avoid a precise delimitation to the outer boundary of resource jurisdiction. Under conditions of uncertainty, vague claims to larger rather than smaller areas of the ocean had the potential for enclosing more resources.

The extent of each nation's desired resource jurisdiction probably would differ according to differences in local geographic conditions, expectations of finding resource supplies that were worth extracting, the distances of such supplies from shore, the costs of enforcing wider claims, and the enclosures made by other nearby countries. Some combination of these factors would determine the criterion by which a claim was asserted, its seaward boundary, and its timing.

The three most likely candidate criteria for enclosure were water depth, distance from shore, and the geology of the continental margin. Nations seeking control over primarily shallow water fisheries could base their enclosures on the depth of water, choosing the particular isobath contour that yielded the desired areal jurisdiction.[19] On the other hand, nations seeking control over migrating fisheries in deep waters would find it more rewarding to draw a simple outer boundary roughly at the distance from shore that would enclose the area through which the fishery usually swam. Nations wanting to exploit offshore minerals and having broad adjacent continental margins would have incentives to justify a resource zone on the basis of the actual prolongation of the geological shelf. If the rewards were relatively great and the enforcement costs low, such claims could extend past the shelf to include the entire continental margin.

Truman's Proclamation: The First Degree

The United States, by 1945, had established a lead in mineral exploration technologies, and petroleum deposits had been located off the coasts of Texas and California.[20] In view of the diminished postwar oil reserves and the advice of petroleum geologists that the seabed beyond the three-mile limit of the U.S. territorial sea offered attractive mineral possibilities, President Truman, on September 28, 1945, declared that "the Government of the United States regards the natural resources of the subsoil and seabed of the continental shelf beneath the high seas but contiguous to the coasts of the United States as appertaining to the United States, subject to its jurisdiction and control."[21] Truman's definition of the continental shelf "as an extension of the land-mass of the coastal nation and thus naturally appurtenant to it" was not at all precise, however. At the time a number of "equally plausible" definitions of the shelf had currency.[22] One specified its outer limit as the 200-meter isobath line. Another limited the shelf at its geologic junction with the continental slope regardless of the depth of the junction. Still another equated the shelf with the full continental margin. A White House press release which accompanied the proclamation stated that the shelf was commonly regarded as the seabed and subsoil covered by no more than 200 meters of water, but this language was not included in the proclamation itself.[23] Therefore, U.S. resource jurisdiction had no official boundary.

But this lack of preciseness favored U.S. economic interests at the time. Because the continental shelf of the United States is wide and often extends beyond 200 meters on its Alaskan, Atlantic, and Gulf coasts, the U.S. would acquire a relatively broad economic resource jurisdiction by staking its claim on the criterion of the shelf's geological limits. Truman, lacking reliable information on the precise extent and location of offshore hydrocarbons, in effect erred on the high side by claiming an area that was much broader and deeper even than existing U.S. technologies could exploit. If eventually the geological limits of the shelf proved to be too confining for U.S. economic interests, then the proclamation could be amended to extend the legal limits from the edge of the shelf to the full continental margin.

Between 1945 and 1957 there were 41 additional enclosures.[24] Most countries followed the U.S. practice of claiming resources based on the vague criterion of the continental shelf. Some claimed the entire shelf "whatever the depth and extension of this shelf may be." Others referred to even more general criteria such as the "sea-bed and subsoil of submarine areas," the "submarine platform," or "waters contiguous to [the] coasts." The probable intent behind these enclosures was to garner resources more than ocean territory per se. None of the 41 claims interfered with the rights of other countries to navigate, overfly, or lay submarine cables or pipelines outside of territorial seas. Only nine countries enclosed the waters immediately above the shelf in addition to the minerals lying on or under it.

Enclosures based on the criterion of the continental shelf served the interests of several groups of countries. First, countries having broad continental margins—such as Argentina, Brazil, the U.S., and others shown in Figure 6—would secure exclusive rights to mineral resources over a broad ocean expanse. Second, countries in the Caribbean area could enclose broader areas with the continental shelf criterion than by, say, the 200-meter isobath criterion.[25] In fact, only a half-dozen of the 41 countries based their enclosures on a particular isobath line. By the same token, countries in the Persian Gulf area avoided the geological shelf criterion since the depth there is mostly less than 200 meters (in the strictest geological sense, this region lacks shelves because there is no deep ocean floor to which shelves typically lead). Instead, their enclosures referred to the subsoil and seabed areas that were "contiguous to . . . coasts" or that "border[ed] on territorial waters,"[26] without ever mentioning the shelf per se.

Mention of the shelf was also avoided by countries along the west coast of South America that sought to establish exclusive rights to whales and schools of tunas and anchovies. As Figure 6 shows, their "shelves" are narrow, and so precipitous as barely to exist at all. Therefore, their adjacent submerged land mass would have done them little good as a criterion for enclosure. Instead they adopted a uniform distance of 200 nautical miles, corresponding to the distance then believed to be the range of most whalers and tuna boats.[27]

What caused the rate of claims in the years 1945−57 to be so brisk? In deciding whether and to what extent it should enclose ocean resources, a coastal nation would compare the benefits of increased exclusivity of resource control with the costs of increased enforcement activities, among other things.[28] The coastal states for which the net benefits of enclosure were greater would have the stronger incentives to issue such proclamations. This structure of rewards and costs was shattered during the postwar period by the changes in ocean economics and technologies that I described in Chapter 1. But it was shattered also by the Truman Proclamation and the prospect of an international conference to set boundary limits in the seas.

It is likely that some claims were accelerated by the "prisoner's dilemma" element introduced by the Truman Proclamation. In this situation, when individuals or governments fail to reach a mutual agreement on a specific course of action owing to high costs of bargaining and coordinating their efforts, each party cheats on the other, or takes some rewarding action sooner than would have occurred if coordination costs were lower, in the expectation that the other parties are cheating, too.[29] Possibly coastal states would have had incentives either to avoid enclosures altogether or to issue their claims all at once had bargaining costs within the group been smaller. But if the United States believed that enclosure was necessary to restrict the access of other countries to resources near its coastline, then other nations might perceive similar benefits from making enclosures. If each believed that the others saw the problem in the same way, there would be additional incentives for accelerating enclosures in order to gain an advantage over cohorts.

These incentives would be compounded if it were anticipated that an international conference would soon define the continental shelf in highly ambiguous treaty language. Basil Petrou and R. David Ranson have argued thus:

> an international action or document which blurs the legal situation . . . could generate conflict that might not otherwise have occurred. There may emerge, for example, a treaty which undermines [existing property arrangements] without setting in their place a widely-agreed system of property rights. When a nation is no longer sure that other nations would reject its unilateral actions . . . then the potential benefit from unilateral action is raised. Furthermore, that nation will recognize that other nations, viewing the same clouded situation, are thinking along the same lines. This "prisoner's dilemma" generates a strong incentive to gain a lead in establishing claims.[30]

Other states would have incentives to hasten enclosures if they expected that the conference would define the continental shelf too restrictively for their purposes. Unilaterally established "squatters' rights" that were asserted in advance could raise the cost to the conference of adopting a shelf definition that was contrary to the interests of these countries.

The Geneva Conventions: The Second Degree

The definitions of property rights produced by the first United Nations Conference on the Law of the Sea, held at Geneva in 1958, were ambiguous indeed. One of the major tasks of this conference was to give a precise definition of the continental shelf, since it was feared by some nations that conflicting claims would lead to trouble or that there would be a delay in the exploitation of shelf resources,[31] and the conference had been preceded by eight years of preparatory work by the International Law Commission (ILC), many of whose deliberations dealt with two competing legal definitions. The first was the 200-meter isobath, apparently favored by international legal scholars for the limits it would place on coastal state extensions and for its simplicity and

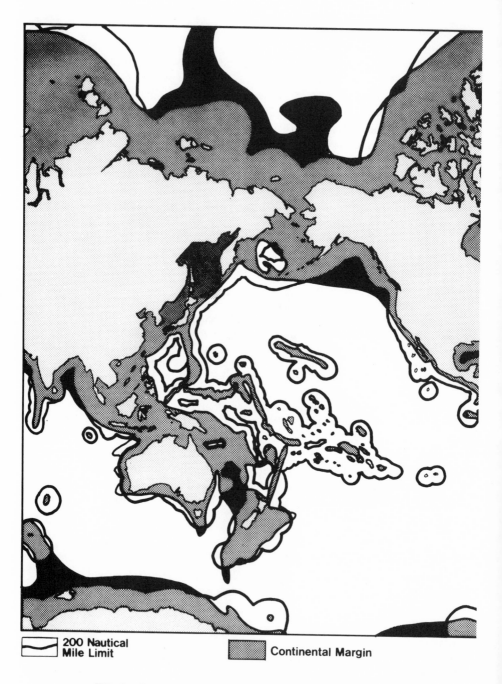

| | 200 Nautical Mile Limit | | Continental Margin |

FIG. 6.   Continental margins of the world in relation to 200-nautical-mile
exclusive economic zones.

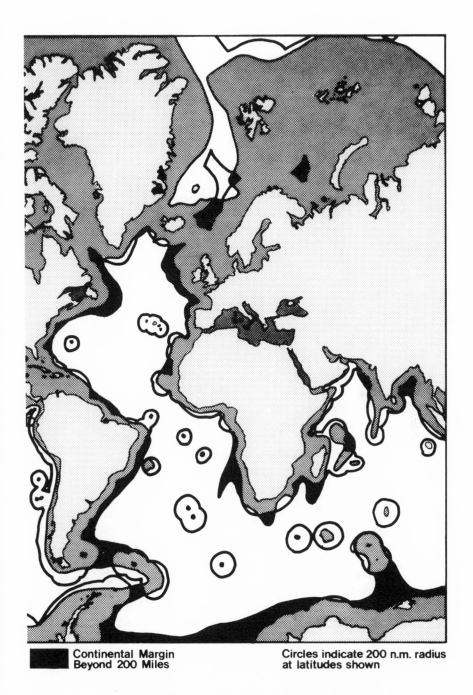

**Continental Margin
Beyond 200 Miles**

**Circles indicate 200 n.m. radius
at latitudes shown**

SOURCE: Office of the Geographer, U.S. Department of State.

clarity.[32] The second was the ''exploitability criterion,'' extending the shelf out to ''where the superjacent waters admit of exploitation of the natural resources of the sea-bed and the subsoil.'' This vague definition was favored by states whose economic interests would be harmed by the 200-meter definition.[33] These included countries in the Persian Gulf area that lacked geological shelves of any kind as well as nations in the Caribbean Sea and along the west coast of Central and South America that had precipitous shelves.[34] The exploitability criterion would work to their advantage in that it avoided the rigid rules of either water depth or the geography of their continental margins, providing them instead with exclusive resource rights that were linked to technological feasibility. When costs declined and technologies permitted access to deeper waters, these areas would automatically fall within this definition of the shelf.

The ILC debates on the continental shelf were marked by an inability to reach consensus in favor of one definition or the other, and it appears to have reversed its decision on this matter at least twice.[35] The scales tipped in favor of the exploitability criterion when broad-margin nations realized that it facilitated their enclosure of resources beyond the 200-meter isobath. The decisive event occurred in 1956 when the exploitability criterion was adopted by a conference of twenty-one Western Hemisphere nations[36] including the narrow-shelf states mentioned above and the broad-shelf states facing the Atlantic Ocean, Mexico (along its Gulf Coast), and the United States.[37] These nations formed a bloc to secure the ILC's adoption of the exploitability criterion,[38] which was eventually included in the Geneva Convention on the Continental Shelf:

> For the purpose of these articles, the term ''continental shelf'' is used as referring (a) to the seabed and subsoil of the submarine areas adjacent to the coast but out- side the area of the territorial sea, to a depth of 200 meters or, beyond that limit, to where the depth of the superjacent waters admit of the exploitation of the natural resources of said area; (b) to the seabed and subsoil of similar submarine areas adjacent to the coasts of islands.[39]

The effect of this definition in expanding enclosure is illustrated in Figure 7.

This definition is often criticized for its imprecision,[40] but that was its purpose. The intent of a majority of the framers of the convention was to facilitate enclosure, not to create international legal obstacles to its extension. Replacing Truman's geologically based definition of the shelf with the exploita- bility criterion gave the sanction of international law to larger enclosures and represented an escalation of the enclosure movement to a new level.

Moreover, the deliberate imprecision in defining the continental shelf is characteristic of the other Geneva conventions of 1958. The Convention on Fishing and Conservation of the Living Resources of the High Seas created a weak structure of fishing rights that was divided in an ambiguous fashion

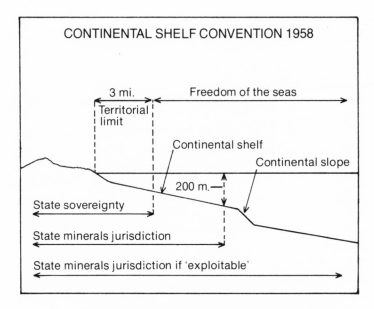

FIG. 7.   The effect of the exploitability criterion of the Continental
Shelf Convention on state resource jurisdiction.

SOURCE: C. Richard Tinsley, "Mining of Manganese Nodules: An Intriguing
Legal Problem," *Engineering and Mining Journal,* October 1973, p. 86. Copy-
right (1973) by McGraw-Hill, Inc., 1221 Avenue of the Americas, New York,
N.Y. 10020.

between adjacent coastal states and other nations.[41] Real conservation was
impossible since no country had exclusive rights to fish and thus restrict the
fishing access of other nations.[42] In addition, the Convention on the Territorial
Sea and the Contiguous Zone avoided a clear definition of the width of the
territorial sea.[43] It was agreed that the combined width of the territorial sea and a
"contiguous zone" for coastal state regulation of customs and fishing should not
exceed twelve nautical miles, but the precise breadth of the territorial sea was left
up to individual coastal states. (This made the Continental Shelf Convention
doubly imprecise since the legal extent of the shelf was supposed to be measured
from the outer boundary of the territorial sea.) The Second UNCLOS convened
in Geneva in 1960 for the single purpose of setting a uniform breadth to the
territorial sea, but it was no more successful than the previous attempts.

UNCLOS III: The Reaction Sets In

The opposition to further enclosure began to mount in 1967. Arvid Pardo, at
that time Malta's ambassador to the United Nations and one of the UN's leading

experts on ocean affairs, eloquently warned the General Assembly of severe consequences if the enclosure movement continued without check:

> The known resources of the sea-bed and of the ocean floor are far greater than the resources known to exist on dry land. The sea-bed and the ocean floor are also of vital and increasing strategic importance. Present and clearly forseeable technology also permits their effective exploitation for military or economic purposes. Some countries may therefore be tempted to use their technical competence to achieve near-unbreakable world dominance through predominant control over the sea-bed and the ocean floor. This, even more than the search for wealth, will impel countries with the requisite technical competence competitively to extend their jurisdiction over selected areas of the ocean floor. The process has already started and will lead to a competitive scramble for sovereign rights over the land under-lying the world's seas and oceans, surpassing in magnitude and in its implication last century's colonial scramble for territory in Asia and Africa. The consequences will be very grave: at the very least a dramatic escalation of the arms race and sharply increasing world tensions, caused also by the intolerable injustice that would reserve the plurality of the world's resources for the exclusive benefit of less than a handful of nations. The strong would get stronger, the rich richer, and among the rich themselves there would arise an increasing and insuperable dif-ferentiation between two or three and the remainder. Between the very few domi-nant Powers, suspicions and tensions would reach unprecedented levels. Tradi-tional activities on the high seas would be curtailed and, at the same time, the world would face the growing danger of permanent damage to the marine environ-ment through radio-active and other pollution: this is a virtually inevitable con-sequence of the present situation.
>
> These are the prospects that the world faces, not in a remote future, but as an immediate consequence of forces and pressures already at work.[44]

"The time has come," Pardo said, "to declare the sea-bed and the ocean floor"—that is, the area beyond the limits of present national jurisdiction—"a common heritage of mankind," and he proposed that "immediate steps should be taken to draft a treaty" based on certain definite principles. First, the area is "not subject to national appropriation in any manner whatsoever"; second, exploration of the area "shall be undertaken in a manner consistent with the Principles and Purposes of the Charter of the United Nations"; third, its "economic exploitation shall be undertaken with the aim of safeguarding the interests of mankind. The net financial benefits derived [therefrom] . . . shall be used primarily to promote the development of poor countries"; fourth, the area "shall be reserved exclusively for peaceful purposes in perpetuity"; fifth, the "proposed treaty should envisage the creation of an international agency (a) to assume jurisdiction, as a trustee for all countries, over the . . . [area]; (b) to regulate, supervise and control activities thereon; and (c) to ensure that the activities undertaken conform to the principles and provisions of the proposed treaty."[45] Pardo estimated that the financial benefits to the proposed agency from the exploitation of the seabeds would amount to approximately six billion 1969 U.S. dollars within five years of its creation.[46]

During 1969, the U.N. General Assembly took additional steps toward convening a Third UN Conference on the Law of the Sea (UNCLOS),[47] but drafted it a mandate that was much broader and more controversial than Pardo had intended. Pardo's proposal had been directed to resolving two basic problems: "the establishment of an equitable international regime and the precise determination of the area beyond national jurisdiction over which the regime would apply."[48] The General Assembly voted to add the subject of "fishing and conservation of the living resources of the high seas," a matter which Pardo felt "was totally beyond the competence" of the organization and of such a "highly controversial" nature that it would become "most difficult to reach agreement in that conference."[49] What is more, the concept of an international regime had grown to include machinery that would have "the power to regulate, co-ordinate, supervise and control all activities relating to the exploration and exploitation of [the resources of the sea-bed and the ocean floor, and the subsoil thereof], for the benefit of mankind as a whole, irrespective of the geographical location of States, taking into account the special interests and needs of the developing countries, whether land-locked or coastal."[50] Another resolution bound states and persons to refrain from all exploitation activities in the area beyond the limits of national jurisdiction and asserted that "no claim to any part of that area or its resources shall be recognized."[51]

Over a period of five years, Pardo's proposals found support across the broad spectrum of UN membership. Chief among the early supporters were countries that expected the proposal to advance their economic interests. The developing low-income countries saw in the oceans one of the planet's "last frontiers" of resources that had yet to be appropriated by the advanced technology countries. Control of the seabeds by some sort of world organization would allow small countries some influence over exploitation without the direct commitment of investment resources. Moreover, a controlling body based strictly on the principle of one nation, one vote would give them control over exploitation. Landlocked or narrow-coastline countries, which account for more than a fourth of the countries in the UN, favored it for similar reasons. Countries that had land-based mineral deposits saw that an international body could be used to support metal prices by cartelizing seabed metal production.[52] Of course, some of these countries also had broad coastlines and thus pro-enclosure interests which tempered their enthusiasm for international restraints.

Other countries, though not all for the same reasons, saw a political advantage in Pardo's proposal. Some viewed the seabeds as a source of financial support for the UN system which would increase its independence from the contributions of advanced technology countries; another group tended to support the proposal out of concern for the destabilizing effect of a "competitive scramble" for military or economic gain from the seabeds. These countries perhaps stood to lose the most if the oceans became an important salient of world politics and if continued enclosure created additional strain on the nation-state system. It was on this basis, for example, that the United States has expressed bipartisan presidential support for an international ocean treaty. In 1966, President Lyndon B. Johnson, who in this regard was a precursor of Pardo, stated that "under no circumstances must we ever allow the prospects of rich harvest and mineral wealth to create a new form of colonial competition among the maritime nations. We must be careful to avoid a race to grab and hold the lands under the high seas. We must ensure that the deep seas and the ocean bottoms are, and remain, the legacy of all human beings."[53] Four years later President Richard M. Nixon, in his Statement on Oceans Policy of 1970, spoke on similar lines: "At issue is whether the oceans will be used rationally and equitably for the benefit of mankind or whether they will become an arena of unrestrained exploitation and conflicting jurisdictional claims in which even the most advantaged states will be losers. . . . With international agreements, we can save over two-thirds of the earth's surface from national conflict and rivalry, protect it from pollution, and put it to use for the benefit of all."[54] The importance of control was again urged in 1975 by Secretary of State Henry A. Kissinger: "The future of the oceans will be shaped in the next few years. At stake are the reach of our navies, the safety of shipping lanes, the rights to vast economic resources, and the choice between chaos and the rule of law across three-quarters of this Earth."[55]

The Third UNCLOS began in 1968 as an ad hoc Sea-Bed Committee of 35 members but gradually expanded to become the largest and most complex international negotiation in history. Participating in 1978 were nearly all the 150-member countries of the United Nations system. After several years of preparatory work, UNCLOS convened in 1973, and since then it has held one procedural and six negotiating sessions consuming 50 weeks of meetings through June 1978. At stake are more than 400 candidate treaty articles covering many ocean issues.[56]

From 200 Meters Deep to 200 Miles Wide:
The Third Degree

The next level of escalation began in the wake of the call for a third UNCLOS. The U.N. General Assembly Resolutions of 1969 and 1970 called for international control of the area of the seabed and ocean floor beyond the present limits of national jurisdiction, bound states to refrain from exploitation activities beyond these limits, and refused to recognize additional enclosures. This situation gave coastal states incentives of the prisoner's dilemma kind to act directly contrary to the UN resolutions—to hasten enclosures in order to push the "present" limits of national jurisdiction seaward before the conference began and thus to leave a proportionately smaller "international area" for an international body, similar to the UN, to control.[57] Between 1967, when Pardo first proposed the Third UNCLOS, and 1973, when its first procedural session was held, 81 states had issued 230 new jurisdictional claims.[58] By 1973, nearly 4.5 million nautical square miles of ocean space had been claimed by countries for their exclusive jurisdiction. This was more than three times the area claimed in 1958 and more than five times what was claimed in 1945.[59]

The first substantive meeting of UNCLOS was held at Caracas in 1974. On that occasion, 110 countries—73 percent of the total United Nations membership of 150 states—spoke in favor of the 200-nautical-mile exclusive economic zone.[60] Lewis M. Alexander and Robert D. Hodgson, both geographers, have calculated that a universal 200-mile EEZ, adopted and enforced, would enclose the resources contained in 35.9 percent of the world's total ocean space. Many geographically enclosed or semi-enclosed seas would become economically enclosed as well. Among these are the Baltic, Black, Caribbean, Celebes, East China, Japan, Java, Mediterranean, North, Persian, South China, and Sulu. Coastal state resource jurisdiction would extend over 37.6 percent of the Arctic and Atlantic oceans, 32.3 percent of the Indian Ocean, and 36.3 percent of the Pacific Ocean.[61] These percentages would increase if more states adopted straight base lines and drew them in a manner that extended their internal waters and territorial seas, and thus the seaward boundary of their EEZs. The effect of a 200-mile EEZ on coastal resource jurisdiction without the construction of straight base lines is illustrated in Figure 8 and can be compared with Figure 7 showing the *status quo ante* according to the exploitability criterion.

The popularity of the 200-nautical-mile EEZ apparently is based on the fact that it provides many coastal states, particularly the so-called developing states, with a broader area of jurisdiction relative to the exploitability criterion, which linked extended jurisdiction to either the possession or the purchase of technologies capable of operation on the continental shelf. In addition, the EEZ enclosures represented a more comprehensive package of rights since they included the living resources of the water column above the submerged land mass in addition to the resources on or under the continental shelf. Of the 148 delegations at UNCLOS in 1974, 118 represented coastal states. Of those, fifteen stood to garner 42 percent of the total area enclosed by a universal 200-mile EEZ, with 30 percent going to the first ten.[62] As Table 4 indicates, the United States stood to gain the most area of all—2.2 million square miles, and twice that if the Pacific Trust Territories were found eligible for full EEZs. At the same time, thirteen nations would acquire EEZs of less than 5,000 square miles each (Table 5). Zaire, for example, the largest nation in Africa, borders the sea for only twenty-two miles and thus would acquire an EEZ of approximately 300 square miles; Jordan has a fifteen-mile coastline and Iraq's is ten, giving each an

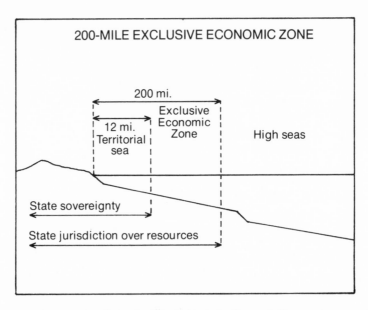

FIG. 8.   The effects of a 200-mile Exclusive Economic Zone on state
resource jurisdiction.

SOURCE: C. Richard Tinsley, "Mining of Manganese Nodules: An Intriguing
Legal Problem," *Engineering and Mining Journal,* October 1973, p. 87. Copy-
right (1973) by McGraw-Hill, Inc., 1221 Avenue of the Americas, New York,
N.Y. 10020.

EEZ of about 100 square miles.[63] Of course, the value of an EEZ is not related
merely to size. Those in the North Sea area, for example, appear to be richer in
hydrocarbons than those along the west coast of Africa although some of the
latter are larger. Table 6 lists nine countries, primarily in the Caribbean and the
South Pacific, that appear to have EEZs of limited economic value.[64]

Countries that are "geographically disadvantaged" with respect to the sea
have found ways of bending the EEZ concept to suit their economic interests as
well. This bloc includes 29 landlocked countries (see Table 7) plus about 20
other coastal states that lack full 200-mile EEZs owing to the presence of
opposite coastal states that lie fewer than 400 miles from their coasts or of
adjacent coastal states whose EEZs obstruct their direct access to the high seas.
Early in the UNCLOS debates the landlocked countries opposed the creation of
EEZs. Later they joined the narrow-shelf and "shelf-locked" states in favoring
EEZs provided that generous terms for international revenue sharing were
created simultaneously. Lately the group has taken the position of agreeing to
strong coastal state rights in the EEZ only on condition that they are given

TABLE 4

<small>STATES HAVING THE LARGEST EXCLUSIVE ECONOMIC ZONES</small>

State	Area (in 1000 square nautical miles approximate)
United States	2,222
Australia	2,043
Indonesia	1,577
New Zealand	1,409
Canada	1,370
Soviet Union	1,309
Japan	1,126
Brazil	924
Mexico	831
Chile	667
Norway	590
India	587
Philippines	551
Portugal	517
Madagascar	377
Total	16,100

<small>SOURCE: Lewis M. Alexander and Robert D. Hodgson, "The Impact of the 200-Mile Economic Zone on the Law of the Sea," *San Diego Law Review* 12 (1975):574–75.</small>

preferential rights in coastal state ports, fisheries, and, for landlocked countries, unhampered transit rights to the sea across their coastal state neighbors.[65]

The Full Margin: The Fourth Degree

The post-1958 enclosure movement would have been dramatic enough if the exploitability criterion had been replaced merely by a universal EEZ at a maximum of 200 miles. Since 1974, however, the delimitation of the EEZ has been equated with either 200 miles or the full continental margin, whichever is farther seaward, by such broad-margin countries as Bangladesh, Canada, Ireland, Korea, South American nations facing the Atlantic Ocean, the United Kingdom, and the United States.[66] Just as the broad-margin states argued for the exploitability criterion in 1958, they have recently realized again that, given the uncertainty of resource locations, jurisdiction over a larger area probably means jurisdiction over more resources.

This brief review of the history of ocean enclosures since 1945 suggests three propositions. First, the nature, extent, and timing of enclosures appears to be related to changes in economic and technological conditions. This conclusion is similar to that of Kenneth W. Clarkson, who traced the development of the international law of fisheries from Roman times to the mid-twentieth century.[67]

TABLE 5

STATES WITH SMALL CONTINENTAL MARGINS OR ECONOMIC ZONES

Less Than 1,000 Square Miles	1,000–5,000 Square Miles	5,000–10,000 Square Miles
Belgium	Albania	Bulgaria
Iraq	Bahrain	Congo
Jordan	Cameroon	Dahomey
Singapore	German Democratic	Gambia
Togo	Republic	Israel
Zaire	Kuwait	Lebanon
	Monaco	Poland
	Syria	Qatar
		Romania
		Yemen

SOURCE: Lewis M. Alexander and Robert D. Hodgson, "The Role of the Geographically-Disadvantaged States in the Law of the Sea," *San Diego Law Review* 13 (1976):564.

Clarkson found that property arrangements became less communal, more exclusive, and more frequently divided among countries where fish consumption was greatest, where technologies permitted the preservation of catches, and where comparative advantages in marine and naval activities permitted these rights to be enforced at relatively low cost.

Second, a controversy between one group of countries favoring a greater degree of enclosure and a second group seeking a lesser degree tends to be resolved in favor of greater enclosure as long as there is uncertainty over resource location and extent. The most far-reaching enclosure criterion having currency in 1958 was adopted at the First UNCLOS and the same is likely to occur at the Third UNCLOS whether or not it is able to conclude its work. Between 1945 and 1977, Truman's proclamation on the continental shelf was expanded markedly by other nations both in its extent of area and by the inclusion of living resources.

TABLE 6

STATES WITH INDICATIONS OF LIMITED RESOURCE POTENTIAL IN THEIR PROSPECTIVE ECONOMIC ZONES

Barbados	Kenya
Dominican Republic	Nauru
Grenada	Tanzania
Haiti	Western Samoa
Jamaica	

SOURCE: Alexander and Hodgson (1976), p. 565.

TABLE 7

LANDLOCKED COUNTRIES

European

Andorra*	Luxembourg
Austria	Switzerland
Czechoslovakia	San Marino*
Hungary	Vatican City*
Liechtenstein*	

*Mini-states

On Other Continents

Afghanistan	Mali
Bhutan	Mongolia
Bolivia	Nepal
Botswana	Niger
Burundi	Paraguay
Central African Republic	Rwanda
Chad	Swaziland
Laos	Uganda
Lesotho	Upper Volta
Malawi	Zambia

SOURCE: Alexander and Hodgson (1976), p. 562.

The third proposition is that the prospect of an international conference designed to settle ocean law tends to stimulate an increase in the rate of enclosure which, if the conference eventually generates a treaty, will be recognized at international law. There is more than a little irony in this result: many who believed (and may still believe) that international procedures are the most effective mechanism for halting enclosures may be somewhat galled to learn that this mechanism actually promotes enclosure. Thus, many of those who favored UNCLOS as the last chance to halt creeping jurisdiction find that their efforts contributed to galloping enclosure instead.

4. THE ECONOMIC STANDARD: AVOIDING INEFFICIENCY

The scarcity of resources in the oceans compels society to choose not only how particular resources should be used but also which persons or institutions should make these decisions. As many economists recognize, the question of who makes the decisions is the more important, because it obviously has a great deal to do with the kinds of decisions that are made; that is, the institutional framework for decision making usually affects individuals' incentives to make certain choices, in that there are inevitably particular costs and rewards which influence decision makers as they weigh competing resource-use options. Different institutional rules give them varying incentives to make choices that are "better" or "worse" according to some standard. Few would accept the proposition that economics should be the sole standard for determining the rules to govern resource use in the oceans. Usually some attention is paid also to questions of national security, for example. On the other hand, few would suggest that the economic element of resource-use decisions should be ignored, especially during an era of rising demands for ocean resources.[68]

Usually, the economic consequences of an event are divided into two categories. The distributional effects refer to changes in the relative wealth—the size of the "slices" of the economic "pie"—accruing to individuals or nations as circumstances and policies change. The best example is establishing a tariff. If the United States government places a tax on foreign shoes, the sales of American shoe producers will increase relative to shoes made in Italy, the leading exporter. Assuming that the size of the economic pie is held constant, the redistribution of wealth between the two groups of producers is analogous to that of a zero-sum poker game in which the gains of the winners of the pot exactly equal the losses of the other players. Economics can compare the distributional shares of the various players before and after the tariff is imposed and in some cases can predict which participants will gain or lose. But economics does not make flat statements about the "ideal" distribution of wealth since there are no noncontroversial theorems that demonstrate the logical superiority of one wealth distribution over another. Economics demonstrates that the gains of all participants can increase only if the size of the pie grows, a positive-sum game in which the percentage shares of individuals may remain fixed.

The efficiency effects refer to changes in the size of the pie. The value of production obtainable from the existing stock of resources would be greatly increased when each productive resource is assigned to its highest valued use, and resource allocation is efficient when no further rearrangement of resources between uses would yield a net increase in the value of production. In our example, imposition of a tariff on foreign shoes will result in some inefficiency in both the Italian and the U.S. economies. The reduced American purchase of foreign shoes will cause idleness in Italy and reduce the size of the Italian economic pie, and the American pie will also shrink because Americans, one way or another, will have to spend more for shoes than before—either for American shoes or for Italian shoes on which a tariff has been imposed. Furthermore, more American resources will have to be allocated to shoe production than before, leaving fewer resources for other goods (which may in turn push up the prices of some of these items). Thus neither economy will maximize its value of production, as a direct consequence of the higher tariff (as long as all other economic forces remain the same).

Economic efficiency is not, however, a criterion that everyone is obligated to accept as a matter of logic. Most of us as individuals attach different weights to the goal of efficiency just as we adopt different notions of distributional fairness. But almost everyone will attach *some* value to reducing pure waste. Roland N. McKean has described this clearly:

> While few persons regard economic efficiency in the [technical] sense described above as their overriding objective or [standard], most of us have enough to gain from this kind of efficiency to keep it in mind as *one* of our important objectives. Congressional debates and hearings suggest that congressmen do give some weight to economic efficiency. . . . They do not have in mind the precise technical meaning of efficiency, yet the imprecise concepts they do have in mind certainly appear to be related to the technical concept. The weight placed on efficiency by congressmen strongly suggests that most voters—most persons in the society—attach *some* value to economic efficiency. They are willing to trade some efficiency for other objectives (for instance, fairness) when it is too expensive to bargain for efficiency plus the other objectives, but they are not willing to forget about economic efficiency entirely. For these reasons, the policy consequences that economics can trace out are relevant not merely because they are among the consequences but because they are consequences that most persons feel are important.[69]

The direction of the change in wealth for an individual or a nation following some event is determined by the net impact of the distributional and efficiency effects. For example, I may favor certain policies or institutional rules that put society as a whole at an inefficient point of resource use if it greatly increases my returns because the distribution of income happens to twist more than proportionately in my favor. I may also favor certain inefficient policies which, though yielding a zero net change in my own wealth, sharply improve the distributional share of individuals or countries which I happen to think are especially deserving. By the same token, I may oppose policies that yield a more equitable income distribution (as *I* judge it to be equitable) because they may drastically reduce the size of the pie. Economics is useful because it yields predictions about the direction, and occasionally the magnitude, of some of these impacts, and therefore shows to society the cost (the resources sacrificed) of pursuing a particular distributional goal, or vice versa. This is what McKean means by considering the trade-offs between efficiency objectives and fairness objectives.

The transition from high seas freedoms to enclosure represents a fundamental change in the institutional rules governing resource use in many coastal areas of the globe. The primary institutional choice that statesmen must now make is between (1) a continuation of past trends which stress increased resource control by coastal states, (2) granting increased authority to international institutions mainly at the expense of coastal states, and (3) returning to the era of strictly communal ownership.

The distributional consequences of the enclosure movement have received the most attention in the literature on oceans and in official policies. To take just one example, Ambassador Pardo's remarks appeared to stress the gains that enclosure offers to advanced technology countries at the expense of developing countries, to coastal nations at the expense of landlocked nations, and to countries intent upon ocean mining at the expense of existing mineral producers. The "competitive scramble" for resources that Pardo and others have predicted seems analogous to the zero-sum poker game. In this instance the value of resources available to potential winners is limited by the existing wealth of the other participants seated around the game table. The main questions to be settled are who will be winners or losers and what will be the extent of redistribution— both of which depend upon the skills of the individual players as well as upon the deal of the cards. It is possible that a game of the zero-sum type for the oceans could produce the destabilizing international political consequences that Pardo predicted if the resources at stake are extremely valuable and if no mechanism exists for making almost every "player" a "winner."

However, a destabilizing outcome is less likely if the enclosure movement substantially increases the size of the total economic pie. Greatly increasing the size of the pie will affect the distribution of wealth among countries, to the advantage of some and the disadvantage of others. In some countries the efficiency gains may reinforce the distributional gains, but in others the two effects may pull in opposite directions. Nonetheless, if enclosure yields both a greater value of production from ocean resources and creates at least some efficiency gains for a wide variety of nations that consume or produce ocean goods and services, the "game" at hand may be more akin to the positive-sum than the zero-sum type. The greater the size of the efficiency gains relative to the distributional losses for certain countries, the weaker will be the potentially destabilizing consequences of enclosure that several statesmen have hypothesized. The destabilizing consequences would be especially weak if the countries that benefited most from enclosure, either as producers or as consumers, also were in the strongest position to affect the stability of the international political system. Depending upon the size and influence of the efficiency and distributional impacts, it is conceivable that the net result of enclosure would be to *increase* international stability. The hypothesis that enclosure will be destabilizing to the international community cannot be eliminated as a matter of logic, but the strength of the argument has probably been exaggerated by a failure to take into account the efficiency impacts.

The standard measure of efficiency is economic rent.[70] Detailed estimates of economic rents for several resources in ocean areas that the United States now controls or is likely to control in the future are shown in Table 8. These estimates, calculated by Robert R. Nathan Associates of Washington, D.C., for the United States Senate, although far from definitive, suggest that the rents from oil and gas extraction will be several times more than the combined rents for the other resources. (The possible exception to this statement is that the rent for using the oceans as a receptacle for wastes, which is difficult to estimate, may be very large.) The practical implication of this finding is that where multiple ocean uses conflict or impose adverse spillover effects on one another, devoting the area in question to the use having the highest economic rent will provide the greatest cost saving to society at large. This action avoids inefficiency by avoiding or postponing wasteful activities.

A study of the efficiency implications of different institutional rules to govern ocean resources use—for example, the choice between the authority of coastal states versus international bodies over international straits—is equivalent to comparing the economic rents associated with each decision rule. Hence, a

TABLE 8

CRUDELY ESTIMATED AND PROJECTED ANNUAL ECONOMIC RENTS ATTRIBUTABLE TO SELECTED OCEAN RESOURCES CONTROLLED BY THE UNITED STATES, 1972/73−2000

(In billions of 1973 dollars)

Activity	1972	1973	1985	2000
Mineral resources:				
Oil and gas		3.90+	7.70+	9.40+
Manganese nodules			0.03−0.05	0.06−0.09
Living resources:				
Food fish	[1] 0.15−0.22		.19− .48	.27−1.20
Industrial fish	[1] .01− .02		.01− .02	.01− .04
Nonextractive uses:				
Energy[2]			.04− .07	.32− .54
Transportation[3]			.14− .34+	(?)
Recreation	[4]		[4]	[4]
Receptacle for waste	[5]		[5]	[5]

[1]Theoretical value, assuming nonexistent entry control; actual value is zero.

[2]Attributable to power generation offshore.

[3]Offshore deep-water ports for U.S. crude oil imports only.

[4]Large rents certain, but unmeasurable.

[5]Possibly significant, but unmeasurable.

SOURCE: U.S. Congress, Senate Committee on Commerce, *The Economic Value of Ocean Resources to the United States,* prepared by Robert R. Nathan Associates at the request of Hon. Warren G. Magnuson pursuant to S. Res. 222, National Ocean Policy Study (Washington, D.C., December 1974), p. 6. (Several errors in the original have been corrected.)

policy of maximizing economic rent is equivalent to a policy of avoiding inefficiency.

5. THE ECONOMIC PARADIGM

Although a universal Exclusive Economic Zone at least 200 miles in breadth is nearly an accomplished fact whether or not UNCLOS produces a comprehensive treaty for the oceans, the extent to which coastal states may exclude in these areas the competing uses of other countries remains a controversial issue. Coastal states emphasize their EEZ ''rights,'' but their ''duties'' are emphasized by nations with interests in distant-water fishing, marine commerce, scientific research, or mineral extraction off foreign coasts. The costs of these activities could rise if coastal states obtained unrestricted EEZ rights. Hence such countries favor imposing international constraints to ''induce'' coastal states to recognize ''their'' interests. At the heart of this controversy is the extent to which coastal property rights will be intruded upon by the powers of an international regime.

The economic element of this problem, as I stressed before, is to decide which individuals, firms, countries, other entities, or international authorities would make ''better'' or ''worse'' allocations of ocean space among competing uses and users according to the criterion of avoiding economic inefficiency. This problem becomes easier to deal with if it is broken into two subproblems. First, which type of ocean institution—coastal state or international authority—usually would have stronger incentives to recognize accurately and to weigh *all* the costs and benefits of different options? Second, which type of institution usually would face less difficulty (or, more precisely, have fewer transactions costs) of assigning and enforcing the structure of property rights that is associated with the highest economic rent? The growing literature on the economic theory of property rights has brought out many facets of the efficiency implications of different structures of ownership.[71] Two propositions of this literature appear to have special application to the selection of ocean institutions.

Exclusivity of Property Rights

The strength of a decision maker's incentives to invest in gathering information on alternative resource uses to the economical degree, to compare data on the economic rents of different uses, and to select the option having the highest rents depends on the amount of the resulting benefits and costs that belong exclusively to him. The greater (or smaller) the amount of benefits that the resource owner can capture for his exclusive use, the stronger (or weaker) his incentives to refrain from allocating resources to inefficient purposes that generate low rents.

Which type of ocean institution—coastal state or international authority—would in most cases have the stronger incentive to recognize accurately and to weigh the full benefits and costs of different ocean uses, and then to avoid the options that yield economic inefficiency? The answer to this question, which was first raised in section 2 of the preceding chapter, depends upon the extent of the spillovers associated with alternative uses and the degree to which they can be internalized within each of the alternative structures of ownership.

Returning to the example of tanker pollution, the spillover costs of oily beaches and destroyed marine life would be borne almost exclusively by the coastal state involved unless someone was strictly liable for the damage he caused. Since such liability is rare, a few coastal states have sought to reduce the risks to their shores by creating pollution control zones as a way of restricting tanker navigation. But since restrictions of this sort, especially if widespread, would naturally tend to raise somewhat the total cost of petroleum transport and the prices of oil imports, many oil-importing nations oppose them. The coastal states themselves would be little concerned with these extra costs—even though they represented a portion of the real opportunity costs of unpolluted coasts—unless imported oil formed an important fraction of their total use of petroleum and the increased costs of imported oil were a larger dollar amount than the expected cost of pollution abatement. Thus, coastal states having oil imports of relatively small value would generally find it inexpensive to trade off the higher costs of oil shipments borne by other nations against their reduced pollution abatement costs. At the extreme, coastal states that import relatively little petroleum would have weak incentives even to gather information on the opportunity costs of restricting tanker navigation, let alone to give these foregone opportunities much weight in actual decision making.

The manner in which an international authority reckoned benefits and costs would depend upon the characteristics of the pollution and the structure of the institution. Consider first the case where pollution damaged mainly the shore lines of the state(s) closest to its origin. An international authority composed mostly of nations far removed from the pollution site probably would attach the most weight to benefits that accrued to many of its members and to discount benefits or costs that were borne by only a few affected coastal states. Among the benefits that most member states could appropriate at least to some degree would be the lower costs of imported petroleum associated with unfettered tanker transportation. Among the costs that most nations belonging to the authority would not have to bear would be spillovers in the form of reduced values of polluted coastlines along established tanker routes. Therefore, as long as the effects of the pollution were confined to few countries and international decisions were made according to the rule of one-nation, one-vote, the international authority would usually find it rewarding to attach relatively little weight to localized pollution costs even though they represented the real opportunity costs of unrestricted tanker navigation near coasts. At the extreme, an international authority in this case, as with the coastal state in the previous situation, might find it unrewarding even to gather information on the pollution threats to coastal states from tanker navigation as long as the number and strength of affected states were small.

But it sometimes happens that pollutants are carried great distances via ocean currents and take their toll on the EEZs of states far distant from the pollution source. The larger the number of states that perceived an environmental threat from tanker pollution wherever it occurred, the greater the likelihood (*ceteris paribus*) that the international authority would take into account the full opportunity costs of unrestricted tanker navigation in a reckoning similar to that of the coastal state. The same result would occur if tanker routes exposed many coastal nations to the threat of polluted shore lines.

The point is that there are significant risks to generalizing about the degree of exclusivity of ocean property arrangements either for coastal states or for international authorities. Although there is a clear relationship between exclusivity per se and the avoidance of economically wasteful activities, the degree of exclusivity that different institutional structures offer is unclear. The example of spillovers from tanker pollution is a vivid illustration of this problem, but I shall argue later that this is really a ''worst case'' relative to the spillover problems from other ocean uses. Nevertheless, the oceans are mobile enough to offer some spillover potentials from almost every ocean use. This makes it necessary to attempt to reckon the relative incentives for efficiency on a case-by-case basis, taking into account also differences among resources and geography.

Costs of Transactions and Enforcement

To avoid inefficiency, once the property rights associated with the highest economic rents have been identified, they must be assigned to the most productive users and enforced against unauthorized users. The process of defining, assigning, negotiating, enforcing, exchanging, or subdividing property rights consumes both time and other real resources. These transactional arrangements are the costs of operating an economic or legal system, domestically or internationally. Generally, the higher the transactions costs are, the lower the probability that resources will be allocated to the uses or users that will avoid inefficiency. For example, assume that economic rents could be increased by $100 million over a 25-year period by shifting certain coastal areas from fishery use to an oil drilling field, but that the transactions costs of accomplishing this would amount to $101 million over the same period (including the cost of purchasing the implicit property rights of existing fishing fleets). Any coastal state or international authority devoted to avoiding inefficiency would, in this case, refrain from reallocating this ocean area to its highest rent use since the transaction would cost more than it would gain. Some of the extra economic rent could have been obtained if transactions costs had been smaller.

Because of the historic principle of freedom of the seas, unfettered navigation has long headed the list of property rights assignments in the use of the oceans, with other uses far behind.[72] The exceptions have been in certain areas where fishing has rivaled navigation, or surpassed it, to the extent that all other uses were forced to locate in ocean areas where no conflict existed. At certain times this was no doubt economical, since the number of uses of the oceans and the number of states having major ocean interests were relatively few; but as the variety of uses and users has increased, so have the transactions costs of sharing certain ocean areas between long-standing primary uses and new activities that offer potentially greater economic rents. The reason for this is that transactions costs tend to increase along with increases in the number of individuals or nations that must be included in agreements to restructure or reassign property rights.[73] Primarily because of the transactional impediments to joint action, ocean areas that would naturally be reassigned to higher rent purposes if transactions costs were trivial are instead locked in traditional uses. When the consent of many countries is required to rearrange long-standing patterns of ocean use, the resulting increase in efficiency often amounts to less than the transactions cost of achieving it.

Consider the use of the oceans as a sink for man's wastes. Historically, this has been one of man's primary uses of the world's oceans. Today, as the economic rents of certain ocean areas in nonpolluting activities appear to be rising, it seems evident that if the rents from cleaner seas begin to exceed the cost savings of using the seas for waste disposal, some reassignment of property rights should be made to fix more of the costs of polluting firmly on those who are responsible for the polluting. But the transactions costs of reversing the liability for ocean pollution must also be recognized; these would be enormous, owing to the large number of pollutants, individual polluters, and nations involved. Thus the initial assignment of rights is perpetuated in policy in spite of the seemingly uneconomic results because the costs of overturning it appear large relative to gains.

The same high cost of transactions as compared with potential gains can also prevent the internalization of beneficial spillovers. A notable example is that of the lack of investments in anadromous fisheries, even though they might greatly improve yields. These transactions costs are of two kinds, both extremely high. One is that of effectively enforcing the partitioning of the oceans in order to allow a home nation to harvest all the extra fish its husbandry could produce, with zero poaching by other countries. The other costs are those of negotiating and enforcing an agreement to divide husbandry investments and the resulting catch in some equitable fashion among the various fishing nations, each of which naturally tries to get the others to pay for most of the investments. As a result, communal arrangements are perpetuated, the productivity of a fishery becomes inefficiently small, overfishing is the rule, and economic rents are trivial at best.

In contrast to the difficulties of generalizing about the relative incentives of coastal states versus international institutions in the case of the exclusivity-of-property-rights proposition, the implications of the proposition on transactions costs are clear. Thus: the greater the number of participating nations and the more diverse their interests are, the larger the transactions costs of gathering information to the economical degree and of comparing data on the opportunity costs of alternative resource uses. Diversity of interests can also raise decision-making costs within a single country. If different pressure groups have vastly different goals in ocean uses, the costs of reaching agreement on a comprehensive national ocean policy may be even higher for a single state than for an international authority. (As we shall see in Chapter 10, the United States appears to be one of these special cases.) Generally, however, the costs to a group of states of reaching and enforcing agreements are greater than the decision-making costs for a single state. That being true, it follows that the probability that an international authority composed of many states would avoid inefficient uses of the ocean is smaller than the probability for individual coastal states. These higher costs of reaching and enforcing decisions appear to be an abiding characteristic of international procedures. The level of transactions costs is plainly one of the things that cannot, at least in this analysis, be held constant between institutions of different types.

Conclusions and Qualifications

The economic analysis to this point, which has been limited to applying the two propositions to a few examples of each type of spillover situation, does not suggest a general presumption in favor of one type of ocean institution over the other. The proposition on transactions costs implies that coastal states often will find it less expensive (more rewarding) to avoid inefficient ocean outcomes, but the exclusivity-of-property-rights proposition gives ambiguous results. Depending upon the degree to which particular benefits and costs are internalized, decision making in institutions of either type may occasionally be biased toward inefficient choices. This suggests that a detailed analysis of the implications for spillovers and transactions costs of each ocean resource will be necessary in order to learn whether the two propositions are reinforcing or conflicting. This is done in Chapters 3–7 for coastal resources and in Chapter 8 for the deep seabed minerals. In each chapter the economic analysis follows a discussion of important physical characteristics of the resource and the technologies for exploitation. This is based on my judgment that the economics can be deduced straightforwardly once the characteristics of the resource and the means for extracting it from nature are well understood.

At the outset, three specific qualifications to the analysis should be made. First, comparisons between coastal states and international bodies for their relative incentives to avoid economic inefficiency must be to some extent hypothetical, especially for international authorities. Some coastal states have had experience in controlling ocean resource exploitation under 200-mile enclosures, and I have used the available information to assemble case studies wherever possible. But the available information is scanty in most situations owing to the novelty of 200-mile zones. Comparisons between coastal state outcomes and the results of decision making in international bodies are even more difficult to draw since an international authority for the oceans has yet to be created. As we shall see, there are at the present time roughly half a dozen international bodies that have some control over shipping or fishing, but none has the jurisdiction or power to allocate ocean resources between uses or users to the degree that the proposed international seabed authority presently under debate at UNCLOS would have. Indeed, this authority "would magnify by many orders of magnitude beyond current practice the regulatory activities of international organizations with regard to the oceans."[74] This, of course, is the principal reason why the creation of this proposed authority is so controversial.

Second, for those comparisons that are possible, the "model" dichotomy that I employ most frequently is between coastal states that do not share authority over some ocean resource with other countries, and international bodies that by their very nature divided control according to the rule of one-nation, one-vote. Obviously, these two situations represent polar extremes at either end of a continuum of institutional structures. For example, the United States enclosure of hydrocarbons in 1945 represents an absolute degree of coastal control, and the 150-nation UNCLOS represents the opposite extreme, with institutional mixes lying somewhere in between. Regional groups of countries designed to solve particular spillover problems is one obvious possibility, which I shall discuss in the chapters on fisheries and pollution. Another possibility would be an international body in which decisions were made according to weighted voting or other rules that made it less expensive for individual countries with strong interests to register either their power or their preferences. Some present international bodies contain weighted voting systems of some kind for quasi-executive functions, but these are usually tied to an overall policy-making legislature in which all members vote equally.[75] To avoid confusing the analysis with the many forms of weighted voting that could be devised, the discussion is limited to only the most prominent possibilities that have received attention at UNCLOS. Dwelling on too many of these variations would detract from comparisons between the two polar institutional types and their economic implications.

The third qualification concerns the importance of economic interests in the oceans in relation to other national objectives. By focusing on the standard of avoiding inefficiency, I do not mean to suggest that nations rarely attach value also to noneconomic objectives, much less that they should systematically avoid inefficiency to the exclusion of other objectives.[76] I can easily imagine that in some cases a nation's leadership would be willing to trade important economic objectives for other goals (such as political prestige or improvement of the incomes of certain domestic groups), just as I am unable easily to imagine that many national leaders would for very long systematically pursue goals that yielded substantial economic waste. A nation might, for example, because of its domestic political structure, take a position at UNCLOS that generated $5 million in benefits to its military by trading away other economic rents which in the aggregate reduced its national wealth by $6 million. But one would expect trade-offs of this sort to be made less frequently (or with more strings attached) when the rents sacrificed were ten times greater and even less so when the rents sacrificed were one hundred times greater. The larger the economic rents that are given up, the greater the opportunity cost to the nation of taking positions that yield either reduced wealth or inefficient resource-use outcomes.

Notes

1. G. Etzel Pearcy, "Geographical Aspects of the Law of the Sea," *Annals of the Association of American Geographers* 49 (1959):11.

2. Bruce C. Heezen, Marie Tharp, and Maurice Ewing, *The Floors of the Oceans: I. The North Atlantic*, Geological Society of America Special Paper no. 65 (1959), p. 18. My description of the geomorphology of the continental shelf and margin is based on pp. 17−21.

3. K. O. Emery, "The Continental Shelves," *Scientific American*, September 1969, p. 108.

4. Often the demarcation between the shelf and slope (called the shelf edge) is more easily observed than the junction between the slope and rise (sometimes called the base of the continent or the base of the slope). See Hollis D. Hedberg, "The National-International Jurisdictional Boundary on the Ocean Floor," *Ocean Management* 1 (1973):83−102.

5. Heezen et al., p. 83.

6. In general, see Sir Edward Bullard, "The Origin of the Oceans," *Scientific American*, September 1969, p. 69; H. W. Menard, "The Deep-Ocean Floor," ibid., pp. 126−42. Sea-floor spreading is integral to the theory of continental drift (called plate tectonics). This theory views the earth's surface as composed of about six giant

slabs, each of which may contain portions of a continent and an ocean basin, which are "floating" in convergent or divergent directions on an underlying layer of molten material. These movements create new oceans as plates move away from each other as in the case of the Red Sea, or earthquakes where plates collide as in the case of the northern and eastern rims of the Pacific Ocean.

7. Convention on the Territorial Sea and Contiguous Zone, done at Geneva, April 29, 1958, art. 7, 15 U.S.T. 1606, T.I.A.S. No. 5639, 516 U.N.T.S. 205.

8. Anglo-Norwegian Fisheries Case (1951), I.C.J. 116.

9. The usual juridical definition of a fjord is a deep indentation of the coast (bays are semicircular) surrounded on three sides by land, not islands.

10. Robert D. Hodgson and Lewis M. Alexander, *Towards An Objective Analysis of Special Circumstances* (Kingston, R.I.: Law of the Sea Institute, Occasional Paper no. 13, 1972), pp. 23–44; hereafter cited as Alexander and Hodgson (1972).

11. Ibid., p. 29.

12. Ann L. Hollick, "United States and Canadian Policy Processes in Law of the Sea," *San Diego Law Review* 12 (1975):530–31.

13. Agim Demirali, "The Third United Nations Conference on the Law of the Sea and an Archipelagic Regime," ibid. 13 (1976):749–50. See also Choon-Ho Park, "The South China Sea Disputes: Who Owns the Islands and the Natural Resources?," *Ocean Development and International Law Journal* 5 (1978): 42.

14. See U.S. Department of State, Bureau of Intelligence and Research, Office of the Geographer, *Limits in the Seas, No. 36: National Claims to Maritime Jurisdictions* (3d. rev., Washington, D.C.: December 23, 1975), pp. 26, 124, and passim.

15. Several other terms have been used to describe the same jurisdictional claim. Among these are Coastal State Economic Area, Coastal Economic Area, and Coastal Economic Zone.

16. Convention on the Continental Shelf, art. 5, done at Geneva, April 29, 1958 (effective for U.S. June 10, 1964), 15 U.S.T. 471, T.I.A.S. No. 5578, 499 U.N.T.S. 311.

17. Lewis M. Alexander and Robert D. Hodgson, "The Role of The Geographically-Disadvantaged States in the Law of the Sea," *San Diego Law Review* 13 (1976):562; hereafter cited as Alexander and Hodgson (1976).

18. Park, passim.

19. An isobath contour is a map line everywhere along which the ocean has a given depth.

20. "Proclamation Concerning United States Jurisdiction over Natural Resources in Coastal Areas and the High Seas," White House Press Release to accompany U.S. Presidential Proclamation No. 2667, September 28, 1945, reprinted in U.S. Department of State, *Bulletin*, vol. 13, no. 327 (September 30, 1945), pp. 484–85.

21. U.S. Presidential Proclamation No. 2667.

22. Myres S. McDougal and William T. Burke, *The Public Order of the Oceans* (New Haven and London: Yale University Press, 1962), p. 670.

23. White House Press Release, September 28, 1945.

24. UN, *Synoptic Table Concerning the Breadth and Juridical Status of the Territorial Sea and Adjacent Zones: Notes by the Secretary General*, Doc. A/CONF.19/4 (February 8, 1960); reprinted in *Conventions on the Law of the Sea*, Hearing before the U.S. Senate Committee on Foreign Relations, 86th Cong., 2d Sess. (January 20, 1960), pp. 27–38. A different accounting of these claims is given in McDougal and Burke, pp. 669–70; and in Northcutt Ely's testimony in *Law of the Sea and Peaceful Uses of the Sea-beds*, Hearings before the Subcommittee on International Organizations and Movements of the U.S. House Committee on Foreign Affairs, 92d Cong., 2d Sess. (April 1972), pp. 50–53. See also Marjorie M. Whiteman, *Digest of International Law* (Washington, D.C.: U.S. Department of State Publication 7825, 1965), IV, 789–814; Richard Young, "The Continental Shelf in the Practice of American States," *Inter-American Juridical Yearbook 1950–1951* (Washington, D.C.: Pan American Union, 1953), pp. 27–36; and Sir Hersh Lauterpacht, "Sovereignty over Submarine Areas," *British Yearbook of International Law: 1950* (London: Oxford University Press, 1951), vol. 27, pp. 376–443.

25. Richard Young, "Further Claims to Areas Beneath the High Seas," *American Journal of International Law* 43 (1949):790.

26. Territorial Waters of Saudi Arabia, Decree No. 6/4/5/3711, May 28, 1949, reprinted in ibid., (Suppl. 1949), pp. 154–57; Bahrain Government Proclamation No. 37/1368, June 5, 1949, reprinted in ibid., pp. 185–86.

27. Ann L. Hollick, "The Origins of 200-Mile Offshore Zones," *American Journal of International Law* 71 (1977):494–500. This source argues that Chile and Peru, which were among the first countries to establish 200-mile fishing zones, could just as well have established 50-mile zones since few of their fleets ventured beyond this distance. However, this reasoning fails to account for other incentives for erring on the high side.

28. These could include strategic considerations and the internal strengths of various interest groups. Chapter 10 describes competition within the U.S. government between the navy, which opposed enclosures, and the oil industry, which generally favored them.

29. In the classic case, two persons who are apprehended for joint commission of a crime have strong incentives to remain silent if there is neither witness nor independent evidence that would otherwise convict them. But if the authorities separate the two and offer immunity to the first one who confesses, behavior that would be irrational becomes logical owing to the high cost to each suspect of monitoring the other's statements.

30. Basil N. Petrou and R. David Ranson, "Resources from the World's Deep Seabeds: The Law and Economics of an Unborn Industry" (Washington, D.C., mimeo draft, 1975), p. 20. The argument expressed in the quoted passage in the original source pertains to competitive claims to deep seabed areas, but it applies with equal force to coastal resource enclosures.

31. A lucid history of these concerns and deliberations is given in McDougal and Burke, pp. 671–87.

32. Ibid., pp. 678–79.

33. Statements that reflect the national economic interests of these countries can be found in, e.g., ibid., pp. 672–73; United Nations, *Yearbook of the International Law Commission*, 1950, I, 218–24, 304–6; also 1951, I, 270, 273, 299; and 1956, I, 131.

34. The Caribbean area contains a large number of coastal states in close proximity.

Although the exploitability criterion extended the area of each state's exclusive resource jurisdiction relative to the 200-meter delimitation, it did not solve the problem of determining boundaries between the jurisdictions of states opposite or adjacent to one another. These boundaries would have to be determined by separate agreements among the nations involved.

35. See the *ILC Yearbook*, 1951, I, 273; and ibid., 1953, I, 77−82.

36. *Inter-American Specialized Conference on "Conservation of Natural Resources: The Continental Shelf and Marine Waters," Ciudad Trujillo, March 15−28, 1956, Final Act* (Washington, D.C.: Pan American Union, 1956), p. 13, reprinted in UN, *ILC Yearbook*, 1956, II, 251−52.

37. Evidently the affirmative vote of the U.S. for the Resolution of Ciudad Trujillo was related directly to its status as a "broad margin" nation. According to one State Department official, the U.S. went to this conference with the intention of supporting a 200-meter delimitation to the continental shelf. During the negotiations, the delegation was provided with "a detailed bathymetric chart of the East Coast, which showed that a curious platform exists off New York a short distance down the Continental Slope at a depth slightly greater than 100 fathoms. On the basis of the possible strategic importance of this special area, the U.S. Delegation cabled home and was authorized to support the 'feasibility' rule, which was adopted by this Conference." See Norman V. Breckner et al., *The Navy and the Common Sea* (Washington, D.C.: U.S. Office of Naval Research, 1972), p. 223.

38. See *ILC Yearbook*, 1956, I, 130−41; Whiteman, *Digest of International Law*, IV (1965), pp. 829−42.

39. Convention on the Continental Shelf, art. I (1958).

40. See, e.g., McDougal and Burke, pp. 671−72.

41. April 29, 1958 (effective for the U.S. March 20, 1966), 17 U.S.T. 138, T.I.A.S. 5969, 559 U.N.T.S. 285.

42. This issue will be discussed further in Chapter 5.

43. April 29, 1958 (effective for the U.S. September 10, 1964), 15 U.S.T. 1606, T.I.A.S. No. 5639, 516 U.N.T.S. 205.

44. UN General Assembly Official Records, First Committee, *Examination of the Question of the Reservation Exclusively for Peaceful Purposes of the Sea-Bed and the Ocean Floor, and the Subsoil Thereof, Underlying the High Seas Beyond the Limits of Present National Jurisdiction, and the Use of Their Resources in the Interests of Mankind*, 22d sess., Agenda Item 92, Doc. A/C.1/PV.1515 (November 1, 1967), pp. 12−13.

45. UN General Assembly, *Declaration and Treaty Concerning the Reservation Exclusively for Peaceful Purposes of the Sea-Bed and of the Ocean Floor, Underlying the Seas Beyond the Limits of Present National Jurisdiction, and the Use of Their Resources in the Interests of Mankind*, Note verbale dated 17 August 1967 from the Permanent Mission of Malta to the United Nations Addressed to the Secretary General, 22d Sess., Doc. A/6695 (August 18, 1967).

46. UN Doc. A/C.1/PV1515, p. 2.

47. UN General Assembly Official Records, *Resolutions Adopted During its 24th*

Session, September 16–December 17, 1969, Suppl. No. 30, Doc. A/7630, 1833d Plenary Meeting, Resolutions 2574A-D (December 15, 1969), pp. 10–11.

48. UN General Assembly Official Records, *Question of the Reservation Exclusively for Peaceful Purposes of the Sea-Bed and the Ocean Floor, and the Subsoil Thereof, Underlying the High Seas Beyond the Limits of Present National Jurisdiction, and the Use of Their Resources in the Interests of Mankind: Report of the Committee on Peaceful Uses of the Sea-Bed and the Ocean Floor Beyond the Limits of National Jurisdiction,* Agenda Item 32, 24th Sess., Doc. A/PV.1833 (December 15, 1969), p. 4.

49. Ibid. As it turned out the opposite was true. UNCLOS had much more difficulty reaching agreement over the division of the mineral resources of the "common heritage" than the division of coastal fishing rights between the adjacent countries and those that fish at a great distance from their home waters. This issue is discussed in Chapter 9.

50. UN General Assembly, First Committee, *Question of the Reservation Exclusively for Peaceful Purposes of the Sea-Bed and the Ocean Floor, and the Subsoil Thereof, Underlying the High Seas Beyond the Limits of Present National Jurisdiction, and the Use of Their Resources in the Interests of Mankind,* 24th sess., Agenda Item 32, Doc. A/7834 (December 9, 1969), p. 15.

51. Ibid., p. 16.

52. References to each of these groups of countries as likely supporters of the proposal can be found in UN Doc. A/C.1/PV1515, p. 4 (para. 29), and p. 9 (para. 70).

53. Comments made by President Johnson at the commissioning of the research vessel *Oceanographer* on July 13, 1966, *Weekly Comp. Pres. Doc.,* vol. 2, p. 931 (1966).

54. Richard M. Nixon, Statement on United States Oceans Policy, ibid., vol. 6, p. 667 (May 23, 1970).

55. Henry A. Kissinger, "The Challenge of Peace," speech before the St. Louis World Affairs Council, St. Louis, Mo., May 12, 1975.

56. The conference does not include every law-of-the-sea issue; for example, it has not seriously attempted to curtail the practices of coastal states in drawing base lines or common boundaries.

57. Ambassador Pardo appears to have anticipated this problem and warned the General Assembly of it on the day the first UNCLOS resolutions were passed: "Those States which have extended their national jurisdiction to vast distances from their coasts will find support in this resolution for the claims they have already made, while those States, such as mine, which have been modest in their claims and which have been respectful of the rights of others, find that their interests are ignored." UN, General Assembly Official Records, 24th Sess., Doc. A/PV.1833 (December 15, 1969), p. 5. In reply, the U.S. delegate, Mr. Phillips, argued, as I have here, that the more important cause of accelerated enclosures was the fact that another law of the sea conference per se had been scheduled. "In practical effect," he said, "this draft resolution is likely to encourage some States that may feel it useful or necessary to engage in exploration or exploitation of sea-bed resources to move towards unjustifiably expansive claims of national jurisdiction solely in order to remove those exploitation activities from the scope of the prohibition contained in the draft resolution and thus, render them, in their view, legitimate." Ibid., p. 2.

58. John Temple Swing, "Who Will Own the Oceans?" *Foreign Affairs* 54 (1976): 531.

59. "From Pole to Pole: Nations Race to Grab Sea's Riches," *U.S. News and World Report*, Aug. 13, 1973, p. 49.

60. Eight states opposed the proposal and 33 either abstained or did not address the subject at Caracas. Lewis M. Alexander and Robert D. Hodgson, "The Impact of the 200-Mile Economic Zone on the Law of the Sea," *San Diego Law Review* 12 (1975):570; hereafter cited as Alexander and Hodgson (1975).

61. Ibid., pp. 572−73. These percentage calculations are based on the assumption that all islands regardless of size are given EEZs of 200 miles; the slightly lower percentage for the Indian Ocean is due to its having fewer islands than the other oceans. Bodies of water that would be nearly enclosed by a 200-mile EEZ are the Bay of Bengal, the Gulf of Mexico, and the Norwegian and Arabian seas.

62. Ibid., pp. 572−75; Lewis M. Alexander, "Geography and the LOS Debate: Geographical Factors and the Patterns of Alignment," in *Perspectives on Ocean Policy*, report of the Conference on Conflict and Order in Ocean Relations, held October 21−24, 1974, at Airlie, Va. (Washington, D.C.: National Science Foundation, NSF-75-17, 1975), pp. 319−24. All the following measurements are in terms of nautical miles, where one nautical mile equals 1.151 statute miles.

63. Alexander and Hodgson (1975), pp. 574−75; Alexander and Hodgson (1976), p. 564.

64. These inferences, however, can be misleading unless total national wealth is taken into account. For example, Nauru, the tiny island mentioned previously, has guano deposits which, since 1973, have given it the highest per capita income in the world, a situation likely to continue for at least another fifteen years. See Walter McQuade, "The Smallest, Richest Republic in the World," *Fortune*, Dec. 15, 1975, pp. 132−40.

65. See Arvid Pardo, "Future Prospects for Law of the Sea," in *Perspectives on Ocean Policy*, p. 391; Alexander, p. 321.

66. Alexander and Hodgson (1975), p. 594.

67. "International Law, U.S. Seabeds Policy, and Ocean Resource Development," *Journal of Law and Economics* 17 (1974):117−25.

68. Dividing resources or rising resource values may also increase the political element of decision making, as the recent experience with petroleum indicates.

69. Roland N. McKean, "Products Liability: Trends and Implications," *University of Chicago Law Review* 38 (1970):42.

70. Recognizing that interest in this subject goes beyond economics to such fields as ecology, politics, and international law, I have placed in the notes explanations of certain basic economic concepts that might not be familiar in other disciplines.

Economic rent measures the cost advantage of either superior resources or superior ways of doing things. It is a residual value that is left over after all costs have been accounted for and all subsidies have been excluded. For example, if an opera singer's next-best employment is selling shoes, then the difference between the two wages would be the scarcity rent attributable to the specialized singing talent. A coastal area that is worth more as a field for offshore oil drilling than as a shipping lane would show a larger rent in the former use. Similarly, the difference between the profits in drilling for oil on a parcel of land that is expected to yield 500 barrels per day at a well depth of 5,000 feet would be worth more than the right to drill for the same quality of oil on a different parcel that is expected to give the same barrel output but at a depth of 10,000 feet, and this difference in returns (the rent) would be reflected in a higher market value of the first parcel.

The concept of economic rent was first developed by economists of the eighteenth and nineteenth centuries who used the term to describe the returns from the use of land. Land is an input into productive processes that is fixed in its total amount but not in its division between various economic activities. For example, the total quantity of land along the New York waterfront is absolutely limited, but the amount that can be used for warehouses versus apartment buildings is usually variable. The same applies to the division of most ocean areas among competing uses. Economists now apply the term to the returns to any factor of production that cannot be augmented. The returns to "human capital," such as the opera singer, are usually called *quasi* rents—for not only is human capital transitory in its life span but also the returns captured by one opera singer tend to stimulate other individuals to develop competitive singing talents.

71. For a sample of this literature, see Armen A. Alchian, *Some Economics of Property* (Santa Monica: Rand Corporation, Report No. P-2316, May 26, 1961); A. A. Alchian and Reuben A. Kessel, "Competition, Monopoly, and the Pursuit of Money," in Universities-National Bureau of Economic Research, *Aspects of Labor Economics* (Princeton: Princeton University Press, 1962), pp. 156–75; R. H. Coase, "The Problem of Social Cost," *Journal of Law and Economics* 3 (1960):1–44; Harold Demsetz, "Toward a Theory of Property Rights," *American Economic Review Papers and Proceedings* 57 (1967):347–59; "Some Aspects of Property Rights," *Journal of Law and Economics* 9 (1966):61–70; Eirik G. Furubotn and Svetozar Pejovich, "Property Rights and Economic Theory: A Survey of Recent Literature," *Journal of Economic Literature* 10 (1972):1137–62.

72. Clarkson, pp. 118, 142.

73. This argument is based on R. H. Coase, "United States Policy Regarding the Law of the Seas," in *Mineral Resources of the Deep Seabed*, Hearings before the Subcommittee on Minerals, Materials, and Fuels of the U.S. Senate Committee on Interior and Insular Affairs, 93d Cong., 2d Sess., pt. 2 (1974), pp. 1166–67.

74. David A. Kay, "International Ocean Organizations and Their Regulatory Functions," in *Perspectives on Ocean Policy*, p. 291. The International Telecommunications Union does have limited jurisdiction over international uses of the radio spectrum resource, and in Chapter 9 it will be compared with hypothetical ocean authorities.

75. The obvious model is the United Nations itself, where the General Assembly votes on the basis of strict equality of members, but the Security Council does not.

76. Most of the economic analysis of transactions costs has been based on individual behavior assuming wealth maximization. See Coase (1960) and James M. Buchanan and Gordon Tullock, *The Calculus of Consent* (Ann Arbor: University of Michigan Press, 1962), pp. 63–84. The analysis of these authors has been extended from individual behavior to the behavior of nation-states without the assumption of wealth maximization.

CHAPTER 3

Regulating Navigation

The most striking implication of ocean enclosure for navigation users has been the extension of territorial seas from three to twelve miles. In 1958, 46 or about 60 percent of the countries participating in the First UNCLOS adhered to the three-mile limit,[1] but by 1977 only 26 or about 17 percent of those participating in the Third UNCLOS did.[2] A universal twelve-mile territorial sea would enclose approximately 121 straits of less than 24 miles in breadth. Most lack commercial or military significance owing either to low demand for transit or to the availability of alternatives.[3] Several are important, however, and if closed would force ships to follow detours of sometimes thousands of miles. Among these are the Bering Strait, joining the Arctic and Pacific oceans, Bosporus-Dardanelles, Dover, Gibraltar, Bab el Mandeb and Hormuz, two Middle Eastern straits connecting the Indian Ocean with the Red Sea and the Persian Gulf, respectively, and four straits in Southeast Asia—Lombok, Luzon, Malacca, and Sunda—which link the Pacific and Indian oceans, making it unnecessary to circumnavigate Australia.

The high seas principle means essentially that the ships of any nation may navigate and exploit riches without having to rely exclusively upon the strength and inclination of the coastal state for their safety or well-being.[4] The opposite principle applies to internal waters, through which foreign ships may not sail without express consent. Lying between internal waters and high seas is the territorial sea. Navigation in this area is subject to the vague rule of "innocent passage" as stated in the 1958 Geneva Convention on the Territorial Sea and Contiguous Zone. According to this rule, coastal states may prevent the transit of surface ships that would be "prejudicial to the peace, good order, or security of the coastal state."[5] The Convention declares that unannounced submerged passage or overflight by aircraft of the territorial sea are not innocent, but beyond this it offers no interpretation of what is "prejudicial."

The trend in coastal state interpretations of innocent passage is in harmony with other aspects of the enclosure movement of the oceans. Increasingly, coastal states are restricting ships to specified sea-lanes, forcing navigational users to share certain areas with oil rigs, threatening to exclude supertankers above a certain size and other vessels with dangerous cargoes, and contemplating charging tolls through high-demand straits. Elizabeth Young predicts that the definition of prejudicial will eventually be expanded so that "no under-insured, ill-equipped, ill-navigated, chartless, flag-of-convenience-registered, 250,000-ton tanker can ever be 'innocent' in the English Channel or the Malacca strait, or, should it find itself there, in the Canadian Arctic. Liquid natural gas and petroleum carriers cannot long fail to be subjected to special regulations throughout their journey, particularly in crowded waters."[6] The nuances of prejudicial and innocent transit become moot, of course, where archipelagic or coastal nations construct base lines that enclose straits as internal waters.

1. RISING DEMAND FOR NAVIGATION

Queen Elizabeth of England, in 1580, replying to complaints by Spain about Drake's exploits in the West Indies and the Pacific, stated the English point of view about *mare clausum*. "The use of the sea and air is common to all," she said; "neither can any title to the ocean belong to any people or private man, forasmuch as neither nature nor regard of the public use permitteth any possession thereof."[7] In the sixteenth century, the vastness of ocean space relative to demands in most areas of course made the seas a free good that was "common to all." But their use as unobstructed trade routes in a few relatively congested areas required rationing processes which either complemented or substituted for the usual method of first come, first served. During the age of sail, ocean users were few in number and their passage was slow and more or less predictable along the lanes of known trade winds and tides. The rules of the sea were correspondingly simple and inexpensively enforced. They included common practices concerning ships lightings, sound signals, channel markings, and rights of way—notably the rule that approaching ships avoid collision by each turning to starboard, which appears to have been based on little more than the right-handedness of 90 percent of the world's population.[8]

As the advent of steam after 1830 markedly increased the speed and maneuverability of ships, navigational rules of the road were adjusted as the number of accidents rose, and the precedent of admiralty court rulings in favor of the keep-to-the-right rule was codified into international agreements for ocean (and eventually air) navigation.[9] But recent technological progress in the size and speed of vessels apparently has not been matched by technological improvements in aids to navigation, and thus the margins for navigational safety have steadily declined.[10] More hazardous cargoes have increased the cost of miscalculating depths, distances, and speeds of approaching ships. It is possible that some rules are now so out of date that under certain circumstances they actually raise the probability of collisions.[11]

Congestion is related to both the number and size of ships. Table 9 indicates that total world ship cargo increased more than threefold between 1959 and 1974, and that tanker cargo increased by nearly fourfold during the same period. Table 10 estimates that non-fishing vessels at sea will rise by about 22 percent between 1969 and 1980, and oil tankers will increase by almost 20 percent. Increased

TABLE 9

Goods Loaded in International Seaborne Shipping by Type of Cargo, for World in Various Years

Year	Tanker Cargo	Dry Cargo (millions of metric tons)	Total Cargo
1937	105	389	494
1950	225	325	550
1959	478	518	996
1969	1,276	1,036	2,312
1970	1,440	1,165	2,605
1971	1,526	1,173	2,669
1972	1,654	1,219	2,873
1973	1,867	1,407	3,274
1974	1,838	1,450	3,288

SOURCE: United Nations, *Statistical Yearbook—1975*, table 17, p. 63.

TABLE 10

Vessels at Sea, Estimated for 1969 and Projected in 1980

Vessel Type	1969 Population	Number at Sea	1980 Population	Number at Sea
Tankers	5,869	4,637	7,039	5,559
Ore and bulk carriers	2,378	1,474	5,370	3,519
General cargo and passenger	26,100	5,269	19,565	4,935
Others	3,980	270	2,984	254
Subtotal	38,327	11,650	34,958	14,267
Fishing	11,949	9,323	19,156	14,946
Total	50,276	20,973	54,114	29,213

SOURCE: Robert P. Thompson, "Establishing Global Traffic Flows," *Journal of Navigation* 25 (1972):484, 491. Reproduced from *The Journal of Navigation* (1972), by courtesy of the Council of the Royal Institute of Navigation.

speed and containerization over the past two decades have effectively doubled cargo ship capacity by reducing turnaround times. Rising traffic relative to the space available has caused more groundings and other mishaps,[12] and larger ships mean that the potential consequences of each mishap are also greater. In the year 1970, 7 percent of the merchant fleet was involved in at least one two-ship collision, and in the period 1964–70 dollar losses to insurers increased by 41 percent.[13]

The growth of the world's tanker fleet is illustrated in Table 11. About 5,000 tankers were in operation in 1976, of which 50 were expected to be in excess of 400,000 deadweight tons (dwt) and 1,100 feet in length.[14] A giant tanker is similar to an iceberg, having only one-fifth of its hull visible above water and a draft of between 70 and 95 feet. A ship of this mass is suited to operations in deep water and relatively few ports. It requires a large area for turning, tends to be unmaneuverable at low speeds, and may require three miles to come to a complete stop at full speed (which can be twenty knots). These same character-istics, and especially its huge hull, make it vulnerable to collision with smaller vessels under less skilled masters. Its hull shape and hydrodynamics cause it to

TABLE 11

CHARACTERISTICS OF THE WORLD TANK SHIP FLEET, 1900–1976

Year	Number	Deadweight Tons	Average Speed (Knots)
1900	109	530,725	9.03
1910	208	1,248,718	9.38
1920	540	4,417,041	10.01
1930	1,191	11,060,794	10.29
1940	1,637	17,581,257	11.18
1945	1,768	21,667,642	12.67
1950	2,056	26,957,200	13.30
1955	2,681	41,623,100	14.00
1960	3,264	65,780,400	15.10
1965	3,436	93,171,900	15.70
1966	3,524	102,908,800	15.70
1967	3,613	112,366,200	15.70
1968	3,748	126,454,200	15.80
1969	3,893	146,029,100	15.80
1970	4,002	167,940,000	15.80
1971	4,207	193,891,000	15.80
1972	4,342	221,204,000	15.80
1973	4,572	256,822,000	15.80
1974	4,892	302,276,800	15.70
1975	5,112	348,586,400	15.70
1976	5,140	382,534,000	15.70

SOURCE: Sun Oil Company, Sun Shipbuilding and Dry Dock Company, *Analysis of World Tank Ship Fleet*, eds. 1–35 (Chester, Pa.: 1942–77); reprinted in American Petroleum Institute, *Petroleum Facts and Figures*, 1971 ed., p. 246.

"squat" at the bow as it slows down, thus increasing its draft, and the Bernoulli effect in narrow waters tends to pull it toward shallow banks. All these things add to the risk of transit through straits, where its size alone contributes to congestion. The size and design of giant tankers also make them vulnerable to the 80-foot freak waves that sometimes occur in continental shelf areas, particularly off the Cape of Good Hope, one of the world's busiest and most treacherous stretches of sea, where tankers ride fast and dangerous currents along the edge of the shelf to save on transit time and fuel.[15] Their cargoes pose a potential environmental risk. The increasing number of tanker accidents, including strandings and groundings (Table 12), is a source of concern to coastal states and will perhaps eventually lead to their placing certain restrictions on tanker passage.

One of the most serious problems of maritime congestion occurs in the straits of Malacca and Singapore, which together form the major artery between the Indian Ocean and the South China Sea and thence to the Pacific Ocean.[16] The geography is illustrated in Figure 9. The Strait of Malacca is about 500 miles long and lies between the island of Sumatra, belonging to Indonesia, and the west coast of the Malay Peninsula. It narrows at one point to less than nine miles and then continues for another sixty miles as the Strait of Singapore, where it narrows to a little over three miles. Both Indonesia and Malaysia claim twelve-mile territorial seas, and Singapore has a three-mile claim. The substitute route, skirting Sumatra to the west, involves roughly three additional days and 900 miles via the Strait of Sunda, between the islands of Sumatra and Java, or about

TABLE 12

ANNUAL SHIP ACCIDENTS, INCLUDING GROUNDINGS AND
STRANDINGS, 1959–1968.

Year	Tankers in N.W. European Waters	All Ships in N.W. European Waters	Tankers Worldwide
1959	258	1,354	1,078
1960	240	1,067	1,247
1961	310	1,177	1,370
1962	267	1,196	1,187
1963	305	1,091	1,290
1964	304	1,217	1,354
1965	299	1,336	1,358
1966	249	951	1,555
1967	230	1,030	1,384
1968	287	1,082	1,556
Totals	2,749	11,501	13,379

SOURCE: C. Grimes, "A Survey of Marine Accidents with Particular Reference to Tankers." *Journal of Navigation* 25 (1972):497. Reproduced from *The Journal of Navigation* (1972), by courtesy of the Council of the Royal Institute of Navigation.

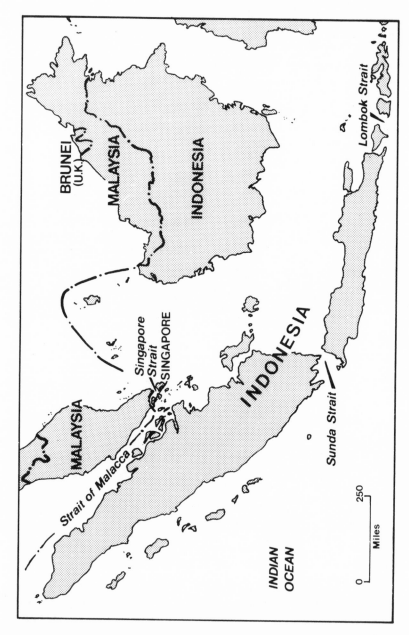

FIG. 9. Southeast Asia, showing the straits of Malacca and Singapore and the straits of Sunda and Lombok.

four additional days and 1,200 miles via the Strait of Lombok, east of Bali, and thence through the Macassar Strait.

In 1972, about 40,000 ships—100 to 150 per day—navigated the Malacca and Singapore straits. Most were large petroleum tankers bound for Japan, which obtains 85 percent of its oil from the Persian Gulf via the two straits. Depths in the area rarely exceed 75 feet, and tankers larger than 200,000 dwt clear the bottom with no more than one fathom to spare. Shoals, swift currents, and the agitation of powerful screws cause the bottom to shift much like sand dunes, making navigation charts unreliable. Groundings are common and at least one major collision occurs there each month. The straits also appear to be among the world's most polluted waterways, as a result of which fishing in the area has declined drastically. Navigational tolerances are so close and the giant ships have so little room to maneuver that there are many cases in which tankers allegedly have been unable to avoid smaller craft, with attendant loss of life.[17]

The 1972 grounding of the *Showa Maru*, a Japanese tanker of 1,075 feet and 237,000 dwt, spilled about 20,000 barrels of petroleum in the straits. This led Indonesia and Malaysia to consider closing the straits to vessels in excess of 200,000 dwt. Japan estimated that detours through the Strait of Lombok might add as much as a billion dollars annually to their oil bill, and for a time apparently it considered the possibility of constructing either a canal or a pipeline across the Isthmus of Kra in Thailand.[18] Japan also argued at UNCLOS that the straits should be controlled by an international authority, but this is a proposal that the three straits states categorically reject. Both Indonesia and Malaysia have established joint patrols of the straits and have accepted Japan's offer to finance a fresh navigational survey of the area. They have also considered imposing transit tolls, which would discriminate according to the value of the cargo ($5,000 for tankers and $3,000 for other ships); these could have yielded about $147 million in the year 1972.[19]

2. ECONOMIC RENTS TO USE OF STRAITS

How much would shipping costs increase if key straits were closed? Although there are relatively few data suggesting the magnitudes of economic rents to ocean transportation, several a priori factors suggest that they should not be relatively great. First, merchant shipping is typically a low-profit activity. Ship construction and operations appear to require low-wage labor, and few big-income countries engage in either activity without subsidization.[20] (These subsidies must, of course, be subtracted from shipping earnings so that the resulting net economic rent reflects an actual cost advantage.) Second, the closure of straits increases the cost of transportation along the affected route, but it does not end ocean transportation between the two ports. There are ocean substitutes for almost every strait (the extreme substitute of circumnavigation of the globe would be a rarity) and there are land substitutes for Gibraltar. Third, the per-mile operating cost of shipping is relatively low, so the resulting impact of straits closure on goods prices should be small for substitute routes short of circumnavigation.

In 1972, Robert R. Nathan Associates attempted to estimate the economic rents to the United States from several ocean resources.[21] The three straits having the greatest economic importance for the U.S. are the English Channel, Gibraltar, and Malacca. Based on several restrictive assumptions about detours, it was estimated conservatively that the additional shipping costs incurred in avoiding these straits in 1972 would have been at least $51 million.[22] (This very rough estimate is sensitive not only to the assumptions made about detours but to both the growth in U.S. trade and the rate of oil importation from Alaska to West Coast ports, which would reduce the U.S. demand for oil shipments through Malacca.)

A second estimate of U.S. economic rents from shipments of crude oil from the Middle East was prepared for the U.S. Department of the Treasury by David B. Johnson.[23] Johnson estimated the extra costs of shipment if each nation along the route imposed an extended territorial sea or pollution control zone which forced U.S.-bound tankers to remain at least 200 nautical miles from coastlines. For the trip from the Persian Gulf around the Cape of Good Hope to Philadelphia, the estimated extra cost was ten cents per barrel of oil; this was half the cost differential of twenty cents per barrel that Johnson attributed to the closure of the Suez Canal. The cost differential for the trip between the Persian Gulf and San Francisco around Australia rather than through the Straits of Malacca and Singapore was thirty-five cents per barrel or about 30 percent of the shorter trip. These data are given in Table 13. After projecting U.S. oil imports for the period 1976 to 2000, Johnson concluded that the annual increase in U.S. oil shipping costs—that is, the loss of economic rent—would amount to about $137 million, or a total of $3.4 billion (nondiscounted) over the 25-year period. Two qualifications must be attached to Johnson's study, however: the cost differentials depend on the charter rates for tankers, which tend to swing widely, and on bunker fuel costs, which tend to rise; also, it is feasible for tankers to remain at least 200 miles from the Cape of Good Hope, but it is a less safe route owing to the greater occurrence of freak waves in deeper areas.[24] For these reasons the strong incentives of tankers to sail within twelve miles of the South African coast give South Africa much greater potential for extracting either a fee or political concessions that would nearly equal the cost savings of avoiding the substitute routes.

In a third study, Johnson and Dennis E. Logue estimated that the loss in

TABLE 13

ROUND-TRIP TANKER TRANSPORTATION COSTS UTILIZING ALTERNATIVE
ROUTES FROM THE PERSIAN GULF

	To Philadelphia			To San Francisco		Differential Costs Between Normal Routes & 200-Mile Regime Routes
	Suez Canal	Cape of Good Hope	200-Mile Regime	Malacca-Singapore Strait	200-Mile Regime	
Per barrel costs (dollars)	1.00	1.20	1.30	1.13	1.48	–
Total annual costs ($ millions)						
Assuming 2.5 mmb/d to Atlantic Coast	913	1,095	1,186	–	–	91
Assuming 2.0 mmb/d to Atlantic and .5 mmb/d to Pacific Coast	730	876	949	206	270	137
Nondiscounted costs, 1976-2000 ($ millions)						
Assuming 2.5 mmb/d to Atlantic Coast	22,825	27,375	29,650	–	–	2,275
Assuming 2.0 mmb/d to Atlantic and .5 mmb/d to Pacific	18,250	21,900	23,725	5,510	6,750	3,425

NOTE: It is assumed that all trips are made in 250,000 dwt tankers at 1973 time-charter hire rates and that bunker fuel is priced at $70 per ton. Light loading for the winter weather zone located 200 miles off Cape of Good Hope is included in cost estimate for 200-mile regime as well as a small time differential for an adverse current.

SOURCE: David B. Johnson and Dennis E. Logue, "U.S. Economic Interests in Law of the Sea Issues," in Ryan C. Amacher and Richard James Sweeney, eds., *The Law of the Sea: U.S. Interests and Alternatives* (Washington, D.C.: American Enterprise Institute for Public Policy Research, 1976), p. 67.

economic rent to the U.S. from the closure of the English Channel, through which between 22 and 27 percent of U.S. imports typically pass, would amount to about $35 to $45 million per year.[25] Therefore, the three studies of economic rents to navigation are reinforcing but not definitive. Each suggests that the value of straits transit to the U.S., though positive, is not overwhelming, and that the closure of such straits would affect the U.S. in ways that are less than devastating. Furthermore (see Table 14), of the straits that are most important to the U.S., only Malacca is expected to increase in traffic through 1980; thus the previous estimates of rents to the U.S. from straits use probably are not underestimated by a failure to project the growth in shipping. For other nations, however, the cost savings from the use of straits would be considerable—for example Japan, which as we have seen imports almost all its petroleum through

TABLE 14

ESTIMATED GLOBAL TRAFFIC FLOWS BY REGION, 1969 AND 1980

| | Ships per Day | |
Region	1969	1980
English Channel	400	340
Strait of Gibraltar	215	180
Strait of Malacca	85	180
Cape of Good Hope	160	225
Coast of Japan	100	190
Masqat (Persian Gulf)	80	180

SOURCE: Robert P. Thompson, "Establishing Global Traffic Flows," *Journal of Navigation* 25 (1972):488, 494. Reproduced from *The Journal of Navigation* (1972), by courtesy of the Council of the Royal Institute of Navigation.

Malacca and Singapore. The closure of the straits there would by no means cut off Japan's access to oil, but there is no question that the cost of transporting it would rise by the cost of detours through the straits of Sunda or Lombok, or an amount equal to the economic rents captured by Japan from the use of the more direct route.

3. COMPARING INSTITUTIONAL INCENTIVES

Which type of institutions would have stronger incentives for avoiding uses of straits that yield inefficient ocean outcomes? Restricting navigation through straits would reduce the economic rents to shipping, a cost borne mostly by maritime countries, and would result in benefits in the form of reduced pollution, a gain captured mostly by the state or states controlling the straits. The paradigm presented in the preceding chapter suggests that coastal states would internalize a greater fraction of the full benefits and costs from straits use and would enforce the associated structure of property rights at a lower transactions cost, depending upon two factors: the extent to which the coastal state itself engages in foreign trade, and the cost of collecting tolls for passage through the straits.

Restricting the passage of ships through straits is analogous to imposing a tariff: it raises somewhat the prices of imported goods and services to the coastal nation and lowers somewhat the net prices received by its exporters. This tariff is therefore an opportunity cost that will be borne by the coastal state in direct proportion to the importance of international trade in its gross national product. The same point applies either to regulations that exclude all oil tankers from straits or that exclude only those tankers above a certain size. The greater the degree to which a coastal state's oil consumption is imported, the greater the extent to which these regulations are self-defeating. In either case the restrictions impose costs on the coastal state as well as on other states; the greater the amount of such costs that the coastal state bears, the less one would expect to see of this sort of restriction.

This is not to argue that the gains of unfettered ocean transportation exceed the potential costs of pollution abatement for every straits state. The net impact of this mix of gains and costs is an empirical matter that will vary from country to country. All things considered, the costs of pollution abatement may turn out to exceed the gains from freer trade for countries along tanker routes having valuable coastal fisheries or recreational opportunities, and just the reverse is likely to apply more often to straits states that are major oil exporters. I venture to say, however, that most straits states will recognize that there is at least some cost that they incur by restricting navigation, and that this realization will lead these states to internalize at least some of these costs either by postponing the introduction of restrictions or by making them weaker, if not avoiding them altogether. The greater the value to the straits state of either the foreign trade or the oil import, the proportionately stronger its incentives to internalize more spillover benefits and costs.

The different possibilities for internalizing navigational rents are illustrated in the positions taken by the three states bordering the straits of Malacca and Singapore.[26] Singapore is the world's fourth busiest port and is a major stopover for bunkering and refitting all but the biggest ships. It would have much to lose from restricting navigation through the straits. It has steadfastly maintained a three-mile territorial sea and, contrary to the views of Indonesia and Malaysia, continues to recognize both straits as international waterways. Malaysia's port interests are relatively few in number, and of the three states it would no doubt suffer the most damage from a major pollution incident. Indonesia, according to Michael Leifer and Dolliver Nelson, has an economic interest in building up its ports at the expense of Singapore. Thus it is in its own interests to force ships to reroute through the straits of Lombok or Sunda, which it controls. In other words, two of the three straits states do take into account at least some of the spillover benefits of navigational use, although one of them has perverse incentives owing to the area's unique geography.

The second condition that would lead straits states to take into account the cost consequences of restricting navigation is the possibility of collecting a portion of shipping rents through tolls. The greater the potential income from tolls, the less bias straits states would have in favor of pollution reduction and against pollution-prone navigation, especially if toll income exceeded the increases in the prices of their imports and exports that were caused by tolls. Therefore, the incentives of straits states to prohibit or restrict navigation in certain areas would be fewer, the greater the costs that they would bear from diminished maritime trade, and the smaller the costs of pollution abatement relative to the combined costs of diminished trade and foregone toll income.

The literature on the law of the sea has always viewed shipping tolls as an undesirable and disruptive impediment to international trade and has tended to minimize their affirmative implications for promoting trade by inducing straits states to refrain from restricting navigation. This bias in the literature reflects the fears of maritime nations that they will be "blackmailed" by straits states. As James L. Johnston has pointed out, the blackmail hypothesis is weak in its basic assumption:

> . . . that countries with the ability to restrict passage through straits and other areas will in fact stringently restrict passage through straits. There are several reasons to question this result. First, a coastal state accrues costs by restricting navigation, both the direct costs of detecting violations by ships or aircraft, patroling and enforcing the restrictions, administering the penalties, and collecting the fees, and the indirect costs of distinguishing among ships so that the prices of imports and exports are not raised to the straits states and their allies, and coping with animosity and possible retaliation from maritime powers on whom these states otherwise depend.
>
> The most important straits are bordered by more than one country. Thus, for the straits states to close an important strait would be equivalent to their forming a viable monopoly—always a costly business. To enjoy whatever monopoly rents would accrue from restricting passage, it would be necessary for several states to act in concert. This arrangement contains an inherent destabilizing factor, however, since it would be in the interest of any one of the states bordering on the strait to reduce prices enough to draw for more than its share of the monopoly rent. In the limit, this behavior would reduce the monopoly rents to zero. This would be the expected result if the countries bordering on the strait were generally on friendly terms. The same result would come much more quickly if the states were not on friendly terms, like Spain and Morocco which border the Strait of Gibraltar.[27]

Tolls would serve an economic purpose by reducing the number of navigation users in those straits where congestion was rising and could reach dangerous levels. Some ships that carried lower valued cargoes could afford to incur delays either in the form of detours or by planning in advance to use the strait at less congested times.[28] Income would be redistributed somewhat from maritime states to straits states, but maritime users also would gain assurance of a passage with fewer interruptions. Moreover, the extent of the redistribution would probably be small since the economic rents to ocean shipping do not appear to be large.

A somewhat different problem arises if a ship traveling a given trading route encounters a series of coastal state territorial seas or EEZs, each of which constitutes a quasi-monopoly geographical position. For example, the problem of "successive monopolies" could arise for westbound tankers leaving the Persian Gulf for Rotterdam. The trip through the Mediterranean encounters two straits, Suez and Gibraltar, plus the EEZs of several intervening littoral countries. This raises the prospect of each nation demanding a toll for transit rights, much in the same way as along the Rhine River during the Middle Ages when German "robber knights" used the strategic positions of their castles to exact "safe conduct" tolls from merchants.[29] The possibility of this actually occurring is remote, however, for two important reasons. In the first place, the aggregate amount that all coastal states along the Mediterranean route could collect, either by a concerted effort of the group or by a series of individual actions, could not exceed the maximum amount that any one of them could obtain. This would be the economic rent of avoiding a more circuitous and expensive passage. Trying to collect more than the economic rent would cause traffic and revenues to fall, and this would signal the countries involved to lower their tolls to more reasonable levels. This incentive to set tolls at an aggregate level that did not exhaust economic rents probably explains why the Rhine trade thrived during the Middle Ages in spite of the large number of tolling stations. The second reason why aggregate tolls along the Mediterranean would be unlikely to exceed available rents is the fact, as the Mediterranean states and all shippers recognize, that a substitute route exists around the Cape of Good Hope involving no straits and fewer unavoidable EEZs than through the Mediterranean.

The familiar experience of the Suez Canal illustrates the inherent limits to the exercise of a geographical monopoly. The canal's reopening to international shipping on June 5, 1975, was proclaimed by President Sadat as Egypt's "gift to the world,"[30] but it is a gift for which the Egyptians levy a charge. The director of the canal authority, viewing the reopening prospectively in 1974, stated that "we expect to be able to set dues that will make it in the interest of a ship to use the canal if it physically can."[31] The actual "dues" were about double the 1967 rates or almost $1.00 a ton; the highest fee paid in 1976 was $200,000 for the passage of a 249,000 dwt tanker.[32] Evidently this structure of fees did not maximize the wealth of the canal authority in 1975−76 since the toll revenues were significantly lower than the $400 million that the canal authority anticipated. Traffic averaged only 20−25 ships per day versus the pre-1967 average of 63.[33] The fees were too high because it was now cheaper for many ships to take the substitute route, circumnavigating Africa. As oil shipments declined after 1974, the demand for tanker charters fell relative to the number of tankers available and the rates for charters dropped sharply; as a result, the opportunity cost of taking the long way around fell in both time and dollars, and there was less demand for use of the canal than Egypt had anticipated. The canal, for example, reduces the trip from the Persian Gulf to Rotterdam by twelve days.[34] Assuming a daily operating cost of $7,000 for a large tanker,[35] the rate of $1.00 per ton means that tankers of more than 100,000 dwt can usually break even by taking the longer trip around the Cape of Good Hope (leaving aside the greater risks associated with this voyage). Egypt is planning to improve the canal by deepening it for even larger tankers, but since the economic rents for large tankers would probably be less than the fees based on the 1976 rate, it may be obliged to reduce the tolls somewhat. The director of the canal authority has been quoted as saying that "After the improvement [canal deepening] program we have to reexamine the toll structure because perhaps it may be a bit high."[36]

There is little evidence to suggest that congestion in straits is rapidly increasing, so the imposition of tolls on a broad scale is unlikely at least for the present. Straits states are wary of imposing tolls even where the threat of pollution damage is relatively great, as in the Strait of Malacca. Conditions may change, however, and the economic function served by tolls—both as an inducement to coastal states to avoid restrictions on navigation and to reduce traffic congestion—should be kept in mind. Instead of tolls, strait states could perhaps establish certain tie-in arrangements that would be more palatable politically to maritime states but would serve the same purpose as tolls. Ship owners might be asked to insure their vessels with firms licensed by strait states and pay higher-than-competitive premiums. Alternatively, they could be asked to purchase bunker fuel or have their ships overhauled in the ports of straits states in exchange for rebates on or exemptions from tolls. Either policy would induce higher-cost firms to enter the insurance or repair industries, thereby inducing some inefficiency, but these costs may be worth the political gains from avoiding tolls outright. Still another possibility is that tolls could be used to create a fund for abating pollution damage and improving navigational aids, or even to purchase up-to-date navigation charts and other information.[37] Moreover, if tolls are imposed, the Suez experience suggests that there is definitely an upper limit to the amount that a state can extract from shippers using a particular route.

In sum, the low economic rents to navigation suggest that straits states have little to gain economically by placing unreasonable restrictions on navigation. This appears to explain why the UNCLOS negotiations on straits and the territorial sea, which will be detailed in Chapter 9, have yielded only minor new impediments to navigation.[38] But a strong case can be made on efficiency grounds for straits states levying tolls where shipping in confined waters has potentially drastic spillover consequences. The imposition of tolls permits the straits state to pursue not only its own self-interest in garnering a larger distributional slice of the ocean economic pie but also a general efficiency interest in having navigational users bear a larger share of the full costs they create.

Straits states would have incentives to avoid prohibitive toll rates that would reduce their revenue and raise the costs of their imports and exports.

A one-nation, one-vote international authority with jurisdiction over straits navigation would have higher costs of assigning and enforcing regulations relative to coastal state jurisdiction. Also, it would be very unlikely to offer an offsetting advantage in the internalization of spillovers since it probably would attach greater weight to the widespread benefits of lower shipping costs than to the hazards that some shipping imposes on just a handful of coastal nations. Internalization of spillovers would occur only if the authority were required to make an accurate appraisal of the pollution damage, and to make compensation for it fairly in usable currencies. Existing international financial institutions, such as the International Bank for Reconstruction and Development and the several regional development banks, do not appear to be suited to this purpose, since they customarily extend loans and grants for the purpose of economic development rather than as compensation for spillovers. Moreover, the straits states that are vulnerable to pollution damage include not only developing nations but wealthier countries such as France, Spain, Turkey, the United Kingdom, and Persian Gulf nations. (Most of the countries in this group transfer resources to, rather than receive resources from, international institutions.) Coastal state authority appears to offer greater prospects that more spillovers will be accounted for while consuming fewer resources in transactions and enforcement.

4. CONFLICTING USES IN OTHER OCEAN AREAS

In the past, masters of vessels could correctly consider navigation to be the paramount use of the oceans. In the course of their voyages they had to be concerned mainly with the weather, the location and speed of other ships, and such natural obstacles as reefs. This era has ended as the number of threats to navigation increased owing to an increase in nonnavigation uses of the oceans. In straits, ships carrying dangerous cargoes now must compete for space with other uses that require a relatively unpolluted water column. In other coastal areas, even around ports, ships of all kinds compete for space with oil rigs, dredges, and various kinds of new installations mentioned in Chapter 1. The same acre of ocean space cannot be used both as a shipping lane and as a site for offshore oil drilling without risking a catastrophe, and institutional rules must be devised for giving preference to one use among the various competing uses in ways that take into account the associated economic rents.

International law, according to the Geneva Convention on the Continental Shelf, offers no firm rule for trading off navigation uses versus nonnavigation uses. The convention states that "the exploration of the continental shelf and the exploitation of its natural resources must not result in any unjustifiable interference with navigation," but it permits coastal states "to construct and maintain or operate . . . installations and other devices necessary for its exploration and the exploitation of its natural resources, and to establish safety zones around such installations and devices and to take in those zones measures necessary for their protection." The convention also declares that "neither the installations or devices, nor the safety zones around them, may be established where interference may be caused to the use of recognized sea lanes essential to international navigation."[39] What are justifiable or reasonable interferences with navigation, and who is to make this determination?

The extension of coastal state nonnavigation activities into areas that were once strictly the preserve of navigation users raises the question of whether coastal states will recognize the resulting spillover costs in their decision-making calculus. At the extreme, it is feared that coastal states could "blackmail" maritime states by threatening to establish oil rigs or other fixed installations in areas that had previously been used largely for shipping. Recognizing these concerns, Kenneth W. Clarkson has proposed an international agreement which would require coastal states to dedicate certain areas for the exclusive use of ships. As he describes it:

> The most efficient international agreement governing the assignment and enforcement of ocean rights requires a closer tailoring of regulations and other constraints with existing and expected economic conditions. . . . For example, the agreement might establish two separate types of navigation rights, one to regulate areas where relative values of navigation and nonnavigation uses are unlikely to change and one where change is more likely to occur. . . . Where navigation uses are likely to remain the highest valued use of the ocean, primary ocean navigation routes with international modification procedures could be instituted. Rights to primary navigation routes would reflect existing and near term future usage and would be defined with respect to location or potential harm (open seas vs. bays) and degree of competition (continental shelf vs. high seas). Furthermore, these rights should be *firmly* established requiring renegotiation of the initial international agreement when change is desirable. However, the agreement must also allow for low cost reassignment to higher valued uses when changes in the relative values of navigation and nonnavigation are likely to occur. . . . This may be accomplished by creating secondary, but transferable, navigation rights in areas where navigation is currently less valuable but likely to change. Such areas might include navigation routes bordering the primary navigation routes to facilitate possible increased usage or new technology in ocean vessels.[40]

Clarkson's argument in favor of international regulations would be unnecessary if coastal states took navigation into account before constructing fixed installations or determining other ocean uses, and there is evidence that they do.

There were approximately 700 active oil platforms along the United States coast in the Gulf of Mexico in 1976, some of them located 100 miles from shore.[41] Since these rigs could pose serious hazards for ships, certain areas have been designated as shipping "fairways" in which no permits are granted for oil drilling (see Fig. 10).[42] Shipping is not required to use fairways, but masters of vessels are assured of obstruction-free passage through these areas.[43] The fairway program began in 1954, and in the early years fairway locations were occasionally changed if they were found to be superimposed over important fields of oil and gas. Later, as the number of oil rigs increased, it became more expensive to relocate the fairways than for oil firms to use slant drilling to penetrate these fields. The United States publishes navigational charts showing the precise locations of each oil rig and submersible installations, and abandoned rigs must be removed. Its procedures for fairways appear to be in harmony with the provisions of the Continental Shelf Convention pertaining to interferences with navigation, and they are probably enforceable at low cost relative to Clarkson's proposal for international jurisdiction over sea-lanes.

The higher transactions costs associated with international procedures are also apparent in the attempts of the Inter-Governmental Maritime Consultative Organization (IMCO) to cope with navigational safety in the English Channel. IMCO is a specialized agency of the United Nations which, among other things, drafts conventions that for signatories set standards for the operation of vessels and recommends routes for sea-lanes in high-density areas. The English Channel is the world's most heavily traveled waterway. Its east-west traffic amounts to roughly 350 ships per day in addition to more than 200 crossings between the English and French coasts.[44] It is shallow and often of uncertain depth owing to shifting sandbanks and fixed natural obstacles. Between 1959 and 1973, there were an average of 12.4 collisions annually; two-thirds of these occurred in fog, which is present in the Channel about one percent of the time.[45] Nearly one-half of all the world's ship collisions in 1970 occurred in and around the Channel.[46]

Transactions costs appear to be large relative to gains for the few littoral states along the Channel even to agree on a division of the cost of navigational aids having spillover benefits. The British regularly remove shipwrecks along the English coast even though this creates spillover benefits for other countries. But as of 1971 at least a dozen wrecks remained along the coasts of Belgium, France, and Holland, and some of these were left unmarked.[47] One agreement among several countries to improve navigation took eight years to complete because the group had to wait upon France to pay for a lightship along its coast that would essentially be a "present to the world at large."[48]

In 1961, several governments in the area proposed a traffic-separation scheme, and it was adopted by IMCO in 1967. Sea-lanes direct eastbound traffic along the French coast and westbound traffic along the English coast, with channel ferries being required to cross at right angles to the sea-lanes. (The system is illustrated

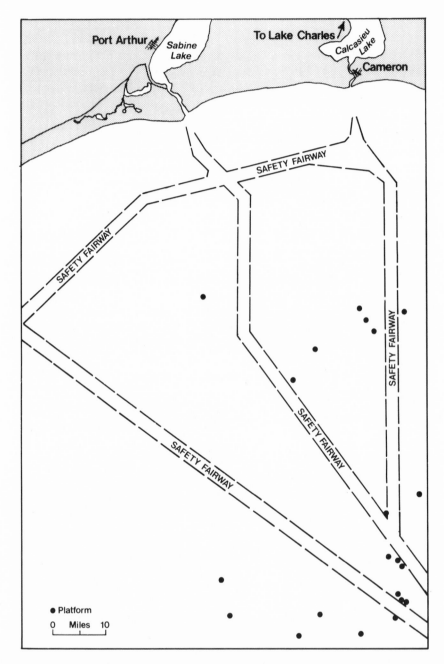

FIG. 10.   Safety fairways in the Gulf of Mexico near entrances to Port Arthur and
Orange, Texas (left), and Lake Charles, Louisiana (right).

SOURCE: Portion of U.S. Nautical Chart No. 11340, "United States Gulf Coast: Mississippi
River to Galveston," 37th ed., June 10, 1978 (Washington, D.C.: U.S. Department of Commerce, National Oceanic and Atmospheric Administration, National Ocean Survey).

in Fig. 11.) Even these relatively simple regulations, much like a system of traffic lights or freeway signs, tended to improve safety. Table 15 reveals that the number of collisions (or "meetings") declined by about 40 percent in the five years after the system was introduced compared with the preceding five years.[49] IMCO has since recommended similar plans for the ports of Boston, Brest, Chesapeake Bay, Los Angeles, New York, Piraeus, Rotterdam, and San

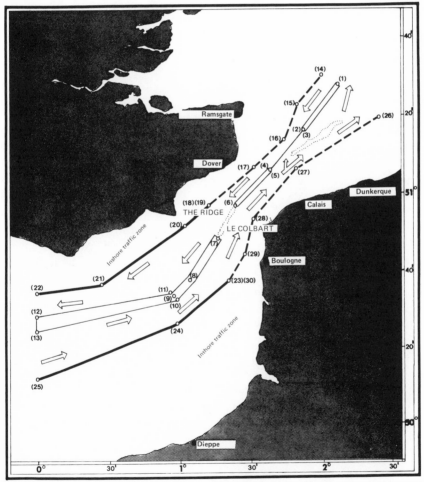

IN THE STRAIT OF DOVER AND ADJACENT WATERS

FIG. 11. Traffic separation scheme in the English Channel.

SOURCE: Inter-Governmental Maritime Consultative Organisation, *Ships' Routeing*, 3d. ed. (London, 1973), p. 47.

TABLE 15

EFFECTS OF TRAFFIC SEPARATION SCHEME ON SAFETY IN
DOVER STRAIT, 1962—1972

	5 Years Before (1962)	5 Years After (1972)
Total number of major happenings	73	70
Total number of collisions		
(meeting, crossing, overtaking)	62	50
Collision-encounter situations		
Meeting	46	28
Crossing	7	6
Strandings	11	20

SOURCE: T. Macduff, "The Probability of Vessel Collisions," *Ocean Industry*, September 1974, p. 144.

Francisco, also for the Baltic Sea, waters near the English and French coasts, the Skagerrak, and several straits.[50]

IMCO's experience appears to support the proposition that the costs of reaching and enforcing agreements, whether to establish property rights or less complex regulatory schemes, increase with the number of countries whose consent is required. By its charter, IMCO can only invite and exhort member governments to ratify traffic-separation agreements or to prevent the shipping under their jurisdictions from violating these rules of the sea. IMCO agreements must be approved by countries having two-thirds of the world's merchant tonnage in order to have standing at international law, and only one of the three conventions that IMCO has sponsored over the past decade is even close to obtaining approval by the necessary number of states.[51] Ships of some countries may of course abide by the new rules even without ratification, but in the English Channel, enforcement remains a problem since IMCO must rely entirely upon the efforts of individual countries. The United Kingdom imposes small fines of up to £100 on ships of British registry that violate the rules and has persuaded Belgium, Denmark, Liberia, Norway, Sweden, and West Germany to take action against violators under their registries. Other signers have taken weaker actions, however, and the ships registered in countries that have not signed the agreement (notably Cyprus and Panama) violate the rules routinely.[52]

5. CONCLUSIONS

Since the close of World War II, the use of the oceans as a commons for navigational purposes in coastal areas has declined with the almost universal extension of territorial seas to twelve miles. This realignment of rights and duties has paralleled a steady upward trend in the number and size of ships in the world merchant fleet as well as a trend toward more dangerous cargoes. Coastal states have, in a few situations, established new regulations which have tended to internalize on navigation users the spillover consequences of collisions or groundings, especially of supertankers in environmentally precarious areas.

These trends do not represent an important threat to navigational freedom generally, although they may in certain cases lead navigation users to bear more of the full costs of their actions or their carelessness. So far, the regulations imposed by coastal states have not been arbitrary or uneconomical, and it seems unlikely that they will be so in the future. Any nation that benefits from international trade has an incentive to recognize that jingoistic restrictions on navigation amount to an effective tariff against its own imports and exports as well as those of other countries. Moreover, it is unlikely that navigation would be curtailed sharply even if certain coastal states attempted to take advantage of their geographical quasi-monopoly positions. The fees that they could capture for passage through straits are usually limited by the costs of circumnavigation, and they would have incentives to set fees low enough to avoid huge reductions in traffic. An additional reason why fees would probably be low is that the monopoly rents to navigation uses relative to other ocean uses appear to be relatively low. If navigation uses grow sharply in the future and congestion in key straits tends to increase, then tolls would serve the dual economic purposes of rationing use at peak times and increasing safety.

Notes

1. J. E. S. Fawcett, "How Free Are the Seas?" *International Affairs* 49 (1973):18.

2. See Table 1 above.

3. This is the judgment of Robert E. Osgood based on charts made available by the Office of the Geographer, U.S. Department of State. See "U.S. Security Interests in Ocean Law," *Ocean Development and International Law* 2 (1974):1—36. These calculations are based on measurements from actual coastlines, not hypothetical base lines.

4. H. Lauterpacht, "Sovereignty over Submarine Areas," *British Yearbook of International Law* 27 (1951):378.

5. *Territorial Sea Convention*, art. 14(4), 15 U.S.T. 1606, T.I.A.S., no. 5639. See also H. Gary Knight, "The 1971 United States Proposals on the Breadth of the Territorial Sea and Passage Through International Straits," *Oregon Law Review* 51 (1972):769—70.

6. Elizabeth Young, "New Laws for Old Navies: Military Implications of the Law of the Sea," *Survival* 16 (1974):265.

7. T. W. Fulton, *The Sovereignty of the Sea*, p. 107.

8. The supporting evidence is mostly anecdotal. In order to keep their right hands free for drawing swords, soldiers have usually carried their scabbards on their left sides. Thus, they also mounted horses and escorted ladies on the left. A papal ordinance in the 18th century kept road traffic on the left, but after 1800 Napoleon changed Europe to the right which explains why Englishmen today drive on the left instead. Drivers of horse teams generally sit on the right, as did the pilots of early ships before modern naval architects placed the helm amidships. See L. F. E. Coombs, "Right- and Left-hand Dominance in Navigation," *Journal of Navigation* 25 (1972):359–69.

9. Ibid.

10. C. A. Rhodes, "Traffic Regulation and Pilotage," ibid., p. 475.

11. Existing collision-avoidance rules are based on the headings of two ships approaching or overtaking one another. Alternatively, rules that would maximize the "miss distance" between the two vessels would be based not only on the ships' relative bearings but on their range. See A. W. Merz, "Optimal Evasive Maneuvers in Maritime Collision Avoidance," *Navigation* 20 (1973):144–52.

12. Thomas O'Toole, "Merchant Ships Sink at Rate of One a Day," *Washington Post*, Aug. 7, 1972.

13. See Merz, p. 144, and O'Toole, p. 1. O'Toole does not make any attempt to adjust the data on dollar losses to reflect the intervening inflation, nor do I.

14. Margaret Cashman, "Tankers Will Be Safer in the Future," *Ocean Industry*, March 1975, p. 44.

15. Walter H. Munk, "Huge Waves Can Be Freaky—So Can Huge Tankers," *Los Angeles Times*, Feb. 24, 1977. The Cape is often in fog, and Force 6 winds are common. The area is also strewn with islands, rocks, and wrecked ships. The Republic of South Africa has established a twelve-mile pollution control zone for laden tankers. See I. C. Little, "The Problems of Operating Mammoth Tankers on the Cape Sea Route," *Navigation* 22 (1975):81–85.

16. See Michael Leifer and Dolliver Nelson, "Conflict of Interest in the Straits of Malacca," *International Affairs* 49 (1973):190–203; "The Grim Lessons of the Showa Maru," *The Sunday Times* (London), Jan. 12, 1975; "Kuala Lumpur Hesitant over Malacca Strait," *Manchester Guardian Weekly*, Mar. 25, 1972, p. 8; David A. Andelman, "Naval and Oil Shipping Plague Strait of Malacca," *New York Times*, Aug. 28, 1975; James Sterbas, "Two Nations Claim Malacca Strait," ibid., Mar. 13, 1972.

17. George McArthur, "Supertankers Lord It Over Asian Strait," *Los Angeles Times*, July 28, 1976. Troubles occur elsewhere, too, as when the *Torrey Canyon* stranded on Seven Stones Reef while attempting to avoid fishing vessels near the Scilly Isles. See Robert P. Thompson, "Establishing Global Traffic Flows," *Journal of Navigation* 25 (1972):483.

18. McArthur.

19. UN Doc. A/AC.138/SCII/SR.4–23 (1971), pp. 88, 113; "Kuala Lumpur Hesitant over Malacca Strait," p. 8.

20. James L. Johnston, "The Likelihood of a Treaty Emerging from the Third United Nations Conference on the Law of the Sea," reprinted in *Deep Seabed Mining*, Hearings before the Subcommittee on Oceanography of the Committee on Merchant Marine and Fisheries, U.S. House of Representatives, 94th Cong., 2d Sess., May 1975, February and March 1976 (Serial no. 94-27), p. 504, hereafter cited as James L. Johnston (1976a).

21. *Economic Value of Ocean Resources to the United States*, pp. 94–96.

22. The simplifying assumptions were that (1) each ship movement requires on the average only one additional day's voyage time one way (implying typical diversion of more or less than 400 miles each way); (2) 50 percent of the traffic has no return cargo; and (3) average daily shipping costs at sea for all types of cargo combined are around 30 cents per ton. Ibid., p. 96.

23. David B. Johnson, "Comparative Costs for Oil Shipped by Alternative Routes from the Persian Gulf to the United States," Office of the Assistant Secretary for International Affairs and Research, U.S. Department of the Treasury, Washington, D.C. (May 24, 1974); portions reprinted in David B. Johnson and Dennis E. Logue, "U.S. Economic Interests in Law of the Sea Issues," in Ryan C. Amacher and Richard James Sweeney, eds., *The Law of the Sea: U.S. Interests and Alternatives* (Washington, D.C.: American Enterprise Institute for Public Policy Research, 1976), pp. 65–68.

24. I am indebted to Robert L. Friedheim for discussions of this point.

25. Johnson and Logue, p. 65.

26. This discussion of the comparative national interests of Indonesia, Malaysia, and Singapore is drawn from Leifer and Nelson (n. 16 above), pp. 191–94.

27. James L. Johnston, "Epilogue," in Amacher and Sweeney, eds., 182–83; hereafter cited as James L. Johnston (1976b).

28. Michael E. Levine has made this argument for rationing airport runway space at peak hours of the day. See "Landing Fees and the Airport Congestion Problem," *Journal of Law and Economics* 12 (1969):79–108.

29. "The Rhine River . . . had 19 tolls along its course at the end of the twelfth century, 35 or more at the end of the thirteenth, 50 at the end of the fourteenth, and in excess of 60 at the end of the fifteenth. Fortunately, merchants were frequently able to avoid the more heavily taxed routes by traveling alternative routes opened by treaty or agreement." Warren C. Scoville and J. Clayburn La Force, *The Middle Ages and the Renaissance*, p. 12.

30. "Recent Developments in the Law of the Sea: Suez Canal Reopens," *San Diego Law Review* 13 (1976):559.

31. Quoted in Joseph A. Gribbin, *Potential Effects of Reopening and Expanding the Suez Canal on the Shipment Cost of Crude Oil*, U.S. Department of Commerce, Maritime Administration (Washington, D.C., July 1974), p. 3n.

32. Jack Foisie and Don Schanche, "Canal Thrives, Egyptians Say," *Los Angeles Times*, May 16, 1976. Inflation, of course, would account for some portion of the increase in dues.

33. Ibid.

34. "Recent Developments in the Law of the Sea: Suez Canal Reopens," pp. 660–61.

35. Foisie and Schanche.

36. Ibid.

37. Arvid Pardo, "Future Prospects for Law of the Sea," in *Perspectives on Ocean Policy*, p. 394. In the 19th century, the Danish government levied tolls on passage to and from the Baltic through the Danish Sound. The fees were commuted into lump-sum payments in 1857 in exchange for Denmark's pledge to dredge the sound and to provide for navigational aids. (Richard T. Cooper, "An Economist's View of the Oceans," in ibid., p. 152n.) The Convention on the Territorial Sea, art. 18, permits charges to be "levied upon a foreign ship passing through the territorial sea as a payment only for specific services rendered to the ship. These charges shall be levied without discrimination."

38. James L. Johnston (1976b), p. 183, makes this point.

39. Art. 5, sections 1, 2, and 6.

40. Kenneth W. Clarkson, "International Law, U.S. Seabeds Policy, and Ocean Resource Development," *Journal of Law and Economics* 17 (1974):129–30.

41. "Gulf of Mexico: Map of Federal Waters," *Offshore*, June 20, 1976.

42. "Safety Aspects of Offshore Installations in the Gulf of Mexico," Note by the Government of the United States submitted to the Inter-Governmental Maritime Consultative Organization, Maritime Safety Committee, February 27, 1967, reprinted in *Outer Continental Shelf Policy Issues*, Hearings before the U.S. Senate Committee on Interior and Insular Affairs, 92d. Cong., 2d Sess., March–April 1972, pt. 3, pp. 1364–71. See also U.S. 33 C.F.R. 67; W. L. Griffin, "Accommodation of Conflicting Uses of Ocean Space with Special Reference to Navigation Safety Lanes," in Lewis M. Alexander, ed., *The Law of the Sea: The Future of the Sea's Resources*, Proceedings of the Second Annual Conference of the Law of the Sea Institute, University of Rhode Island, Kingston, R.I., 1968, pp. 73–83.

43. For ships that do deviate from fairways, positioning by satellite and the new Loran-C navigational systems now enable them to ascertain their location within a 50-foot accuracy. Larry Pryor, "Navigation System Will Pinpoint Ships and Cars," *Los Angeles Times*, Jan. 18, 1976; "Satellite Navigation," 36 *Offshore*, February 1976, pp. 54–55.

44. Anne Robinson and Tony Dawe, "Why the Channel Watchdogs Can Only Watch and Hope," *The Sunday Times* (London), Jan. 26, 1975; Robert P. Thompson, "Establishing Global Traffic Flows," *Journal of Navigation* 25 (1972):488.

45. E. R. Hargreaves, "Safety of Navigation in the English Channel," *Journal of Navigation* 26 (1973):400–402.

46. Ibid., pp. 399–400.

47. Ibid., p. 400; L. Oudet, "The Economics of Traffic Circulation," *Journal of Navigation* 26 (1973):63.

48. Evidently this is a "present" for which the French have elected not to levy a fee. R. H. Coase has shown that the costs of collecting fees for lighthouses (or other navigational aids) are not prohibitively expensive, or at least were not for the British lighthouse authority in the 19th century. See "The Lighthouse in Economics," *Journal of Law and Economics* 17 (1974):357–76.

49. The number of strandings increased by more than 80 percent, however. Perhaps the traffic separation plan increased the confidence of ships' masters that the likelihood of their meeting other vessels had declined, and that as a result they paid less attention to natural obstacles and variations in the depth of the Channel. Yoram Barzel suggested to me that this result parallels Sam Peltzman's finding that auto safety legislation requiring automobiles in the U.S. to be equipped with seatbelts led motorists to drive less safely, thereby injuring more pedestrians. See "The Effects of Automobile Safety Legislation," *Journal of Political Economy* 83 (1975):677−725.

50. Inter-Governmental Maritime Consultative Organisation, *Ships' Routeing*, 3d ed. (London, 1973).

51. By January 1975, only twelve states, with half the world's merchant tonnage, had ratified the IMCO scheme for the English Channel, and most of these countries were located near the Channel or were heavy users of it. See Robinson and Dawe, "Channel Watchdogs."

52. Ibid.

CHAPTER 4

Property Rights in Offshore Hydrocarbons

1. RESOURCE EXTENT AND ECONOMIC RENTS

The processes that create petroleum and natural gas are not well understood, but they appear to begin with the slow decay of concentrated deposits of marine and plant biota in shallow seawater.[1] Through a relatively short span of geological time, the organic materials must be covered by layers of sedimentary rock, either by the action of volcanoes or by the drift of continents. These rocks provide the pressure and heat to "cook" the biota and change their chemical structure.[2] The overlying strata also serve as a reservoir to hold the resulting hydrocarbons. Initial layers of porous rock, such as limestone or sandstone, provide the necessary cracks and interstices for the petroleum or natural gas to fill. Since the lighter hydrocarbons will separate from the heavier seawater and eventually rise to the earth's surface, a mechanism for trapping them underground must be laid down in succeeding geological generations. Trap formations are called anticlines—the technical term for folds, arches, or domes in the earth's crust. They consist of either salt domes or sheets of impermeable rock such as clays and shales deposited by rivers or volcanoes. The more pronounced the trap formation and the more impermeable its structure, the more fluids or gases that will be contained as they migrate upward from distant reservoirs (see Fig. 12).

Petroleum, as with most minerals, is found in "patches" or concentrations rather than in an even distribution throughout the globe. It cannot be found precisely without drilling, but scientific techniques can locate anticlinal structures that often are associated with oil. Reflection seismographs transmit waves of energy into the earth's crust which bounce off layers of rock and return to radio receivers on the surface. A study of the waves received permits geologists to construct a picture of the underlying structure. Where strata are arched or faulted, drilling may be promising. These techniques can increase the odds of

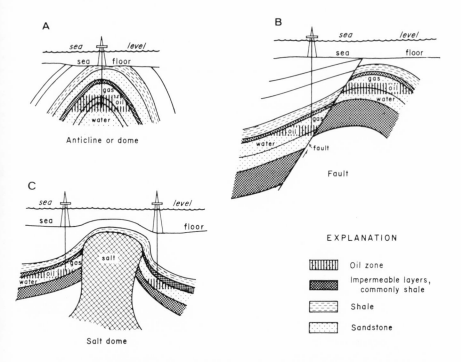

FIG. 12.   Geological structures associated with the discovery of petroleum resources.

SOURCE: David W. Allen et al., *Effects on Commercial Fishing of Petroleum Development off the Northeastern United States* (Woods Hole Oceanographic Institution, April 1976), p. 27.

finding hydrocarbons from one in one thousand for drilling at random to one in fifteen or twenty.

Deposits of oil and gas hydrocarbons are concentrated particularly in North America and Asia, but the quantity of economically usable deposits varies with changes in extraction costs, technologies, and world prices. Through 1972, for example, more than one-third of the world's cumulative production (of 151 countries) came from the United States. However, Saudi Arabia holds about one-quarter of the world's proved reserves that are estimated to remain in the ground, and its offshore reserves amount to about 160 percent of the offshore reserves estimated for the remaining 150 countries combined. The United States Geological Survey (USGS), which has estimated the reserves, defines "proved reserves" as that portion of known resources that are recoverable with current technology at present prices, essentially "inventories." Thus, resources that are known to exist but can be extracted only at a cost that exceeds present market prices (for example, Arctic deposits) are not counted as proved reserves. As time passes and prices of hydrocarbons increase and technologies improve, the USGS subtracts deposits from the resources category and adds them to the proved reserves category.[3] Hence, future estimates of proved reserves should increase relative to 1972 data (net of production) since prices of hydrocarbons have more than tripled in the interim. The higher prices, in turn, have increased economic rents, making it more important than before to divide the ownership of offshore hydrocarbons between coastal states and international institutions in a way that avoids economic inefficiency. ,

Offshore reserves for 151 countries in 1972 were about 15 percent of combined onshore and offshore reserves of oil, and about 6 percent of gas. Data for offshore reserves are limited by the lack of current knowledge concerning the offshore potential of Canada and the U.S.S.R. in the Arctic Ocean and of China in the Yellow and East China seas, an area that some speculate will eventually rival the Persian Gulf.[4] Moreover, USGS estimates of offshore reserves are limited to waters within the 200-meter isobath, and technology already permits exploitation at greater depths.

For the United States, the USGS has estimated that domestic proved reserves were about 6 percent of total world reserves in 1972.[5] Table 16 shows USGS estimates of the division of U.S. reserves between onshore and offshore categories in 1974. Almost 10 percent of all U.S. reserves of oil and 15 percent of natural gas were offshore within the 200-meter isobath. Table 16 also shows USGS estimates of "undiscovered recoverable resources," that is, deposits that are likely to be found in favorable geologic settings and can be extracted with current technologies. These estimates, owing to their relatively speculative nature, are provided in a range with the high probability (95 percent) associated with finding the lower limit of the range and the lower probability (5 percent) associated with finding the amount of oil or natural gas indicated by the upper limit. Table 17 shows that these estimates have changed markedly as new geologic information has been acquired, and predictions in 1975 were significantly reduced from earlier forecasts. Even so, the hydrocarbons available to the U.S. are substantial and would be still larger if deposits beyond the 200-meter isobath were included. The continental shelf of the United States within the 200-meter isobath alone is one of the world's largest (545,000 square nautical miles) and the USGS believes that there are more hydrocarbons to be discovered in offshore U.S. areas than in onshore areas.

Petroleum explorers have generally sought deposits that would yield the highest economic rents. At first, these were relatively shallow deposits found in the main petroleum provinces. Subsequent technical advances in drilling made it possible to exploit deeper fields having higher extraction costs and smaller economic rents. Eventually, rising petroleum prices and tremendous jumps in underwater capabilities enabled oil companies to earn economic rents from offshore exploitation that were on a par with the savings in costs from new drilling on land. Drilling is riskier at sea than on shore, and therefore costlier, but part of

TABLE 16

Production, Reserves, and Undiscovered Recoverable Resources of Crude Oil, Natural Gas, and Natural Gas Liquids for the United States, December 31, 1974

(onshore and offshore to water depth of 200 metres)

Area	Cumulative Production	Reserves Demonstrated Measured[2]	Reserves Demonstrated Indicated[3]	Inferred[4]	Undiscovered Recoverable Resources Range[5] [6] (95%-5%)
Crude Oil[1] (billions of barrels)					
Lower 48 Onshore	99.892	21.086	4.315	14.3	20 - 64
Alaska Onshore	0.154	9.944	0.013	6.1	6 - 19
Total Onshore	100.046	31.030	4.328	20.4	37 - 81
Lower 48 Offshore	5.634	3.070	0.308	2.6	5 - 18
Alaska Offshore	0.456	0.150	Negligible	0.1	3 - 31
Total Offshore	6.090	3.220	0.308	2.7	10 - 49
Total Onshore and Offshore	106.136	34.250	4.636	23.1	50 - 127
Natural Gas[1] (Trillions of cubic feet)					
Lower 48 Onshore	446.366	169.454		119.4	246 - 453
Alaska Onshore	0.482	31.722		14.7	16 - 57
Total Onshore	446.848	201.176		134.1	264 - 506
Lower 48 Offshore	33.553	35.811	Not Applicable	67.4	26 - 111
Alaska Offshore	0.423	0.145		0.1	8 - 80
Total Offshore	33.976	35.956		67.5	42 - 181
Total Onshore and Offshore	480.824	237.132		201.6	322 - 655
Natural Gas Liquids (billions of barrels)					
Total Onshore and Offshore	15.730	6.350	Not Applicable	6	11 - 22

[1]Cumulative production and estimates of reserves and resources reflect an assumed recovery of about 32 percent of the oil and 80 percent of the gas-in-place. Some portion of the remaining oil-in-place is recoverable through application of improved recovery techniques. Estimates are based on figures released by the American Petroleum Institute (API) and the American Gas Association (AGA) in April 1975.

[2]Identified resources that can be economically extracted with existing technology. Estimates are the "proved reserves" of the API and AGA.

[3]Identified resources, economically recoverable if known fluid injection technology is applied. Estimates are from the API.

[4]Resources estimated to be recoverable in the future as a result of extensions, revisions of estimates, and new pays in known fields beyond those shown in indicated reserves.

[5]The low value of the range is the quantity associated with a 95 percent probability (19 in 20 chance) that there is *at least* this amount. The high value is the quantity with a 5 percent probability (1 in 20 chance) that there is at least this amount. Totals for the low and high values are not obtained by arithmetic summation; they are derived by statistical methods.

[6]The reader is cautioned against averaging ranges.

Source: Betty M. Miller et al., *Geological Estimates of Undiscovered Recoverable Oil and Gas Resources in the United States* (Washington, D.C.: U.S. Department of the Interior, Geological Survey Circular 725, 1975), pp. 4-5.

TABLE 17

Trend in U.S. Geological Survey Estimates of U.S. Offshore
Undiscovered Recoverable Resources of Petroleum Liquids
and Natural Gas

(to a depth of 200 meters)

		Estimates	
Resource	1968[1]	1974[2]	1975[3]
Crude oil (billions of barrels)	660-780	65-130	10-49
Natural gas (trillions of cubic feet)	1640-2220	395-790	42-181

Sources:

[1] V. E. McKelvey et al., *Potential Mineral Resources of the United States Outer Continental Shelf* (Washington, D.C.: U.S. Department of the Interior, Geological Survey, March 11, 1968), reprinted in *Outer Continental Shelf Policy Issues,* Hearings before the U.S. Senate Committee on Interior and Insular Affairs, 92nd Cong., 2d Sess., Serial No. 92-27, pt. 1 (March 23, 24, April 11, 18, 1972), pp. 192−96.

[2] U.S. Department of the Interior, Geological Survey, *News Release,* March 26, 1974, p. 3, quoting Dr. V. E. McKelvey, USGS director.

[3] B. M. Miller et al., pp. 4−5, cf. Table 16. Unlike the estimates published by the USGS in 1968 and 1974, the data published in 1975 did not predict that the ocean area between the 200- and 2,500-meter isobaths would contain about the same quantity of hydrocarbons as between the zero- and 200-meter isobaths.

this extra cost is offset by the higher cost of drilling to greater depths for new land-based producing wells. Also, seismic reconnaissance is cheaper and quicker at sea, where instruments are towed by boats (exploration on land requires drilling and blasting with dynamite) and are accurate in water depths up to 5,000 feet.

Experience and further technological improvements also have steadily reduced the cost of setting wells farther from coastlines (see Fig. 13). In 1965, the deepest water in which wells were routinely set was 100 meters.[6] By 1975 wells in 200 meters were routine and more than thirty countries had granted oil concessions in waters beyond this depth.[7] Stationary surface drilling platforms could be placed in waters up to 350 meters deep and hold as many as 60 wells. They could withstand earthquake conditions off California, gales that produced 100-foot waves in the North Sea, waves of the same height plus ice and fast currents in the Gulf of Alaska, and hurricanes in the Gulf of Mexico.[8] Platform cost is influenced by such factors as weather, reservoir type and depth, physical features of the ocean bottom, distance from shore, location of pipelines, and the number and spacing of wells. But water depth appears to be a critical element of cost. Beyond 400 meters the cheaper technology involves a submerged and diverless platform that is anchored to the ocean bottom with drilling pipes extending from vessels moored on the surface above.

Between 1960 and 1971, approximately 5 percent of the world's total production of petroleum and about 6 percent of its natural gas were taken from offshore areas, and by the end of 1972 more than 130 firms were exploring the

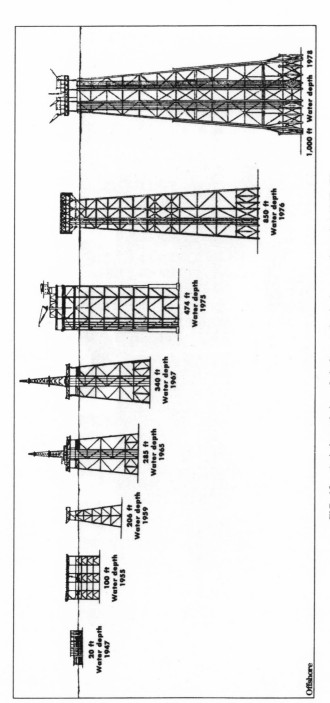

Offshore

FIG. 13. Artist's rendering of platform technologies over the period 1947–78.

SOURCE: Griff C. Lee, " 'Deep' Thoughts on Conventional Concepts," paper presented at the Offshore Southeast Asia Conference, February 21–24, 1978, Singapore Society of Petroleum Engineers, reprinted in *Offshore*, April 1978, p. 92.

coastal areas of 80 countries.[9] Tables 18 and 19 show the annual growth of world offshore production between 1969 and 1975, when it was estimated that offshore production was about 17 percent of world oil and more than 20 percent of world natural gas. Table 20 shows the same information for the United States. Offshore exploration has moved into progressively less hospitable regions—from the swamps of Louisiana to the shallow Gulf of Mexico, the cold North Sea, and the frigid Arctic—which offer higher extraction costs but also economic rents that are at least equal to the next-best drilling opportunities on land. Eventually exploration will move to the deeper regions of the continental rise which geologists now believe have rich petroleum reservoirs.[10] This transition will be faster the more prolonged the period that cartelization is anticipated to govern petroleum supplies from the Middle East.

The economic rent to the United States of offshore oil and natural gas production in 1973 was estimated by Robert R. Nathan Associates. They concluded that the opportunity cost of this output, measured by the cost of replacing it with oil imports, was in excess of $3.9 billion.[11] In estimating future economic rents to the U.S., they assumed that hydrocarbon prices would rise relatively little above 1974 levels owing to the possibilities of substituting coal, oil from shale deposits, and coal liquefaction. This yielded predicted rents of $7.7 billion in 1985 and $9.4 billion in 2000, which dwarf their estimates of future economic rents to the United States from all other ocean uses combined. Data are not

TABLE 18

ESTIMATED WORLD PRODUCTION OF CRUDE OIL, ONSHORE VS. OFFSHORE

(thousands of barrels)

Year[1]	Onshore Production	Offshore Production	Total World Production	Offshore Production as a % of World Production
1969	12,961,336	2,261,175	15,222,511	14.9%
1970	13,969,418	2,749,290	16,718,708	16.4
1971	14,585,273	3,077,520	17,662,793	17.4
1972	15,283,638	3,317,107	18,600,745	17.8
1973	16,585,248	3,782,733	20,367,981	18.6
1974[r]	17,015,414	3,522,313	20,537,727	17.2
1975[p]	16,178,454	3,295,585	19,474,039	16.9

[r]Revised
[p]Preliminary
[1]Data not available prior to 1969
SOURCES:
1969–75: Total world production, U.S. Bureau of Mines.
1969–75: Offshore production, United States, U.S. Geological Survey and U.S. Bureau of Mines; rest of the world, *Offshore*.
Provided by American Petroleum Institute, Washington, D.C.

TABLE 19

Estimated World Production of Natural Gas, Onshore vs. Offshore

(millions of cubic feet)

Year	Onshore Production	Offshore Production	Total World Production	Offshore Production as a % of World Production
1970[r]	32,832,941	5,261,020[1]	38,093,961	13.8%
1971[r]	34,662,198	6,148,461[1]	40,810,659	15.1
1972[r]	36,639,035	6,824,375[1]	43,463,410	15.7
1973[r]	49,295,292	7,697,045	56,992,337	13.5
1974[r]	39,164,595	8,088,727	47,253,322	17.1
1975[p]	37,497,838	9,532,076	47,029,914	20.3

[r]Revised

[p]Preliminary

[1]Reflects free world offshore production since Communist nations production figures are not available.

Sources:

Offshore production, *Offshore* and U.S. Geological Survey.
Total world production 1970−74: U.S. Bureau of Mines; 1975: U.S. Bureau of Mines and *Oil and Gas Journal*.
Provided by American Petroleum Institute, Washington, D.C.

available for the rents accruing to other countries, but if the relative magnitudes for the world at large are similar to those for the United States, then the potential cost of wasteful use of hydrocarbons would appear to be relatively high.

The combination of rising economic rents to continental shelf oil resources plus rapid changes in offshore exploitation technologies is causing a realignment of property rights toward more exclusive structures which are better attuned to new market opportunities. This has occurred not only because of national self-interest but also because communal exploitation of oil deposits is now widely recognized as economically inefficient. Competition to acquire these rents has occurred in almost every ocean and sometimes has led to diplomatic friction between countries that have traditionally had friendly relations as well as between countries that have often been at odds with one another. There have been the disputes between China and other countries over the Paracels and Spratlies, referred to earlier, as well as over the Senkaku Islands in the East China Sea; also disputes of varying degrees between Greece and Turkey over islands in the Eastern Aegean off the Turkish coast; between Norway and the U.S.S.R. over Norwegian plans to exploit shelf deposits off the coast of Spitsbergen in the Barents Sea; between the United Kingdom and Denmark over exploitation off Rockall Island, northwest of Scotland; between the U.K. and Argentina over the ownership of the Falkland Islands (called the Malvinas by Argentina) in the South Atlantic; between the U.K. and Ireland over shelf areas in the Irish Sea; between Spain and Morocco over several islands off Morocco's

TABLE 20

Onshore-Offshore Production of Hydrocarbons for the United States

Year	Crude Oil and Condensate (Thousands of Barrels)				Natural Gas (Millions of Cubic Feet)				Year
	Onshore	Offshore	Total	Offshore as a % of Total	Onshore	Offshore	Total	Offshore as a % of Total	
Cumulative to 1953	47,336,529	477,188	47,813,717	1.0%	142,838,325	91,675	142,930,000	0.06%	Cumulative to 1953
1954	2,266,387	48,601	2,314,988	2.1	8,657,781	84,765	8,742,546	1.0	1954
1955	2,425,289	59,139	2,484,428	2.4	9,277,192	128,159	9,405,351	1.4	1955
1956	2,543,889	73,394	2,617,283	2.8	9,938,516	143,407	10,081,923	1.4	1956
1957	2,533,249	83,652	2,616,901	3.2	10,506,021	174,237	10,680,258	1.6	1957
1958	2,362,773	86,214	2,448,987	3.5	10,772,251	258,047	11,030,298	2.3	1958
1959	2,474,511	100,079	2,574,590	3.9	11,692,755	353,360	12,046,115	2.9	1959
1960	2,458,170	116,763	2,574,933	4.5	12,330,577	440,461	12,771,038	3.4	1960
1961	2,488,382	133,376	2,621,758	5.1	12,775,881	478,144	13,254,025	3.6	1961
1962	2,513,972	162,217	2,676,189	6.1	13,236,310	640,312	13,876,622	4.6	1962
1963	2,564,621	188,102	2,752,723	6.8	13,903,285	763,274	14,666,559	5.2	1963
1964	2,572,003	214,819	2,786,822	7.7	14,612,386	849,757	15,462,143	5.5	1964
1965	2,605,862	242,652	2,848,514	8.5	15,100,329	939,424	16,039,753	5.9	1965
1966	2,727,493	300,270	3,027,763	9.9	15,833,431	1,373,197	17,206,628	8.0	1966
1967	2,847,565	368,177	3,215,742	11.4	16,333,573	1,837,752	18,171,325	10.1	1967
1968	2,857,851	471,191	3,329,042	14.2	17,001,069	2,321,331	19,322,400	12.0	1968
1969	2,845,919	525,832	3,371,751	15.6	17,853,564	2,844,676	20,698,240	13.7	1969
1970	2,941,736	575,714	3,517,450	16.4	18,702,524	3,218,118	21,920,642	14.7	1970
1971	2,839,160	614,754	3,453,914	17.8	18,742,333	3,750,679	22,493,012	16.7	1971
1972	2,847,796	607,572	3,455,368	17.6	18,774,283	3,757,415	22,531,698	16.7	1972
1973r	2,781,905	578,998	3,360,903	17.2	18,672,212	3,975,337	22,647,549	17.6	1973
1974r	2,658,949	543,636	3,202,585	17.0	17,370,769	4,229,753	21,600,522	19.6	1974r
1975p	2,550,828	501,220	3,052,048	16.4	15,851,200	4,257,461	20,108,661	21.2	1975p

pPreliminary
rRevised

Sources for oil: Total U.S. production, U.S. Bureau of Mines; U.S. offshore production, 1973–74, U.S. Bureau of Mines; all other years, USGS. Distribution of production computed by the American Petroleum Institute.

Sources for gas: Total U.S. production, U.S. Bureau of Mines; U.S. offshore production, USGS. Distribution of production computed by the American Petroleum Institute. Provided by American Petroleum Institute, Washington, D.C.

Mediterranean coast near Gibraltar; between Iraq and Kuwait over islands in the Persian Gulf; between the United States and Canada over the Georges Bank area between Maine and Nova Scotia; and numerous disputes between Egypt and Israel over deposits in the Gulf of Suez as well as off the coast of Sinai in the Red Sea.[12] The prospect of oil deposits has even produced division within countries. Metropolitan Denmark has had disagreements with Eskimos in Greenland and with the inhabitants of the Faeroes over the division of oil revenues.[13] In the North Sea, huge oil and gas deposits opposite the coast of Scotland have led to debates over its secession from the United Kingdom.[14]

2. ECONOMICS OF THE COMMON POOL

Economic analysis demonstrates that exploitation of a hydrocarbon deposit, whether on land or at sea, will be inefficient unless control is assigned to a single decision maker by property rights or by regulations.[15] On land, the inefficiency arises where multiple oil or gas producers have exclusive rights to their parcels of land overlying the reservoir, but none have the exclusive rights to extract hydrocarbons. The first producer to sink a well obtains some fluids or gas without pumping since the reservoir pressures push hydrocarbons out the hole. As extraction continues, the reservoir pressure declines and pumping must substitute for the natural forces of the field. However, sinking multiple independently owned wells will cause pressures to decline more rapidly owing to the larger number of holes, and the various producers thus are forced to spend more and more for pumping. Furthermore, as additional wells are drilled, the first producer realizes that some of the oil that would have flowed out of his well instead moves in the direction of his neighbors' land and out their wells. This realization leads each producer to increase his rate of pumping defensively, which raises the pumping costs of all producers. The oil would have been extracted at a rate that would avoid inefficiency under the condition of exclusive ownership. But with nonexclusive or communal "ownership," it is instead extracted through cost-increasing competition which in the end dissipates all economic rent. The amount of oil recovered is the same under each mode of ownership, but exclusive property rights ideally accomplish the job without the waste of resources.

The uneconomically rapid exploitation of common pools can rarely be eliminated by independent actions. The rational action for each producer is to raise his rate of pumping, because a reduction means that his neighbors will capture the oil that he foregoes. Group actions to convert the multiple parcels of land to single ownership are an obvious attraction since the value of the drilling rights is greatest when they are held by just one producer. This gain from sole ownership would be the maximum that any driller would pay to his cohorts in a bargain to acquire the exclusive rights, which equals the cost savings of avoiding competitive pumping. Alternatively, the group either could form a corporation to share the costs and gains of exploiting the reservoir or could enter into an agreement to reduce the combined rate of pumping to a level that would avoid inefficiency.

The success of each type of group action depends on the number of producers (the owners or lessees of overlying land parcels), the total area of the pool, and the transactions costs of making and enforcing agreements. Where only two or three producers are involved, transactions costs might be low relative to the cost savings of reducing extraction rates. This would make exchanges of drilling rights, incorporation, or agreements to reduce output appear relatively attractive. But the costs of taking and enforcing these actions are almost bound to rise as the size of the group increases. Any single producer would have reasons to hold out, simply by refusing to join in the production cuts, and perhaps simultaneously to increase his own rate of pumping while others were reducing theirs. Others might join in the agreement but immediately start cheating in the classic prisoner's dilemma expectation that their cohorts would also cheat. Even if existing producers could agree to divide output rates or pumping costs in some equitable fashion, the resulting reduction in inefficiency could lead additional landowners to "slant drill" into the pool, an action which would of course also raise the transaction cost of reaching new agreements.

In the United States, government regulations have been introduced when voluntary arrangements failed. Usually, these regulations have the effect of forcing all independent producers working the reservoir to act as a unit, as if the field were under sole ownership, and new entrants are restricted. Under "unitization," each producer relinquishes his right to drill competitively in exchange for an assured share of the lower output rate determined by the governmental agency. Of course, unitization does not eliminate all problems. Individual producers must be prevented from clandestinely exceeding their quotas while cohorts adhere to the pact, and regulatory agencies do not always have either the necessary information to know the economically optimal exploitation rate for the reservoir or the necessary incentives to select that particular rate.[16]

Experience with communal inefficiencies on land suggests ways of avoiding them in offshore exploitation. First, competitive extraction of hydrocarbons from a single reservoir should be limited, ideally to just one producer. Second, the area over which rights are granted should be larger than the typical mineral rights of onshore exploitation. The possibilities for common pool inefficiencies are large onshore since hydrocarbon fields can usually be tapped by drilling slant wells from many different parcels of land. Property rights in ocean space, however, may be created *de novo* without preexisting titles. Thus, ocean tracts should be made large enough to enclose the expected deposit plus perhaps some additional area to account for uncertainty—in effect to err on the high side in case the actual deposit turns out to be larger than anticipated. Both these conditions suggest that the ocean authority assigning tracts should first engage in some amount of search to determine if the proposed pattern of drilling deeds overlaps major hydrocarbon fields.

Third, property rights to extract hydrocarbons in all ocean areas should be clearly assigned to one type of ocean authority or another in order to avoid the potential wastes of either zero or apportioned ownership. Multiple drilling into a single reservoir is more likely to occur in a no-man's area where neither coastal states nor international institutions have the authority to grant exclusive drilling licenses. Similar problems would arise in other areas of unclear jurisdiction if institutions of both types share the right to grant licenses. In short, coastal authority should begin where international authority ends and the two should not overlap. On the one hand, if control by international authorities offers efficiency gains, then international jurisdiction should extend landward to the outer edge of the territorial sea. On the other hand, if coastal state control is preferred on economic grounds, then coastal jurisdiction should extend to the outer edge of the continental margin (to include the continental rise) or to whatever distance beyond the margin that hydrocarbons are expected to be found. Delimiting the boundary between coastal enclosures and international control according to some rule of thumb, such as the full continental margin or the 200-mile EEZ, raises the certainty of ownership and thus increases the likelihood that deposits at greater depths will be exploited when costs and technologies permit. Where geophysical information suggests that automatic boundaries in a few cases could overlap major deposits, however, some initial exploratory effort may be prudent before final boundaries in these areas are established, especially if the potential for common pool inefficiencies is relatively great.

Fourth, automatic rules for delimiting the boundaries between the EEZs of nearby coastal states sometimes may yield inefficient results. Two such rules were established in the Convention on the Continental Shelf.[17] In the case of two or more states whose coasts are opposite one another, the suggested boundary is the median line of which every point is equidistant from the base lines used to measure each country's territorial sea. In the case of adjacent states, the suggested boundary is a simple extension of the landside boundary. Either rule, however, may lead to important common pools being divided, and some attempt should probably be made by the states involved to compare these economic losses with the gains of simplified negotiations when rules of thumb are used. As before, it might be rewarding for the coastal states involved to engage in some preliminary amount of search activity in order to gauge the potential for common pool inefficiencies. The greater the probable losses in efficiency, the bigger the payoffs to all parties of more extensive search effort to determine the extent of important reservoirs. Where major fields become likely, the exploitation rights should be held ideally by just one of the countries involved.

The division of common deposits between countries could be accomplished by exchanges of money or other resources, or in some cases of political principles worth no more than the extra gains stemming from exclusive as opposed to communal ownership. Another approach, illustrated in Figure 14 for two countries facing a common sea, would be for country A to establish initial boundaries by drawing straight base lines, and then permit country B to redefine new boundaries that enclose expected pools near the base lines. This would permit an early establishment of initial boundaries and would permit adjustments to reflect deposits of oil or other resources when technology lowers the cost of properly identifying them.[18] Usually both countries would gain from exchanges of this sort, and therefore usually would have incentives to explore an agreement of this kind. This is especially so where the number of participants is few and exchange costs are relatively low.

Both the exclusivity-of-rights proposition and the transactions cost proposition imply that coastal state control over offshore hydrocarbons offers a good opportunity for avoiding inefficient resource-use outcomes. The benefits of petroleum extraction would be concentrated in the case of coastal state control but diffused under international authority. This raises the relative cost to coastal

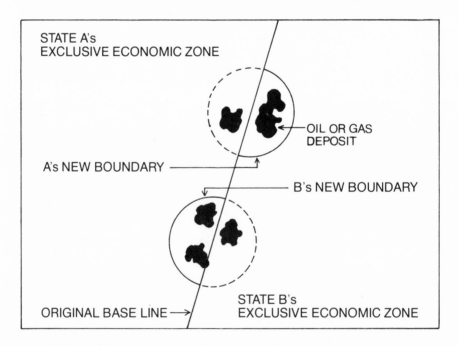

FIG. 14.   Hypothetical division of continental shelf in the vicinity of oil deposits by
two opposite coastal states.

SOURCE: Kenneth W. Clarkson.

states of exploiting these high-rent resources in a wasteful fashion. The benefits of avoiding common pool inefficiencies could be so small when spread over 151 countries that the international authority would usually have relatively weak incentives even to gather information on the potential cost savings. Assuming that coastal and international authorities could capture equally the benefits of avoiding inefficient resource use, the procedures for reaching and enforcing agreements in a one-nation, one-vote international authority would probably be relatively high. Increased decision-making costs would mean longer delays in deciding which deposits should be exploited and when exploitation should begin, the rate of extraction, and the conditions imposed on licensees.

International options for control of hydrocarbon exploitation become even less attractive when they are compared to the seabed regime to control deep-sea hard mineral exploitation that UNCLOS is most likely to adopt. This organization would not be based on the principle of one-nation, one-vote. It would vest policy and administrative functions in an executive council in which the interests of ocean mining countries, which best approximate the interests of efficiency in resource use, would not be protected from the terrestrial mining countries who seek to limit seabed production.[19] Their purpose would be to create a monopoly gain either to benefit themselves or to go into a fund to finance new investments for developing countries. If this were done, mineral prices would be higher than otherwise owing to the smaller output, and economic inefficiency would be the result. The analogous but hypothetical regime to regulate oil and gas would amount to an ocean-based Organization of Petroleum Exporting Countries (OPEC) which would probably limit seabed hydrocarbon production to benefit terrestrial producers and possibly developing nations as well. (A group of coastal states could band together for the same purpose, of course, but the probability of effective cooperation would decline as the size of the group increased owing to higher transactions costs.) Thus, international institutions of either the one-nation, one-vote kind or the weighted-voting kind are probably inferior to coastal state resource jurisdiction.

3. SKETCHES OF COASTAL STATE CONTROL: U.S., U.K., AND NORWAY

A brief survey of offshore leasing practices by three countries with extensive hydrocarbon deposits suggests that coastal states do not consistently pursue policies that avoid economic waste, although certain key features of each country's policies do.

The United States Outer Continental Shelf Lands Act of 1953 created comprehensive procedures for the development of mineral resources in all offshore lands claimed by the U.S. in the Truman Proclamation and subsequent actions.[20] The outer continental shelf (OCS) area is divided into tracts of 5,760 acres (nine square miles), but even this size is too small to prevent some overlapping of individual reservoirs. For example, in 1975 an enormous reservoir was discovered near the Mississippi River in the Gulf of Mexico by one petroleum company holding leases of three tracts, but the field extended beneath a fourth tract that was licensed to a different firm.[21] The unitization of a common pool in Prudhoe Bay in 1975 involved eight oil companies which had drilled a total of 138 wells.[22] Usually three or four wells are sufficient to explore the potential of an anticlinal structure of relatively simple geology, but where a single structure is overlaid by four adjacent OCS tracts and each is leased to a separate firm, two or three wells per tract are required. Fewer total wells would be required, often by as much as 40 percent, if a single firm could test the entire fault structure with a single hole near the junction where the four corners meet.[23] The amendments to the OCS Lands Act that Congress was considering (but has so far not enacted through June 1978) would give the Secretary of the Interior additional power to regulate unitization and pooling.[24]

A second cause of common pool inefficiencies is that the United States government acquires relatively little preleasing information on the oil potential of various tracts. After the government draws up the tract boundaries, oil companies may engage in geophysical searches and then nominate certain tracts for cash bidding. Each firm is permitted to nominate more tracts than it intends to bid on, so its proprietary rights in the search information are protected. However, no exploratory wells are drilled either by government or by industry until after tract leases have been auctioned off. Some of this search effort is duplicative, and resources might be saved if the government did a more extensive survey which included at least some drilling and published the results before lease bidding began.[25] Since oil companies would be willing to pay higher prices for those tracts that appeared to have exceptional promise, such a survey would not actually increase the cost to the taxpayer. However, both Congress and the oil companies seem opposed to such a plan, Congress on the ground that the resulting program would be bureaucratically inefficient, and the oil industry because it considers it a first step toward the creation of a nationalized oil company.[26]

Hydrocarbons were first discovered beneath the North Sea continental shelves in 1959. By 1976 the area was yielding oil and was reckoned as one of the world's major petroleum provinces.[27] The countries along the North Sea littoral, only seven in number with a long history of international dealings, were able to agree during 1963−64 that the area should be divided among them according to the median-line rules of the Convention on the Continental Shelf.[28] Median lines were drawn for the boundaries separating Norway from the others even though Norway's geological shelf terminates abruptly at the Norwegian Trench, a depression more than 200 meters deep which follows the general contours of the coast of Norway at a distance of less than 50 miles. Strict adherence to the geological continental shelf criterion rather than to that of median lines would have shifted the boundary between the zones of Norway and the United Kingdom almost back to the Norwegian coastline, which all contracting parties at the time regarded as unfair. A separate agreement between the United Kingdom and Norway binds them to joint consultations in the event that oil-bearing structures extend beneath the common boundary and to arbitration if agreements cannot be reached bilaterally.[29] There was no geophysical investigation prior to the division of the North Sea.

Ironically, one of the most important geologic features of the North Sea basin is a "fault bounded . . . rift valley," the axis of which is "roughly north-south, coinciding rather remarkably with the [median] line."[30] Most of the oil and gas fields discovered in the British and Norwegian sectors thus far are close to the median line, and, as Figure 15 illustrates, three straddle it. One of these is "Frigg," an enormous field of high-quality natural gas. Following two years of negotiations, the reservoir was unitized and the gas will be piped to Britain owing to the delay in designing a pipeline that can span the 300−600-meter-deep Norwegian Trench.[31] The investment cost in developing Frigg—building three British and two Norwegian platforms, plus the pipeline to and terminal facilities in Britain—will approach the combined Anglo-French costs of developing and building the SST airplanes.[32] It is, however, not clear what fraction of this cost is attributable to Frigg's status as a common pool, apart from its enormous size.

The second common pool is "Statfjord," Europe's largest oil reservoir, 90 percent of which is on Norway's side of the median line.[33] The Norwegians plan to lay pipe from Statfjord across the Trench to the mainland, but the British will probably complete their pipeline to the Shetland Islands before then. Another factor raising transactions costs is the United Kingdom's preference for early exploitation of oil deposits, whereas Norway, with less than one-tenth the U.K.'s population, seeks a slower rate of recovery and of economic growth generally.[34] Therefore, the potential for communal inefficiencies at Statfjord is relatively high, including competition in pumping and perhaps a duplicate line of pipes. At least some of these costs might have been avoided if even modest search expenditures had been made before the boundaries were drawn. This possibility could be worth remembering before new boundaries are drawn for the areas north of the Shetlands, in the Irish Sea, and in the western approaches to the English Channel.[35]

All three countries have used offshore production as a source of governmental revenue, but the efficiency consequences of these taxes are mixed. The ideal tax would fall exclusively on economic rents. Taxes on nonrent elements of earnings necessarily cause some inefficiency by discouraging some investments that would otherwise have been economic. Economic analysis suggests that the auction bid is the only tax instrument that raises revenues exclusively from rents and at the same time allocates the license rights efficiently. At an auction, a firm will bid up only to the amount where it can still obtain at least the normal return

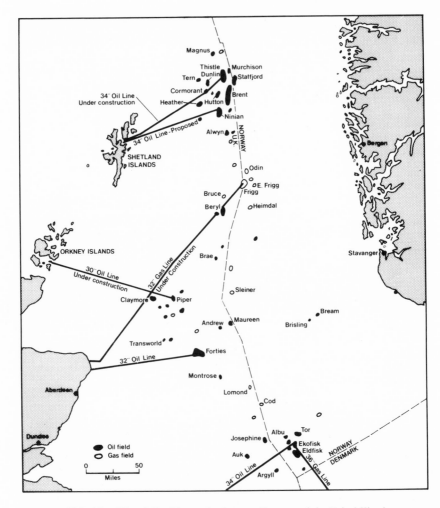

FIG. 15.   Oil and Gas Discoveries between Norway and the United Kingdom
in the North Sea.

SOURCE: *Offshore*, June 20, 1975, p. 262.

on investment in the lease including the cost of exploration and production. This
bid will be based on the geophysical data concerning various tracts that are
available for lease. The firm bidding the highest is likely to be the one that is able
to put the lease to its most productive employment, and competition among firms
tends to weed out those that are less productive (revealed by the fact that they bid
less). Thus assigning leases according to the unambiguous criterion of highest
bids at auction accomplishes the dual purpose of (1) assuring that the most
efficient firm obtains particular lease rights, and (2) maximizing the govern-

ment's share of economic rents.[36] There are, moreover, several easy steps that can be taken to assure that auctions remain competitive.[37]

Practices of the United States and the United Kingdom for assigning offshore tract leases differ sharply. Until 1978 the U.S. used auctions exclusively, and between 1961 and 1975 about $15.5 billion in revenues (economic rent) were paid by the oil companies to the U.S. government.[38] Congress in 1978, however, seemed to think that the government should experiment with bidding systems other than the "front-end" cash bonus, based on the assumption that it is cheaper for larger oil companies to borrow the huge sums required for front-end bidding and that this system therefore reduces competition from smaller companies. Although there is little evidence to support this view, the OCS amendments being debated in 1978 would limit cash-bonus bidding to a maximum of 70 percent of lease sales and would test the "unfair advantage" hypothesis by requiring bid competitions on the basis of royalties, work effort, and other criteria which I shall argue are inferior to cash-bonus bidding.[39]

In the United Kingdom, cash-bonus bids have been avoided in favor of "bidding" in terms of work effort programs, that is, the resources that firms offer to devote to exploration and exploitation of particular tracts (measured by the platforms they will erect or holes they will drill). Kenneth W. Dam (1965) argued that this licensing system has two purposes: to hasten the rate of exploitation beyond what competition would ordinarily provide, and to assign preferentially a disproportionate number of offshore licenses to British Common-wealth firms.[40] The ministry in charge of licensing avoids stating in advance the precise work effort that is required to win a license, so firms are led to compete by offering greater rates of exploration and presumably extraction. This ambiguous basis for awarding leases enhances the ministry's discretionary authority, especially where there is intense competition for a few tracts. Dam suggested that inefficiency results if the firms that would have bid the most at a hypothetical auction do not obtain the same licenses in the work-program competition. His hypothesis was not rejected by data from the one-time cash auction that occurred in 1971, when Commonwealth firms secured only one-half the number of licenses that they formerly obtained under the discretionary work-program competition and the total auction revenue collected by the government on a per-tract basis was about ten times the average per-tract cost of work programs.[41] Dam concluded from this that discretionary licensing fell short of collecting the economic rents created by the British policy.

Another source of inefficiency for all three countries—the United States, Norway, and the United Kingdom—is that they tax offshore output on the basis of royalty, during 1977 at 16 2/3 percent of each well's production in the case of the U.S., and 12 1/2 percent in the case of Norway and the U.K. Royalty taxes do not capture economic rents: since production costs are not subtracted from the value of production before calculating the tax, the royalty amounts to an extra cost on each barrel of output.[42] Certain fields that would have been profitably exploited without royalties become submarginal with them, especially since field productivity inevitably declines as the natural reservoir pressures diminish. When economic incentives are interfered with, exploiting firms will prematurely abandon some tracts and fail to work others. This reduces hydrocarbon supplies and prices go up. Ergo: the higher the royalty, the greater the inefficiency.[43] Norway has imposed a sliding-scale royalty to circumvent this cause and effect, but the royalty has the disadvantages of being difficult to implement, of failing to distinguish between fields in shallow versus deeper waters that are more expensive to work, and of encouraging the operator to reduce production in order to reduce his tax obligations. In addition, the scale of royalty taxation is not sensitive to variations in the optimal rate of extraction over the life of the reservoir, and therefore incentives are still distorted.

The consequences of higher royalty rates on oil and gas production decisions have been estimated by the National Petroleum Council of the United States. The higher the royalty tax rate, the less attractive it becomes for industry to set marginal wells in greater depths or in locations where more severe weather conditions prevail. For example, Table 21 shows that a relatively large oil reservoir (containing more than 100 million barrels) can be economically worked in waters 1,000 meters deep and in all but the most severe climatic conditions as long as the governmental take is relatively "low," defined as the absence of royalty taxation of the U.S. kind. But if the same reservoir were subject to "high" governmental taxes similar to those of the U.S., the same field could be economically worked only in mild to moderate climates and at depths 500 meters or less.[44] The higher the royalty, the smaller the supply of oil that is produced and therefore the higher its price.

Other than royalties, all three countries under comparison impose taxes on the income from offshore drilling. The United Kingdom in 1976 declared its right to purchase 51 percent of the output of most fields at market prices, and Norway is a "partner" in the ownership of all wells in its sector although its share usually is "carried" by its oil company partners as a credit against future royalty payments.[45] None of these arrangements is found in U.S. offshore licensing, and it is unclear to what extent they capture rents. Both Norway and the U.K. have used their participation rights to urge licensees to give special consideration to local firms in their purchase of equipment and other supplies.[46] Such devices are simply taxes on production and hence do not capture rents directly. Both nations, according to Dam, appear to be aware of the resulting inefficiency but continue the practices for various political reasons.[47]

4. CONCLUSIONS

The structure of property rights in offshore hydrocarbons established by Norway, the United Kingdom, and the United States appears to have avoided

TABLE 21

APPROXIMATE ECONOMICS OF VARIOUS SEABED CRUDE OIL RESERVOIRS BASED ON 20 PERCENT RETURN ON INVESTMENT AND DIFFERENT LEVELS OF GOVERNMENTAL TAKE

Water Depth (Meters)	Large Reservoir (100 - 200 MMB) Climatic Conditions			Medium Reservoir (50 - 100 MMB) Climatic Conditions			Small Reservoir (10 - 50 MMB) Climatic Conditions		
	Mild	Moderate	Severe	Mild	Moderate	Severe	Mild	Moderate	Severe
Low Government Take									
200	E	E	E	E	E	E	E	E	-1.5E
500	E	E	E	E	E	-1.5E	E	-1.5E	-2.5E
1,000	E	E	-1.5E	-1.5E	-1.5E	-2.5E	-2E	-2.5E	-4.5E
Medium Government Take									
200	E	E	E	E	E	-1.5E	E	E	-2E
500	E	E	-1.5E	E	-1.5E	-2.5E	-2E	-2E	-4E
1,000	E	-1.5E	-2E	-1.5E	-2E	-3.5E	-3E	-3.5E	-6.5E
High Government Take									
200	E	E	-1.5E	E	E	-1.5E	E	-1.5E	-2.5E
500	E	-1.5E	-2E	-1.5E	-1.5E	-2.5E	-2E	-2.5E	-4.5E
1,000	-1.5E	-1.5E	-2.5E	-2E	-2E	-4E	-3E	-3.5E	-6.5E

E = Economic (20% ROI as a guide) at projected long-term value of seabed crude oil ($11 - $13/Bbl. in constant 1974 dollars).

Negative multiples of E (e.g., -2E) are uneconomic and indicate the degree by which such cases would fail to meet assumed economic standards.

Figures are based on current technology levels. It is possible that future technological advances may lower the costs of finding and producing oil in deeper waters and less favorable climatic conditions. Thus, some of the areas shown above as being uneconomic may move into the economic range at some point in the future.

Table is based on a minimum 20 percent ROI on exploratory drilling, development, and production expenditures. Includes substantial royalty, moderate taxes, but no lease bonuses or other acquisition costs. Also, geological and geophysical costs and normal compensation for exploration project risk are excluded.

Includes additional investment equal to present value equivalent to $1/Bbl. on total recoverable oil, i.e., $175 million for a large reservoir, $65 million for a medium reservoir, and $25 million for a small reservoir. This added expense is intended to illustrate the impact on ROI and economics of additional cost burdens such as lease bonus, etc.

SOURCE: National Petroleum Council of the U.S., *Ocean Petroleum Resources* (Washington, D.C., March 1975), pp. 35-37.

inefficiencies of several kinds. First, the right to extract hydrocarbons in a given ocean area is almost always assigned exclusively to a single producer. Second, tract size ordinarily is large enough to avoid common pool inefficiencies.[48] Third, coastal authority extends across the full continental margin unless shelf boundaries must be delimited with opposite nations, and "grey" or "no-man's" areas have for the most part been avoided. Fourth, the cost to coastal nations of enforcing their structures of property rights appears to be relatively low.[49] Nevertheless, policies of the three nations have also yielded inefficiencies. First, they have not always erred on the high side in establishing tract sizes, resulting in some common pool inefficiencies. Second, each country might have benefited from some additional preleasing information before drawing tract boundaries and especially before the division of the North Sea among the several nations involved. Third, the taxes imposed on offshore production appear to have had a mixed effect on efficiency. Two of the three countries appear to have distorted resource allocation through royalty schemes. Only the U.S. has adopted a consistently efficient scheme to assign licenses and to tax economic rents, but even this system may be modified after 1978.

Still, coastal enclosures, in spite of these imperfections, appear to be a better system of dealing with the change in hydrocarbon values and technologies than international institutions would be. At best, international authorities would achieve the same efficiencies as coastal states have achieved at a greater transactions cost, and probably with greater delays before production began. At worst, international authorities in which the votes of major oil-producing countries were weighted unequally would probably have incentives to create an "OPEC of the oceans" which would limit production for monopoly purposes. (Some coastal states might attempt to form a cartel, but it would be less effective owing to prisoner's dilemma incentives.) Because the economic rents from offshore oil exploitation appear to be relatively high, and therefore the wastes from inefficient exploitation potentially large, coastal state jurisdiction for control of petroleum resources appears to be one of the most economically desirable aspects of the enclosure movement of the oceans.

Notes

1. For descriptions of these processes see Edward Wenk, Jr., "The Physical Resources of the Ocean," *Scientific American*, September 1969, pp. 166–69; P. A. Rona,

"New Evidence for Seabed Resources from Global Tectonics," *Ocean Management* 1 (1973):153−55; Alexander and Hodgson (1975), p. 576; T. F. Gaskell, "Position Fixing for North Sea Oil," *Journal of Navigation* 27 (1974):207; B. M. Miller et al., *Geological Estimates of Undiscovered Recoverable Oil and Gas Resources in the United States*, U.S. Department of the Interior, Geological Survey Circular 725 (1975), pp. 17−18.

2. The desirable temperature is between 150 and 180 degrees Fahrenheit. The organic material must accumulate on the sea floor quickly enough, and be buried under sedimentary rock rapidly enough, to prevent its decomposition either by the oxygen in seawater or by microorganisms that would change it into gases. See George Getze, "Oceans of Oil Believed Brewing in Deep-Sea Basins," *Los Angeles Times*, Feb. 17, 1974.

3. For example, U.S. proved reserves are roughly 24 billion barrels or a ten-year supply of oil at 1975 consumption rates, but it is estimated that the total U.S. onshore and offshore resources exceed 330 billion barrels, more than a 50-year supply at current rates of use.

Rising oil prices also affect the type of technology employed. At the present time, there are three principal techniques for recovering oil. The cheapest, called primary recovery, is when the oil flows to the surface under the natural pressure of the reservoir or is pumped. Secondary recovery methods involve the injection of water or heat back into the reservoir to raise the pressure lost by primary extraction methods. Tertiary methods, even more expensive than secondary methods, involve the injection of chemical detergents of varying kinds (called surfactants) to stimulate reservoir production. At present, primary methods apply to only 20−30 percent of all the underground oil in the U.S. Secondary methods could double that production, and tertiary techniques could raise the total potential recovery to 75 percent. Secondary techniques that were uneconomic at barrel prices of $2−3 are now considered profitable at prices of $9 or more, and U.S. annual production could more than double in five years. Still higher prices would increase the extent of tertiary recovery, now in the experimental stage since extraction costs exceed the value of the oil obtained. See Sanford Rose, "Our Vast, Hidden Oil Resources," *Fortune*, April 1974, pp. 104−7, 182−84. See also Sherwood E. Frezon, *Summary of 1972 Oil and Gas Statistics for Onshore and Offshore Areas of 151 Countries* (Washington, D.C.: U.S. Department of the Interior, Geological Survey Professional Paper 885, 1974), esp. table pp. 157−62.

4. Nicholas C. Chriss, "Offshore Oil—China Has Plenty for Lamps and Maybe for World," *Los Angeles Times*, Apr. 27, 1974; Ann Cozens, "Exploratory Efforts Are Escalating in the Arctic," *Offshore*, April 1976, pp. 60−62.

5. Frezon, pp. 157−62.

6. "Drilling Technology Keeps Pace with Deep Water," *Offshore*, June 5, 1975, p. 46.

7. The deepest exploratory well drilled by 1974 was off Gabon in 2,300 feet of water. In United States waters, wells in depths of 1,497 feet were drilled in the Santa Barbara Channel and 696 feet in the Gulf of Mexico. The deepest producing well in 1974 was in water 416 feet deep in the North Sea, but an 850-foot platform was planned for Santa Barbara waters. See Judy Feder, "Many Countries Have Offered Concessions over 600

ft," *Offshore*, June 5, 1975, pp. 55−56; "Drilling Technology Keeps Pace with Deep Water," ibid., pp. 46−51; National Petroleum Council of the U.S., *Ocean Petroleum Resources* (Washington, D.C., March 1975), p. 32.

8. "Platforms for Deep Water and Rough Climates Come in Varied Exotic Styles," *Offshore*, November 1975, pp. 108−11.

9. See John P. Albers et al., *Summary Petroleum and Selected Mineral Statistics for 120 Countries, Including Offshore Areas* (Washington, D.C.: U.S. Department of the Interior, Geological Survey Professional Paper 817, 1973), p. 14; Gilbert Corwin and Henry L. Berryhill, Jr., "Interim Revision and Updating of World Subsea Mineral Resources" (Washington, D.C.: U.S. Department of the Interior, Geological Survey, Miscellaneous Geologic Investigations, Map I-632, 1973), reprinted in *Mineral Resources of the Deep Seabed*, pt. 1, pp. 716−47, esp. p. 719.

10. Getze, p. 1.

11. *Economic Value of Ocean Resources to the United States*, pp. 7−13. Their analysis suggests that most of this amount was captured by the U.S. public at large. Producers captured only about one-fifth of these rents owing to the continuation of petroleum price controls, reduced tax incentives for drilling, tighter environmental controls, increased drilling at greater depths, increased entry by new oil producers, and higher "front end" bonus payments to U.S. federal and state governments for offshore leases (these exceeded $3.0 billion in 1973 alone).

12. Leonard LeBlanc, "Nations Scramble for Unclaimed Seabed," *Offshore*, March 1977, pp. 41−46.

13. "Where North Sea Rigs are Drilling," ibid., September 1976, p. 125; Bernard D. Nossiter, "Danes, Eskimos Near Accord on Control of Greenland Oil," *Washington Post*, July 13, 1977.

14. Ray Perman, "Oil and Devolution," *Financial Times* (London), Dec. 7, 1976.

15. Excellent analyses of this sort can be found in Jack Hirshleifer, James C. De Haven, and Jerome W. Milliman, *Water Supply: Economics, Technology, and Policy* (Chicago: University of Chicago Press, 1960), pp. 59−66, and in Alan E. Friedman, "The Economics of the Common Pool: Property Rights in Exhaustible Resources," *U.C.L.A. Law Review*, 18 (1971):855−87. Portions of the following paragraphs are taken from R. D. Eckert, "Exploitation of Deep Ocean Minerals: Regulatory Mechanisms and United States Policy," *Journal of Law and Economics*, 17 (1974):159−63.

16. Examples of both situations can be found in the regulation of giant fields in Texas. See Rose, pp. 105−7.

17. Art. 6(1).

18. This approach was suggested to me by Kenneth W. Clarkson.

19. The details of these institutions are developed in Chapters 8 and 9.

20. 43 U.S.C. 1331 et seq. For comprehensive legislative history see Robert B. Krueger, "The Background of the Doctrine of the Continental Shelf and the Outer Continental Shelf Lands Act," *Natural Resources Journal* 10 (1970):442−514. "Outer continental shelf" is a legal term referring not to the underlying geomorphology of the continental shelf but to the part of it that is subject to federal rather than state jurisdiction.

21. Jim Carmichael and Susan Thobe, "Deepwater Field Shapes Up Off Louisiana in Prospect Cognac," *Offshore*, September 1975, p. 76.

22. "Prudhoe Bay Operators Agree to Unitization in the Set Areas," ibid., February 1976, p. 179.

23. "Will Unitization Solve the Problem?" ibid., September 1974, pp. 82−83. See John C. Whitaker, *Striking a Balance: Environment and Natural Resources Policy in the Nixon-Ford Years* (Washington, D.C.: American Enterprise Institute for Public Policy Research and the Hoover Institution on War, Revolution and Peace, 1976), pp. 280−81.

24. *Outer Continental Shelf Lands Act Amendments of 1977*, report of the U.S. Senate Committee on Energy and Natural Resources to Accompany S. 9, Report No. 95-284, 95th Cong., 1st. Sess, June 21, 1977, p. 8; Report of the U.S. House of Representatives Ad Hoc Select Committee on the Outer Continental Shelf to Accompany H.R. 1614, Report No. 95-590, 95th Cong., 1st Sess., August 29, 1977, p. 9.

25. David Hughart, "Informational Asymmetry, Bidding Strategies, and the Marketing of Offshore Petroleum Leases," *Journal of Political Economy* 83 (1975):969−85.

26. See "OCS Leasing Fight to Be Replayed," *Congressional Quarterly*, July 9, 1977, pp. 1409−11. Other critics within government and without it have argued for more extensive preleasing data gathering. See Robert A. Rosenblatt, "U.S. Accused on Southland Sale of Offshore Oil Rights," *Los Angeles Times*, Mar. 8, 1977, and "Recent Developments in the Law of the Sea: Seabed Resources," *San Diego Law Review* 13 (1976):652. For other criticism of the current policy see *Outer Continental Shelf Oil and Gas Development*, Hearings before the U.S. Senate Committee on Interior and Insular Affairs, Subcommittee on Minerals, Materials, and Fuels, 93d Cong., 2d Sess., May 1974, statement of Walter J. Mead, p. 246; testimony of Robert B. Krueger, pp. 303, 311; statement of Frank Ikard, p. 487; statement of Carl H. Savit, p. 706.

27. J. M. Watson and C. A. Swanson, "The North Sea—A Major Petroleum Province," *Oil and Gas Journal*, Oct. 28, 1974, pp. 94−97. The U.S. Geological Survey as of December 31, 1972, put North Sea reserves at 12.2 billion barrels of oil and 95.5 trillion cubic feet of natural gas. (According to Frezon, p. 157, USGS estimates for the U.S. are 7.6 billion barrels of oil.)

28. This is described in Kenneth W. Dam, "Oil and Gas Licensing and the North Sea," *Journal of Law and Economics* 8 (1965):52−54, hereafter cited as Dam (1965). I also benefited from a paper prepared by Les Niemi, "A Look at Common-Pool Problems in North Sea Oil and Gas and Specifically How They Affect Norway and Great Britain," Stanford University, June 10, 1975.

29. Dam (1965), pp. 54, 68.

30. Watson and Swanson, pp. 95−96. See also Richard Selley, "The Jurassic North Sea Play Is Rewarding But Not Easy," *Oil and Gas Journal*, Aug. 25, 1975, pp. 134−37.

31. Niemi, pp. 11−16; Frank J. Gardner, "Frigg Becoming World-Class Gas Area," *Oil and Gas Journal*, June 23, 1975, pp. 64−66; "Frigg Field May Be One of North Sea's Largest," ibid., May 8, 1972, p. 40.

32. Robert Burke, "International Cooperation Speeds Frigg to Production," *Offshore*, June 5, 1976, pp. 41−44.

33. See Niemi, pp. 16−21; "Statfjord Production Delayed Until 1978−79," *Offshore*, September 1976, p. 152; "Ekofisk-Teesside Crude-Oil Pipeline Begins Operation," *Oil and Gas Journal*, Oct. 20, 1975, p. 37; *International Petroleum Encyclopaedia—1976* (Tulsa, 1976), pp. 32−33, 42. A third common reservoir is "Murchison," almost due north of Statfjord and lying about 80 percent on the British side; see Ray Dafter, "Commercial Finds Are Running Out," *Financial Times* (London), Dec. 7, 1976, and "Attractive Markets for U.K. Suppliers," ibid. A fourth Norwegian field, located near the western end of the boundary between Norway and Denmark, was thought to extend into Danish waters. See "U.K. Rethinking North Sea Tax Policies," *Oil and Gas Journal*, Jan. 20, 1975, p. 42.

34. Kenneth W. Dam, "The Evolution of North Sea Licensing Policy in Britain and Norway," *Journal of Law and Economics* 17 (1974): 240−43; hereafter cited as Dam (1974).

35. It might also have been useful to have had geologic information before the Persian Gulf was divided among the littoral countries. Several offshore fields are overlaid by the boundary between Saudi Arabia and Kuwait in the so-called Neutral Zone, between Bahrain and Saudi Arabia, and between Abu Dhabi and both Iran and Qatar. "Middle East Report," *Offshore*, January 1977, pp. 66−67; *International Petroleum Encyclopaedia—1976*, pp. 64, 69−70, 75−76, 78, 80.

36. The highest bids received for any U.S. OCS auction through 1977 occurred in March 1974 when $2.1 billion was offered for 421,000 acres off the coast of Louisiana, an average of $4,988 per acre. In late 1975, OCS sales off southern California drew only $417 million for 312,000 acres, or $1,336 per acre. See Dan Fisher, "Lease Sales: Gambling on a Slick Game," *Los Angeles Times*, Dec. 11, 1975; and "U.S. Accepts Majority of Southland Oil Lease Bids," ibid., Dec. 20, 1975. The sale of about 80,600 acres off the U.S. east coast in 1978 drew only $100.7 million, or about $1,247 per acre. See "Bids on 14 Tracts in Oil Lease Sale Rejected by U.S.," *Wall Street Journal*, Apr. 14, 1978.

37. The government forbids the nine largest oil companies from submitting joint bids, and it secretly prepares reservation prices for each tract in advance of the auction. Bids smaller than the minimum are rejected, although this procedure means that some economical tracts are not being worked owing to the government's insufficient a priori data for determining minimum bids.

38. The 12 million acres leased during this period amounted to about 5 percent of the U.S. continental shelf area and about one percent of the U.S. continental margin. Jim Carmichael, "A New Era Could Be Ahead for Louisiana," *Offshore*, November 1974, p. 59.

39. See Senate Report no. 95-284, pp. 9−13; House Report no. 95-590, pp. 10−15.

40. Dam (1965), pp. 55−66.

41. The fifteen tracts leased according to cash-bonus bids at the 1971 auction brought revenues of £37 million. This exceeded by £7 million the cost of the work programs for 127 tracts assigned in one round of leasing according to the discretionary work program bidding system, and exceeded by £3 million the cost of the work programs for 106 tracts allocated in the succeeding round. See Dam (1974), p. 216.

42. Ibid., pp. 252−54; Basil N. Petrou and R. David Ranson, "Resources from the World's Deep Seabeds" (1975), p. 43.

43. Royalties are sometimes favored on the grounds that bonuses raise entry costs and thus reduce the number of potential bidders at an auction. Studies suggest, however, that the cost of drilling is the main entry cost and that removal of the bonus bid would not significantly affect the rate of entry. See *Outer Continental Shelf Oil and Gas Development*, statements of Walter Mead, p. 251, and Robert Krueger, p. 306.

James L. Johnston has pointed out to me that the U.S. royalty tax of 16⅔ percent was probably designed to offset the depletion allowance of about the same amount which applied at that time to the income tax calculations of oil producers and can be viewed as a negative royalty. This particular tax, which canceled an economic distortion in the opposite direction, would therefore have no net adverse effect on resource use.

44. *Ocean Petroleum Resources*, pp. 35−38.

45. See Dam (1974), pp. 229−38, 256−61; Robert A. Kolbe, "Britain's Approach to Participation Jells," *Offshore*, April 1976, pp. 45−48; Dow Jones, "Britain Reaches North Sea Pact with Oil Firms," *Los Angeles Times*, Dec. 22, 1976.

46. Dam (1974), p. 260, and J. Dickson Mabon, "The Government View," *Financial Times* (London), Dec. 7, 1976. Canada's system of offshore licensing is much the same as that of the British. See Rob Robertson, "Political Decisions Remain at Top of List in Canada's Industry," *Offshore*, June 20, 1976, pp. 116−24.

47. Dam (1974), pp. 261−63.

48. The sizes of U.K. tracts are approximately 250 square kilometers.

49. British naval ships patrol the North Sea and have intercepted Russian surveillance vessels that sail within 500 yards of oil platforms. See the Reuters dispatch, "British Navy Ship Intercepts Russ Spy Vessel at Oil Rigs," *Los Angeles Times*, Feb. 18, 1976.

CHAPTER 5

Property Rights in Fisheries

More than 90 percent of the world's catch of fish is taken within 200 miles of coastlines.[1] The world catch in 1973 totaled 65.7 million metric tons, of which 90 percent was taken by 34 countries and 41 percent by just three—China, Japan, and the U.S.S.R.[2] It provided approximately 15 percent of mankind's consumption of animal protein but only a small fraction of the total daily caloric intake.[3] Fish constitute about half of the total animal protein consumed in Japan, Taiwan, and many countries of South and Southeast Asia.[4] Fish constitute a significant fraction of the national incomes of only a few other countries or provinces—the Canadian Maritime area, the Faeroes, Iceland, Norway, Peru, and Portugal.[5]

Fish are among the oldest and most variegated of species on the planet, but it is uneconomic to take more than a few of them for man's consumption. American fleets catch very few species, and Asian fleets many more. Such species as cod and sole inhabit continental shelf areas almost exclusively, while flounders, hake, herring, mackerel, and prawns move seasonally between coastal and deeper offshore waters. Tunas and whales migrate continuously over a vast portion of the globe, and such species as salmon and some eels return to coastal rivers for spawning after a life of wandering throughout the world's oceans.

A complex interaction between biological and geophysical forces makes coastal areas the most fertile for fisheries.[6] The essential process that creates and sustains sea life is photosynthesis. The initial product of this process is phytoplankton, a microscopic sea plant that is the foundation of the oceanic food chain. Its growth requires a delicate mixture of radiation, temperature, dissolved organic chemicals, mineral salts, and other nutrients. Phytoplankton can grow only where sufficient sunlight exists, generally to a depth of between 30 and 300 feet depending upon latitude and water transparency, and its density varies geographically, seasonally, and cyclically. Some animals, such as whales, graze on phytoplankton directly. But most is consumed by other small sea organisms, which are then consumed by small fish and animals, which are themselves consumed by larger species.

Once grazing species have exhausted the supply of plankton, it must be replaced with waters that are rich in the necessary nutrients. Resting on the continental shelves are minerals and decomposed biological materials which through the geological ages have been washed off land by rivers and weather. These materials can produce fertile feeding grounds near coastlines when they are exchanged with surface waters through powerful hydrographic processes. In the northern latitudes the process is called "winter overturn." With winter cooling, the surface waters become heavier and more dense, and as they sink the relatively warm and mineral-intensive waters rise in exchange. With the coming of spring the period of sunlight lengthens and photosynthesis creates food. Winter overturn in the North Atlantic and the North Sea is complemented by horizontal currents which exchange and enrich enormous quantities of water through the great distance between Greenland and the Antarctic. In lower latitudes, exchange occurs through "upwelling." The rotation of the planet combines with the weather to create giant gyres, wind-driven currents in the surface layer of the ocean which move in a clockwise direction in the northern hemisphere and in a counterclockwise direction in the southern hemisphere.[7] This causes surface waters to move away from the west coasts of North and South America and Africa, and for nutrient-rich waters to move up from the lower reaches of the water column just above the continental shelf to where sunlight can again stimulate the growth of phytoplankton. The massive Humboldt Current off Peru makes this area one of the world's richest fisheries, principally for anchovita and tuna, and the Benguela Current has a similar effect off the southwestern coast of Africa. The coastal areas of Japan in the Pacific Ocean contain valuable fisheries owing to the convergence between the Japanese Current moving clockwise to the north and the Bering Sea currents that move south to meet it. The convergence between the Gulf Stream that moves northward along the east coast of the United States and the Labrador Current heading south from Greenland causes productive fisheries to be found on the Grand Banks off Newfoundland and Georges Bank off Cape Cod.

Competition among fishermen is most keen in the coastal areas mentioned, and it is in such areas that the greatest economic inefficiencies also occur owing to inappropriate property rights or regulations. In this chapter I shall first analyze the fundamental problem of fisheries management and show why communal inefficiencies are inevitable unless economical regulations or property arrangements are imposed. Second, I shall apply this analysis to the current situation where numerous coastal states have extended their jurisdiction over fisheries out to 200 miles. The likely consequences of these coastal enclosures will then be compared with the results of fisheries regulations by various international organizations.

1. COMMUNAL FISHERIES AND THE
DISSIPATION OF RENT

As with oil reservoirs, competitive processes may lead to the inefficient exploitation of living resources unless appropriate structures of property rights or regulations are created and enforced. Most species of fish are highly mobile or "fugitive" resources to which ownership is established only by capture. Because of the wandering characteristics of fish, fishermen cannot benefit by postponing a catch in the hope of netting a larger and more valuable fish later since that fish is likely to be caught in the meantime by someone else. The opportunity cost of taking a fish at a given moment is virtually zero because there is usually no alternative for production at a later time. Therefore, each fisherman takes the behavior of his competitors into account by keeping anything that he catches, and the rate of production under communal ownership exceeds the rate that would be associated with a regime of private property. Oysters and other bottom species are, of course, an exception owing to their relatively low mobility. This enables property rights to be established in certain beds and feeding grounds at lower cost, and raises economic rents significantly.[8]

The inefficiencies of communal fisheries caused by mobility are compounded by the biological properties of the species: the size of the stock determines its rate of growth. The species can be decimated if fish are caught more rapidly than they can reproduce. A single fisherman cannot affect the size of the stock by reducing his rate of catch unless all the other participants in the fishery agree to abstain proportionately. Without an agreement to limit catches, the main result of a single fisherman's reduced rate of catch is to lower costs for his competitors. Therefore, the unconstrained incentives of each fisherman are to hasten the rate of catch and thus raise the total cost to the industry of catching a given quantity.[9] These problems of diminishing returns are compounded by a positive income elasticity for fish and rising incomes, which increase entry.[10]

This increase in cost has an important economic consequence: it dissipates the economic rent attributable to the fishery. Without an effective constraint on the number of fishermen, any new fisherman is willing to enter the fishery as long as some amount of rent is still captured by his cohorts. Similarly, economic incentives alone make established fishermen willing to add resources to their fishing effort in the form of faster boats, improved gear, or new technologies such as radar. The result is to raise the total costs of fishing by vastly duplicating harvesting efforts. But the extra capacity adds little or nothing to output. Over-investment continues to the point where the total costs of fishing are equal to the total revenue obtained. At this point the economic rent attributable to the stock of fish remaining in the water is zero. Many of the resources devoted to fishing effort are wasted, and the incomes of fishermen decline as their numbers rise.

This unhappy result arises solely from the fact that there is no economic incentive for participants to halt investments short of the point where some economic rent remains. Rents are not dissipated in the other resources connected with fishing—nets, boats, fuel, and so on—because these resources are privately owned and therefore their use must be paid for. Consequently, investment in the industries supplying nets, boats, and fuel will be organized so as to maximize rents rather than dissipate them. However, no one owns the swimming fish and therefore no payment must be given for their capture. Without an owner to collect the payment and a policeman to prevent poaching by nonpayers, the value of the fishery is destroyed along with the physical quantity of the resource itself, and the price of fish is higher than it would otherwise be.[11]

The waste associated with open access to fisheries will rarely be eliminated by means of strictly voluntary arrangements. If the transactions costs of assigning catch limits and policing the agreement were sufficiently low—as they appear to be for oyster beds, certain clams, and lobsters—the fishermen involved could limit catches to maximize the economic rent and then divide it among themselves in some equitable fashion.[12] But the mobility of fish drastically raises the cost of assigning to individuals the property right to particular fish or schools of fish. The large number of fishermen (as in the case of multiple oil producers) raises the cost of reaching group decisions, increases the incentives of some to hold out by refusing to join the group, and heightens the incentive to cheat if they do join by secretly catching more fish than permitted. Even if these costs could be overcome, new entrants would eventually dissipate any rents that the agreement created.

All the studies that have been made of common pool fisheries indicate that substantial economic losses have been incurred. For example, James A. Crutchfield and Giulio Pontecorvo found that 80 percent of the resources employed in the Alaskan salmon fishery in the 1950s represented excess costs, whereas only 8 percent were redundant in the 1930s.[13] According to Crutchfield, the waste associated with communal ownership in this fishery can be illustrated in ``one simple and appalling statistic—the total number of fishing units has tripled over a period in which the total catch has declined substantially.'' In the Pacific halibut fishery, Crutchfield found that the number of vessels nearly tripled while the catch rose by only about 50 percent.[14] In a study of the Georges Bank haddock fishery off Cape Cod, Edward Lynch et al. concluded that economic rent would have been maximized with a 50 percent reduction in fishing effort.[15] Another study of the same area by Lawrence Van Meir indicated that as catch increased, the days of fishing effort (a measure of average costs) went up even faster. Moreover, the catch in 1945 was two and one-half times larger than the catch in 1964.[16]

For U.S. fisheries as a whole, Robert R. Nathan Associates estimated that the potential economic rent in 1972 was on the order of at least $150 million and could have been as high as $200 million, or between 20 and 30 percent of the value of the harvest.[17] This estimate is based on the assumption that sufficient entry controls were adopted to preserve the economic value of fish *in the water*. In practice, of course, the rents to the fishery were essentially zero. In 1976, Francis T. Christy, Jr., estimated that the overcapitalization and excess of labor in American fisheries was on the order of $300 million per year. At a 6 percent rate of interest, the capitalized value of this annual economic rent would be $5 billion.[18]

Manifestations of this wasteful structure of communal rights are easy to find. Congestion along the coast of France is now so great that as many as 400 boats crowd into an area no larger than sixteen square miles.[19] Both diplomacy and force have been employed in attempts to create property rights. Icelandic patrol boats have engaged in celebrated cat-and-mouse tactics with British frigates to prevent British fishermen from working coastal areas. Ecuador has impounded and fined American tuna boats. The Norwegians have fired on U.S.S.R. fishing vessels.[20] Evidence of overfishing is revealed in Table 22. Although it is difficult to separate the effects of overfishing from disease and other natural events, the worldwide catch of fish appears to have peaked in 1970−71 after a rapid increase in the preceding decade. The worst reduction occurred in South America, an area believed to be overfished of tuna, where the total catch in 1973 was only a third of that in 1971.[21]

2. EXPERIENCE WITH COASTAL FISHERIES CONTROL

For an economic rent in uncaught fish to be created and sustained, two conditions must be met. First, exclusive property rights must be vested in a single authority which can assign and enforce them at low cost. Second, decision makers in this authority must have incentives to acquire information to the economical degree about the rents associated with different ocean uses, and then to select the use having the highest rent. Both of the propositions of economic analysis used in earlier chapters imply that the opportunities for avoiding communal inefficiencies in fisheries would be greater if authority were assigned to coastal states despite some attributes related to the wandering characteristics of living resources.[22] The economic benefits of organizing fisheries to generate rents would be concentrated, and the cost of enforcing this structure of property rights would be relatively low. Usually, however, coastal states have given more weight to the political goal of maintaining traditional levels of employment in the fishery than to the economic factors that would rationalize incentives, create rents, and avoid the destruction of stocks.[23] The key omission has been the assignment of exclusive fishing rights for a single area to a single operator.

TABLE 22

WORLD AND REGIONAL CATCHES OF FISH, SELECTED YEARS

(millions of metric tons)

	1938	1948	1955	1960	1965	1966	1967	1968	1969	1970	1971	1972	1973	1974	1975
World	21.1	19.6	28.9	40.2	53.2	57.3	60.4	63.9	62.7	70.0	70.9	66.2	66.8	70.5	69.7
Africa	0.6	1.0	1.8	2.3	3.1	3.4	3.8	4.2	4.3	4.4	4.3	4.8	5.0	5.1	4.5
America, North and Central	3.2	3.6	4.0	4.1	4.4	4.4	4.4	4.6	4.6	4.9	4.9	4.7	4.8	4.7	4.8
America, South	0.2	0.5	0.8	4.4	9.0	11.1	12.2	13.0	11.4	14.8	13.1	6.8	4.4	6.7	6.0
Asia	9.7	6.8	11.9	17.4	20.0	21.2	22.1	23.8	24.4	26.1	27.9	28.6	30.0	30.8	30.7
Europe	5.7	6.2	7.8	8.1	10.8	11.6	12.1	11.9	11.3	12.0	12.1	12.4	12.7	12.7	12.6
Oceania	0.08	0.09	0.10	0.13	0.15	0.17	0.18	0.19	0.17	0.2	0.24	0.23	0.26	0.28	0.24
U.S.S.R.	1.5	1.8	2.5	3.0	5.0	5.4	5.8	6.1	6.5	7.2	7.3	7.8	8.6	9.2	9.9

NOTE: Regions may not add up to world owing to rounding errors and revisions in data.

SOURCES: United Nations, Food and Agriculture Organization, *Yearbook of Fishery Statistics—1965*, vol. 20, table A1-0 (1966); *Yearbook of Fishery Statistics—1973*, vol. 36, tables A0-1, A0-2 (1974); *Yearbook of Fishery Statistics—1975*, vol. 40, table A-1, D-1 (1976).

Although coastal states often have recognized the importance of exclusive property rights, they have preferred to rely on regulations designed to limit certain forms of competition.

In one way or another, all these regulations have been ineffective because it has been impossible for governmental authorities to anticipate all the margins along which rents could be dissipated. Regulations can alter the form of competition among fishermen but cannot eliminate the pervasive force of competition itself. A typical regulatory approach has been to forbid fishing in certain areas until overfished stocks can be rehabilitated. This has usually led fishermen to substitute different means for catching the same quantity of fish as before, that is, by fishing more intensively in nonrestricted areas and stocks or making greater efforts to catch whatever fish occasionally venture outside their sanctuaries. Reductions in the fishing season have had a similar result, tending to shorten turnaround times in port and stimulating the rate and cost of fishing effort in what remains of the season. Efforts by governments to require layovers of a certain period each time a ship returns to port have led to longer periods of time at sea, and once the boats have returned to port, they vividly illustrate the idleness of labor and capital caused by excessive investment in the industry.[24] Attempts to set quota limits on catch have stimulated the rate of catch (often by new equipment and techniques) or else have led to fresh entry. In some cases, states have attempted to reduce catches by restricting the type of fishing gear used, such as net mesh, but these, too, have been circumvented by employing more men or using larger boats. Restriction on boat size in turn has led to the introduction of radar or more powerful boats. In every instance, the imposition of some new rule may be temporarily effective in creating rents, but the incentives for its avoidance lead to the dissipation of rent through new entry or investments.

Other approaches would appear to be more fruitful in eliminating communal inefficiency. Licensing vessels would reduce the number of fishing boats, but rents would still be dissipated unless licensing was accompanied by appropriate rules to control the intensity of fishing effort. Similarly, taxes on the catch would raise the cost of fishing effort and reduce it by some amount, but there are problems in determining the precise amount. Not only are there difficulties in determining the size of extant stocks and their growth rates, but the government may not have incentives to adopt the licensing or taxation policy that would reduce inefficiency to manageable levels. Ideally, a total limit on catch would be divided among existing fishermen; these rights would be exchangeable and new fishermen could not enter these fisheries without purchasing a quota. However, the rents created by such policies usually put governments under almost irresistible political pressure to relax entry restrictions, which dissipates rents and returns the industry to a point of resource misallocation.

The structure of costs and rewards that leads fisheries officials in many countries to maintain or increase inefficiency rather than to reduce it is a subject that deserves more treatment than is given here, but even the most general observations reveal the difficulties involved. Consider first the problem of gathering the appropriate amount of information on resource values under different circumstances. Fisheries biologists long have argued that the desirable rate of fishing effort is the one that maximizes the fishery's sustainable yield—that is, the largest quantity of fish that can be caught year after year without depleting the stock. On the one hand, these specialists argue that "too little" effort would result in too small a catch in the near term, a relatively large resource population, and high mortalities from natural forces. These mortalities could be reduced by increasing the rate of catch up to some point. On the other hand, beyond some point a higher level of effort would yield "too great" a catch. This would reduce the population of fish now, and eventually future stocks as well since some young fish would have been caught before they had an opportunity to reproduce. The "some point" in each case, which it is argued should be the appropriate biological target of fisheries management, is the level of effort that generates the maximum sustainable yield.

Economists, on the other hand, have argued universally that the economically optimal yield from the fishery is something different, because the cost of fishing effort per unit of catch tends to rise as the stock declines.[25] The smaller the stock, generally, the more difficult (expensive) it becomes for fishermen to sustain previous levels of catch. In addition, the extra cost of increased fishing effort tends to rise more rapidly than the extra revenue of this catch. The smaller quantity of catch associated with the economically optimal yield (and the lower costs of fishing relative to the value of fish) represents the level of effort that would maximize rents. A greater quantity of fish is taken when the maximum sustainable yield is achieved, but the economic rent attributable to the fishery is lost with the increased entry that brings the greater catch. The field of study most intimately associated with fisheries—namely, fish biology—has produced an exploitation criterion that contributes to the inappropriate economic organization of the industry: the low incomes associated with fishing occupations, the dissipation of economic rents to uncaught fish, wasted resources, and high fish prices.[26]

The regulators of fisheries have, for their own reasons, tended to accept the information given to them by the noneconomist fisheries specialists. Accordingly, they have usually failed to impose the condition of sole ownership (or regulations akin to this condition) which would generate the rent-maximizing yield consistent with healthy fisheries. Not only have regulators usually attempted to hit the wrong target of maximum sustainable versus economically optimal yield, but they often have overshot their target by permitting a level of fishing effort that is too great even by the standards of the maximum sustainable yield. Strict entry restrictions have usually been imposed only after all parties concerned, including the fishermen, realized that fish stocks had declined to levels that were alarmingly low. Thus, fisheries regulators not only accepted erroneous information, but their incentives to act upon these data were relatively strong. Although the maximum sustainable yield does not maximize the value of uncaught fish or the total incomes of fishermen, it does maximize, at least in the short run, the quantity of employment in the industry. Nations having large and concentrated populations of fishermen probably found the maximum sustainable yield criterion to be more to their advantage politically, at least as long as the fish survived.

The pre-1976 fisheries policies of the United States, Japan, and Canada illustrate the inefficiencies of this type of regulation. In the U.S. the federal government had the power to control all fishing out to the twelve-mile limit but elected to exercise this jurisdiction only for those U.S. coastal areas affected by a treaty or an executive agreement. Otherwise, jurisdiction was held by the individual U.S. states out to the three-mile limit, and they exercised control over the fishing activities of their residents out to the twelve-mile limit. This division of authority among the twenty-one littoral U.S. states usually gave each one of them control over an area that was too small to provide effective conditions for sole ownership. The mobility of fisheries within adjacent U.S. coastal areas, especially those on the East Coast, seriously limited the opportunity for avoiding inefficient resource use even if this had been the dominant goal of fisheries regulation.

Regulators of the U.S. coastal states gave little weight to the goal of avoiding economic waste relative to the competing goal of maintaining short-term employment in fishing industries, and therefore created a host of inefficient and sometimes outmoded regulations. For example, Virginia oystermen are required to use unwieldy twenty-foot tongs rather than more efficient dredges.[27] In Maryland, until recently, oystermen could use dredges but had to tow them from sailboats on all but two days of the week when motorized boats were allowed.[28] In Alaska, some fishing boats are limited to 50 feet in length.[29] After studying a large body of data, Crutchfield concluded that "The [U.S.] states have generated an ever-increasing mass of restrictive legislation, most of it clothed in the shining garments of conservation, but bearing the clear marks of pressure politics. An overwhelming proportion of regulations affecting fisheries in the individual states, whether statutory or administrative, reflects power plays by one ethnic group of fishermen against another, by owners of one type of gear against another, or by fishermen of one state against those of another state."[30] Before 1976, the U.S. negotiated bilateral deals for fishing beyond the twelve-mile limit by Japan, Mexico, Poland, and the U.S.S.R. Foreign fleets were granted limited access to certain areas within the twelve-mile band in exchange for an agreement to abstain from fishing in other areas off U.S. coasts.[31] Enforcement of these limits was weak, however; violators were lightly penalized and inspection was not mandatory. The Russians permitted inspection of their trawlers by the U.S.

Coast Guard but did not allow inspectors to remain on board for continuous observations. Japan permitted observers on board but confined them to quarters when catch was being offloaded from trawlers to factory ships.[32] As stocks continued to decline, enforcement by the U.S. was stepped up and in 1975 certain vessels of Cuba, Poland, and South Korea were seized.

In Japan, a single national agency has the power to control almost every aspect of fishing including seasonal, species, and geographical limits. The agency's policy has been to create rents intermittently by limiting entry, but then to dissipate rents usually by permitting fishermen to compete by increasing boat tonnage or, at other times, by relaxing certain entry controls in response to political pressures.[33] Since 1952, the agency has allowed minor increases in the tonnage of smaller boats without requiring new licenses but has permitted substantial increases for larger replacement boats depending upon the tonnage of the decommissioned vessel. The average vessel size increased from 91 gross tons in 1952 to 230 gross tons in 1962. As a measure of the corresponding rents, licenses sold for about $100 per ton in 1955 and for about $1,200 per ton in 1962—a value about equal to the cost of boat construction. Raising the "free entry" tonnage limit in 1955 from 20 to 40 gross tons led to a sixtyfold increase in the number of "39.9-tonners" by 1962. According to the assessment of Japanese fisheries policy by Francis T. Christy and Anthony Scott, "the political problems are indeed great, but they are not insurmountable. A stronger central control or a reduction in the incentive to acquire [license] rights may help to overcome the difficulties."[34]

The Canadian government in 1968 adopted a program to control boat licenses in the British Columbian salmon fishery.[35] The purposes of the program were four: (1) to reduce overcapitalization and idle labor, (2) to raise the incomes of fishermen, (3) to capture for the government a portion of the resulting rents, and (4) to avoid distortions in resource allocation. The size of the fleet was frozen at its 1968 level and two types of licenses were introduced: "A" licenses were for larger boats, which could be enlarged, retired, and replaced; "B" licenses were for smaller boats, which had to be phased out over a ten-year period. Annual fees for "B" licenses were only $10, but the fees for "A" licenses were increased from $100 to $400 in three years, and with each increase the number of vessels declined. G. Alexander Fraser and W. McKay report that the whole salmon fleet declined by about 15 percent during 1969–77 (see Table 23).[36] Table 24 shows changes in the value of the fleet based on estimates given by vessel owners and without adjusting for inflation. Estimates of vessel values include license values since a license can be transferred only when the vessel is sold.

The British Columbian program reveals a variety of adjustments that fishermen may make to dissipate economic rents. First, salmon boat construction increased in anticipation of the controls that were imposed in 1968. Blake A. Campbell indicates that the construction rate during 1967–68 was more than 20

TABLE 23

Number of Vessels in the Active British Columbian Salmon Fleet
According to Category of Fishing Gear, 1967–1977

	1967	1968	1969	1970	1971	1972	1973	1974	1975	1976	1977
Seiners	233	278	286	293	253	249	229	233	230	224	221
Seine combination	182	120	84	132	152	146	230	255	242	289	294
Subtotal	415	398	370	425	405	395	459	488	472	513	515
Gill net	2,388	2,286	2,474	2,325	2,151	2,098	1,831	1,950	1,701	1,573	1,543
Gill net combination	1,479	1,542	953	1,171	1,064	948	1,163	1,019	1,177	1,286	1,291
Subtotal	3,867	3,828	3,427	3,496	3,215	3,046	2,994	2,969	2,878	2,859	2,834
Troll	2,232	2,245	2,215	2,138	2,046	1,960	1,600	1,563	1,540	1,600	1,591
Troll combination	126	132	125	127	140	123	180	187	129	187	352
Subtotal	2,358	2,377	2,340	2,265	2,186	2,083	1,780	1,750	1,669	1,787	1,943
TOTAL	6,640	6,603	6,137	6,186	5,806	5,524	5,233	5,207	5,019	5,159	5,292

Source: G. Alexander Fraser, Canadian Fisheries and Marine Service, Pacific Region, Vancouver, B.C., August 1978.

TABLE 24

Total Value in $Millions of the Active British Columbian Salmon
Fleet by Category of Fishing Gear, 1967–1977

	1967	1968	1969	1970	1971	1972	1973	1974	1975	1976	1977
Seiners	7.7	11.6	13.1	13.4	12.2	11.2	12.9	24.5	24.2	24.6	25.9
Seine combination	11.0	5.2	5.0	8.3	8.2	9.0	21.4	42.6	41.8	54.9	63.8
Subtotal	18.7	16.8	18.1	21.7	20.4	20.2	44.3	67.1	66.0	79.5	89.7
Gill net	12.6	12.9	17.7	17.3	17.7	19.1	22.6	44.5	34.9	33.8	36.8
Gill net combination	14.1	14.5	11.9	15.9	15.4	14.6	24.9	36.2	39.4	45.8	48.3
Subtotal	26.7	27.4	29.6	33.2	33.1	33.7	47.5	80.7	74.3	79.6	85.1
Troll	25.0	25.3	29.8	30.7	32.5	36.1	42.8	61.5	57.2	69.9	73.0
Troll combination	1.5	3.9	2.6	3.2	3.8	3.7	8.4	9.8	6.2	12.7	25.2
Subtotal	26.5	29.2	32.4	33.9	36.3	39.8	51.2	71.3	63.4	82.6	98.2
TOTAL	71.9	73.4	80.1	88.8	89.8	93.7	143.0	219.1	203.7	241.7	273.0

Source: G. Alexander Fraser, Canadian Fisheries and Marine Service, Pacific Region, Vancouver, B.C., August 1978.

percent above the average rate for 1961—65 and about 40 percent greater than the rate for either 1966 or 1969.[37] Second, the salmon fleet expanded as owners of boats that mainly fished other species claimed to be salmon fishermen in order to be eligible for one of the grandfathered licenses. Third, the capitalization of the total fleet soared: Fraser and McKay estimate by 241 percent (in nominal terms) for 1969—77 (see Table 24). Smaller vessels were "retired" before they were fully depreciated and were replaced by larger boats that could dissipate more rent. This form of competition was curtailed in 1970 when replacements were restricted to a tonnage basis rather than a boat-for-boat basis. Salmon boats also were limited in length, but purchasers and builders of boats responded to this restriction by ordering heavier and beamier boats which effectively increased the capacities of fish holds by two- or threefold.

Most important, the British Columbian government failed to limit the number of different types of fishing gear that each boat could employ. Table 23 illustrates that the number of boats in categories that employed just one fishing technology—either seine nets, gill nets, or troll—declined during 1969—77 following the imposition of restrictions in 1968; for the most part, these were also the smallest boats. And during the same nine-year period, boats that adopted combinations of gear technologies increased in both number and valuation. The sub-fleet of seine combination boats, which have the most expensive combinations of gear technologies, accounted for the largest percentage increase of any of the three types of gear combinations. Moreover, the gill-net boats often adopted trolling as their combination technology since the conversion costs were the lowest and there were no limitations on the number of days per week that boats could troll.

In sum, the Canadian policy, although headed in the right direction for reducing inefficiencies, neither eliminated inefficiency nor captured a share of the rents for the government owing to an inability to anticipate all the margins along which fishermen would compete. Plans to restrict vessels to one specified type of gear, to limit boats to a single salmon fishery, and to levy fees for licenses as a percentage of the value of catch offer more promise.[38]

3. THE NEW ERA OF 200-MILE ENCLOSURES

The problem of dividing the property rights to coastal fisheries has been a preoccupation of international legal arrangements since ancient times.[39] As in the case of recent continental shelf claims, the impetus for an increased rate of fisheries enclosure was a proclamation issued by President Truman in 1945. At the same time as he advanced the U.S. Continental Shelf Proclamation, Truman issued a "Proclamation Concerning the Policy of the United States with Respect to Coastal Fisheries in Certain Areas of the High Seas."[40] His purpose was to establish conservation zones in areas traditionally fished by U.S. nationals that would also apply to foreign fishermen if and when they began to work these waters. (His timing was based on the expectation that Japanese vessels would soon enter the Alaskan salmon fisheries.) The proclamation did not assert exclusive U.S. use of these areas or interfere with navigational freedoms, but was aimed at creating exclusive U.S. authority to regulate domestic and foreign fishing activities. Where fisheries had been used jointly by U.S. and foreign fleets, boundaries were to be established through bilateral agreements.

Truman's action was followed by more extensive fisheries enclosures. In 1952, Chile, Ecuador, and Peru claimed 200-mile territorial seas to control the valuable tuna fisheries that migrated through these waters, and the anticipation of the First UNCLOS in 1958 and the Third in 1974 probably created a bandwagon effect among other countries. Table 25 illustrates that by April 1, 1974, 33 nations had extended fisheries jurisdiction beyond the twelve miles stipulated in the 1958 Geneva conventions. During 1975–76, 200-mile enclosures were announced by Canada, Iceland, Mexico, Norway, the U.S., the U.S.S.R., the U.K., and other countries of the European Economic Community.[41] Some of these countries had held back their claims because of extensive fishing interests off the coasts of other nations such as the operation of the U.S. tuna fleet in the tropical Pacific and the shrimp fleet in the south Atlantic, the British cod fleet off Iceland, and the Japanese and Russian fleets in various locations. Eventually the fishing interests of each country became dominated by coastal rather than distant-water interests. By September 1, 1977 (see Table 2), 68 countries had enclosed fisheries beyond twelve miles from shore, of which 51 were 200 miles.[42] Even Japan, the nation with perhaps the most to lose from coastal fisheries enclosures, ceased to oppose the trend. Japan announced its intention to establish its own 200-mile zone and began to negotiate bilaterally for continued access to the fisheries zones of other nations at reduced levels of catch.[43] Japan also had entered into competition with the United States to be the first nation to claim two emerging volcanic islands in the Pacific Ocean near the Marianas, and thus the 200-mile fisheries zone that would surround them.[44]

Benefits of Sole Ownership and Enforcement

The effectiveness of a universal 200-mile fisheries conservation zone (or EEZ) in creating economic rents depends upon the species that are enclosed and the costs of enforcement. The stocks that are enclosed will vary according to geography and ocean conditions. Enclosures offer greater opportunities for reducing communal inefficiencies when stocks remain largely within a single EEZ, migrating neither between adjacent EEZs nor between an EEZ and the

TABLE 25

Country	Exclusive Fishing Jurisdiction (nautical miles)	Notes
Argentina	200	
Bangladesh	200	
Brazil	200	
Cameroon	18	
Chile	200	
Congo	3–15	15 unconfirmed.
Costa Rica		"Specialized competence" over living resources to 100 miles.
Ecuador	200	
El Salvador	200	
Gabon	100	
Gambia	150	Unconfirmed; apparently some confusion in drafting of Act No. 9, 1969.
Ghana	30	
Guinea	130	
Haiti	15	Congressional Decree 25 of Jan. 17, 1951, set a 200-nautical-mile territorial sea. Article 5 of the Honduran Constitution accepts a 12-nautical-mile limit, but the earlier 200-mile limit is still on the books.
Iceland	50	
Iran	50	Limited in Persian Gulf to continental shelf boundaries.
Korea, Republic of		Archipelago principle.
Madagascar	50	
Maldives	100*	Maximum 150, letter to FAO, May 11, 1959.
Mauritania	30	
Morocco	70	Except for Strait of Gibraltar.
Nicaragua	200	
Nigeria	30	
Oman	50	
Pakistan	50	
Panama	200	
Peru	200	
Philippines		Archipelago principle.
Senegal	122	
Sierra Leone	200	
Somalia	200	
Tanzania	50	
Tonga		Archipelago principle.
Tunisia	12	Exclusive fisheries zone follows the 50-meter isobath for part of coast (maximum 65 miles).
Uruguay	200	
Vietnam, North	20†	
Vietnam, Republic of	53	

*Approximate.

†Kilometers.

SOURCE: U.S. Senate, Committee on Commerce, *A Legislative History of the Fishery Conservation and Management Act of 1976* (Washington, D.C., October 1976), p. 1077, from U.S. Department of State, Office of the Geographer, *Limits in the Seas No. 37, National Claims to Maritime Jurisdiction*, revised (Washington, D.C., April 1, 1974).

"unowned" high seas areas. For example, demersal (groundfish) species such as the cods, haddocks, and herrings usually cling to continental shelf areas. Therefore, economic rents are likely to be fostered by the enclosures of Icelandic cod banks, the Grand Banks areas of Canada, and the Georges Banks, the Gulf of Mexico, the coastal areas off California, and the Bay of Alaska of the United States. Similarly, the longer the coastline, the greater the fraction of coastal species that are likely to be enclosed. On this basis the enclosures of Brazil, Canada, Chile, India, Norway, the U.S., the U.S.S.R., and various archipelagic countries should be relatively effective. Stocks that regularly venture beyond the 200-mile limit could be enclosed by extending coastal jurisdiction to the edge of the continental margin or even farther if enforcement costs warrant.

Communal inefficiencies in other coastal fisheries may be eliminated only through bilateral or multilateral arrangements. This is likely to be the case in the North Sea, the Caribbean, and along the west coast of Africa owing to the location of political boundaries and the numerous countries in each region. A universal 200-mile EEZ, subject to ad hoc delimitation of adjacent and opposite boundaries, could still offer some gains, however, particularly in making clear the number of nations that would necessarily be included in fisheries negotiations as well as the property rights of each country before negotiations began.

The universal EEZ of 200 miles might also reduce inefficiencies in some highly migratory fisheries. Several tunas are fished in the eastern tropical Pacific Ocean from southern California to northern Chile, a distance of about 4,500 miles through the coastal regions of thirteen countries or possessions.[45] As Figure 16 illustrates, however, between 60 and 90 percent of the catch during the period 1967–74 was taken within the 200-mile limit. The younger fish tend to stay closer to shore, and fishermen habitually avoid deeper areas because of the greater risk of bad weather.[46] The two major tuna fishing nations, Japan and the United States, each take 60 to 80 percent of their Pacific catch within 200 miles of the west coast of South America and 100 percent of their Atlantic catch within 200 miles of the west coast of Africa.[47] In the Pacific, tunas follow anchovies and other bait fish that usually move close to the coasts of Chile, Ecuador, and Peru owing to the upwelling actions of the Humboldt and other currents. Therefore the 200-mile EEZs of these three nations are strategically placed in spite of the fact that the species move through other EEZs as well. (The choice of 200 miles as the limit appears to allow for some error on the high side, as I argued in Chapter 2.)

The effectiveness of coastal state fisheries control also depends upon enforcement costs. Some states already have enforced twelve-mile limits. The United Kingdom used armed service helicopters and naval vessels to patrol its coastal areas, and employed frigates to escort trawlers when they entered Iceland's EEZ. Iceland, engaged in a conflict that dates back to 1946, patrolled its waters with smaller naval craft which were sometimes involved in gunfire or collisions with the larger British ships.[48] China, Korea, and the U.S.S.R. have intermittently

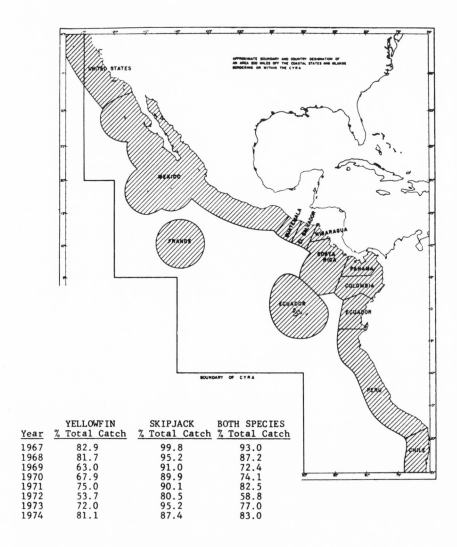

Year	YELLOWFIN % Total Catch	SKIPJACK % Total Catch	BOTH SPECIES % Total Catch
1967	82.9	99.8	93.0
1968	81.7	95.2	87.2
1969	63.0	91.0	72.4
1970	67.9	89.9	74.1
1971	75.0	90.1	82.5
1972	53.7	80.5	58.8
1973	72.0	95.2	77.0
1974	81.1	87.4	83.0

SOURCE: INTER-AMERICAN TROPICAL TUNA COMMISSION

FIG. 16.   Catches of yellowfin tunas within 200 miles of thirteen countries and islands within
the Regulatory Area of the Inter-American Tropical Tuna Commission, for 1967–74.

SOURCE: F. David Froman, "The 200-Mile Exclusive Economic Zone: Death Knell for the
American Tuna Industry," *San Diego Law Review* 13 (1976):722.

restricted Japanese boats from fishing in coastal areas depending upon the overall state of political relations between each of the three countries and Japan.[49] The United States has employed its Coast Guard to board and seize foreign boats that violated its twelve-mile limit, and from time to time has revoked the loan of warships to other nations when they have been used against U.S. fishing vessels.[50]

Enforcement activities will increase with the universal 200-mile EEZ, and instruments of force will be allocated to fisheries having the highest potential economic rents. During the "cod war," for example, Iceland used a handful of patrol boats to ward off six British frigates.[51] In 1976 the British planned to employ three frigates, eight minesweepers, and nine other ships along with patrol aircraft to monitor their 270,000-square-mile EEZ.[52] Norway and Mexico (which has a 772,000-square-mile EEZ) were purchasing additional patrol vessels and converting others to this purpose.[53] The U.S. planned to employ a mix of Coast Guard cutters, helicopters, short- and long-range aircraft, transponders, and satellites to enforce its 2,222,000-square-mile EEZ.[54] During 1975 to 1977, these countries established quota limits on foreign catches in their zones and fines for violators. One of the highest was set by the U.S.S.R. at $132,000.[55]

Fees, licenses, and quotas have been a commonplace in Latin America.[56] Ecuador and Peru require foreign tuna boats to purchase licenses before fishing in their 200-mile EEZs, and unlicensed boats are seized and fined. The Ecuadorian fee reached $77,000 in 1974 after increasing threefold in the previous two years. Between 1961 and 1973, the two countries levied a total of $6,000,000 in fines on U.S. vessels.[57] (During this period the U.S. government refused to recognize enclosures beyond the three-mile territorial sea, and compensated vessel owners for fines and lost incomes to discourage them from purchasing licenses. The rate of exploitation in this fishery would have declined had the U.S. avoided paying these subsidies.) In another Latin American fishery, an agreement was negotiated in 1972 to limit U.S. access to Brazilian shrimps.[58] The U.S. fleet was initially limited to 326 vessels of which no more than 160 were permitted to fish at one time, but these limits were tightened when the agreement was renegotiated in 1975. The length of the season was reduced, certain kinds of gear were restricted, some areas were reserved for Brazilian use exclusively, and the U.S. agreed to pay Brazil about $360,000 per year to cover enforcement costs plus fines of $100 per ship per day. In 1976 Mexico was engaged in similar negotiations with Cuba over the number of vessels that can fish the Gulf area and the fees that they must pay for access rights.[59]

An Example: U.S. Fisheries Conservation Zone

The importance of U.S. coastal fisheries is illustrated in Figure 17 and Tables 26–30. Of all commercial catches by U.S. fishermen, approximately 82 percent

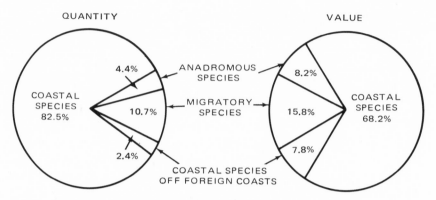

FIG. 17.   The importance of the United States as a coastal fishing nation.

SOURCE: U.S. Senate, Committee on Commerce and National Ocean Policy Study, *A Legislative History of the Fishery Conservation and Management Act of 1976,* 94th Cong., 2d Sess. (Washington, D.C., October 1976), p. 667.

of the tonnage and 68 percent of the value was taken from U.S. coastal areas within 200 miles. Of this catch, about 62 percent of the value in 1974 was taken between the twelve-mile and the 200-mile contours, and about 78 percent of this amount was taken by foreign fishermen. The tonnage and value of U.S. commercial fish landings increased between 1960 and 1974 (Table 27), but catches in some fisheries declined sharply (Table 28). Table 29 lists 48 species found in U.S. coastal waters, of which 62 percent are either "fully utilized" or "overfished" according to the criterion of maximum sustainable yield. Of the fourteen overfished species, seven were exploited by foreign fleets, six by U.S. fleets, and one (the yellowtail flounder) by both. Table 30 shows the extent of overfishing of certain northeastern Pacific Ocean species by comparing the catch in 1975–76 with the estimated maximum sustainable yields, and Figure 18 shows the decline in the share of catch in the Atlantic Ocean by the United States as compared with foreign fishermen between 1960 and 1972.

The U.S. Congress took these data and others as evidence that coastal fisheries should be enclosed to the 200-mile limit. The Fishery Conservation and Management Act of 1976[60] established a Fisheries Conservation Zone, in which the U.S. has exclusive control over continental shelf species and anadromous species except where they are found within another nation's territorial sea, continental shelf, EEZ, or fisheries zone. The Act does not include highly migratory species. It authorizes eight independent regional fisheries management councils to develop management plans for each species that is overfished within its region. These plans must specify the beginning and length of fishing seasons, allowable gear, and the total permitted catch. The law applies to both Americans

TABLE 26

TOTAL VALUE OF U.S. COMMERCIAL AND FOREIGN CATCH WITHIN 200 MILES
OF U.S. COAST

(exvessel, 1974 dollars)

	0 to 200 miles	0 to 12 miles	12 to 200 miles
Total catch	1,516	570	946
United States	780	570	210
Foreign	736	0	736

NOTE: 176.8 U.S. in foreign waters.

SOURCE: *A Legislative History of the Fishery Conservation and Management Act of 1976*, p. 358.

TABLE 27

U.S. LANDINGS OF FISH AND SHELLFISH, 1960−1974

(corrected to include Puerto Rico tuna landings by U.S. vessels)

Year	Million pounds	Million dollars
1960	4,962.9	356.5*
1961	5,218.1	365.8*
1962	5,382.7	399.6*
1963	4,884.0	380.7
1964	4,589.4	394.0
1965	4,831.6	452.1
1966	4,430.7	481.4
1967	4,152.9	450.0
1968	4,267.7	512.6
1969	4,433.3	541.9
1970	5,001.9	626.7
1971	5,146.8	675.7
1972	4,894.1	765.5
1973	4,926.3	970.8
1974	5,118.8	957.4

*Puerto Rico tuna values calculated using average dollars per pound from U.S. landings each year for yellowfin and skipjack.

SOURCE: *A Legislative History of the Fishery Conservation and Management Act of 1976*, p. 957, from Fisheries of the United States, Annuals of NMFS and Fishery Statistics of the U.S., 1971, *Statistical Digest* no. 65, NMFS.

and foreigners, but it is clear that its implementation is intended to favor American fishermen. Foreigners are allowed to take only the portion of the total permitted catch that Americans do not intend to harvest, and foreign quotas are granted only if other nations will give reciprocal access rights to American fishing vessels in their equivalent zones. In 1976, quotas were established for the

TABLE 28

TRENDS IN U.S. COMMERCIAL FISH LANDINGS, SELECTED SPECIES AND YEARS

(in millions of pounds)

State and Species	1960	1965	1973 (or other)
Rhode Island—Total	68.7	48.7	96.7
Menhaden and industrial	39.7	16.5	40.4
Flounder	5.8	9.8	25.3
Sea herring	0.2	0.4	9.3
Maine—Total	294.6	204.8	143.3
Sea herring	152.3	70.2	37.2
Perch	78.3	60.3	36.1
Lobster	23.9	18.9	17.0
Massachusetts—Total	443.9	408.7	257.1
Haddock	100.6	115.6	7.7
Whiting	84.7	44.8	25.4
Flounder	52.2	99.9	59.4
Alaska—Total	358.5	490.5	422.4
Salmon	207.1	274.8	136.5
Herring	77.9	25.6	34.8
Halibut	28.4	30.2	24.8
Oregon—Total	49.2	69.1	91.7
Flounder and sole	13.9	12.3	12.5 (1974)
Dungeness crab	9.3	7.5	2.3
Salmon	5.6	11.8	16.9
Washington—Total	113.1	127.4	117.3
Halibut	22.0	9.4	3.7 (1971)
Salmon	16.5	30.4	55.0 (1971)
Flounder and sole	16.3	11.9	5.8 (1971)
California—Total Other than Tuna	N.A.	95.3	107.6
Sole (all)	Do	20.2	30.4
Crab (all)	Do	5.1	2.1
Squid	Do	18.6	12.1
California—Tunas and Related	N.A.	358.0	610.4
Tuna	Do	279.9	293.7
Jack mackerel	Do	66.7	20.6
Anchovy	Do	5.7	265.3

SOURCE: *Emergency Marine Fisheries Protection Act of 1975*, Hearings before the U.S. Senate Committee on Commerce, 94th. Cong., 1st Sess., on S.961, Serial No. 94-27, pt. 2, September 19, 1975, pp. 135—40.

Mexican, Japanese, and Russian fleets at levels that were well below their previous catches.[61] Individual foreign vessel owners are required to purchase permits that specify the vessel's size and gear and the areas that it is allowed to fish. The Act is enforced by the United States Coast Guard, and officers are authorized to board and inspect fishing vessels, and if necessary to seize cargoes and arrest individuals. Enforcement began on March 1, 1977, and during the following month Russian vessels operating off Cape Cod were boarded, seized, and fined.[62]

TABLE 29

A Partial List of Species of Economic Importance to U.S. Fisheries
Showing Their Status in June 1974

Potential for increased catch—18 species

Pacific rock sole	Jonah crab
Alaska herring	Surf clam
Northeast Pacific shrimp	Ocean quahog
Sea trout	Gulf of Mexico clupeid
King mackerel	Oysters
Mullet	Hard clam
California anchovy	Calico scallop
Blue crab	Pacific salmon
Rock crab	Skipjack

Fully utilized—16 species

Atlantic mackerel	Pacific hake
Red hake	Atlantic cod
Silver hake	Atlantic ocean perch
Atlantic herring	Bluefish
Atlantic squid	Menhaden
Bering Sea cod	American lobster
King crab	Gulf shrimp
Tanner crab	Eastern Tropical Pacific Yellowfin tuna

Overfished—14 species

Yellowfin sole. Foreign.	Haddock. Foreign.
Alaska pollock. Foreign.	Yellowtail flounder. United States-Foreign.
Pacific ocean perch. Foreign.	California sardine. United States.
Pacific halibut. United States.	Pacific mackerel. United States.
Atlantic halibut. Foreign.	Atlantic sea scallop. United States.
Bering Sea herring. Foreign.	Northwest Atlantic shrimp. United States.
Bering Sea shrimp. Foreign.	Atlantic bluefin tuna. United States.

Percent of total number of species fully utilized or overfished: 62 percent

Source: *A Legislative History of the Fishery Conservation and Management Act of 1976,* pp. 358–59; data prepared by the U.S. National Marine Fisheries Service, Washington, D.C.

Avoiding economic inefficiency is one of the objectives of the Act. The statute stipulates that fishery management plans may "establish a system for limiting access to the fishery in order to achieve optimum yield." Optimum yield must take into account (1) present participation in the fishery, (2) historical fishing practices in and dependence on the fishery, (3) the capability of fishing vessels used in the fishery to engage in other fisheries, (4) the cultural and social framework relevant to the fishery, and (5) the economics of the fishery.[63] The Act does not mandate the standard of maximum sustainable yield, and states that "Conservation and management measures shall, where practicable, promote efficiency in the utilization of fishery resources; except that no such measure shall have economic allocation as its sole purpose."[64] The regional councils àre

TABLE 30

RELATION BETWEEN MAXIMUM SUSTAINABLE YIELD AND EXPECTED CATCHES OF
TRADITIONAL GROUNDFISH SPECIES IN THE EASTERN BERING SEA AND THE
NORTHEASTERN PACIFIC OCEAN, 1975–1976
(in thousands of metric tons)

| | | | Expected Catch or Quota | | | | | |
Region and species	Japan	U.S.S.R.	Poland	United States	Others	Total	MSY	MSY Total
East Bering Sea and Aleutians:								
Pollock	1,100*	210.0*	0	0	3.0	1,313.0	1,000	−313.0
Herring	18*	30.0*	0	0	0.3	48.3	40	−8.3
POP	11*}	148.0*	0	0	0 }	373.0 }	350 }	−23.0
Others	214*}		0	0	0			
Total	1,343*	388.0*	0	0	3.3	1,734.3	1,390	−344.3
Gulf of Alaska:								
Rockfishes	54*	10.0*	0	0	3.5	67.5	50	−17.5
Pollock	7	40.0*	9	0	1.0	57.0	100	+43.0
Sablefish	30*}		0	1	5.0 }		30 }	
Flounders	24 }	30.0*		0	0 }	100.0	90 }	+45.0
Others	1 }		9	0	0 }		25 }	
Total	116*	80.0*	18	1	9.5	224.5	295	+70.5
Washington and California:								
Hake	0	150.0*	44*	6	1.0	201.0	150	−51.0
Rockfishes	4*	2.5*	1	10	0	17.5	15	−2.5
Flounders	0 }	3.0*	0	20	0 }	33.0	20 }	+7.0
Others	0 }		0	10	0 }		20 }	
Total	4*	155.5*	45	46	1.0	251.5	205	−46.5

*Agreed quota; all others based on recent performance.

MSY = maximum sustainable yield.

SOURCE: *A Legislative History of the Fishery Conservation and Management Act of 1976*, p. 632, prepared by the U.S. National Marine Fisheries Service, Seattle, 1975.

permitted to draft management plans that limit entry by Americans as well as foreign fishermen when overfishing occurs, and two or more councils must coordinate efforts and manage a species "as a unit throughout its range" when the range extends outside a single council's jurisdiction.

It is still too early to judge the effectiveness of the legislation. During the first year of the 200-mile zone, the National Marine Fisheries Service, which administers the law, reduced the allowable catch of U.S. fleets as well as foreign fleets.[65] But the appointments to the regional councils went mainly to individuals connected with commercial fishermen, with little representation for consumers or scientists, so the possibility arises that the councils could mainly become cartels in behalf of local fishing interests.[66]

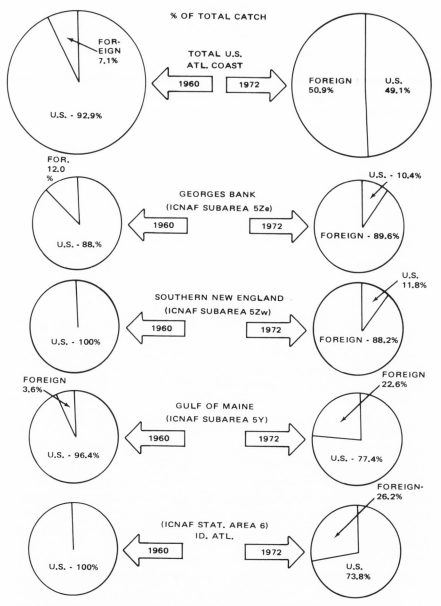

% OF TOTAL CATCH

FOR-EIGN
7.1%

TOTAL U.S.
ATL. COAST

1960   1972

FOREIGN
50.9%

U.S.
49.1%

U.S. - 92.9%

FOR.
12.0
%

GEORGES BANK
(ICNAF SUBAREA 5Ze)

1960   1972

U.S. - 10.4%

U.S. - 88.%

FOREIGN - 89.6%

U.S.
11.8%

SOUTHERN NEW ENGLAND
(ICNAF SUBAREA 5Zw)

1960   1972

U.S. - 100%

FOREIGN - 88.2%

FOREIGN
3.6%

GULF OF MAINE
(ICNAF SUBAREA 5Y)

1960   1972

FOREIGN
22.6%

U.S. - 96.4%

U.S. - 77.4%

FOREIGN-
26.2%

(ICNAF STAT. AREA 6)
ID. ATL.

1960   1972

U.S. - 100%

U.S.
73.8%

FIG. 18.   Trends in foreign vs. U.S. domestic catches from coastal U.S. fisheries in the
Atlantic Ocean, 1960 and 1972.

Source: National Marine Fisheries Service, National Oceanic and Atmospheric Administration,
Department of Commerce, June 1973.

Note: ICNAF is an abbreviation for the International Commission for the Northwest Atlantic
Fisheries, which regulates catches between Greenland and Rhode Island, U.S.

4. EXPERIENCE WITH BILATERAL AND MULTILATERAL AGREEMENTS

Joint action among two or more countries to delimit and enforce efficient structures of property rights may be required when fish migrate between adjacent or opposite EEZs, but joint action is apt to be more costly than independent action since different countries may have different preferences for the rate at which resources are utilized or different cost structures of their fishing industries. Although each nation would reap benefits from an enforced agreement to determine the economically optimal yields and to hold down catches to those levels, each also has reasons for holding out for a larger distributional gain or to increase its rate of catch secretly while others adhere to agreed limits. Nations may well recognize the inefficiencies inherent in multiple enforcement patrols and yet be reluctant to hand over exclusive enforcement rights to other nations. The more expensive monitoring becomes, the more likely cheating is and therefore the more temporary the gains from joint agreement are.[67]

I have chosen several examples of fisheries agreements as a way of highlighting the transactions costs involved, going from the lowest cost to the highest according to the number of participating nations, in ascending order. Bilateral agreements, involving two countries, are here assumed to be the lowest category of transactions costs, trilateral agreements the next lowest, and so on, with international agreements involving a variety of states outside a particular region representing the highest category. My hypothesis is that inefficiency should rise as the size of the group increases.[68]

Modern fisheries regulation began in 1923 with the first of a series of conventions between Canada and the United States. The International Pacific Halibut Commission was created to restore the depleted halibut fishery of the northeast Pacific Ocean.[69] It achieved maximum sustainable yields, but only after 40 years of effort, and the economic waste associated with its regulation has been significant. The commission set a combined catch quota for the two nations and severely restricted the fishing season. This led fishermen to invest in additional fishing effort, which in turn led the commission to restrict fishing areas and gear. Aside from the commission's inability to foreclose every avenue for raising fishing effort, its principal defect has been constitutional: it lacks the power to limit entry. As a result, the industry is drastically overcapitalized, unemployment and superannuation of fishermen are common, and layovers in port are required to preserve the resource population. The commission is generally viewed as a "technical" success, but it has been an economic failure in spite of encompassing only two nations that share a long history of cooperative dealings.

Another agreement that is thought to be relatively effective in noneconomic terms is the 1952 trilateral treaty between Canada, Japan, and the United States.[70] This treaty established the principle of "abstention," whereby Japan agreed not to exploit the salmon fisheries east of the 195° W. meridian which were subject to efforts at conservation and investment by the other two nations. Canada and Japan also agreed to abstain from the Alaskan salmon fishery. The treaty created a commission to engage in biological research leading to recommendations as to which species should be placed on or removed from the "abstention list." The commission adopted the criterion of maximum sustainable yields, but lacked powers to halt investment in effort. Enforcement is by Canada and the U.S. only. The fishery continues to generate economic waste, but observers still consider this agreement to be something of an accomplishment as fishery treaties go.

Continued success of even this limited kind, however, is uncertain. The treaty must be renewed by all parties on an annual basis and the continued participation of Japan is not assured. The Japanese believe that the abstention principle is discriminatory toward them because the treaty was concluded as part of the overall peace settlement at the close of World War II. The treaty has become steadily less popular with successive Japanese governments. Even more potentially destructive is the failure of the treaty to include two formidable distant-water fishing nations, Korea and the U.S.S.R. The transactions costs for five nations reaching agreement would increase owing to basic differences in technologies, costs, and domestic tastes for fish. Canadian and American fishermen seek to catch a limited number of species that can be caught with high-cost "traditional" technologies. But the Japanese and Russians employ lower-cost factory technologies and harvest a larger variety of species that are acceptable in their domestic and export markets.[71]

The fur seal treaty, a quadrilateral agreement among Japan, the United Kingdom, the United States, and the U.S.S.R., dates from 1911 and was a response to the horrifying pelagic (high seas) slaughter of these mammals.[72] The treaty prohibited pelagic sealing and confined all kills to the island rookeries owned by the U.S. and the U.S.S.R. These two nations paid Japan and the U.K. 15 percent each of the annual kill in return for their abstention; the research costs for determining optimum kills were divided among all four nations, with enforcement activities undertaken by each nation separately. The U.S. Pribilof Islands contained the largest herds and the U.S. adopted an exploitation criterion equivalent to the economical yield.[73] A renegotiated treaty in 1957 replaced the U.K. with Canada, retained the 15 percent quotas for Canada and Japan, and substituted the criterion of maximum sustainable yield for the economically optimal yield. The property arrangements are effective and transactions costs are low since a large fraction of the herds stays close to land. Certainly the agreement is a technical success and it may be economically successful even now. For the 30 years following 1911 it was probably the closest approximation to an economically efficient fishery that the world has experienced.

The Inter-American Tropical Tuna Commission was formed in 1949 by five parties—Colombia, Costa Rica, Ecuador, Panama, and the United States—to study and make recommendations on the several species of tuna and bait fish that migrate through the eastern Pacific Ocean (see Fig. 19).[74] It adopted the maximum yield criterion, but by 1960 the long-distance fleet from California had seriously reduced the stock. Fishing effort increased to the point where the season had to be cut to 69 days.[75] Quotas were set but for the most part ignored since only the U.S. chose to enforce them. By 1975, entry had increased to eight nations, stocks were declining, and agreements on quotas could not be reached.[76]

The International Commission for the Northwest Atlantic Fisheries (ICNAF) was formed in 1949 to deal with the exploitation by multiple nations of the coastal fisheries between Rhode Island and Greenland.[77] Originally composed of ten member-states, the commission grew to sixteen owing to the trawler activities of Japan, Poland, Spain, the two Germanys, and the U.S.S.R. Transactions costs are high because of the large number of interrelated groundfish species under ICNAF's jurisdiction, the large number of contracting parties (it is the largest of all ongoing international fisheries organizations), and the required rule of unanimity for reaching decisions.

ICNAF has a reputation for being slow, cumbersome, and generally incapable of adopting rules that are contrary to the interests of any one of its members. Its regulation has been accompanied by huge inefficiencies. Although ICNAF has had the power to set annual quotas, the limits for each nation have rarely been less than catches of the previous year. It has advocated the maximum yield criterion, but these limits are hard to learn since the area includes many species that are ecologically related. ICNAF adopted season and gear restrictions, but they have not kept pace with advances in fishing effort. The inability to control entry, especially by nations with modern trawler fleets, led to drastic congestion and overfishing by the mid-1960s.

Although the coastal states most affected by ICNAF's policies, Canada and the United States, have sought to enforce the agreement, their inspections have revealed that quotas often have been ignored and sometimes foreign boats have fished species that were on the prohibited list.[78] Canada and the U.S. have lobbied within ICNAF to cut quotas, but these efforts were unavailing until 1975 when Congress appeared ready to enact the 200-mile fisheries limit.[79] Quotas were reduced in 1976 by as much as 50 percent for some species, which even at these levels will require five to seven years to recover from overfishing and restore maximum yields (see Table 31). In the future, U.S. enforcement of its 200-mile fisheries conservation zone offers new possibilities for avoiding communal inefficiencies.

The Geneva Convention on Fishing and Conservation of the Living Resources of the High Seas of 1958 has been ratified by 33 nations, which makes it the largest international agreement to date (in number of participants) that deals with the problems of fisheries.[80] The treaty adopts the maximum sustainable yield criterion as the appropriate rate of catch and recognizes the high seas fishing rights of all nations as well as their duties to conserve resources and to prevent

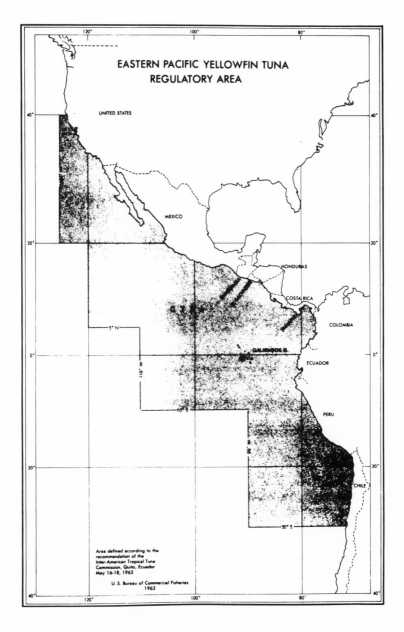

FIG. 19.   Eastern Pacific Yellowfin Tuna Regulatory Area of the Inter-American
Tropical Tuna Commission, 1962.

*CYRA = Commission's Yellowfin Regulatory Area.

SOURCE: F. David Froman, "The 200-Mile Exclusive Economic Zone: Death Knell for the
American Tuna Industry," *San Diego Law Review* 13 (1976):721.

TABLE 31

1976 ICNAF Catch Quotas (TACs) for Areas 5 and 6, and the Estimated
Recovery Time for Stocks to Reach Levels Associated with
Maximum Sustainable Yields (MSYs)

Species	ICNAF Area	1976 TAC* (thousands of tons)	Years to Recover Including 1976
Cod	5Y	8	5
	5Z	35	0
Haddock	5	6	7
Redfish	5	17	4–5
S. hake	5Y	10	5
	5Ze	50	3–4
	5Zw+6	43	4–5
R. hake	5Ze	26	3
	5Zw+6	16	4–5
Pollock	4VWX+5	55	0
Yellow tail	5(E 69°)	16	>7
	5(W 69°)+6	4	>7
All flounders except yellow tail	5+6	20	7
Herring	5Y	†	†
	5Z	†	†
Mackerel	5Y and 6	254	4–5
Other finfish (+20 species)	5 and 6	150	5–6
Squid-illex	5 and 6	30	0
Squid-Loligo	5 and 6	44	0
All finfish and squids	5 and 6	650	7

*TAC refers to the total allowable catch under species quotas recommended by ICNAF for 1976.

†Indicates that these species have seriously depressed stocks that may require 20 years to recover at present levels of recruitment.

Source: *A Legislative History of the Fishery Conservation and Management Act of 1976*, p. 633 (prepared by the U.S. National Marine Fisheries Service).

overfishing. But the treaty is inconsistent with that recognition when it also declares that a coastal state "has a special interest in the maintenance of the productivity of the living resources in any area of the high seas adjacent to its territorial sea." Article 6 stipulates that coastal states have the right to "adopt unilateral measures" to regulate adjacent fisheries, and to participate on "an equal footing" with regulatory efforts taken by other states in these areas even if their own nationals do not carry on fishing there. And coastal states also have the right (Article 7) "to adopt unilateral measures" if negotiations with other states concerned have not led to an agreement within six months, provided that there is "a need for urgent application of conservation measures" and that these measures "do not discriminate in form or fact against foreign fishermen."

In other words, the treaty does not assign anything like exclusive property rights in uncaught fish to coastal states. Instead, rights are apportioned in some ambiguous manner between coastal states and distant-water fishing states. Coastal states are allowed a "special interest" in fisheries which reflects the series of enclosures before 1958, but this right must be shared with states far removed from the fishery; no state has the exclusive right to fish or to restrict entry. The maximum yield clause permits many of the hard issues concerning the economically justified rate of utilization to be skirted. Relatively high levels of transactions costs produced an agreement which, like the other Geneva conventions of 1958, places no effective international constraint on the activities of any state seeking to exploit a commonly owned resource and thus fails to lessen the economic waste associated with communal fisheries.

But this brief survey of six international fisheries regulatory organizations provides little support for my hypothesis that transactions and enforcement costs steadily rise, and that therefore the effectiveness of regulation declines, as the size of the group increases. Instead, if these data support any proposition it is that fisheries agreements are unproductive for groups of countries of any number. The only successful international agreement involved four countries, rather than two or three, and it apparently was successful because of geographical factors which confined enforcement to a relatively small area. The basic proposition about transactions and enforcement costs is, I suspect, valid, but its impact was masked in each of the case studies by other important variables that could not be controlled.

These data do tend to support my earlier argument that extensions of coastal state authority will probably provide the fewest resource misallocations, especially where coastlines are relatively long and coastal fisheries do not migrate much between adjacent EEZs. Although the record of coastal countries in regulating fisheries efficiently is very poor, the chances of improvement are probably higher for coastal arrangements than for international ones. More research on this question might separate the costs of transactions from the costs of enforcement for groups of different sizes, since the data suggest that transactions costs tend to be smaller for groups of two or three countries than for large groups such as ICNAF or the signatories of the 1958 Geneva Convention (although this relationship does not appear to be either strong or linear).[81] It is, for example, relatively easy for a large number of countries to reach agreements about airline hijacking, but apparently this does not hold true for strictly economic issues on which national interests sharply diverge.

5. ANADROMOUS SPECIES

Some fishes, particularly salmon and eels, spend most of their adult lives in ocean waters but regularly return to the coastal rivers of their home country to spawn in fresh water. Though they may be caught on the high seas, the total costs of fishing effort are markedly lower if they are caught in coastal or inland areas. The productivity of anadromous fisheries can be affected by the actions of coastal fishermen and the policies of the home country. On the one hand, there is greater potential for overfishing in spawning areas owing to denser fishery populations. On the other hand, there is the potential for higher fishery yields if the home country limits catches and invests in hatcheries, fish runs, research, and pollution controls. The home country will have relatively few incentives to make such investments if most of the fishery it cultivates is likely to be caught before maturity by distant-water fleets. Nonetheless, in the absence of some agreement to permit a fishery to be worked jointly at the economically optimal rate, pelagic fishing represents the only method by which distant nations can capture anadromous species.

Solutions of two sorts for this situation have been proposed by Francis T. Christy, Jr.[82] One sort would grant the home country exclusive rights to catch the anadromous species in local waters or on the high seas. Some share of the catch would then be granted to all states that agreed to abstain from pelagic fishing. Foreign fishing would be prohibited without the permission of the home country, perhaps in exchange for a fee. The second sort of agreement would guarantee the home country a fixed share of all catches as compensation for protecting the spawning area and for undertaking investments that increased harvests. A variant of this scheme would induce pelagic states to share in the costs of home country cultivation according to some equitable formula. The exact amount of each country's share of the total benefits from reducing the rate of catch would of course, be a matter for hard bargaining. Substantial wastes would be avoided under either of these schemes as long as economical catch limits were imposed. But agreements of the first sort would yield the largest reduction in waste because the total costs of a given rate of catch would be minimized by fishing at the mouths of coastal streams where fish densities are highest at spawning time and because enforcement costs would also be relatively small.

Transactions costs can be substantial even when only two countries are involved. Several species of salmon and trout spawn in Russian rivers along the Kamchatka Peninsula after traversing either the western Bering Sea or the Sea of Okhotsk. Russian fishermen work the rivers only, while Japanese boats have traditionally caught these fish on the high seas. Declining catches prompted the Russians in 1956, over Japanese protests, to enclose extensive high seas areas in order to increase the stocks that returned to spawning areas. A fisheries commission set quotas for the Japanese, restricted some types of gear, and prohibited Japanese fishing in some areas. The process of setting quotas has always been acrimonious; in this case in 1959—probably not typical of bilateral fisheries deals owing to the unique political context—the bargaining took 123 days.[83]

6. CONCLUSIONS

The inherent contradictions between using the oceans as a place to generate wealth and maintaining freedom of access are perhaps most vivid in the case of the sea's living resources. Rising human populations and increased demands for protein, as well as changing technologies for extracting it from the sea, have sharply increased the value of resources devoted to marine fishing. As a result of increased demands, the stocks of fish have declined and the costs to society of maintaining communal ownership have increased.

Whereas comparisons in Chapter 4 between coastal state versus international authorities for hydrocarbon resources were to some degree hypothetical, such comparisons for fisheries can be based on actual case studies between organizations of each kind. To say the least, neither type of organization has regulated fisheries efficiently. Of the two, however, coastal states seem likely to capture more of the benefits from organizing fisheries more efficiently, especially where coastlines are long or species do not migrate significantly between adjacent or opposite EEZs. The study of a half-dozen international fisheries commissions also suggests that the costs of reaching and enforcing efficient regulations will usually be smaller for a single country or pair of countries than for international cooperatives. In situations where fisheries migrate between or regularly straddle the boundaries of several zones, compact regional agreements between the relatively few countries involved appear to have distinct advantages over regulation by large groups of states, such as ICNAF. The ineffectiveness of international regulatory bodies even for highly migratory species suggests that coastal state jurisdiction (or small regional groupings at most) offers the best chance for avoiding wasteful outcomes. For each of these situations, the creation of 200-mile fisheries enclosures implies that property rights in the oceans are changing in the direction of avoiding inefficiency, at least to some extent.

The creation of 200-mile enclosures, however, is no more than a necessary precondition for avoiding inefficient outcomes. An economic rent cannot be sustained by restricting the access of foreign fishermen alone. Property rights in fisheries will become relatively "private" only to the extent that coastal states restrict the access of their own nationals as well. It remains to be seen whether the value of fishery rents to coastal states exceeds all the costs, including the political costs, of generating them.

Notes

1. Alexander and Hodgson (1975), p. 586. The term fish commonly includes invertebrates and mammals, such as whales.

2. UN Food and Agriculture Organization, *Yearbook of Fishery Statistics—1973*, vol. 36 (1974), p. 17.

3. Milner B. Schaefer, "The Resources Base: Present and Future," in E. M. Borgese, *Pacem in Maribus* (New York: Dodd, Mead, 1972), p. 111.

4. Hiroshi Kasahara, "International Aspects of the Exploitation of the Living Resources of the Sea," in ibid., p. 124.

5. See Lewis M. Alexander, "Geography and the LOS Debate," in *Perspectives on Ocean Policy*, pp. 325 – 26.

6. This discussion is based on Lionel A. Walford, *Living Resources of the Sea* (New York: Ronald Press, 1958), pp. 71 – 73; John D. Isaacs, "The Nature of Oceanic Life," *Scientific American*, September 1969, pp. 146 – 62; and S. J. Holt, "The Food Resources of the Ocean," ibid., pp. 178 – 94.

7. R. W. Stewart, "The Atmosphere and the Ocean," ibid., pp. 76 – 86. I must also thank Don Walsh for references and discussion of this subject.

8. See two articles by Richard J. Agnello and Lawrence P. Donnelley: "Property Rights and Efficiency in the Oyster Industry," *Journal of Law and Economics* 18 (1975):521 – 33; and "Prices and Property Rights in the Fisheries," *Southern Economic Journal* 42 (1975):253 – 62.

9. This discussion is drawn from Eckert (1974), pp. 159 – 63. See also Jack Hirshleifer, James C. De Haven, and Jerome W. Milliman, *Water Supply: Economics Technology, and Policy*, p. 49; Alan Friedman, "The Economics of the Common Pool," *U.C.L.A. Law Review* 18 (1971):856 – 69; H. Scott Gordon, "The Economic Theory of a Common-Property Resource: The Fishery," *Journal of Political Economy* 62 (1954): 124 – 42; Vernon L. Smith, "On Models of Commercial Fishing," ibid. 77 (1969):181 – 98; Anthony Scott, "The Fishery: Objectives of Sole Ownership," ibid. 63 (1955):116 – 24; Francis T. Christy, Jr., and Anthony Scott, *The Common Wealth in Ocean Fisheries* (Baltimore: Johns Hopkins University Press for Resources for the Future, Inc., 1965), chap. 2.

10. Giulio Pontecorvo, "On the Utility of Bioeconomic Models for Fisheries Management," in Adam A. Sokoloski, ed., *Ocean Fishery Management: Discussions and Research* (Seattle: U.S. Department of Commerce, National Oceanic and Atmospheric Administration, National Marine Fisheries Service, NOAA Technical Report NMFS CIRC-371, April 1973), pp. 13, 18.

11. It has often been taken as a truism in the literature on fisheries that a species will never be overfished to the point of extinction since the cost of taking the last few members will almost always exceed the gains of the extra catch. But this may be incorrect since increased demand and improved technologies (e.g., the substitution of vacuum-type

pumps for common nets) make it more economical to fish lower densities of the stock. This in turn makes the species more susceptible to disease and natural predators. Christy and Scott, pp. 83–84.

12. For an excellent general discussion of this point, see Steven N. S. Cheung, "The Structure of a Contract and the Theory of a Non-Exclusive Resource," *Journal of Law and Economics* 13 (1970):64–70.

13. James Crutchfield and Giulio Pontecorvo, *The Pacific Salmon Fisheries: A Study of Irrational Conservation* (Baltimore: Johns Hopkins Press for Resources for the Future, Inc., 1969), pp. 115–16, 174–75.

14. James A. Crutchfield, "Overcapitalization of the Fishing Effort," in Lewis M. Alexander, ed., *The Law of the Sea: The Future of the Sea's Resources*, p. 24.

15. Edward Lynch, Richard Doherty, and George Draheim, *The Groundfish Industries of New England* (Washington, D.C.: U.S. Fish and Wildlife Service, 1961), p. 121.

16. Lawrence Van Meir, *An Economic Analysis of Policy Alternatives for Managing the Georges Bank Haddock Fishery* (Washington, D.C.: Bureau of Commercial Fisheries, 1969), pp. 91, 95, 100, 108.

17. *Economic Value of Ocean Resources to the United States*, pp. 4–5, 63–64.

18. "The Flaw in the Fisheries Bill," *Washington Post*, Apr. 13, 1976.

19. Christy and Scott, p. 140.

20. Peter Steinhart, "U.S. Enters the Age of 200-Mile Limits," *Los Angeles Times*, Feb. 27, 1977; hereafter cited as Steinhart (1977).

21. Tuna stocks have also declined owing to reduced supplies of the anchovita, a small fish upon which the tunas feed.

22. A slightly different version of this argument is made by Francis T. Christy, Jr., "Distribution Systems for World Fisheries: Problems and Principles," in *Perspectives on Ocean Policy*, pp. 196–98, hereafter cited as Christy (1974); and by James L. Johnston (1976b), p. 184.

23. This point is highlighted by Tom Alexander, "American Fishermen Are Missing the Boat," *Fortune*, September 1973, pp. 192–97, 244–48.

24. Christy and Scott, p. 15.

25. This is the unanimous position of the economic sources cited earlier in this chapter. I have yet to find an economist favoring maximum yields.

26. There appears to be equivocation between the competing goals of the maximum versus the economic yields even by ocean specialists who have access to both literatures. See Borgese, *Pacem in Maribus*, pp. xix–xxiii, and Kasahara, in ibid., pp. 125–27.

27. Tom Alexander, p. 244.

28. Christy and Scott, pp. 15–16.

29. Crutchfield and Pontecorvo, p. 46.

30. James A. Crutchfield, "Resources from the Sea," in T. S. English, ed., *Ocean Resources and Public Policy* (Seattle: University of Washington Press, 1973), p. 115.

31. Francis T. Christy, Jr., "Fisheries: Common Property, Open Access, and Common Heritage," in Borgese, ed., *Pacem in Maribus*, p. 194; hereafter cited as

Christy (1972). The purpose of these agreements appears to have been the interests of the U.S. fishing industry rather than the reduction of common pool wastes, although the latter would also result to some extent if the agreements were enforced. In 1965, U.S. fishing trawlers took 120 million pounds of haddock from the Georges Bank, but by 1972 they took only 11.7 million pounds owing to the entry of Soviet trawlers (Tom Alexander, p. 195). Similarly, in 1961 U.S. fishing fleets took almost the entire catch of cod from the Georges Bank, but by 1973 netted only 12 percent of the total catch. Peter Steinhart, "200-Mile Zones Transform the Sea," *Los Angeles Times*, Mar. 14, 1976; hereafter cited as Steinhart (1976).

32. Steinhart (1976).

33. E. A. Keen, "Limited Entry: The Case of the Japanese Tuna Fishery," in Sokoloski, ed., pp. 146–58.

34. Christy and Scott, p. 119.

35. Blake A. Campbell, *Limited Entry in the Salmon Fishery: The British Columbia Experience* (University of British Columbia Fisheries Programs, Pacific Sea Grant Advisory Program PASGAP 6, May 1972); S. Fraser and W. McKay, *Limited Entry and the Salmon Fishery of British Columbia* (Canadian Fisheries and Marine Service, Pacific Region, mimeo., June 18, 1976). I am indebted to A. G. Zangri, a graduate student at the University of Southern California, for calling my attention to these sources. See also G. Alexander Fraser, *License Limitation in the British Columbia Salmon Fishery* (Vancouver, B.C.: Canadian Fisheries and Marine Service, Technical Report Series PAC/T-77-13, July 1977).

36. Some 350 vessels were retired as part of a governmental "buy-back" scheme that required that the resold boats could not be used for fishing in Canadian waters, and there was attrition from the fleet as some older vessels were unable to meet safety standards. Fraser and McKay, p. 4.

37. Blake A. Campbell, "License Limitation Regulations: Canada's Experience," mimeo. undated, pp. 7–8.

38. These are discussed by Fraser and McKay, pp. 18–20.

39. See Kenneth W. Clarkson, "International Law, U.S. Seabeds Policy, and Ocean Resource Development," *Journal of Law and Economics* 17 (1974):118–25.

40. Presidential Proclamation No. 2668, 16 U.S.C. sec. 741 (1958); *U.N.L.S., High Seas*, pp. 112–13; see also Myres S. McDougal and William T. Burke, *The Public Order of the Oceans*, pp. 966–67.

41. "Recent Developments in the Law of the Sea, 1976–1977: Unilateral Extensions of Sovereignty Over Coastal Waters Declared by Several States," *San Diego Law Review* 14 (1977):724–29.

42. As with Truman's enclosure, most of these contained clauses that indicated clearly an intention to avoid interferences with navigation freedoms.

43. "Japan Maps Fishery Policy in View of 200-Mile Zones," *The Fish Boat*, December 1976, pp. 17–18; "Japan Plans Fishing Zone of 200 Miles," *Los Angeles Times*, Mar. 30, 1977.

44. "Recent Developments in the Law of the Sea: Japan Seeks to Claim New Islands," *San Diego Law Review* 14 (1977):732.

45. John L. Kask, "Present Arrangements for Fishery Exploitation," in Alexander, ed., *The Law of the Sea: The Future of the Sea's Resources*, p. 57.

46. F. David Froman, "The 200-Mile Exclusive Economic Zone: Death Knell for the American Tuna Industry," *San Diego Law Review* 13 (1976):713.

47. Ibid., p. 717.

48. Robin Murray and Frances Murray, "An Examination of the Existing Constabularies and Inspectorates Concerning Themselves with the Sea and the Seabed," in Borgese, ed., *Pacem in Maribus*, pp. 295–321. It was never much of a war, however. No deaths were recorded, the British were permitted to use Icelandic ports in medical emergencies, and the two sides occasionally had tea while untangling their nets. "British Surrender in Iceland 'Cod War'," *Los Angeles Times*, Dec. 2, 1976.

49. Choon-ho Park, "Fishing under Troubled Waters: The Northeast Asia Fisheries Controversy," *Ocean Development and International Law* 2 (1974):93–135. As an example of such controversies, between 1946 and 1968, the U.S.S.R. seized 1,275 Japanese boats and 10,763 fishermen, some of whom have yet to be repatriated. For these data and others see remarks of Manfred C. Vernon, in *The Law of the Sea: National Policy Recommendations*, Proceedings of the Fourth Annual Conference of the Law of the Sea Institute, Kingston, R.I., June 1969, p. 358.

50. David Brand, "The Question of Who Owns Oceans Becomes Vital as Exploitation Grows," *Wall Street Journal*, Sept. 13, 1973.

51. "Britain Suspends Fishing Off Iceland," *Los Angeles Times*, May 31, 1976.

52. "Britain Deploys 20 Ships to Patrol 200-Mile Fishing Limit," ibid., Jan. 1, 1977.

53. Don Cook, "Europe Facing Fishing Rights Wrangle," ibid., Oct. 17, 1976; "Mexico's 200-Mile Sea Limit in Force," ibid., June 7, 1976.

54. Testimony of Admiral Owen Siler, Commandant, U.S. Coast Guard, in *Emergency Marine Fisheries Protection Act of 1975*, Hearing before the Committee on Commerce, U.S. Senate, 94th Cong., 1st Sess., on S. 961, Serial no. 94–27, pt. 1, June 6, 1975, pp. 42–47; Richard C. Paddock, "Satellites May Help Check 200-Mile Zone," *Los Angeles Times*, Apr. 16, 1976; Larry Pryor, "200-Mile U.S. Fish Zone in Effect Today," ibid., Mar. 1, 1977.

55. Reuters dispatch, "Russia to Start Enforcing 200-Mile Fishing Limit," *Los Angeles Times*, Feb. 25, 1977.

56. Imposing taxes or fees to raise marginal costs is a standard means for reducing common pool inefficiencies. See Hirshleifer, De Haven and Milliman, pp. 59–66.

57. "Law of the Sea: A Synopsis," *San Diego Law Review* 12 (1975):670–72; "Recent Developments in the Law of the Sea: Fisheries," ibid., 13 (1976):639–40.

58. Ibid., pp. 638–39; Brazil–United States Shrimp Conservation Agreement, *International Legal Materials*, vol. 11, p. 453 (done at Brasilia, May 9, 1972).

59. Reuters dispatch, "Mexico Starts Sea Zone," *Los Angeles Times*, Aug. 1, 1976.

60. P.L. 94-265, 94th Cong., H.R. 200, April 13, 1976.

61. See Steinhart (1977); Pryor, "200-Mile U.S. Fish Zone in Effect Today"; "Mexico, Russia Sign U.S. Fishing Accord," *Los Angeles Times*, Nov. 27, 1976; Sam Jameson, "Japanese Resentment Expected When U.S. Begins Enforcing 200-Mile

Zone," ibid., Dec. 17, 1976; Associated Press dispatch, "U.S. Sets Japan Fishing Quota," ibid.

The quotas are established by the U.S. Secretary of State. For example, see Department of State Unclassified Cable No. 286063, November 30, 1977, from Secretary Cyrus Vance to American Embassies in Tokyo, Moscow, Warsaw, Copenhagen, Seoul, Taipei, Mexico City, and Ottawa, "Final Allocation of Resources Available for Foreign Fishing Off U.S. Pacific Coast for 1978," 6 pp. I am indebted to Vladimir Kaczynski for providing me with a copy of this cable.

62. Initial enforcement was concentrated in Alaskan and northeastern Pacific waters off the coasts of Washington and Oregon. All foreign fishing in the Gulf of Mexico was halted since no countries have yet applied for permits. On the same day that the U.S. zone went into effect, Cuba announced that it had also declared an EEZ of 200 miles and was prepared to negotiate with adjacent countries over common boundaries. See Pryor, also John Kifner, "U.S. Warned Soviet Before Seizing Ship," *New York Times*, Apr. 11, 1977; "Eight U.S. 'Watchdogs' Live on Soviet Ships," *Los Angeles Times*, Apr. 24, 1977; "Russian Fishing Captain Gets $10,000 Fine, Suspended Sentence in Boston," ibid., May 3, 1977.

63. Sec. 303(b)(6). See also the remarks of Senator Warren G. Magnuson in *Emergency Marine Fisheries Protection Act of 1975*, pt. 1, p. 39, reflecting his perceptions of the theory of limited entry into the fishery.

64. Sec. 301(a) (5). The reports of both the House and Senate committees reflect an understanding of the difference between maximum sustainable yield and economic optimum yield. U.S. Senate, Committee on Commerce and National Ocean Policy Study, *A Legislative History of the Fishery Conservation and Management Act of 1976*, 94th Cong., 2d Sess. (Washington, D.C., October 1976), pp. 676, 691, 1098−99.

65. Bill Drummond, "Fishermen Like 200-Mile Zone But Not Regulations," *Los Angeles Times*, Apr. 24, 1978.

66. Giulio Pontecorvo, "Fishery Management and the General Welfare: Implications of the New Structure," *Washington Law Review* 52 (1977):641−56.

67. George J. Stigler, "A Theory of Oligopoly," *Journal of Political Economy* 72 (1964):44−61.

68. Other sources categorize fisheries agreements according to species or region rather than the number of participants. The treatment here is admittedly abbreviated. For more comprehensive surveys see Christy and Scott, passim; Douglas M. Johnston, *The International Law of Fisheries: A Framework for Policy-Oriented Inquiries* (New Haven: Yale University Press, 1965); William T. Burke, "Aspects of Internal Decision-Making Processes in Intergovernmental Fishery Commissions," *Washington Law Review* 43 (1967):115−78.

69. Douglas M. Johnston, pp. 372−84; Burke, pp. 147−50; Christy and Scott, pp. 14−15.

70. Douglas M. Johnston, pp. 274−82; Burke, pp. 152−53; Christy (1972), p. 192; Crutchfield and Pontecorvo, pp. 190−94.

71. This point is made by James Crutchfield, "The Marine Fisheries: A Problem in International Cooperation," *American Economic Review, Papers and Proceedings* 54 (1964):213–15.

72. Douglas M. Johnston, pp. 264–69.

73. Ibid., pp. 266–67; Burke, p. 147.

74. Douglas M. Johnston, pp. 436–38; Burke, p. 151.

75. Tom Alexander, p. 244.

76. "Recent Developments in the Law of the Sea: Conservation," *San Diego Law Review* 13 (1976):632–33.

77. Douglas M. Johnston, pp. 366–69; Burke, pp. 151–52.

78. Mary Brewer, "ICNAF Rules Are Not Being Followed by Foreign Fishing Fleet," *Boothbay Register*, Dec. 4, 1975, reprinted in *A Legislative History of the Fishery Conservation and Management Act of 1976*, pp. 538–39; letter from Donald C. McKernan to Hon. Warren G. Magnuson, Dec. 4, 1975, reprinted in ibid., p. 542; statement of Hon. Claiborne Pell, ibid., pp. 590–91.

79. "Fish and the Seas," *New York Times*, Dec. 8, 1975, reprinted in ibid., pp. 515–16; "Recent Developments in the Law of the Sea: Conservation," *San Diego Law Review* 13 (1976):633; Roger Worth, "Toward the 200-Mile Limit: Why Canada Feels Overfished and Fed Up," *Financial Post* (Toronto), July 26, 1975; John N. Moore, "Premature Action Would Ruin a High Stakes Game," *Los Angeles Times*, Nov. 2, 1975; "A Law for Some of the Seas," ibid., Oct. 29, 1975.

80. 17 U.S.T. 138, T.I.A.S. 5969 (April 29, 1958, effective March 20, 1966).

81. I am indebted to Michael E. Levine for drawing this distinction to my attention and for his helpful comments on this section.

82. Francis T. Christy, Jr., "A Look at Fisheries Issues," *Marine Technology Society Journal*, July 1974, pp. 56–59.

83. See Douglas M. Johnston, pp. 391–96, 426–27.

CHAPTER 6

Property Rights in the Ocean Environment

One of the oldest uses of the oceans has been as a "sink" for the wastes of man's activities. Lying in hollow basins below the continental elevations, the oceans become the final repository of many pollutants owing to gravity and the other physical forces that have filled the basins with water. The sources of ocean pollution may be classified into four groups. The first is land-based sources: the hydrocarbons, pesticides, and heavy metals that are carried to the sea by atmospheric blowoff, as well as the oil and industrial wastes that are drawn there by rivers and drainage systems.[1] The second group is dumping, the intentional discharge of large and concentrated quantities of pollutants and other materials. It includes untreated municipal sewage, garbage, dredge spoils, munitions, debris, and cannisters containing radioactive or other toxic substances. The third group arises from offshore resource exploitation and includes the petroleum from oil rig spills, leaks, and blowouts and possibly the residues from mining and processing hard minerals. The fourth group is additional petroleum from ships as the result of either accidental collisions, groundings, and leaks or deliberate cleaning and washing of the cargo tanks of crude oil carriers.

The capacity of the oceans to act as a sink is now recognized to be a scarce resource: oceanic ability to accept pollutants and to render them harmless is limited. The injection of chemicals and wastes into marine environments at rates that are greater than the ability of oceans to dispel them and to cleanse itself produces pollution. If mankind has overused the oceans as a sink, it is only because the users have been given incorrect incentives to economize on its limited capabilities for regeneration. This, in turn, is caused by a failure to define and enforce satisfactory property rights in non-sink uses. The chief purpose of this chapter is to show that ocean pollution is largely an economic problem, and that the property rights paradigm employed for other resources in earlier chapters is applicable here as well. The first section describes the nature of ocean pollution spillovers and their geographic determinants. Other sections compare the probable effect on levels of pollution of different property rights assignments between coastal states and international organizations.

1. PHYSICAL CHARACTERISTICS OF OCEAN POLLUTION

Pollution Amounts and Effects

Of all the marine resources discussed in this volume, the self-cleansing properties of the oceans appear to be the least well understood by scientists.[2] Scientific interest in the subject is relatively new, and few of these cleansing processes have been subjected to extensive analysis. Also, scientists do not really know how dirty the oceans are, or the total amounts of various pollutants, or their annual rates of increase from man's activities. It is generally assumed, for the purposes of both science and public policy, that the level of ocean pollution has been rising, especially in coastal areas—that higher populations have led to increased demands for foods and other goods and these in turn have increased the supply of wastes and harmful industrial byproducts. Data to support this premise are scant, however. Provisional time series for a very few pollutants have been compiled from historical U.S. data, but extensive data on annual marine pollution by individual nations, as well as data on world injection rates or aggregate levels of pollution, are nonexistent. The accumulation of knowledge in this field will for some time be slow and piecemeal.

The attention of scientists and policy makers has focused mainly on coastal areas since a large fraction of pollution damage appears to occur there. Continental runoff and atmospheric blowoff cause many land-based pollutants to reach coastal areas first. The costs of transporting municipal sewage, dredge spoils, munitions-laden ships, and heavy debris all increase with the distance from shore. Most oil discharge, intentional or accidental, occurs near shore or in shipping lanes that approach ports. As Michael Waldichuk has put it:

[the] main foci of pollution are in the coastal zone. It is in this area that wastes are discharged from continental sources, and it is here that the greatest damage is generally done. A type of filtration process takes place in the coastal zone removing much of the pollutant, chemically, physically and biologically, before the effluent gets too far out to sea. Long before the open-ocean environment becomes uninhabitable for aquatic organisms, the coastal zone will have lost its use for renewable aquatic resources, amenities, recreation, industrial water use, and possibly, even for navigation.[3]

The cost of pollution is relatively high in coastal areas because of the reduced values for other activities that compete with the use of oceans as a sink.

Navigation is affected by oil slicks that damage hulls, and in some cases ships may be threatened by free-floating dumped debris. Human recreation and health can be affected by the collection of oils and tars on beaches. The cities of New York and San Francisco have lowered their budgeted costs of waste disposal by dumping untreated municipal sewage offshore, but at the added cost of almost devastating nearby beaches.

The effects of pollution on marine organisms and fish, which are usually most productive in coastal regions, can be dramatic.[4] Such materials as heavy metals, sulfides, phosphorus, and pesticides in certain concentrations can be directly toxic to fish. The detonation of dumped munitions can destroy most species within a one-mile radius of the explosion. Petroleum has extremely low solubility in water and can be fatal when it coats surface-swimming ocean birds. The effects of most pollutants are more subtle and indirect, however. The photosynthesis of plankton can be affected by the presence of petroleum or by the dumping of dredge spoils, which cloud the water and prevent the necessary penetration of sunlight. Dumping organic materials such as sewage sometimes reduces the level of oxygen to the point where the diversity of marine species is altered. Concentrations of sewage can cause hepatitis in shellfish. Other pollutants affect the quality of water—for example, its pH or sediment conditions—so significantly that species are either destroyed or induced to seek new feeding areas. Petroleum, usually a very stable compound, will pass through some organisms without alteration but in other organisms may be concentrated to high levels which affect tissue growth and cause cancers. Although the effects of hydrocarbons are complex and poorly understood, there is evidence that they can reduce the ability of some species to reproduce, breathe, or swim. Heavy metals can induce diseases that retard the growth of fish or their ability to escape predators. Concentrations of DDT can limit their capacity to learn and have been shown to prevent salmon from detecting their home stream after migration.

How dangerous is ocean pollution to mankind? Direct ingestion or exposure to gross quantities of some materials can be lethal, of course. But scientific evidence on more subtle relationships is scant and at the present will support only statements that are extremely weak.[5] For example, what is the cumulative effect on human health of ingesting over a long period of time foods that are contaminated with sublethal doses of pollutants? The answer to this question is unknown, although the finding that DDT (which is not soluble in water) persists in the fatty tissues of fish justifies some concern.[6] Does the mixing of chemicals render each pollutant less harmful to man, or is the synergistic compound that results even more toxic than its components? No general answer is possible since some evidence has been found for each type of result.[7] Although mankind has created more than 500,000 separate chemical substances, are these generally more toxic than the pollution created by the natural processes of the planet? Again, no answer is possible until we know the ultimate fates of these materials and the precise proportion between natural and manmade injections. For example, mercury is produced by the oceans themselves as a result of the weathering of the ocean floor, and oil has long entered the marine environment through natural seeps caused by geological faults.[8] One might expect marine species to have developed some resistance to these materials through time, but hard evidence is lacking.

In order to prevent the reduction in coastal values for ocean uses other than a pollution sink, some coastal states have enacted municipal legislation to limit land-based pollution sources and stationary offshore sources. At UNCLOS, some of these nations have favored either "pollution control zones" of as much as 200 nautical miles from shore in which the coastal state could also limit pollution from ships, or the inclusion of pollution control as part of a larger package of EEZ rights. The creation of coastal state rights to cleaner waters is consistent with the enclosure movement for other ocean resources. Whether or not the enclosure movement avoids greater inefficiency in pollution levels relative to international institutions depends, among other things, on local geographic conditions and the extent to which pollutants are dispersed from their sources.

Geography and Jurisdiction

The question of dividing jurisdiction between coastal state and international authorities would be relatively easy to answer if each of four polar physical conditions were met: (1) coastal waters diluted most pollutants poorly and did not disperse them effectively; (2) pollutants in coastal areas did not traverse the boundaries of adjacent or opposite EEZs; (3) most of the important sea-based sources of pollution (for example, ships and oil rigs) occurred in coastal areas and the pollution remained there; and (4) most of the important damage caused by land-based pollution sources, including atmospheric blowoff, occurred in coastal areas. Under these circumstances the economic argument for coastal state jurisdiction would be quite strong. This judgment is formed on the basis of the two propositions employed throughout this book concerning the exclusivity of impacts and the resources consumed in transacting.

The greater the degree to which a coastal state captures both the benefits and the costs of changes in the quantity of pollutants it injects into the oceans, the stronger its incentives to formulate ocean policies that avoid inefficient outcomes. If most of the costs of pollution were internalized on the coastal states involved, it would become more expensive for them to avoid collecting information concerning the reduction in the values of competing uses that pollution causes. The greater the reduction in values, the more rewarding it becomes for coastal states to divert pollution away from the ocean sink toward alternative sites on land. In international authorities, where greater weight probably is placed on widespread benefits and costs, there would be weaker incentives even to gather information on the value of nonpollution uses of coastal areas versus their values as sinks.

The implications of the proposition on transactions costs reinforce this argument. The larger the number of states in the negotiations, the greater the differences in the values that each would attach to additional reductions in ocean pollution levels. Final agreements would be difficult to negotiate unless the nations favoring different antipollution standards could be compensated for their losses, and enforcement costs would rise with the number of signers. Enforcement costs would probably be smaller under coastal control, where the same techniques designed to maintain fishing rights in EEZs of 200 nautical miles in breadth might also be used to monitor pollution activities in such areas.

Unfortunately, there are few scientific data upon which such judgments could be made. Although it is unlikely that the four polar physical conditions mentioned earlier will apply to every coastal area, we do not even know if all four apply anywhere. Even worse, there is very little information on the areas in which any one of the four conditions is met. What scientists do know about the dispersion of pollutants in different geographic settings can be summarized briefly.

The extent to which pollutants that originate along coasts are eventually dissipated depends upon the mass movements of water, atmosphere, and sediments, the migration of organisms, and the chemical reaction of pollutants in solution. Coastal pollutants will be diluted more rapidly in areas where there are strong tides, upwelling and downwelling forces, convergent or divergent currents, onshore winds, agitation from rivers, and high water temperatures. The net effect of such giant forces is still poorly understood by the scientific community.[9] As Gwenda Matthews states: "Pollutants entering the sea from rivers and land runoff are normally limited in the distance they travel. Their potential for damage is not always removed by oceanic processes, however. In spite of all the turbulence we see at the surface, mixing and dilution are far from complete at deeper levels and adjacent bodies of water may remain quite separate from each other as they do, for example, in the lower regions of the Baltic. Not always is 'dilution the answer to pollution.' "[10] Some scientists have argued that pollutants should be disposed of in the deep seas where waters are mixed more thoroughly than coastal waters.[11] Others have argued quite the opposite, that wastes decompose more slowly at greater ocean depths.[12] It would appear that the degree of mixing varies from place to place, but further research is necessary before we can know how much variation there is and what the degrees of difference are.

The effectiveness of pollution transport will also be modified by the movement of marine species and biochemical processes. The migration of birds and fish can distribute some pollutants thousands of miles in one year, and plankton can move them vertically at the rate of several meters a day. In some cases, organisms may transport pollutants more rapidly than the exchange of large bodies of water. Chemical processes also affect the rate at which pollutants spread. Particulate substances tend to settle more readily to the bottom, whereas totally dissolved substances will generally be distributed in accordance with water motion. Scientists have devised theoretical models to explain the movement of pollutants by the transport processes of water exchange, organisms, and chemistry. However, such models have been used successfully only in the case of coastal estuaries. The existing knowledge is too meager to allow an assessment of the effectiveness of pollutant transport even through the immediate coastal area to the waters of the continental shelf.[13]

Every analysis of marine pollution must make some assumption, either understood or expressed, about the degree to which each of the four polar conditions is met in real world pollution situations. For the most part, the literature on the economics of marine pollution has assumed that dispersion of pollutants is so extensive that most spillover problems are international in scope. Accordingly, most of the solutions that are proffered are also international in scope, and coastal state solutions often are ignored or are relegated to the status of trivia.[14] For many situations, however, the common underlying assumption about the effective mixing and dispersing properties of coastal waters for most pollutants appears to be unwarranted. Scientific specialists in this field appear to be reluctant to make general statements about dispersion, and the actual extent of spillovers may vary between different geographical locations. For example, pollutants may remain within the confines of individual EEZs more often along the coasts of North and South America (because of longer coastlines and prevailing east-west winds) than in the North, Baltic, Caribbean, or Mediterranean seas. The most that can be confidently said at the present is that the self-cleansing properties of coastal waters have been questioned and that the tests of the relevant hypotheses have been formulated.[15]

Because it is probably risky to generalize about the extent of spillovers between nations caused by injections of various pollutants at different locations, it is desirable to hedge by investigating the economic impact of both coastal and international mechanisms for pollution control. The next section will outline the essential economic analysis of the most basic and simple pollution problem, and the section following that will attempt to rank sources of pollution according to whether coastal or international controls appear to offer the best opportunities for avoiding economically inefficient outcomes.

2. THE ECONOMIC NATURE OF THE PROBLEM

For centuries the oceans have been available on a free-of-charge basis for use as an abundant sink just as they have been available free of charge for navigation, fishing, and other economic activities.[16] Polluters have used the oceans as a receptacle for wastes without taking into account the fact that such uses are competitive with cultivating fish, deriving foods and medicines from sea plants, and a variety of other activities the market values of which fall drastically in a polluted marine environment. Determining whether the economic rent is greater when oceans are used as a sink rather than for competing purposes is an expensive process even for isolated situations within an individual country. The cost of collecting and analyzing the information required to determine highest valued uses for many nations or the world at large is probably so great as not to be worth the effort. But rising concerns and frequently the demand at UNCLOS and in national legislatures for increased pollution controls may be evidence for the proposition that the value of oceans as a sink is not rising as rapidly as their value in competing uses.

Unpolluted Oceans as a Common Pool Resource

If the oceans have been used as a sink to a degree that is uneconomic, it is probably for most of the same reasons that communal fisheries or offshore hydrocarbons have been overexploited—that is, their use for pollution is also subject to the perverse incentives of the common pool, and international agreements to limit pollution are subject to the problem of the prisoner's dilemma.

As long as the oceans (or other elements of the environment) are unowned and no money charge is made for their use, an individual or state seeking to dispose of waste materials will tend to overuse these sinks without regard to the costs that such activities may impose on others. Consider an individual's decision to dump his daily garbage into the ocean rather than to dig a pit on his own property and dispose of it there. His decision will be based on a comparison of the costs of carrying the garbage to the ocean and the cost of digging the pit and perhaps lining it with concrete to prevent the pollution of the underground aquifer that supplies his well with water. If the costs of carrying are less, he will dispose of the wastes in the ocean even though these costs do not equal the *total* costs of his action. He does not take into account the fact that repeated dumping of wastes into the ocean may damage the beach resources used by his neighbors or reduce the value of the fisheries worked by local fisherman. Unless disposal activities are regulated by some authority or the rights to dispose must be purchased with a money payment roughly equal to the costs that his dumping imposes on others, the individual will have few incentives (other than altruism) to take his pollution costs into account, in the same way that the fishermen in Chapter 5 failed to take into account the full costs of their activities. Sink resources will be overused to an inefficient degree, and the rents attributable to both the uncaught fish and the unpolluted beaches will be sacrificed.

The choice calculations for pollution by a nation are similar to those of the individual provided that the nation itself does not incur a significant or known share of the costs of its polluting activity. Consider the case of a coastal state's decision whether to allow the disposal of cannisters containing radioactive wastes on land or at sea. If land disposal is selected and the cannisters eventually deteriorate, the population in the area surrounding the disposal site will be subjected to some amount of radiation. Few communities would tolerate exposure to such risks without some compensation, so there is an obvious incentive for the government to refuse permits for land disposal but to issue them for ocean disposal. Should the cannisters deteriorate on the ocean bottom, the costs of radiation would be largely borne by the fish and other creatures located nearby. Such exposure could contaminate the food chain and ultimately harm human health, but assuming that some of these creatures would be caught by the fishermen of other countries, only a portion of these spillover costs would be borne by the polluting state. Since no property rights or regulations exist that would allow anyone to control the use of these resources, no fees can be imposed as a way of forcing states to bear the full costs of disposal at sea.

The transport of petroleum in supertankers presents similar problems. Since ship owners are not charged for the use of the oceans in accordance with the risk to the environment that their cargoes pose, ships have grown in size, and they tend to carry more dangerous cargoes and to operate closer to coastlines in order to save on transit time and fuel. The environmental risk is relatively high owing to the concentration of petroleum, natural gas, or other materials that stem from collisions, groundings, or washing cargo tanks, and because of the difficulties of maneuvering these huge ships in confined straits or shallow coastal areas. Obviously, the owners and masters of these vessels do not deliberately operate them in a way that would risk the loss of the ship, its cargo, and possibly lives as well, but their incentive to economize on the use of ocean resources or to reduce environmental harm is certainly lower than it would be if they had to face the full costs of any carelessness. Without appropriate regulations or property rights that would align private with total costs, the amount of petroleum transported and consumed will be higher than otherwise, and the resources that are devoted to preventing and dispersing oil spills and other damage will be smaller.[17]

In each of the three preceding examples, the polluting entity – whether it be an individual, a firm, or a nation—has imposed costs on others because economic incentives have made this form of behavior relatively rewarding. It is unnecessary to assume that the entity either enjoys generating spillover costs or has a preference for vicious behavior. As in the case of fisheries, the culprit is the absence of a mechanism—either regulations or exclusive rights—to control ocean use. Abstention by one polluting firm or nation raises its total costs of waste disposal without making a noticeable dent in the total level of pollution, assuming that the ocean areas near the source tend to transport pollutants effectively, unless all polluters agree to reduce their effluents proportionately. Without prices or liabilities for sink uses, it makes little economic sense for individual polluters to conserve on its use at strictly their own expense unless they incur a significant share of the costs of their behavior owing to weak processes for transporting pollutants.

The economic rent to the use of the oceans as a sink is probably positive, but as a practical matter it is unmeasurable.[18] Ordinarily, rents would be calculated by comparing the dollar cost of disposing of wastes at sea with the dollar cost of increased disposal on land. As the dollar cost of using scarce land increased, the economic rent—the cost advantage in favor of ocean disposal—would also increase, but the straightforward calculation of the cost difference would not measure the economic rent accurately owing to the presence of spillover costs. The extra cost that polluting activities impose on other ocean uses would have to be subtracted from the difference in direct disposal costs in order to arrive at the overall resource gain (or loss) that society enjoys (or suffers) from increased ocean disposal. Since the extent of the spillover costs usually measured by the cleanup or abatement costs is not known, the true economic rent cannot be estimated.

The Position of Liability

The foregoing discussion suggests that an individual coastal state will have few economic incentives to reduce its rate of ocean pollution provided local oceanographic conditions cause the pollutants to be effectively diluted, mixed, and distributed throughout the oceans. Abstention would raise its total disposal costs, and most of the resulting benefits would be gained by other ocean-using nations. This result applies *a fortiori* when the polluter is the owner of a supertanker that is registered in a flag state far distant from the ocean areas in which it customarily operates. But agreement among the community of nations to reduce pollution to manageable levels appears to be at least superficially attractive; if all nations agreed to reduce ocean pollution, all would benefit from a once-and-for-all increase in the quality of the world marine environment. Yet an international agreement to reduce pollution has so far been one of the most difficult issues at UNCLOS. The probability of reaching a useful agreement is small because the transactions costs of writing and enforcing contracts to reduce pollution are relatively high. This situation can best be seen by outlining the necessary conditions for reducing pollution to its economical level.

To simplify the analysis, consider the problems posed by Lake Erie, where Canada and the United States face each other on opposite shores. Assume that winds and other natural forces cause pollutants that are emptied into the lake to mix perfectly, so that one-half of Canada's pollution is a cost to the U.S. and conversely. It might be tempting to conclude that neither state has an incentive to reduce pollution by substituting land-based methods of higher cost since half the cost of its activities is borne by the other. But this conclusion would be false if it were costless for each state to (a) identify the precise source of each pollutant, (*b*) ascertain the damage costs that each pollutant caused, and (*c*) negotiate and enforce contracts with the other.

Assume that Canada intends to release untreated sewage, which Canada knows will eventually reach a concentration along U.S. beaches sufficient to cause total damages of *x* dollars per year. (Recall that it costs nothing for the U.S. to trace the damage to Canadian sources and for each country to assess in advance the accurate damage costs.) What does the U.S. do in this situation? There would appear to be two answers depending upon whether or not Canada was liable for the pollution costs imposed on the U.S., but in fact the answer in each case is the same.[19]

Assume further that the two countries had previously negotiated at zero cost a treaty that made the polluting state liable for 100 percent of the damages caused to the other. Canada has several options for fulfilling its legal duty to the U.S. First, Canada could pollute and pay *x* dollars per year in compensation to the U.S. Alternatively, Canada might install a water-treatment plant that would reduce its sewage effluent to harmless (near zero) levels. Assume that the cost of this plant is *x* dollars minus one. A third option would be for Canada to adopt different technologies and to dispose of its wastes on land. Assume that this cost is *x* dollars plus one per year. If Canada seeks the least-cost solution to the problem, then it would elect to construct the treatment plant rather than shift to different technologies or pay damages to the U.S.[20] Canada's spillover costs imposed on the U.S. have been eliminated. The lake will continue to be used as a beach by the U.S. rather than as a sink by Canada because the damage costs to U.S. beaches exceed the cost to Canada of treating the sewage. It should also be recognized that the community of two countries has selected the most efficient possible use of the lake's resources. But if the assumptions had been turned around and the cost of the treatment plant had amounted to *x* dollars plus two per year, the value of the lake as a sink to Canada would have exceeded its value to the U.S. as a beach, and Canada would logically have continued to pollute while compensating the U.S. in the amount of *x* dollars per year for the cost incurred by U.S. residents of shifting to the next best source of recreation. The spillover effects would be borne by the Canadians because Canada was making compensation to the United States. Whichever of the several alternatives turned out to have the lowest cost, Canada would have continued to pollute only if the cost to the community of two nations of reducing pollution further had exceeded the gains. Owing to the ability of the two to reach and enforce bargains at no cost, the most efficient level of pollution would have resulted in each case.

What would happen if the position of liability were reversed? Assume that a treaty between the two countries has not been negotiated, and that Canada could not legally be held responsible for its pollution. In this situation, the U.S. would calculate the annual damage costs of *x* dollars as compared with the costs of the other options mentioned earlier. (Remember that the U.S. has zero-cost information on these alternatives just as Canada did.) Since the installation of the sewage treatment plant at an annual cost of x dollars minus one remains the smallest dollar cost alternative and the U.S. seeks the least-cost solution to the pollution problem, then the U.S. would pay Canada to install the plant rather than incur x dollars of annual damages. The striking result, as R. H. Coase has demonstrated, is that there are not two answers to the problem but only one: the least-cost alternative that Canada selected when Canada was liable for damages will be the same least-cost option that the U.S. selects when Canada is not liable. The only difference between the two situations involves the distribution of income: instead of Canada's incurring the cost of the cheapest solution when it was liable, the U.S. must pay for the cheapest solution when Canada is not liable. As long as the same course of action is selected in each situation, the resource-use outcome for the lake—that is, whether it is used as a sink or for recreation—will not be affected by the assignment of liability. The most efficient solution is taken no matter which country is liable. Canada's spillover costs were taken into account by the Canadians when they were not liable, because the U.S. either would have offered Canada a payment not to pollute or would have installed the treatment plant at its own expense. As long as information and transactions costs are negligible, the assignment of liability (distributional effects aside) has no influence on how much pollution continues or what is decided upon as the most efficient use of the lake.[21]

Costs of Information and Transactions

Before trying to apply the foregoing analysis to real pollution situations, one must first assess the importance of information and transactions costs. Even a cursory appraisal of the problem of ocean pollution suggests that each of these categories of cost—identifying the polluters, bargaining with them, and monitoring the agreements that are reached—appears to be relatively large.

First, identification costs are large because there are so many different sources of the different kinds of ocean pollution—sewage, dredge spoils, munitions, petroleum from ships and other dangerous materials. It may be relatively easy (inexpensive) for a coastal state to trace the damage to its beaches from a gigantic oil slick to the single supertanker that is grounded nearby. But how can the cause be pinpointed when dozens of ships may have accidentally leaked oil or deliberately washed their tanks in local waters, and hours after the discovery may have traveled some distance from the pollution source? Not only is it expensive to calculate the total costs of damage beyond cleanup costs (these would include damage to wildlife and property), but the damage is always more expensive to apportion when there are multiple sources.

Second, negotiating costs would probably rise according to the number of nations that pollute or suffer damage. The greater the extent to which coastal waters mix thoroughly and disperse pollutants throughout the oceans, the weaker are the incentives of a single nation to reduce its pollution injections and hence the larger the number of states that must be included if an agreement is to be effective. Again, these costs appear to be greatest for pollution from ships. There are many of them, and they are registered in a variety of countries. Although registry nations have the power to control the general condition of ships, they may not exercise this authority unless they are themselves incurring significant pollution damage from ships or are facing penalties for lax regulations. If an agreement to reduce the pollution from ships could be reached, the costs of enforcing it would fall most heavily on the nonregistry states that incurred the most pollution damage.

Third, negotiating costs would increase because different countries would place different values on improvements to the marine environment. The value of a less polluted coastline would probably be greater for coastal states with long coastlines, high coastal populations, productive local fisheries, and high demands for recreation. Lying at the opposite extreme would be countries that are landlocked or have no extensive or productive coastal areas. The former group of countries would benefit the most from agreements that were effective in reducing the quantity of pollutants that circulated throughout the oceans. Different valuations of environmental improvements do not make it impossible (prohibitively expensive) for a group of nations to reach an agreement on cutting back pollution rates, but they do make an agreement of this kind more expensive to achieve and therefore less likely to be realized. Moreover, voluntary actions to decrease pollutants that have worldwide impacts are unlikely owing to the prisoner's dilemma characteristic of the problem, especially if those that agreed to cut back had to incur higher cost forms of disposal.[22]

Fourth, negotiations costs also would increase because different nations would face different opportunity costs of using the oceans as a sink. Those with the highest cost alternative technologies or methods of disposal would probably insist on being compensated for joining the efforts of the group to reduce pollution, and unless they were compensated they might refuse to sign the convention. The states incurring losses would also have incentives to overstate these costs, and the states liable for compensation would tend to understate the losses or insist upon independent verification. If the costs of shifting to alternative technologies were great, the cost of effective group action would definitely increase. Again, this does not mean that an effective international agreement to reduce pollutants is beyond reach, but requiring compensation does make the task somewhat more expensive. States that refused to join the group could continue their polluting activities without compensating the rest, thus imposing more costs on the group than on themselves—assuming that pollutants were effectively dispersed throughout the world's oceans.[23]

Fifth, enforcement costs would be high owing to the difficulty of determining whether or not individual states were reducing pollutants by the amount that they promised when they signed the agreement. In almost any agreement of this kind it will be characteristic of states to have some incentive to cheat for the simple reason that high enforcement costs make it reasonable to expect that their "partners" in the treaty will also engage in some amount of cheating. The higher these costs are—and this depends largely upon the available technologies of enforcement—the smaller the likelihood that an effective agreement to cut pollution will be reached and maintained.

In summary, certain agreements, bargains, or treaties that would have increased the total value of using the oceans when information and transactions had zero cost are less likely to occur when there are transactional impediments to joint action. The rearrangement of rights that would lead polluters to bear the full costs of their actions will not occur if the resources consumed in making and enforcing bargains exceed the resulting increase in the total value of the oceans. As a way of emphasizing this point, assume for a moment that the total value of the ocean uses would be higher if polluters were required to bear all costs of their actions. This outcome would surely occur if transactions could be executed without cost. But assume also that transactions do cost something and that the legal liability for pollution is reversed—that is, that states incurring pollution damage must pay the polluters to reduce spillovers. With positive transactions costs, it could happen that the resources consumed in drawing up and enforcing a treaty to reverse liability would exceed the higher ocean values that would result from reversed liability. As a result, the possibility of a comprehensive treaty (or of bargains among smaller groups of states in lieu of a comprehensive treaty) would be ignored and uncompensated pollution damages would continue. It would appear that this extreme hypothetical case is strikingly similar to the present situation in the real world: total pollution and its cost appear to be rising, the liability of polluters for damages is relatively slight where it exists, and the transactions costs to reduce pollution to manageable levels appear to be high.

Coase's framework for thinking about spillover problems indicates a route for establishing institutional mechanisms that will reduce pollution to more efficient levels. The emphasis of his argument was on the transactions and enforcement costs attached to pollutants of different types and sources. Pending some possibly drastic international reassignment of pollution rights and duties, exchanges between polluters and those they harm in order to internalize a greater amount of spillovers are more likely to occur where the cost of acquiring information and transacting is relatively low. The more these costs can be reduced in the course of structuring property rights to unpolluted (or perhaps less polluted) oceans, the greater the possibility that reassignments or exchanges of such property rights will lead to the level of pollution that increases economic rents from the oceans. With this in mind, the following two sections of this chapter attempt to organize ocean pollutants according to the costs of tracing them to their sources and enforcing liability rules against such injections.

3. SOURCES BETTER SUITED TO COASTAL JURISDICTION

Sources on Land

A significant fraction of all ocean pollution, including the most serious pollutants, originates on land. Man's activities have probably doubled the amount of lead and mercury injected into the oceans by natural processes, and man has introduced entirely new compounds—among them chlorinated hydrocarbons (including DDT), gasoline, and dry cleaning solvents—that may have serious long-term effects.[24] Most of these originate on land and are transported to the oceans by means of rainfall runoff or atmospheric blowoff. The case of petroleum is illustrated in Table 32. Approximately 54 percent of the total estimated quantity of petroleum in the oceans comes from such land-based sources as coastal refineries, the atmosphere, urban drainage and river runoff, and industrial and municipal wastes. Offshore oil production accounts for less than one percent, and the natural seeps caused by fissures on the ocean floor cause about 10 percent. The remaining 35 percent is from vessels.

The costs of reducing many land-based sources would probably be smaller for the concerned coastal state than for an international body. Coastal states would probably have lower costs of discovering precise point sources, of determining the least-cost techniques of reducing pollutants, and of enacting and enforcing legislation. The incentives of coastal states to take spillovers into account would depend upon the degree to which these pollutants both contaminated coastal waters and were contained there by relatively ineffective processes of pollution transport. The most one can say at this point is that coastal states ordinarily would have more incentive to bear responsibility for sewage emissions and other types of ocean dumping than, for example, for the radionucleides that are incidental to nuclear weapons testing. Testing weapons above ground produced such widespread contamination in the higher atmosphere that it could be reduced effectively only by international agreements that were reached despite high transactions and enforcement costs.[25] The same may hold for DDT and similar compounds because of the problems of atmospheric circulation and the migration of species of prey which disperse these pollutants over vast areas.

Ocean Dumping: A Case Study of
Three Forms of Jurisdiction

Ocean dumping is probably not the most severe or the most extensive of the various kinds of pollution, but it appears to fit the model for coastal state control rather well. The coastal state bears a significant fraction of total pollution costs where materials are dumped in waters that have limited properties for effective mixing and transport. Coastal states for the same reason will take into account

TABLE 32

Estimated Budget of Petroleum Hydrocarbons Introduced into the Oceans

Source	Millions of Tons (Metric) Per Year	Percentage
Land-based Activities		
Coastal refineries	0.2	
Atmosphere	0.6	
Coastal municipal wastes	0.3	
Coastal industrial wastes (nonrefining)	0.3	
Urban runoff	0.3	
River runoff	1.6	
	3.3	54
Coastal Activities		
Natural seeps	0.6	
Offshore production	0.08	
	0.68	11
Transportation		
LOT tankers*	0.31	
Non-LOT tankers†	0.77	
Dry docking	0.25	
Terminal operations	0.003	
Bilges bunkering	0.5	
Tanker accidents	0.2	
Nontanker accidents	0.1	
	2.133	35
	6.113	100

*Load on top, i.e., with specially designed tanks to hold oil sludge.
†With ballast in oil tanks.
Source: National Academy of Sciences, *Petroleum in the Marine Environment* (Washington, D.C., 1975), p. 6.

some of the spillover benefits of dumping. For example, dumping inert substances, such as old ships, automobiles, or rubber tires, tends to create new reeflike objects that collect foods and stimulate fisheries.[26] Where most of these gains and costs are coastal, international authorities offer no advantages either in internalization or in enforcement.

During 1972, three different jurisdictions for dumping were created. The United States, having long coastlines and an east-west pattern of winds, enacted domestic legislation that regulated dumping without creating a pollution control zone. In the North Sea, twelve littoral countries with short coastlines adopted a limited convention for essentially the same purpose. At the international level, the Ocean Dumping Convention was signed. Each is analyzed in turn.

United States dumping in tonnage increased more than fourfold between 1949 and 1968 (Table 33). The largest categories of increase during the period

TABLE 33

HISTORICAL TREND IN U.S. OCEAN DUMPING, 1949–1968*

(in tons)

Coastal Area	1949–53		1954–58		1959–63		1964–68	
	Total	Avg./Yr.	Total	Avg./Yr.	Total	Avg./Yr.	Total	Avg./Yr.
Atlantic Coast	8,000,000	1,600,000	16,000,000‡	3,200,000	27,270,000	5,454,000	31,100,000	6,200,000
Gulf Coast	40,000‡	8,000	283,000	56,000	860,000	172,000	2,600,000	520,000
Pacific Coast	487,000	97,000	850,000	170,000	940,000	188,000	3,410,000	682,000
Total	8,527,000	1,705,000	17,133,000	3,426,000	29,070,000	5,814,000	37,110,000	7,402,000

*Figures do not include dredge spoils, radioactive wastes, and military explosives.

†Estimated by fitting a linear trend line between data for preceding period and data for succeeding period.

‡Disposal operations in the Gulf of Mexico began in 1952.

SOURCE: U.S. Council on Environmental Quality, *Ocean Dumping: A National Policy* (Washington, D.C., October 1970), p. 8.

1954−63 were sewage sludge (61 percent) and industrial wastes (114 percent).[27] These trends continued during the period 1968−74 (Table 34), as total dumping increased by 40 percent. By far the largest category of increase, at 290.6 percent, was for construction and demolition debris; sewage sludge increased during this period by 26.8 percent, and industrial wastes by 21.9 percent. The disposal of solid wastes and explosives decreased sharply, and presumably also, as we see from Table 35, there was a decrease in the amount of radioactive wastes dumped by the U.S.

For various reasons, many of the effects of U.S. dumping are concentrated in our coastal areas. Pulp-mill effluents have contaminated some Pacific Coast areas near Washington State with "black liquor" that can kill phytoplankton. The City of New York has dumped sewage and solid wastes into an area outside New York harbor for 40 years. Studies of this area, the "New York Bight," have revealed infections in bottom sediments and inhibited cell division of phytoplankton.[28] Dredge spoils that are barged from inland river locations to offshore dumping sites can smother bottom species and prevent plankton growth by blocking the necessary sunlight.[29] Table 36 shows the composition of dumping by the United States during 1968. Dredge spoils, which were excluded from Table 33, account for 80 percent of the total (34 percent of it, according to the estimate, being existing pollution).[30] Industrial wastes, including such toxic heavy metals as mercury and other compounds such as cyanide and arsenic, amounted to only 10 percent of the tonnage. Sewage amounted to 9 percent.

U.S. legislation was preceded by an Executive Office study of ocean dumping by the Council on Environmental Quality.[31] Its report was devoted mainly to a qualitative consideration of the total costs of dumping, that is, the effect of dumping on competing marine uses and the sometimes higher direct costs that are incurred for next-best methods of land-based disposal. A common finding of the report was that municipalities in the U.S. have regularly disposed of wastes in whatever way involves the least direct (budgeted) cost to themselves without regard to the consequences to other ocean users or to the marine environment. In the case of solid waste, the method of ocean disposal preferred by municipalities was only about 10−20 percent cheaper than either rail-haul to a sanitary landfill or dumping farther from shore. In the case of sewage, the most common current methods of ocean disposal, which are also the cheapest in direct costs, are approximately one-third to one-fifth of the cost of either land-based disposal or methods of ocean disposal that would reduce pollution damages. Dredge spoils, owing to their vast tonnage, cannot be cheaply disposed of on land, but a more careful selection of ocean dumping sites could lessen the damage there. In the case of industrial wastes, the containerization of highly toxic materials can raise direct disposal costs by a factor of twenty. Of course these wastes are thought to be so dangerous that higher direct costs of this

TABLE 34

VESSEL DISCHARGE, U.S. OCEAN DUMPING BY TYPES AND AMOUNTS, 1968–1974

(in tons)

WASTE TYPE	ATLANTIC		GULF		PACIFIC		TOTAL		Percent Change 1968–74
	1968	1974	1968	1974	1968	1974	1968	1974	
Industrial waste	3,013,200	4,767,000	696,000	950,000	981,300	0	4,690,500	5,717,000	+21.9
Sewage sludge	4,477,000	5,676,000	0	0	0	0	4,477,000	5,676,000	+26.8
Construction and demolition debris	574,000	2,242,000	0	0	0	0	574,000	2,242,000	+290.6
Solid waste	0	0	0	0	26,000	200	26,000	200	—
Explosives	15,200	0	0	0	0	0	15,200	0	—
TOTAL	8,079,400	12,685,000	696,000	950,000	1,007,300	200	9,782,700	13,635,200	+39.4

SOURCE: National Academy of Sciences, *Disposal in the Marine Environment: An Oceanographic Assessment* (Washington, D.C., 1976), p. 7.

TABLE 35

HISTORICAL TREND IN U.S. DUMPING OF RADIOACTIVE WASTES, 1946–1970

Year	Number of Containers	Estimated Activity at Time of Disposal (in curies)
1946–1960	76,201	93,690
1961	4,087	275
1962	6,120	478
1963	129	9
1964	114	20
1965	24	5
1966	43	105
1967	12	62
1968	0	0
1969	26	26
1970	2	3
Total	86,758	94,673

SOURCE: U.S. Council on Environmental Quality, *Ocean Dumping: A National Policy* (Washington, D.C., October 1970), p. 7.

magnitude may be required to reduce spillover costs significantly. Generally, the Council did not find ocean dumping to be a critical U.S. problem in 1970, but it argued that it would become more serious in future years as tighter federal regulations on land disposal methods encouraged more ocean disposal.

The details of the 1972 Marine Protection, Research, and Sanctuaries Act are broadly consistent with the findings of the Council's report and represent an attempt to have polluters increasingly take spillover costs into account. The U.S. Environmental Protection Agency is given authority to regulate dumping within the U.S. twelve-mile territorial limits. Dumping of highly toxic substances is prohibited, and less dangerous substances may be dumped only after a permit has been granted. Among the things that the agency must take into account in granting or withholding permits are the availability and cost of alternative disposal methods, including those on land, and the overall impact of various alternatives on the "public interest." The Act establishes fines and other penalties for violation as well as enforcement measures.

In an evaluation of this legislation, Charles S. Pearson found that it was consistent in certain respects with generally recognized economic principles.[32] For example, the Act does not prohibit ocean dumping outright. Different materials are regulated according to their presumed toxicity and potential for pollution damage. The alternatives to ocean dumping and their cost must be reckoned by the agency in its procedures for granting or denying dumping permits. But the legislation also has defects. Its rules establishing maximum

TABLE 36

COMPOSITION AND TOTAL U.S. OCEAN DUMPING, 1968

(in tons)

Waste Type	Atlantic	Gulf	Pacific	Total	Percent of Total
Dredge spoils	15,808,000	15,300,000	7,320,000	38,428,000	80
Industrial wastes	3,013,200	696,000	981,300	4,690,500	10
Sewage sludge	4,477,000	0	0	4,477,000	9
Construction and demolition debris	574,000	0	0	574,000	<1
Solid waste	0	0	26,000	26,000	<1
Explosives	15,200	0	0	15,200	<1
Total	23,887,400	15,996,000	8,327,300	48,210,700	100

SOURCE: U.S. Council on Environmental Quality, *Ocean Dumping: A National Policy* (Washington, D.C., October 1970), p. 3.

permissible concentration may discourage technological innovations in pollution abatement since dumpers have few incentives to reduce pollutants below these levels once they have been met. Most important, the apparatus for regulation of ocean dumping is based on administrative control rather than such market-type controls as effluent taxes. Taxes could be placed on ocean dumping in accordance with the danger of the materials dumped.[33] The level of the tax would be designed to account for the damage costs of dumping, and dumpers facing these taxes would tend to compare the cost of the tax with the cost of the next-best method of disposal. Under the administrative system, the information required in order to reduce dumping to the economical level is so expensive to obtain (for example, discovering which ocean dumpers had the lowest costs for alternative disposal methods) that many economists have concluded that effluent taxation is on the whole more likely to lead to the desired level of environmental protection.[34]

These defects aside, the U.S. legislation appears to represent an enforceable measure on the part of a coastal state that incurs a sizable fraction of the total costs of its ocean dumping activities. Moreover, the legislation appears to be a part of a general process within the U.S. to take into account both marine and continental spillovers (for example, air and inland water pollution). Of course there is no assurance that regulations would reduce marine pollution from dumping in U.S. coastal areas to the economical level; indeed, this result would probably be coincidental in view of the required information costs and the inherent drawbacks of the administrative system of pollution control made necessary by the legislation. But the legislation does prove that there is concern about the problem of competing ocean uses, and it seems to represent at least a crude attempt to avoid certain uses that are inefficient for the U.S.

The Oslo Convention for the Prevention of Marine Pollution by Dumping from Ships and Aircraft represents a regional attempt to reduce pollution spillovers on the part of twelve North Sea states.[35] It is a logical form of joint action for a group of states having short coastlines in a relatively small ocean area. It had been the practice of many of these states to dump pollutants outside their own territorial seas, and to dump farther out to sea as coastal areas became more contaminated.[36] The convention prohibits the dumping of certain substances, such as heavy metals, organohalogen compounds (including pesticides), and known carcinogens. Other pollutants may be dumped only after one of the contracting parties has issued a permit. The criteria for granting a permit include the amount and composition of the substance to be dumped, its form, the rate at which it is to be dumped, and its toxicity and persistence; the characteristics of the dumping site and the method of deposit; and the potential for ''interference with shipping, fishing, recreation, mineral extraction, fish and shellfish culture, areas of scientific importance and other legitimate uses of the sea.''[37] The list of prohibited substances is longer than those in U.S. legislation and the injunction to take into account spillover effects on competing uses appears to be stronger than in the U.S. Areas of the Arctic Ocean and the North Atlantic are included in the convention to discourage governments from shifting pollutants to these sites. On the other hand, implementation is, as one would expect, weaker (more expensive) than in the U.S. because of the fragmented authority and higher transactions costs associated with multi-state authority. Its effectiveness depends on the value that individual states place on non-sink uses of the ocean, the extent to which dumped pollutants are transported by physical and biological processes, the enforcement costs of individual states, and the costs of coordinating joint actions.

The more recent (1972) international Convention on the Prevention of Marine Pollution by Dumping of Wastes and Other Matter was initiated by United States authorities and bears certain similarities to the U.S. domestic legislation discussed earlier.[38] It specifies a group of "blacklisted" substances that are prohibited, and also a "grey list" of substances that require special permits from one of the contracting parties to the convention. Considerations that are to be taken into account in granting permits include the "practical availability of alternative land based methods of treatment, disposal or elimination," "treatment to render the matter less harmful for dumping at sea," and "possible effects on other uses of the sea" such as ship operations, scientific research, conservation, and fishing.[39] The actual methods of granting permits, and the specific criteria for their issuance, are left to the national governments, which are also responsible for monitoring, enforcement, and penalties within their jurisdiction. For the most part, the convention is an international exhortation to individual states to develop municipal legislation to control dumping. Regional arrangements are strongly encouraged, especially for purposes such as monitoring and scientific research that are likely to produce information having spillover benefits among a variety of nations (this issue is discussed in the following chapter). The convention avoids stipulating standards or international maxima for ocean dumping, presumably because the economics of dumping will differ among the signatories, and because the transactions costs of compensating the "losing" states would be relatively high.

Although this convention is probably worth having, it is essentially a very limited measure which can have little impact on dumping apart from the individual efforts of its signatories in adopting, monitoring, and enforcing domestic law. This conclusion is borne out by the stipulation that "nothing in this Convention shall prejudice the codification and development of the law of the sea by the United Nations Conference on the Law of the Sea . . . nor the present or future claims and legal view of any State concerning the law of the sea and the nature and extent of coastal and flag state jurisdiction."[40] The higher transaction and enforcement costs of international processes make such treaty language the only plausible result.

Offshore Oil Production

Offshore oil drilling is one of the least significant sources of marine petroleum pollution. Table 32 indicates that this source contributes about 1.3 percent of all the petroleum found in the oceans. Of the 18,000 wells drilled on the U.S. outer continental shelf area, only 4 have involved major oil spills.[41] One of the most notorious of these, the Santa Barbara blowout of 1969, spilled somewhere between 1 and 3 million gallons—far less than the 29–30 million gallons that had leaked from the *Torrey Canyon* in the English Channel two years earlier.[42]

Because of the enormous cost of drilling at great ocean depths, most offshore oil drilling rigs are located in continental shelf areas. Their proximity to shore has two general implications. First, the cost of detecting oil pollution would usually be lower for the adjacent coastal state than for an international authority possessing a worldwide inspection mandate. The most common forms of pollution from offshore oil drilling—blowouts during drilling, spillage of oil in surface storage tanks, and ruptures in well casings from storms or ship collisions—will usually be first recognized at lowest cost by coastal authorities. The costs of enforcing regulations to reduce pollution from oil drilling also will usually be lower for the coastal state, and they are especially low in territorial sea areas where coastal control is sovereign. How far from shore coastal enforcement will be economical depends upon how high the enforcement costs are in relation to the losses anticipated by the coastal state from oil pollution.

Second, the total costs of offshore oil production are likely to be at their lowest for coastal states where oil rigs are located close to shore and the impact of pollution damage is largely confined to coastal areas. In such cases the coastal state would compare the gains from oil production with the expected incidental damages to shore-line areas and marine life. Where the latter were increasing relative to the value of oil, the coastal state would tend to impose more stringent regulations on oil production, which would increase its cost but at the same time partly compensate for expected damage from oil spills. To some extent, all coastal states would have the incentive to gather information on comparative values of competing uses of coastal resources and to allocate a given area to the use that it valued most highly, but certain geographical features and the like could of course have extraordinary value in particular instances. Thus states having shore-line areas that were relatively populated or used for recreational and tourist purposes would be more apt to favor stronger environmental and coastal protection than would, say, states with coasts that were heavily industrialized or had little value in other uses.

4. DIVIDED JURISDICTION FOR VESSEL
SOURCE POLLUTION

Vessel transportation is the cause of approximately 35 percent of all the petroleum introduced into the oceans, and as a category of petroleum sources is second only to land-based activities. Oil tanker operations and accidents involving tankers together account for at least 60 percent of total vessel pollution and 21 percent of all the petroleum sources listed in Table 32.

Each leg of an oil tanker's round-trip voyage poses a threat to the marine environment. On the laden or cargo voyage, the danger of grounding is relatively high in shallow areas because of deep draughts. Although few in number, these major groundings have always been dramatic events. On March 18, 1967, the *Torrey Canyon* (61,263 gross registered tons) grounded on Seven Stones Reef and spilled 700,000 barrels of crude oil (about 60,000 tons) which contaminated 242 miles of English and French coastline. The costs to the two governments for oil removal alone amounted to more than $16 million.[43] Eleven years later, on March 16, 1978, the supertanker *Amoco Cadiz* lost its steering during a gale about fifty miles from Brest and grounded. As the ship broke up, it spilled its entire cargo of 68 million gallons of crude oil along the beaches of Brittany and for a time threatened the Channel Islands as well.[44] It was the biggest oil spill in history. Other spills, less dramatic, occur frequently. In 1971, some 392 major oil spills were reported within the U.S. twelve-mile limit, and 696 were reported in 1972.[45]

Once its cargo is emptied, a tanker normally must fill 45−60 percent of its tanks with seawater ballast to maintain stability and seaworthiness for the return voyage.[46] During this ballast trip the seawater mixes with the oil residue that remains in the tanks from the cargo voyage. To avoid discharging this mixture at or near port, the tanker usually pumps it out while at sea. After the tanks have been washed, fresh seawater is loaded to provide ballast for the remainder of the trip to port, where the clean ballast is then emptied to make room for a new load of crude oil. In calm waters, the discharge of one hundred barrels of oil will spread to cover an area eight miles square within one week. Since a single tanker deballasting can discharge several hundred barrels, the cumulative effect of normal tanker operations can be enormous.[47] Ballasting operations (identified as ''non-LOT tankers'' in Table 32) are, at 36 percent, the largest single source of pollution from vessels and account for 12.6 percent of all the petroleum injected into the oceans.

One of the critical economic differences between vessel pollution and the various sources discussed in the preceding section of this chapter is the typically higher cost of detecting the particular vessel that is responsible for a known quantity of oil pollution. Huge spills are often traceable at low cost to the vessels involved in collisions or groundings, but these instances of pollution appear to be the exception rather than the rule. More often, it happens that a variety of vessels will have traveled through or been moored in the affected area during the period of time in question. The greater their number and mobility, the higher detection costs are. Even when information costs may be low, the transactions costs of recovering damages from the shipowner increase for ships that are registered in so-called flags-of-convenience states which impose nominal conditions on registration and are intentionally lax in enforcement.[48]

If there are relatively higher costs of information, negotiation, and enforcement against vessel pollution than for the other sources discussed earlier, then a mix of coastal state and international jurisdictions for vessels in some cases might avoid economically inefficient outcomes. For example, vessel pollution that resulted in relatively widespread damage throughout the world ocean and had higher detection costs would be internalized most economically by an international agreement on minimum standards for tanker construction and operation. In the case of lower detection costs or damages that were concentrated in local areas, coastal state jurisdiction would be most efficient.

There are three general approaches to internalizing the spillovers caused by vessel pollution that could be implemented either by coastal states or by international authorities. First, as just mentioned, minimum standards could be imposed either on vessel construction or on ballast operations, or on both. Second, vessel owners could be held fully liable for the total damages caused by petroleum that was leaked or discharged. The implied assumption in both these policies is that actions by ship owners or operators to avoid pollution damage cost less in scarce resources than do actions by others to abate damage once it has occurred.[49] The third approach would be to impose fees on vessels, according to their size, nature of cargo, and route of travel, which would become a fund to compensate those who suffer pollution damage.

Minimum Standards for Tanker Operation
or Construction

Two alternative procedures are available for reducing the amount of oil that tankers discharge into the oceans.[50] The first is called load-on-top (LOT). LOT tankers are equipped with specially designed tanks into which the ballast mixture is collected so that the oil can be separated from the water. The water is pumped out of the ship and the oily sludge is left in the tanks, whereupon a fresh cargo of crude oil is loaded on top of the residue. These techniques, however, are not foolproof, and some emissions still occur. On short voyages there is little time for the water and oil to separate, and rough weather often causes them to re-mix; furthermore, the vertical boundary between the lighter oil and the heavier water is sometimes difficult to determine, and thus the amount of oil that is discharged along with the ballast depends on the skill of the tanker crew. Load-on-top procedures have been adopted by more than three-fourths of all tankers in service during 1975, but they plainly cannot reduce ballast pollution to zero without substantial increases in tanker operating costs. On the other hand, the ballast pollution caused by the tankers that have not adopted load-on-top amounted in 1975 to twice as much as was caused by all the load-on-top tankers, or approximately 36 percent of the total oil pollution from transportation sources (see Table 32).

The second procedure, more expensive than LOT, segregates ballast tanks from cargo tanks. Since the two sets of tanks require independent systems for piping and discharge, the cost can be high, but the method can reduce ballast pollution significantly. The threat of pollution from groundings and collisions can be reduced by adding a second "skin" or bottom to these vessels. Both techniques increase the ship's draught, however, which makes groundings more likely.[51]

A comparison of the direct costs of segregated ballasting versus either unenforced (conventional) or enforced load-on-top techniques has been made by Philip A. Cummins, Dennis E. Logue, Robert D. Tollison, and Thomas D. Willett.[52] Employing data on costs from a variety of nations and tanker sizes, Cummins et al. concluded that segregated ballasting could be expected to add $0.6 to $1.9 billion to shipbuilding costs between 1975 and 1980; double-bottom segregated ballasting could increase costs by $1.3 to $3.6 billion.[53] Converting costs to an annual basis projected for the year 1980 gives the results presented in Table 37. It is clear that segregated ballasting is a relatively expensive means of reducing pollution. Compared with conventional load-on-top, segregated ballasting with single bottoms would raise operating and construction costs in 1980 by as much as 4 percent and would increase the world's freight bill by up to 3.5 percent. Double bottoms raise construction and operating costs by as much as 7 percent and the world freight bill by as much as 10 percent. The higher freight bill for the world is estimated to be as much as $125 million per year if single-skin techniques are adopted, and as much as $358 million if double bottoms are adopted. For the United States, the maximum increase in freight bills would be $26 million per year for single skins and $75 million for double bottoms. The authors also compared the costs of segregated ballasting to enforced load-on-top. Automatic metering techniques for load-on-top have yet to be developed, so the authors assumed that individual human monitors would cost $100,000 per ship per year. Even so, enforced load-on-top was less expensive than segregated ballasting of any type. In short, these initial estimates of costs suggest that segregated ballasting of various kinds will be, depending upon the comparison, between 1.7 and 4.5 times more expensive than alternative load-on-top techniques.[54]

Assuming that segregated ballasting results in less petroleum pollution than load-on-top, is this decrease in pollution worth the additional costs required to modify tankers? This question goes to the heart of the economic problem of

TABLE 37

ANNUAL INCREASED COSTS IN 1980 OF SEGREGATED BALLASTING TECHNIQUES RELATIVE TO LOAD-ON-TOP TECHNIQUES

(Single Skin vs. Double Bottom)

(In millions of dollars per year and percentage increases)

Category of Annual Cost Increase	Cost of Single Skin Relative to				Cost of Double Bottom Relative to			
	Conventional LOT		Enforced LOT*		Conventional LOT		Enforced LOT*	
	Range of Increase	(%)	Range of Increase	(%)	Range of Increase	(%)	Range of Increase	(%)
Construction and operating costs per tanker	.026–.329	1–4	Prev. col. plus 0.1	—	.123–.545	6–7	Prev. col. plus 0.1	—
World freight bill	54–125	1.75–3.5	10–72	0.3–2.1	153–358	5–10	112–305	3.5–8.5
U.S. freight bill								
Method #1†	10–26	1.75–3.5	2–15	0.3–2.1	28–75	5–10	20–64	3.5–8.5
Method #2‡	39–77	1.75–3.5	0–37	0.0–1.7	110–220	5–10	70–180	3.1–8.0

NOTE: Range of increase for each case depends upon assumptions that the authors made concerning sizes of vessels and lengths of voyages.

*Enforced LOT is assumed to add $100,000 to conventional LOT tanker cost.

†Method #1 assumes that the increase in required freight rates pertains only to those new tankers that are built with segregated ballasting.

‡Method #2 assumes that the increase in required freight rates for segregated ballast vessels is applied to all tankers engaged in the international movement of oil.

SOURCE: Philip A. Cummins, Dennis E. Logue, Robert D. Tollison, and Thomas D. Willett, "Oil Tanker Pollution Control: Design Criteria vs. Effective Liability Assessment," *Journal of Maritime Law and Commerce* 7 (1975):178–93.

which standards, if any, to establish. Standards should be imposed only if the value of pollution prevented exceeds the costs, and for a given reduction in pollution the least-cost method of achieving it should be selected.

The same authors then employed "undeniably rough" methods to quantify some of the benefits of reduced pollution.[55] They made two key assumptions. First, damages were proportional to the annual amount of pollution reaching shore-line areas.[56] Second, based on other studies, ballasting pollution that occurs far from shore was estimated to be only 10 percent as damaging as accidental pollution from collisions and groundings near shore. They concluded that the extra cost of segregated ballasting was not worth the pollution that it prevented. Segregated ballasting with single bottoms lowers deliberate ballast pollution, but accidental pollution rises owing to the increased draught and greater risk of collision. The increase was between 2,200 and 8,400 long tons of oil per year (depending upon ship size) as compared with the load-on-top alternative. Segregated ballasting with double bottoms reduced total pollution by between 19,800 and 29,200 long tons per year, but again the reduction was not cost effective. If vessel source pollution damages to the U.S. in 1980 were between $70 and $90 million,[57] the benefit-cost ratio of segregated ballasting with double bottoms for the U.S. would be between 0.002 and 0.020: that is, each dollar spent on segregated ballasting instead of load-on-top would yield the U.S. a trivial $0.002 to $0.020 in benefits.

These authors also used an alternative method of estimating benefits based on cleanup costs alone, which undoubtedly underestimates benefits. Again, the ratios of benefits to costs were low, ranging between 0.016 and 0.213 for double bottoms as compared with load-on-top, depending on ship size and the effectiveness of load-on-top. If cleanup costs were $1,000 per ton, benefits from segregated ballasting would equal its costs only if the value of oil spillage prevented was worth between $5,000 and $63,000 per ton, depending upon the assumptions made.[58] Again, single-skin techniques had negative ratios of benefit to cost owing to the higher probability of accidents.

The trend in international opinion favors standards for ship design and construction instead of load-on-top in spite of evidence in favor of the greater efficiency of load-on-top. The decisive issue in this debate appears to be the differential enforcement costs. Improvements in load-on-top would require either automatic monitoring devices, which are not available at present, or the not always reliable human monitors. Compliance with construction standards is, on the other hand, a simple matter which requires only periodic inspections of the tanker as it is built and at lesser intervals thereafter. Once ship owners have received certificates stating that standards have been met, they are indemnified against liability for pollution damage as long as the required systems remain intact. Thus neither the owner nor the operator of the ship has much monetary incentive to incur additional costs to reduce damage further: the incentives in this case would be purely altruistic.[59]

The trend toward internationally determined tanker standards can be observed by comparing the 1954 International Convention for the Prevention of Pollution of the Sea by Oil with the 1973 IMCO Convention for the Prevention of Pollution from Ships.[60] The 1954 convention (as amended in 1962) prevented the discharge of certain types of petroleum by tankers within 50 nautical miles of land. Enforcement was by flag states unless the offense occurred within the territorial sea of a coastal state. The costs of detecting pollution sources would be high, as would enforcement costs if flag states found it inexpensive to ignore evidence offered to them by coastal states. For these reasons the convention is widely viewed as having been unsuccessful.[61]

The 1973 IMCO convention is much stricter.[62] It makes load-on-top mandatory and limits the total amount of petroleum that may be discharged to 60 liters per mile, not to exceed 1/15,000 of the cargo last carried for existing tankers and 1/30,000 for new tankers. Ballasting operations are prohibited within 50 nautical miles of most coasts and prohibited altogether within certain enclosed seas. Ships are supposed to keep permanent records of all ballasting operations and have them available for inspection by officials of IMCO. Segregated ballasting is required for new tankers of more than 70,000 dwt. Enforcement is delegated to flag states unless violations occur within the territorial sea of a coastal state, but vessels are subject to inspection if either port or coastal states suspect that a violation has occurred.

The least-cost means for meeting the 1973 IMCO standards were estimated by Cummins et al.[63] They found that both conventional and enforced load-on-top were less expensive methods of achieving the 1/15,000 standard (for all but the smallest tanker sizes) than either method of segregated ballasting. The more stringent 1/30,000 standard could be met only by segregated ballasting of some kind. Thus, the techniques required by the convention appear to be appropriate to the standards that were selected.

But an even more important question is whether the 1973 IMCO standards will generate more gains than costs. The hard data required to answer this question are not available but preliminary results presented by Cummins et al. suggest that they are not economically appropriate. Based on U.S. benefit data, they found that segregated ballasting was uneconomical compared with load-on-top procedures where discharges were held either to 1/15,000 or to 2/15,000 of the previous cargo.[64] The limit of 1/15,000 is equal to the IMCO discharge standard for existing tankers, but it is twice the 1/30,000 standard that applies to new tankers. Based on these results, segregated ballasting is unlikely to be economical for the more stringent 1/30,000 standard when it was uneconomical for pollution discharge standards that were one-half or one-fourth as strong.

Two features of the 1973 IMCO conference reinforce the conclusion that the standards agreed to, if enforced, are unlikely to reduce inefficiency. First, there is little evidence that the participating states sought to weigh the total costs and benefits from alternative standards—there is, in fact, some evidence to the contrary.[65] Pearson's account of U.S. policy making before and during the conference suggests that some studies generated within the U.S. government which challenged the preferred policy of segregated ballasting were ignored. For example, the Treasury Department produced a study suggesting that single-skin techniques offered the U.S. a benefit-cost ratio in 1980 of about 0.0005. This result was 30 times smaller than the subsequent calculation by Cummins et al. Although the Treasury paper had certain defects, its conclusion was, as Pearson states, "so striking as to call into question the economic rationale of the mandatory segregated ballasting provision in the convention."[66]

The second feature was the wide disparity of views between the coastal and the maritime states. Some coastal states wanted to establish broad zones for pollution control, and others sought to impose stronger standards for petroleum discharge or ship construction. In opposition, the United States, taking a position more like that of a maritime than a coastal nation, argued thus: "If each of the 120 coastal nations had jurisdiction to set construction standards for vessels, a hodgepodge of conflicting standards would result. Such jurisdiction would also permit decisions on standards to be made solely by coastal nations without the careful balancing of maritime and coastal interests which would result from an international solution."[67] Either shipping construction costs would increase because all new ships would have to be designed to the most severe set of standards enforced by a major coastal or port nation, or operating costs would increase because vessels would be built to engage in limited trading between a few states having similar minimum unilateral standards.[68] The dispute between the two groups of nations was so acrimonious that it nearly broke up the conference.[69] In the end, the United States and other navigation-minded states arrived at a compromise agreement which favored uniform international standards for construction and discharge but fell short of condemning either the 200-mile EEZ for pollution control or the stronger standards that some coastal states wanted to impose. The latter two issues were put over until the following meetings of UNCLOS, at which the compromise remained roughly intact through June 1978.

The emphasis by maritime states on a strictly international solution to vessel pollution is almost certain to yield inefficient results. Can international decision-making processes usually be expected, as the U.S. argued, to make a "careful balancing of maritime and coastal interests" more than coastal nations would? Here the analysis parallels that of the question of unimpeded navigation through international straits discussed in Chapter 3. Coastal or port states are unlikely to impose vessel construction or discharge standards in a capricious or malicious fashion. Their decisions would be influenced to some degree by the benefits and costs that regulation would be likely to bring. Among the benefits would be the value of increased protection to the marine and coastal environment; among the costs would be the value of resources devoted to enforcement and, in the event harsh standards were imposed, the increased expense of trading with other nations. There would probably be incentives for groups of states to harmonize their standards unless local environmental conditions were of enormous importance. In any case, it is probably an exaggeration to claim, as the U.S. did, that there would be 120 different sets of vessel pollution controls simply because there were 120 different coastal nations.

In making trade-off calculations, port states will recognize that they clearly benefit from navigation and commercial activity. The higher these benefits are, the greater the environmental gains would have to be before a major port state sharply curtailed navigation in order to protect competing ocean uses. Coastal states that lack major port facilities might be more willing to trade some amount of navigation costs for some extra environmental protection, especially if the expected damage to the environment is relatively large. An example might be Canada's action to protect the Arctic Ocean, an environmentally fragile area which could be ruined for centuries by a disaster to a tanker transporting Alaskan North Slope oil through these waters. Just as maritime states have worried that coastal states might ignore navigational values in making careful trade-off calculations, some coastal states must wonder whether international decision-making procedures would carefully weigh local environmental values. Moreover, as will be discussed later, nations such as Canada which do attach importance to protecting certain environmental resources are unlikely to be deterred automatically when other states sign treaties that enshrine different behaviors.

Strict Liability for Damages

The rule of strict liability, by which a ship owner would be responsible for the total damages from pollutants that could be traced to his vessel, has three important features as a device for internalizing spillovers from vessels. First, the rule would apply to all vessel source pollution regardless of cause. When liability is strict it becomes unnecessary to investigate the conduct of ships' masters or the circumstances that caused the pollution to occur, such as "negligent" or "willful" ballasting operations, "accidental" groundings, or "unavoidable collisions."[70] Second, when liability is strict, vessel owners or operators are liable for all damages caused to public and private parties alike.[71] Third, owners would be liable for the damages incurred by coastal states that could be traced to particular vessels regardless of where the pollution originated.

The rule of absolute liability appears to offer several economic advantages over control by setting standards for tanker discharge and construction.[72] First, each ship owner would be permitted to select the least-cost method of avoiding pollution damage. Some might prefer to pay damages rather than adopt pollution-reduction techniques, and others might prefer the reverse. Since it is unlikely that the same technique (for example, segregated ballasting) would be the least expensive for all ships, preserving individual incentives to adopt inexpensive solutions would lower the total costs of ocean use. Second, the liability approach would also preserve individual incentives to reduce pollution below the maximum allowed under a regime of discharge and design standards. When standards for ship construction and operations are set, ship owners view rates of pollution that are less than the legal maximums as essentially "free" to them even though they are costly to the world at large. Third, the liability approach would eliminate the administrative cost of selecting the economically appropriate construction and operational standards. Such choices would instead be made by each ship owner as he compared the costs and benefits to him of the reduced liability resulting from safer tanker procedures versus the increased liability resulting from riskier operations.

At the present time, the relatively high costs of detection and transaction referred to earlier in this section constitute the major impediment to administering a universal system of vessel source pollution liability, but there are new techniques being developed which may drastically reduce some of these costs. Consider the problem of accurately detecting vessel sources by examining a sample of polluted water. One alternative would be to tag the cargoes of particular ships by means of chemical or radioactive tracers.[73] (Employing a different isotope or trace element for each shipping company rather than for each ship would probably reduce transaction costs.) Another alternative would be to "fingerprint" petroleum extracted from different countries or fields. This is a system of identifying and recording petroleum based on the chemical structure of hydrocarbons, which differs from field to field according to the size and nature of molecules, their content of sulfur, nitrogen, and other elements, and their sensitivity to light. The United States Coast Guard has demonstrated the effectiveness of four techniques that analyze hydrocarbon samples, according to their ability to absorb infrared radiation (called infrared spectroscopy), their ability to absorb ultraviolet radiation (fluorescence spectroscopy), the contents of gases that have been separated from the petroleum sample (gas chromatography), and the rates at which different components of petroleum migrate as they are passed over a solid substrate.[74] The Coast Guard found a probability of "99.9 percent in the combined ability of the four independent techniques to identify the source of an oil spill."[75] Various techniques are also being investigated and tested by IMCO and other groups.[76] If knowledge in this field were to advance rapidly and lead to markedly lower detection and enforcement costs, then a regime based on liability that was enforced by coastal states might be superior on economic grounds to the existing regime based on uniform international standards for tanker construction and operation.

So far, however, there has been little enthusiasm for the idea of making vessel owners assume more liability for oil pollution damage.[77] In most nations, standard ship insurance policies limit liability to the value of the ship plus its cargo, thus giving little protection to third parties. And since many vessels are separately incorporated, compensation beyond the seizure value of the ship is in practice almost impossible to obtain. In some cases, bankruptcy may be declared before all the costs of a spill have been recovered. Even recently, insurers have opposed the concept of absolute liability on the dual ground that it would force ship owners to disprove negligence rather than the other way around, and that too little data were available to estimate the increase in premiums required to underwrite such coverage.[78] At the international level, liability for the conse-quences of oil discharges was first adopted in the 1957 Brussels Convention on the Limitation of Shipowners' Liability, but the ceilings specified by the convention were low.[79] (This treaty and other tanker liability measures are summarized in Table 38.)

Perceptions of this problem were almost universally shattered in the aftermath of the *Torrey Canyon* disaster of 1967. Under the ceilings set by the 1957 pact, the owners of the vessel were liable only to a maximum of $3.6 million even though cleanup costs (not including damages incurred by third parties) amounted to at least $16 million. This led the owners of more than 90 percent of the world tanker tonnage to form voluntary industry associations to provide some relief for pollution damages caused by tanker accidents but not ballasting operations. In 1969, it was agreed that governments would be compensated up to $10 million per incident for cleanup costs provided that the tanker owners could not disprove negligence.[80] Zero compensation was provided for damages to the property of private parties. A second industry agreement in 1971 provided for some compensation to governments and private parties that had been unable to obtain relief from any other source, but limited the claims payable on a single incident to a maximum of $30 million including the amounts paid by tanker owners under the 1969 agreement.[81] The priority of payments under this arrangement favors tanker owners rather than coastal state governments or their citizens who may incur damage to property. In cases of large-scale pollution damage, it is clear that private parties would legally be entitled to zero compensation. Also excluded is compensation for "ecological impairment" and for losses caused by fires or explosions from spilled oil.[82]

Subsequent international actions have somewhat strengthened the principle of vessel liability. The 1969 International Convention on Civil Liability for Oil Pollution Damage doubled the limits of the 1957 Brussels Convention up to a maximum of $14 million per incident. Liability is strict unless the vessel owner can prove that the damages were due to an act of war, the wrongful act of a third party, or negligence by a government in maintaining navigational aids. Liability is unlimited when pollution has occurred as a result of willful conduct.[83] The 1969 agreement was supplemented by the 1971 International Convention on the Establishment of an International Fund for Compensation for Oil Pollution Damage. If ratified, this convention will provide additional compensation up to a total of $30 million from all sources, but the claimant must prove that the damages were caused by a ship rather than by a fixed installation. The fund would be made up entirely from contributions by cargo owners, which amounts to a tax on imported oil. Unlike the voluntary agreements mentioned earlier, which will lapse when this convention is ratified, there is no priority of payment and all claimants share proportionately in the recovery.[84]

International law has recognized the rights of coastal states in certain circumstances to reduce damages from vessel accidents by pursuit onto the high seas. The 1969 International Convention Relating to Intervention on the High Seas in Cases of Oil Pollution Casualties authorizes coastal states to take undefined measures against all seagoing nonmilitary vessels that have been involved in a "maritime casualty" which poses a "grave and immediate danger" to coastal interests.[85] These interests include tourism, living marine resources, and the livelihood of persons engaged in fishing. Except in cases of "extreme urgency," the coastal state is required to contact the vessel's flag state and any other coastal states that may be affected by the casualty in order to disclose its "proposed measures" for dealing with the situation. Preventative measures must be "proportional to the damage, actual or threatened."

It is evident that the trend toward larger and larger oil tankers has not been matched by a trend toward making owners fully responsible for all the costs of pollution from their ships. Liability for damage resulting from accidents to tankers has increased, but it is still limited, and the maximum damages payable under international law often are small in comparison with the total costs of major pollution incidents. Moreover, claims are subject to a variety of restrictions. Incidents must occur within territorial seas. Damages from ballasting operations are excluded regardless of where they occur. Compensation to private parties for property damage is voluntary. Coastal states may pursue vessels to the high seas once pollution has occurred, but their internationally recognized rights to prevent pollution are few and weak. Although international law has plainly moved in the direction of strict vessel source liability—especially for accidents involving tankers owned by multinational oil companies, not only because of law but because of increased governmental and public pressures—the results so far may be unsatisfying to coastal states that are intent upon protecting special environments. Indeed, Table 38 suggests that the tanker liability laws of certain coastal states of the United States—namely, Florida, Maine, and Washington—are more stringent than either U.S. federal law or the voluntary tanker agreements. One would expect to see similar differences at an international level, between the liability imposed by certain coastal nations and that of international bodies.

The disparity between potential pollution damages and the available international sanctions against them has led some coastal states to take unilateral action to maintain the value of environmental resources. The most striking of these is

TABLE 38

Major Provisions of Treaties, Statutes, and Private Schemes to Increase Liability for Damages from Oil Pollution by Ships, Both International and U.S. Domestic

	Limitation of Liability (46 U.S.C. § 183 [1851])	Brussels Convention on Limitation of Liability (1957)	Intergovernmental Maritime Consultative Organization (IMCO)	U.S. Public Law 91-224 (1970)
Source of compensation	Owner or charterer of vessel	Owner of vessel	Owner at time of incident	Owner or charterer of vessel
Coverage	Any vessel	Seagoing vessels	All ships carrying 2,000 T oil	Vessel in U.S. territorial waters
Basis of liability	Any damage due to fault	Any damage from fault	Strict liability for all damages	Strict liability for cleanup expenses
Exceptions	Liability always obtains upon fault	Liability always obtains upon fault	1. War; 2. Phenomenal act of nature; 3. Act of third party; 4. Negligence; 5. Interference of plaintiff	1. Act of God; 2. Act of war; 3. Act of negligence of U.S. government; 4. Act of a third party
Limit of liability	Value of vessel and freight pending for property damage $60 per net ton for personal injury or loss of life	$67 per net ton for property damage, $207 per net ton for personal injury or loss of life	$134.40 per net ton or $14,112,000, whichever is lesser minus the defendant's cleanup expenditures	$100 per net ton or $14,000,000, whichever is the lesser
Court with jurisdiction	U.S. district court with admiralty jurisdiction	U.S. district court with admiralty jurisdiction	Any country where damage occurs	U.S. district court with admiralty jurisdiction
Relationship with other laws	Exclusive remedy is in federal court except for "savings to suitor" cases	Exclusive remedy is in federal court except for "savings to suitor" cases	Exclusive remedy for oil pollution damages	Supplemental to other remedies
Instances of unlimited liability	Privity or fault of owner or charterer	Privity or fault of owner or charterer	If fault or privity of owner	Willful negligence or willful misconduct of owner or in privity with the owner
Financial responsibility required	None	None	To extent of potential liability	For vessels larger than 300 gross tons
Statute of limitation	Laches	Laches	3 years after damage discovered but not more than 6 years after the incident	Laches

	Maine Public Laws, Chapter 572, 11-A, § 552	Florida Statutes Annotated, Chapter 376, §.12, et seq	Revised Code of Washington 90.48.315	TOVALOP	CRISTAL
Source of compensation	Coastal protection fund pays plaintiff and is reimbursed by oil terminal operators	Coastal protection fund pays plaintiff and is reimbursed by oil terminal operators	Person having control over oil	Owner of tanker	Oil Companies Institute for Marine Pollution Compensation Ltd.
Coverage	State waters	State waters	State waters	Damages to coast line	Same as IMCO
Basis of liability	Strict liability for all damages	Strict liability for all damages	Strict liability for all damages	Rebuttable presumption of fault for cleanup cost	Same as IMCO
Exceptions	1. Act of war; 2. Act of government—federal, state, or municipal; 3. Act of God	1. Act of war; 2. Act of government—federal, state, or municipal; 3. Act of God; 4. Act of third party	1. Act of war or sabotage; 2. Negligence of United States or Washington State		Same as IMCO proposed Convention on Civil Liability
Limit of liability	No limit	No limit	No limit	$100 per gross registered ton or $10,000,000 whichever is the lesser	Accumulated total to $30,000,000 for all expenses
Court with jurisdiction	Maine state courts	Florida state courts	Washington state courts	Any country where damage occurs	Same as IMCO proposed Convention on Civil Liability
Relationship with other laws	Supplemental	Supplemental	Supplemental	Supplemental	Supplemental
Instances of unlimited liability	Always	Always	Always	None	None
Financial responsibility required	None	Depends on tonnage, etc.		None	None
Statute of limitation	6 months	3 years			Same as CLC

SOURCE: John G. Gissberg, "Civil Liability for Oil Pollution Damage from Tankers and Other Ocean Going Vessels" (unpublished Ph.D. dissertation, University of Michigan, 1972), pp. 118–25; reprinted in Kenneth W. Clarkson, "International Law, U.S. Seabeds Policy, and Ocean Resource Development," *Journal of Law and Economics* 17 (1974):135–37.

the Canadian action to prevent pollution of the Arctic Ocean. The Arctic area is highly vulnerable to oil spills. Once petroleum has entered the marine environment, large supplies of oxygen and microorganisms are required to render it harmless. Because of the very low temperature, below 10 degrees Centigrade, bacterial oxidation in the Arctic takes place so slowly that fifty years could pass before pollutants had been dispersed and the area cleansed.[86] Moreover, the presence of ice floes and other natural obstacles would limit the processes of dispersal and raise cleanup costs. If the costs of restoration were large in comparison with the economic rents that would otherwise result from choosing passage through the Arctic instead of an alternate route, then coastal state control would appear to be desirable on economic grounds.

Canadian action was prompted by the voyage of the tanker *Manhattan* in 1969, which demonstrated the technical feasibility of using the so-called Northwest Passage to transport petroleum between Alaska and the U.S. East Coast.[87] The Canadian Arctic Waters Pollution Prevention Act of 1970 applies to all Arctic areas extending 100 nautical miles from land and to dumping of any nature that would "degrade or alter . . . those waters to an extent that is detrimental to their use by man or by an animal, fish or plant that is useful to man."[88] Sources of waste include land-based activities, fixed offshore installations, and all ships regardless of size, type, or registry. Ships are strictly liable for the cost of cleanup or other remedial action but not for the value of lost marine or wildlife. Ships entering the area must demonstrate financial responsibility for the damage they could cause, and the Canadian government may order the removal or destruction of a ship or its cargo in the event of danger, seize or require the forfeiture of ship cargo, and levy fines for violations. Canada claims that this act of functional enclosure is based on a unique environmental consideration and that no claim of sovereignty is expressed or implied.[89] The legislation also permits the government to establish "shipping safety control zones" in other Canadian Arctic areas through which ships may not navigate unless they meet minimum standards of construction, maintenance, crew size, navigational aids, pilotage, and so on. Any ship within a zone may be boarded and inspected by Canadian "pollution prevention officers" to determine whether the ship complies with Canadian standards. In a parallel action, the Canadian Parliament also established a twelve-nautical-mile territorial sea to enclose the Barrow Strait and the Prince of Wales Strait.[90]

These actions were taken after the Canadian government had concluded that its basic coastal interests in avoiding serious pollution in the Arctic and elsewhere were not likely to be protected by international agreements.[91] Subsequent events proved that this forecast was accurate. The United States and other maritime nations opposed the Canadian unilateral approach to a problem which they believed should be met by international solutions emphasizing uniform tanker standards and eschewing coastal authority over navigation as embodied in the 1973 IMCO Convention on the Prevention of Pollution from Ships. But the Canadian Arctic, an area which requires "a careful balancing of maritime and coastal interests" owing to relatively high pollution costs that are for the most part borne locally, seems particularly unsuited to an international solution.[92] Enforcement costs by Canada would appear to be relatively low, and the popularity of the legislation among the Canadian public suggests that it will be enforced.[93]

United States legislation for vessel source liability implements the 1969 Civil Liability Convention and is significantly weaker than the Canadian law. The U.S. Water Quality Improvement Act of 1970 (summarized in Table 38) holds ship owners liable to the U.S. government for cleanup costs up to a maximum of $14 million per incident and compensation to private parties is ignored.[94] The only defenses permitted by the law are proof that the pollution was caused by an act of war, by the negligence of a third party, or by the negligence of the U.S. government. Liability is unlimited when willful misconduct can be demonstrated. Jurisdiction is limited to the U.S. navigable inland waters and the three-mile territorial sea. Masters of vessels must notify the U.S. authorities when discharges in "harmful quantities" occur or else face fines and possible imprisonment. Vessels must demonstrate financial responsibility to the limits of liability and they may be boarded for inspection by the U.S. Coast Guard.

Pollution Fees for Shipping

The third approach to the problem of vessel source pollution would be for coastal states to enclose adjacent areas for the purpose of imposing fees for the transit of ships that posed environmental dangers. This approach might be more attractive than setting construction standards if the particular standards that would protect the environment would also raise drastically the cost of the country's imports and exports. It might be more attractive than setting liability standards if the costs of tracing individual oil spills or tank washings to each of many ships were high. Fees could not exceed the economic rent to ship owners of using the particular strait or coastal area, but the total revenues from such fees might be sufficient to constitute a sort of insurance fund to cover expected costs of cleanup and compensation in the event a major spill occurred.

Pollution fees share a common weakness with construction standards, however, in that the masters or owners of vessels would have no great incentive to find new ways of reducing spills or to set stricter standards of operating care, as they would no doubt have if strict liability were imposed. Under strict liability ship owners or operators cannot escape bearing the full consequences of the ship's action merely by adding a second hull or paying a transit fee. Economic analysis thus suggests that the liability system is the best way of cutting down on ocean pollution by ships.

5. CONCLUSIONS

The central argument of this chapter has been that the apparently high level of marine pollution can best be explained through economic reasoning, and that success in reducing pollution depends upon creating an economical realignment of property rights in alternative uses of the oceans. In order for these new property rights to be appropriate to the situation, however, biochemical data on the extent and impact of pollutants and oceanographic data on the dispersion of pollutants must first be available.

Until recently, polluters have generally had an unrestricted right to pollute in whatever amounts they chose regardless of the consequences. Those who were damaged would have offered to pay polluters to reduce these costs if by so doing they could have increased the economic rent from ocean uses, and if transactions had cost nothing to make and enforce. In fact, however, the value of resources consumed in negotiating and enforcing agreements usually exceeded the extra rents captured by other users if pollution declined. This being so, it appears reasonable to conclude, even though there is little hard evidence, that the levels of certain marine pollutants (especially petroleum from ships) have increased over the years.

Preliminary analysis suggests that although the enclosure movement of the oceans is not an inefficient means of controlling land-based pollutants and coastal dumping in situations where a large amount of the related benefits and costs fall on the watchful nation, it is of less help in solving the problem of pollution from ships, for which some division of authority between coastal states and inter-national institutions appears to be economically desirable. There is evidence to suggest, however, that the present tendency for international negotiations to emphasize universal standards of tanker operation and construction is a less efficient way of stopping pollution than rules that impose strict liability on ship owners (or users) or national legislation whereby coastal states may protect unique marine environments.

Notes

1. The natural processes of the planet also create pollutants such as oil seeps along submarine faults on the continental shelf and mercury deposits on the ocean floor. But the attention of this chapter is on pollutants of man.

2. The absence of such information is well documented in National Academy of Sciences, *Marine Environmental Quality* (Washington, D.C., 1971), and in *Assessing Potential Ocean Pollutants* (Washington, D.C., 1975), hereafter cited as National Academy of Sciences (1975a).

3. Michael Waldichuk, "Coastal Marine Pollution and Fish," *Ocean Management* 2 (1974):47−48.

4. See, e.g., ibid.; also U.S. Council on Environmental Quality, *Ocean Dumping: A National Policy* (Washington, D.C., October 1970), pp. 12−18; National Academy of Sciences, *Petroleum in the Marine Environment* (Washington, D.C., 1975), pp. 73−103, hereafter cited as National Academy of Sciences (1975b).

5. The following statement is representative of our ignorance of the effect of petroleum: "Neither a single rate nor a mathematical model for the rate of petroleum biodegradation in the marine environment can be given at present. On the basis of available information, the most that can be stated is that some microorganisms capable of oxidizing chemicals present in petroleum (under the right conditions) have been found in virtually all parts of the marine environment examined." National Academy of Sciences (1975b), p. 66.

6. Oysters have been found to amplify small concentrations of DDT by 70,000 times in one month. Robert A. Shinn, *The International Politics of Marine Pollution Control* (New York: Praeger, 1974), p. 32.

7. Gwenda Matthews, "Pollution of the Oceans: An International Problem?" *Ocean Management* 1 (1973):164−65.

8. Oil seeps were spotted along the coast of Santa Barbara, California, by the Spanish discoverers as early as 1776. "Oil Pollution Reported in Offshore California: First Time was 1776," *Offshore,* May 1974, p. 248. Estimates for the two sources of mercury are given in National Academy of Sciences (1971), pp. 12−14.

9. National Academy of Sciences (1971), pp. 42−43.

10. Matthews, p. 163.

11. D. W. Hood, B. Stevenson, and L. M. Jeffrey, "The Deep Sea Disposal of Industrial Wastes," *Industrial and Engineering Chemistry* 50 (1958):885−88.

12. H. W. Jannasch and C. O. Wirsen, "Deep Sea Microorganisms: In situ Response to Nutrient Enrichment," *Science* 180 (1973):641−43. This source and the one preceding were cited in *The Economic Value of Ocean Resources to the United States,* p. 103.

13. The limited extent of current scientific knowledge about these processes is the theme of a panel of the National Academy of Sciences (1971), pp. 36−37, 40−44, 54−59, 99−100.

14. See, e.g., Seyom Brown et al., *Regimes for the Ocean, Outer Space, and Weather* (Washington, D.C.: Brookings Institution, 1977), chaps. 1−8; Ralph d'Arge, "Transfrontier Pollution: Some Issues on Regulation," in Ingo Walter, ed., *Studies in International Environmental Economics* (New York: John Wiley & Sons, 1976), p. 260; "Observations on the Economics of Transnational Environmental Externalities," in OECD, *Problems in Transfrontier Pollution* (Paris, 1974), pp. 147−77 passim; Robert E. Osgood et al., *Toward a National Ocean Policy: 1976 and Beyond* (Washington,

D.C.: National Science Foundation, NSF-RA-X-75-006, 1975), p. 103; Ingo Walter, *International Economics of Pollution* (New York: John Wiley & Sons, 1975), pp. 156, 194.

15. According to Matthews (p. 164), the discriminating evidence involves the ultimate resting place of most pollutants: "If the sea floor is their last home, then we can confidently assert that the oceans are self cleansing; but if the ocean and its biota are stable reservoirs for pollutants, the long-term picture is not so bright." A similar statement is given in National Academy of Sciences (1971), pp. 3–4.

16. L. H. J. Legault, "The Freedom of the Seas: A License to Pollute?" *University of Toronto Law Journal* 21 (1971):211–21.

17. An analogous situation can be found in the pollution of the atmosphere by automobiles. The ability of the atmosphere to dissipate automobile pollutants is limited and represents a scarce resource for society at large. But automobile designers, builders, and users have little incentive to economize on it since no charge is made for its use. Until recently, automobiles have been designed with little or no thought to emission pollution, and drivers have been given no incentive to avoid driving at certain times and in certain places as a way of reducing pollution. More stringent automobile emissions standards on the construction of cars in the United States is only a substitute for pricing the pollution of the atmosphere.

18. See *The Economic Value of Ocean Resources to the United States,* pp. 98–103.

19. This example is based on the classic study of spillover effects by R. H. Coase, "The Problem of Social Cost," *Journal of Law and Economics* 3 (1960):1–44.

20. The assumption here that states seek the least-cost solution to such problems might be challenged on the grounds that states do not always seek to maximize their wealth. This challenge is, of course, correct. A weaker version of the hypothesis, but one that is still useful and probably accurate, is that states would ignore the least-cost option less frequently the greater the cost, that is, the greater the loss of resources from avoiding the cost-minimizing use.

21. This proposition has come to be known in the economic literature as the Coase Theorem and is considered to be one of the most important propositions in modern welfare economics. It should be noted that the "invariance" result will be affected by the position of liability only if there are drastic differences in the level of wealth between the two countries. For example, if one country is rich and x dollars is a trivial fraction of its wealth, then its payment of this amount to the other country generally will not affect the total allocation of resources between the two. But if the rich country is not liable and x dollars is a substantial fraction of the other country's wealth, then the latter under some circumstances could elect to incur the damages rather than pay to have pollution reduced to economical levels. A misallocation of resources that included too much pollution might be the result. As we shall see later on, a misallocation could also occur if the transactions costs were positive and high compared with the increase in the value of production obtained by reducing spillover costs to economical levels.

22. I am indebted to Michael E. Levine for his criticism of an earlier draft of this section.

23. This is emphasized by Pearson in *International Marine Environment Policy: The Economic Dimension,* pp. 48–50, and "Environmental Policy and the Ocean," in *Per-*

spectives on Ocean Policy, pp. 209–12. Pearson also suggests that some countries, particularly coastal developing states, could place such a low value on the reduction of worldwide pollution that they could become "pollution havens." See Osgood et al., *Toward a National Ocean Policy: 1976 and Beyond,* p. 107. This argument presumes, of course, that pollutants mix thoroughly in the world ocean. Recent drafts of the treaty under negotiation at UNCLOS bear out Pearson's concern somewhat, since the obligations of developing coastal states to avoid pollution are weaker than those for developed coastal states.

24. U.S. Council on Environmental Quality, *Ocean Dumping: A National Policy* (Washington, D.C., October 1970), p. 34.

25. The transactions costs were high in spite of the fact that the agreement involved only two major powers. Such costs would probably rise as the number of states having nuclear capabilities rose.

26. Richard B. Stone, "Building Reefs for Better Fishing," *Exxon, U.S.A.* 14, no. 3 (1975):13–15; William C. Rempel, "Liberty Ship's Last Trip Will Be a Blast," *Los Angeles Times,* Nov. 8, 1976.

27. U.S. Council on Environmental Quality, p. 8.

28. Ibid., p. 13; National Academy of Sciences (1975b), p. 10.

29. National Academy of Sciences (1975a), pp. 228–67, and (1971), p. 96.

30. U.S. Council on Environmental Quality, p. 3.

31. Ibid., pp. 12–29.

32. Pearson (1975), pp. 64–83.

33. Even more efficient would be the creation of license rights to dump or to pollute which would be auctioned off to the highest bidders like the U.S. oil drilling rights described in Chapter 4.

34. An excellent exposition of this argument is Larry A. Ruff, "The Economic Common Sense of Pollution," *The Public Interest* 19 (1970):69–85.

35. Convention dated February 15, 1972, *International Legal Materials,* March 1972, p. 262–66.

36. Michael Hardy, "International Control of Marine Pollution," *Natural Resources Journal* 11 (1971):310, 312.

37. Convention, Annex III.

38. *International Legal Materials* vol. 11, November 1972, pp. 1291–1313; Pearson (1975), pp. 65–67.

39. Convention, Annex III.

40. Convention, art. XIII.

41. Statement of Frank Ikard, American Petroleum Institute, in *Outer Continental Shelf Oil and Gas Development,* p. 483.

42. Robert B. Krueger, "An Evaluation of the Provisions and Policies of the Outer Continental Shelf Lands Act," *Natural Resources Journal* 10 (1970):769–70.

43. Charles F. Goria, "Compensation for Oil Pollution at Sea: An Insurance Approach," *San Diego Law Review* 12 (1975):717; Henry J. McGurren, "The Externalities of a Torrey Canyon Situation: An Impetus for Change in Legislation," *Natural*

Resources Journal 11 (1971):348; Lance D. Wood, "An Integrated International and Domestic Approach to Civil Liability for Vessel-Source Oil Pollution," *Journal of Maritime Law and Commerce* 7 (1975):1.

44. Paul Treuthardt, "Towing Mystery Emerges in Disaster," *Los Angeles Times,* Mar. 30, 1978.

45. Wood, p. 54.

46. In severe weather, a ballast of 80 percent of tank capacity may be required. These issues are discussed in Pearson (1975), p. 86; Philip A. Cummins, Dennis E. Logue, Robert D. Tollison, and Thomas D. Willett, "Oil Tanker Pollution Control: Design Criteria vs. Effective Liability Assessment," *Journal of Maritime Law and Commerce* 7 (1975):172−73. Both these sources cite a technical paper.

47. See Wood, pp. 30−31.

48. Liberia, Greece, and Panama are among the most "convenient" (least demanding) of flag states for the registration of oil tankers. For a discussion of this issue see A. V. Lowe, "The Enforcement of Marine Pollution Regulations," *San Diego Law Review* 12 (1975):633.

49. The importance of this assumption in formulating pollution policies that avoid inefficiency is exceeded only by the frequency with which it is employed in the literature (see, e.g., Cummins et al., p. 193). Subjecting it to a more careful scrutiny is beyond the scope of this study, however.

50. The following description of tanker technologies is drawn from Cummins et al., pp. 172−74.

51. Ibid., p. 200.

52. Ibid., pp. 178−93; this describes the various assumptions and procedures used to generate these data.

53. Ibid., p. 182.

54. Ibid., p. 172.

55. Ibid., pp. 198−204.

56. By dealing exclusively with the annual rates of petroleum injections, the authors ignore the cumulative effect that continuous pollution may eventually have. The assumption is reasonable enough, however, since scientists have yet to ascertain physical accumulations. When that is accomplished economists may attempt to place values on pollution reductions.

57. This estimate is based on the prior work of Dennis P. Tihansky, "An Economic Assessment of Marine Water Pollution Damages," in Thomas F. P. Sullivan, ed., *1973 Pollution Control in the Maritime Industries* (International Association for Pollution Control, 1973), pp. 284−324.

58. Cummins et al., p. 204.

59. Ibid., p. 177.

60. See UNTS, vol. 327, p. 26, and *International Legal Materials* 12 (1973): 1319−87.

61. See Pearson (1975), p. 42; Legault, p. 213.

62. Its requirements are summarized in Pearson (1975), pp. 121−24.

63. Cummins et al., pp. 193−98.

64. Ibid., p. 200.

65. See Pearson (1975), pp. 89−98. Evidently "it was impossible to establish damage estimates that had minimal support among the participants." Several preliminary cost-benefit comparisons were prepared as background papers for the conference by the U.K. Department of Trade and Industry, the U.S. Treasury, and the U.S. Coast Guard. Although only the latter paper found a ratio of costs and benefits that favored segregated ballasting, this became the basis for the U.S. position on that matter. Each paper was surrounded by "considerable professional controversy" and allegations of bias in one direction or another. Ibid., pp. 90−92.

66. Ibid., p. 96.

67. U.S. Department of State, *U.N. Law of the Sea Conference 1975* (Washington, D.C.: Bureau of Public Affairs Publication 8764, February 1975), p. 6. It has also been stated that non-uniform coastal controls would lead to a "crazy quilt" of regulations that would tempt ship operators to go "jurisdiction shopping" for regulations that were more favorable to world commerce. (See National Petroleum Council, *Law of the Sea: Particular Aspects Affecting the Petroleum Industry*, Washington, D.C., May 1973, pp. 28−29). A related argument against broad pollution control zones made by the U.S. government is that zone-locked states would have reduced access to open ocean areas outside their own EEZ without the permission of their neighbors. (See U.S. Department of State, p. 6.) This problem applies to 66 coastal and 6 landlocked states. See statement of John N. Moore in *Status Report on Law of the Sea Conference*, Hearings before the U.S. Senate Subcommittee on Minerals, Materials, and Fuels of the Committee on Interior and Insular Affairs, 93d Cong., 1st Sess. (September 19, 1973), pp. 221−22.

68. National Petroleum Council (1975), p. 71. In the United States, at least, the advocacy of uniform international standards for environmental protection appears to be an issue on which the federal government, the petroleum industry, and some organizations intent upon environmental quality can agree. See statement of Richard A. Frank, in *Mineral Resources of the Deep Seabed*, pt. 2, p. 1071.

69. Pearson (1975), p. 57.

70. The rule of strict liability is much like the rule against trespass. If my next-door neighbor accidentally builds his fence a few inches on my side of the boundary between our two lots, then the fence must come down if that is my desire. The nature of his intentions and skills is beside the point.

71. If the operator or lessee of an oil tanker can affect the quantity of oil discharged more directly than the ship's owner, then perhaps the operator should be assigned the liability instead. But since there are more lessees of ships than there are owners, assigning liability to owners would lessen transactions and enforcement costs of a liability system. If it proved to be more economical for the operator to be liable, the two parties could exchange it at a price. These possibilities for exchange are implicit in the following discussion, which refers only to the "ship owner."

72. Some of these issues are analyzed by Pearson (1975), pp. 94−95.

73. See, e.g., Peter N. Swan, "International and National Approaches to Oil Pollution Responsibility: An Emerging Regime for a Global Problem," *Oregon Law Review* 50 (1971):531 and the sources cited therein.

74. See U.S. Department of Transportation, U.S. Coast Guard Research and Development Center, *Oil Spill Identification System,* Interim Report on Project No. CG-D-41-75 (Springfield, Va.: National Technical Information Service, October 1974); A. P. Bentz, "Oil Spill Identification," *Analytical Chemistry* 48 (1976):454A−472A.

75. *Oil Spill Identification System,* p. 5.

76. See, e.g., National Petroleum Council (1975), p. 70; National Academy of Sciences (1975b), pp. 19−31.

77. Most of the following discussion is drawn from Wood, pp. 4−10, and Goria, pp. 717−21.

78. McGurren, pp. 367−68; Goria, pp. 733−35.

79. Goria, p. 718.

80. This is referred to as the Tanker Owners Voluntary Agreement Concerning Liability for Oil Pollution (TOVALOP). Ibid., pp. 726−27.

81. This is referred to as the Contract Regarding an Interim Supplement to Tanker Liability for Oil Pollution (CRISTAL). Ibid., pp. 728−29.

82. Wood, p. 10.

83. Goria, pp. 722−24.

84. Ibid., pp. 724−26.

85. *International Legal Materials* 9 (1970):25−44. This document is often referred to as the Public Law Convention. The discussion here is drawn largely from Swan, pp. 544−47.

86. Shinn, pp. 10 and 77, citing a Canadian document by Paul St. Pierre, "Draft Report on the Threat of Ecological Disaster in Arctic Regions" (Ottawa: North Atlantic Assembly, October 1970), p. 5.

87. Ann L. Hollick, "United States and Canadian Policy Processes in Law of the Sea," *San Diego Law Review* 12 (1975):531−32.

88. 18 and 19 Eliz. 2, C. 47 (Can. 1970), reprinted in *International Legal Materials* 9 (1970):543−54. See also Swan, pp. 565−70.

89. No state would be zone locked as a result of this Canadian action.

90. Hollick (1975), pp. 531−32; *International Legal Materials* 9 (1970):553.

91. Hollick, pp. 532−33. Canada has consistently favored stronger international agreements than those that were reached in the conventions noted earlier. It abstained from voting on the Public Law Convention on the ground that intervention by a coastal state was undesirably limited, and it voted against the Civil Liability Convention on the ground that vessel liability should be unlimited in addition to being strict. Legault, p. 220.

92. Some writers have suggested, however, that pollution in the Arctic would alter weather patterns throughout the Northern Hemisphere. See Shinn, p. 77.

93. Hollick (1975), pp. 531−33.

94. For details of this act and a comparison between it and the 1969 Civil Liability Convention see Swan, pp. 547−65.

CHAPTER 7

Property Rights in Marine Science

Marine research, broadly defined, is the scientific procedure of formulating explanations of the characteristics and processes of the oceans, and of gathering the information that would support or refute these explanations. The range of subjects that it encompasses is enormous. These include such physical features as ocean depth, temperature, bottom configurations and sediment conditions; such biological features as the extent and management of living resources; and such basic oceanic processes as horizontal currents, vertical upwelling, meteorology, movement of the planet's surface, and the transport and assimilation of pollutants.

Marine science has, of course, played only a minor role in the historical development of ocean uses and services, but recently it has been very important in helping to create sometimes startling new uses and services. A better understanding of the geology of continental shelf areas, for example, has led to the discovery of offshore minerals. Ocean biology has contributed to the attempt to stabilize fishery yields. Ocean chemistry may eventually provide better techniques for abating pollutants and thus improve water quality. Knowledge of bathymetry has opened many ocean areas to the use of submarines for military and civilian uses.

Both basic and applied research activities tend to concentrate in coastal areas. The continental shelf is the most valuable ocean area for man's purposes and a logical place for applied oceanography. And for basic science the shelf area represents a unique "region of transition between land and sea."[1] The oceanic processes in the shelf areas are markedly different from those in the deep seas and must be investigated in order to develop an understanding of the oceans as a whole.

The activities of marine science in coastal areas imply that it may occasionally compete with other activities for access, especially when there are conflicts between uses. For example, scientists who drill wells to explore the geological strata beneath the continental shelf employ the same mobile drilling rigs that are used by the petroleum industry, and drilling of both types creates the possibility of oil pollution. The use of such exploration techniques as explosions and seismic tests can harm fisheries.

The technical requirements of oceanographic research are substantial. Research vessels are highly specialized, containing extensive laboratories and such equipment as drills, grab dredges, seismic and acoustical devices, and mechanisms to measure gravitational and magnetic forces. Their charters must be arranged one to three years in advance and costs are high (in 1973 as much as $4,000 per day).[2] As a result, oceanographic research is skewed toward wealthier nations. In 1968, according to United Nations data, there were approximately 478 research and oceanographic vessels of more than fifteen meters in length. Of these, 436 were owned by sixteen nations in North America, Europe, Japan, and South Africa; all Latin American and all other Asian and African nations combined had only 42.

> The United States alone spent more on ocean research than all other countries of the world together, and the ocean research budget of Sweden alone was higher than the ocean science budget of all African countries. Every year American oceanographic vessels can be found working off the coasts of Latin America and of Asian and African nations. In contrast, no requests for research permits from any of the developing countries, and few from developed countries, have been received by the State Department.[3]

The most prominent American oceanographic organizations include about a half dozen universities, the United States Navy and Coast Guard, and several civilian bureaus of the U.S. government.

1. EXPANDED JURISDICTION BY COASTAL STATES

The extension of ocean research into the world ocean and the significant intrusion of coastal states into scientific activities developed during the postwar era. Milner B. Schaefer describes the situation:

> Before World War II, ocean scientists had little difficulty in conducting their investigations when and where they wished. Of course, nations had full jurisdiction over all activities in their internal waters and jurisdiction over activities, except navigation in innocent passage, in their territorial seas. However, scientists mostly worked in waters of [either their own country or] nearby friendly nations who readily permitted observations even in internal waters. The scientists took samples of water, biota, and even the sea bottom while passing through the territorial sea, only informally notifying the government having jurisdiction. This

notification was often made through their scientific colleagues in that nation. Far-ranging oceanographic investigations . . . were not numerous and were generally welcomed by everyone concerned; so research operations, port calls, and other activities were scheduled without any considerable formalities.[4]

Following the war, science budgets for both military and civilian research increased sharply, especially in the U.S. and the U.S.S.R. This led to rising concern by coastal states about the consequences of granting foreign scientists unfettered access to offshore areas. There appear to be two reasons for this concern.

First, coastal states found it increasingly difficult to distinguish between bona fide research for scientific purposes as opposed to clandestine military activities. Both the United States and the U.S.S.R. seem to have contributed to this confusion. Not only did U.S. military research increase after 1945, but nearly two-thirds of the civilian research in this country was carried out with funds provided by the U.S. Navy's Office of Naval Research even though most of the programs appear not to have had any direct military application. Moreover, some naval vessels, such as the *Pueblo*, were categorized as "environmental research vessels" though they were in fact engaged almost entirely in surveillance and military intelligence work.[5] The Hughes *Glomar Explorer* and its accompanying barge were alleged to have been developed to extract manganese nodules off the ocean floor, but they, too, turned out to have been operated initially for intelligence purposes.[6]

Second, coastal states have also found it increasingly difficult to distinguish between marine research for scientific purposes and marine research for commercial purposes. This is particularly true of coastal states undergoing economic development, which seem to fear that even basic research by scientists of foreign developed countries on "their" shelves could give those countries an advantage when exploitation begins or even earlier during bargaining over lease rights and royalties.[7] Many coastal states have maintained this position in spite of the recognition by all parties that coastal governments will be in a position to control many of the details of actual exploitation.[8]

At the core of coastal state arguments against any recognition of unrestricted scientific access to shelf areas is the difficulty of distinguishing between fundamental and applied research. For example, scientific investigation into the geology of shelf areas may reveal basic principles of the motion of the continents and ocean basins. But it may also be of use to firms intent upon exploration for offshore petroleum. The uses that scientists make of their observations and samples cannot be inexpensively monitored by the coastal state. If these results are publicized widely or given discreetly to petroleum firms, then the coastal state would have lost its right to collect a fee for the sale of valuable information. The same point applies to fisheries research. Fisheries scientists sometimes have to catch several tons of fish to provide a sufficiently large sample to estimate fish populations. If monitoring costs are high, fish could be surreptitiously taken in commercial quantities or information about fishery locations could be transmitted from "research" vessels to trawler fleets.[9] The greater the monitoring costs, the fewer the net benefits coastal states can capture from foreign scientific investigations of their shelves. In a few cases coastal interests may be harmed since, quite understandably, the continental shelf areas of developing countries are more in demand for research by scientists of developed countries than are the shelves of developed areas by scientists of developing countries.[10]

Marine scientists in universities and some governmental agencies have generally employed two arguments to support their goal of absolutely free access to continental shelf areas.[11] First, many have claimed that their activities are entirely devoted to fundamental science, and not to applied research for either commercial or military purposes.[12] But it is not easy to find objective standards by which a division between the two categories of research could firmly be made. In the first place, both types of research employ similar techniques and equipment. John A. Knauss has described the overlapping as follows:

> I am not going to draw a line between the kind of scientific research that is done for science and that kind of scientific research that is done for oil exploration because I don't understand the difference. It really is a matter of degree. When we [scientists] do research on the continental shelf we use seismic methods, we use magnetic methods, we use gravity methods, and the difference between what we do and what the oil industry does is a matter of quantity not of quality. That is, we use the same techniques but obviously if you are going to put the investment that is needed into finding oil you need to do the work more intensively.[13]

Even if a firm difference could be established between the techniques of fundamental research and applied research, there would still be no clear distinction in the uses to which the results of research were put. It often happens that fundamental research is soon found to have concrete and commercial application.[14] For example, the initial discoveries of widespread deposits of manganese nodules made by university oceanographic laboratories led rather quickly to more detailed research by mining firms, and they may eventually result in actual mining operations. Other university projects led to the discovery of hot brines in the Red Sea, which also are likely to have eventual commercial value. Drilling on the continental shelves for strictly scientific purposes led to accurate predictions about the location of offshore petroleum deposits. Basic geological research suggesting that the surface of the earth is in motion has applications to seismology and to the location of offshore mineral resources. The investigation of upwelling forces has led to improved yields from fisheries, and the study of horizontal currents has implications for the placement of oil drilling rigs. Each of these relationships lends credence to the statement of a Brazilian diplomat that "in the last analysis, every particle of scientific knowledge could be translated into terms of economic gain or national security and, in a technological society, scientific knowledge means power."[15]

Second, scientists have maintained that coastal state interests in avoiding either military or commercial research would be protected by pledges to publish all findings in public sources. Since the value of applied research usually depends in some measure on secrecy, scientists say that their vow of "open publication" would logically be made only in connection with basic research. Such promises would constitute a litmus test for establishing the bona fides of legitimate scientific institutions and their personnel.[16] However, not only do some coastal states seem to be skeptical of these arguments, but scientists themselves may in some cases refuse to publish their findings regardless of prior pledges, especially when the results of research cruises are too skimpy to justify publication or fail to support scientific predictions.[17] Scientists may even occasionally decline to publish all that they have learned. Either situation would raise the cost to coastal states of "enforcing" their "contract" with scientists unless future dealings between the two were likely. In other cases coastal states appear to place little value on open publication since they often lack the trained scientific personnel necessary to evaluate these results,[18] although it is not clear why impartial expertise could not be purchased from friendly nations. This raises the possibility that some coastal states have incentives to avoid open publication and to retain exclusive rights to the information themselves. The discussion below suggests that these incentives are relatively great in situations where the line between pure and applied science is not absolutely clear and where expectations as to the value of the resources under investigation vary widely.

There has been an unmistakable trend during the past quarter-century toward increased coastal control over marine science. The Truman Proclamation of 1945 and the additional enclosures that followed it avoided specific reference to controls over research, but the idea had become explicit by the time the First UN Conference on the Law of the Sea convened at Geneva in 1958. Numerous marine scientists attended the conference and urged that the "freedom of scientific research" be included in the list of freedoms contained in the High Seas Convention. But the framers of that convention, believing for the most part that freedom of research was equivalent to freedom to test nuclear weapons, skirted their request.[19] Even more galling to the scientists was the extension of the principles of enclosure for research to the status of international law with the "consent regime" in the Continental Shelf Convention:

> The consent of the coastal State shall be obtained in respect of any research concerning the continental shelf and undertaken there. Nevertheless, the coastal State shall not normally withhold its consent if the request is submitted by a qualified institution with a view to purely scientific research into the physical or biological characteristics of the continental shelf, subject to the proviso that the

coastal State shall have the right, if it so desires, to participate or to be represented in the research, and that in any event the results shall be published.[20]

By 1971, the convention had been ratified by 33 of the 86 states that participated
in the Geneva Conference. Attitudes favoring restrictions on scientific research
had hardened by the time of the Third UNCLOS. At the Caracas meetings in
1974, 29 states spoke approvingly of coastal consent, another 54 agreed with
them, and only 21 states favored removal of most restrictions on marine
science.[21]

Coastal states have rarely intervened in the details of planning research
cruises, in the selection of foreign personnel to organize and conduct the cruise,
or in the use of the samples and data in the laboratory once the cruise is completed. Usually participation is confined to the stage of research where sampling,
observation, and measurement are actually carried out.[22] Of course, this part of
the voyage is critical to its overall success. It is here that the coastal state can
exercise its authority with the lowest cost of enforcement.

Aside from the U.S.S.R., Latin American coastal states have been in the
vanguard of imposing terms and conditions on the cruises of research vessels,
especially those of the United States. These states generally view the control over
foreign scientific research as an extension of the sovereign rights that are implicit,
if not express, in their continental shelf or 200-mile enclosures. Their stated goals
are to prevent pollution or harm to fisheries, and to spur the type of research that
will be of assistance to their programs for economic development. Twenty Latin
American states met at Lima in 1970 to lay out the several conditions which they
deemed necessary for scientific research in their jurisdictions. These were: (1) all
cruises had to secure prior authorization; (2) the coastal state had the right to
participate in the cruise and to benefit from its results; (3) all samples collected
during the cruise would be the property of the coastal state and could be
appropriated by the nation sponsoring the cruise only with the express permission
of the coastal state; (4) scientific research in the territorial sea would not be
subject to the usual rule of innocent passage.[23]

Controls of this kind have caused delays, inconvenience, and expense for
marine researchers.[24] Time is lost in securing approval for the cruise as a whole
and for specific port calls. In a number of instances approval has been denied on
the grounds of insufficient advance notice. Scientists are uncertain of the types of
research that coastal states seek to control and also of the precise areas in which
consent is required since the width of the territorial sea differs from country to
country and the definition of continental shelves is usually ambiguous. In some
cases the fate of a research cruise has been determined by foreign policy. Some
coastal states have refused access if the vessel has previously visited nations in
which they do not have an embassy.[25] Also, the U.S. Department of State in the
past has refused to assist in securing clearances from foreign embassies if, as was

often the case, scientists intended to do research in waters where the U.S. did not officially recognize coastal state claims, generally the 200-mile categorical enclosures of living resources by Latin Americans.[26]

Most research cruises have been completed in spite of these restrictions, but the cost of marine research has increased. Judith A. Tegger Kildow has also reported that the number of flat refusals has increased. Between 1967 and 1971 there were twenty-nine instances of refusals just for American research boats.[27] Almost half of these cases were refused on grounds of military security, usually by the U.S.S.R. or Turkey. Other reasons for rejection included concern for harm to water quality or fisheries, possible commercial applications of the proposed research, and the state of overall political relations between the countries involved. Countries in Latin America accounted for about half of this group of refusals, with France and Portugal accounting for another quarter. Brazil appears to have imposed the most stringent requirements of all. In addition to the restrictions mentioned above, which are common to most Latin American states, Brazil requires information on all sources of financial support for the cruise, biographical data on all personnel, photographs and specifications of the research vessel, a description of all on-board equipment, nautical charts illustrating all tracks, routes, and port calls, and a willingness to comply with all Brazilian laws including inspection by civilian and military authorities. Final approval for clearances can be given only by the president of Brazil. As a result, the activities of many American scientific research organizations had virtually ceased in the Brazilian EEZ by 1973.[28]

2. COASTAL INCENTIVES TO ACQUIRE INFORMATION

One of the principal themes of this book is that coastal states, to the extent they are motivated to increase their wealth, have incentives to collect information about the extent and value of different ocean uses up to the point where the cost of extra search exceeds its worth. These incentives are stronger, the greater the extent to which the coastal state can capture the benefits of making use of the resulting information. These benefits would include the higher net values from ocean services by avoiding inefficient uses. Yet the evidence presented in this chapter suggests that coastal states are, in various situations, attempting either to control the nature of oceanic research that takes place in their EEZs or to restrict the use of information that is generated by research, or occasionally to prevent research altogether. Moreover, this behavior imposes an external cost on world society, to the extent that fundamental scientific research is curtailed, by retarding the rate of growth in knowledge of basic planetary processes.

Behavior of this type raises two questions. First, are coastal state actions relating to oceanic research consistent with the behavioral incentives that have been attributable to these countries? If not, then how can the model of incentives be modified to explain these actions? Second, what actions might be taken by other countries to induce these coastal states to recognize the external costs of their behavior that have limited the acquisition of marine knowledge? Can these costs be "internalized" to the coastal states involved?

A tentative answer to the first question can be found by applying the recent contributions to the economic theory of information by Jack Hirshleifer and John M. Marshall, both of whom have analyzed the incentives to generate information privately and then to release it publicly.[29] The basic point can be illustrated in terms of a concrete example.

Assume that I own 200 square miles of land in the Nevada desert and that uranium was recently discovered on my neighbor's property adjacent to mine. Stimulated by this discovery, mining firms have offered to purchase the mineral rights to my land at prices that are substantially higher than what those rights would have fetched *ex ante*. Naturally, they are based on the higher probability— greater than zero but less than certainty—that these firms now assign to the discovery of uranium on my property. The firms that attach the higher probability to finding ore will offer the higher prices for the mining rights.

Assume also that I reject these offer prices, preferring to hold open the option that I will exploit the resource myself, assuming that ore is found, by forming my own mining company. One of the firms then makes a counteroffer: it volunteers to search my land for uranium ores and to report its findings to me without any obligation on my part to hire this or any other firm to exploit the resource. This offer appears to promise me substantial benefits. Information on the extent of ore is hidden from view. Since the data must be extracted from the earth at some cost, the information itself would be a valuable commodity. All these discovery costs would be borne by the mining company, so it is difficult to see how I could lose by this transaction. Depending on what the mining company finds, I could then decide whether investment in uranium exploitation would be profitable, whether this investment should be made by me or should be contracted to mining specialists, and so forth.

Further reflection reveals, however, that my acceptance of this offer exposes me to new risks. This is because I do not know what the findings of the research will be or in which direction they will point. If the research findings eventually become public, the value of my mineral rights could change drastically. If uranium ore is found in amounts that exceed the expectations that influenced the first prices offered, it is probable that further offers will be even higher. If ore is found in quantities that are less than these expectations, the new offers will be less. And if no ore is found, the value of the mineral rights will tumble to the prices that prevailed before the first discovery was made.

My decision in this situation depends upon how I feel about taking risks. If I permit the mining company to search, I am taking an all-or-nothing gamble. If I prohibit the search, I am opting for the relatively high probability of a moderate gain. I would take the zero-priced offer to search if I enjoy gambling, such as playing for high stakes at Las Vegas or refusing to take fire insurance on my house. I would refuse the offer to search if I am disinclined to take risks and prefer on the whole to pay a small, certain amount and know that there is no possibility of a huge loss of greater expected value. As Hirshleifer says, an individual of this sort "would actually pay something to a knowledgeable outsider not to reveal, in advance of market trading, which [result] will obtain!"[30] Depending upon the degree of change in my wealth that I thought search and discovery could cause, I might even employ resources to patrol my land to prevent unauthorized exploration by mining companies.

There are two different circumstances under which I would have stronger incentives to accept the offer to search. The first would be the availability of a market in which I could purchase an insurance policy that would protect my wealth from the consequences of an unfavorable discovery—that is, learning that the ores on my land were, relative to expectations, either of low quality, present in small quantities, or nonexistent. If I could purchase this insurance hedge at relatively low cost, then I would have fewer incentives either to prohibit the search or to try to suppress the resultant information if it were unfavorable. (If the information were favorable, I would have incentives, as Hirshleifer notes, to "push" it publicly since this would probably increase my wealth.) This sort of transaction, however—which Marshall calls "insuring the [unfavorable] impacts of public information"—requires the existence of a separate hedge market that can be utilized *ex ante*.[31] If the information arrives before I am able to hedge its unfavorable impact or if insurance markets of this sort are not available at low cost, then it would still pay me to suppress the data or to delay their arrival.[32]

Second, I would have stronger incentives to authorize search if I could write a contract with the mining company that would grant me the exclusive right to possess and to use the information and could enforce the contract at low cost. My decision in this case would depend upon the cost to me of monitoring the company's search activities, of keeping the results secret, and of preventing unauthorized disclosure of the data by officials or employees of the company.

The position of the coastal state with respect to the resources located in its EEZ appears to be similar to the uranium example. Resource values are uncertain since the location and extent of resources cannot be inexpensively determined by observation from the surface of the ocean. Firms seeking to exploit these resources would be willing to pay different sums for extraction rights depending upon the probabilities that they assign to finding profitable deposits. The highest of these potential payments is the opportunity cost to the coastal state either of exploiting offshore resources on its own account or of postponing exploitation in the hope of obtaining still higher prices in the future. Allowing foreigners to engage in applied research relating to EEZ resources may generate information which, depending upon its direction, will raise or lower these future offer prices. From this perspective, the coastal state takes on the risk of additional losses of wealth if the information turns out to be unfavorable and publicly known. Moreover, if the distinction between basic and applied research is expensive to draw or to maintain, then the coastal state's incentives to authorize basic research become just as weak as its incentives to authorize applied research. These incentives will vary among countries depending upon local circumstances and the importance that each state attaches to gaining additional wealth by "speculating" on the value of its EEZ resources. On the whole, it appears that these incentives would be weaker the greater (1) the anticipated variance in future prices for EEZ mineral rights, once reliable information on the extent of these resources becomes publicly known; (2) the aversion to bearing additional risk; and (3) the cost of distinguishing between research of different types and of monitoring the uses to which the results of either type of research are put.

On the basis of this analysis it would appear that the incentives of coastal states to permit oceanic research could range all the way from total access to zero access depending upon each of the factors noted above. Coastal state policies toward marine research can probably be divided into three categories, although placing a particular state in the appropriate category requires more information than I have presented in this chapter. The first category would include states that had weak incentives to restrict applied research and thus basic research as well. Policies of unrestricted access would be consistent with either the willingness of the state to bear additional risk or an assessment that the value of resources in its EEZ was low relative to the costs of enforcing restrictions on research.

The second category would include coastal states that restrict marine research but do not prevent it altogether. An individual state in this category could seek increased wealth and could be averse to risk, but it might have at hand techniques for inexpensively differentiating between various types of research and controlling the uses to which research was put. States in this group would permit fundamental research but would subject it to certain contractual controls—a state might, for example, insist on a property right in all samples and data that are collected, and an agreement to carrying its own personnel on board the ship at all times to monitor activities. Techniques of this sort could also be used, as James L. Johnston has suggested, to channel research away from the subjects most desired by foreign scientists and toward those most valued by the coastal state.[33] The total amount of research that is permitted by states falling into this category would be less than under a regime of zero restraints on scientific access, but there would be more research of direct use to the coastal state.[34]

In the third category would be the coastal states which, in addition to having all the characteristics of states in the second category, also faced high costs of distinguishing between basic and applied research and of monitoring the uses of research. These states would restrict research of any kind under a blanket policy. On the basis of available information, the number of states in this category appears to be smaller than those in the second category.[35]

3. STRENGTHENING COASTAL INCENTIVES TO ALLOW RESEARCH

Coastal state restrictions on fundamental marine research that are incidental to restrictions on applied research impose costs on the rest of the world in that they hamper the acquisition of knowledge about basic oceanic processes. How can some of these costs be brought to bear on the coastal state so that it sees the value of allowing basic research?

Associations of scientists have suggested several solutions. First, it has been proposed that the Intergovernmental Oceanographic Commission of UNESCO be permitted to certify the bona fides of universities and marine research organizations seeking access to foreign offshore areas.[36] The commission would not certify details of individual projects, but it would attest to the reputation of the specific organization for performing fundamental as opposed to either commercial or military investigations. But this procedure would not affect the problem of basic scientific research being used for applied purposes either before or after publication: this would still be difficult for the coastal state to control. For the same reason it would be almost useless for the U.S. government to coordinate and certify the legitimacy of research programs of American universities in foreign waters.[37]

Second, scientists have urged that the United States unilaterally open its internal and territorial waters to the research activities of foreign scientists, provided that U.S. scientists have the right to participate in the research, that the results will be available to the U.S. after the completion of the cruise, and that the results will eventually be published in open sources.[38] A generous offer of this kind by the United States would probably not be reciprocated, however, since few foreign countries have shown interest in engaging in research in U.S. ocean areas.

Third, scientists have urged that a separate international conference be called to remove the "consent regime" from the 1958 Continental Shelf Convention and to write a new convention that would firmly establish the principle of freedom of access for scientific purposes.[39] Since they recognize that this outcome is unlikely in the near future, they also have proposed that bilateral agreements be made between the United States and other countries, or that multilateral agreements be made between the United States and regions that are important for scientific activities, whereby restraints on access would be reduced or eliminated.[40] But the prospect of reaching agreements of this sort is not very good unless coastal states are offered some form of compensation for relaxing their restraints on research access. One cannot expect coastal states to surrender something for nothing, since it is plain that some of them capture benefits by curtailing scientific access.

Raising the issue of direct compensation suggests a variety of solutions to the problem. Although the coastal states that benefit most from restricting scientific access would demand the largest payments of either cash or other resources to induce them to remove at least some of these restrictions, it is unlikely that transfers of this kind would be employed even by wealthy nations since the value of additional basic oceanic research would be difficult to estimate. Less sweeping arrangements are more likely. For example, the United States could offer a flat fee to coastal states in return for each research cruise that was permitted access to desired coastal areas. The fee might increase with the length of the stay in each nation's coastal area, or it could be the subject of bargaining between the United States and the coastal state. Agreements could be negotiated in terms other than cash, such as technical assistance or the training of coastal state scientific personnel.[41]

Another long-run solution to the problem would be for coastal states to sell either to firms of their own nationality or to foreign entities the full rights to explore and exploit all resources in the EEZ. If these firms had greater incentives to distinguish between basic and applied research, they would develop skills to separate the two. This would weaken the incentives to impose blanket prohibitions on research, as some coastal governments have done.

Still another alternative would be simply to do nothing in the short run, recognizing that much of the problem will have passed by the time an international solution of some kind can be agreed to and become effective. It is to be expected that once the value of coastal resources becomes better known and exploitation begins, coastal states will have fewer incentives to hold information secret by restricting research generally. Gradually, information about the extent and value of offshore resources will leak to the public, thus making it less and less reasonable to restrict either the gathering of information or the dissemination of information that has already been collected. As Friedheim and Kadane concluded, ''we can offer no panacea for those ocean scientists who would like to assure themselves of stable working conditions with the stroke of a pen.''[42] But one can suggest with some confidence that their problems will, if left alone, steadily diminish over time.

4. CONCLUSIONS

The enclosure movement that applied initially to continental shelf minerals and then to fisheries has been extended to coastal marine research activities by foreign scientists. Property rights in marine science may have been established in a few cases for reasons of nationalist zeal. But a coastal state that seeks to increase its wealth often will find that its interests lie in restricting research of any kind as long as it finds it relatively expensive to draw and enforce a line between purely scientific projects and other activities that may have commercial payoffs. To allow research on the value of coastal resources poses a risk to the wealth of the coastal state since the research may reveal that resources are worth less than prospective buyers thought. Risk-avoiding countries may prefer to suppress such information, at least until the bargaining over the terms of exploitation, royalties, and other contractual items are completed.

The distributional gains that coastal nations capture by restricting even basic scientific research almost certainly impose a cost on the world community by reducing the rate at which we learn more about the basic processes of the planet. Property rights in marine science have also placed some inconvenience on scientists themselves, and in many cases the cost of research projects, and especially the time delays in obtaining coastal state consent, have increased. But the number of absolute refusals has been relatively small and the instances where research activities have been halted altogether have been fewer yet. A few coastal states, notably the U.S.S.R. and Turkey, have a history of restricting research by foreign scientists and are unlikely to alter their policies. In other cases, changes in policy toward marine science will depend upon relatively narrow calculations by the nation sponsoring research. In the future, such nations increasingly will have to determine whether the value of their research activities is equal to the cash, resources, or other political objectives that they must sacrifice to compensate certain coastal nations for the risk to their wealth that additional scientific research and related activities can impose.

Notes

1. Warren S. Wooster and Michael D. Bradley, "Access Requirements of Oceanic Research: The Scientists' Perspective," in W. S. Wooster, ed., *Freedom of Oceanic Research* (New York: Crane, Russak, 1973), p. 31.

2. Ibid., p. 29.

3. Herman T. Franssen, "Developing Country Views of Sea Law and Marine Science," in ibid., pp. 163–64. I have based the numbers in my text on the data contained in Franssen's table on p. 164, which is slightly at variance with his text.

4. Milner B. Schaefer, "Freedom of Scientific Research and Exploration in the Sea," *Stanford Journal of International Studies* 4 (1969):60–61.

5. Franssen, p. 162.

6. See Chapter 8 below.

7. This point is made by James L. Johnston (1976b), p. 188; Franssen, pp. 137–77; and Robert L. Friedheim and Joseph B. Kadane, "Ocean Science in the UN Political Arena," *Journal of Maritime Law and Commerce* 3 (1972):487.

8. William L. Sullivan, Jr., "Freedom of Scientific Inquiry," in Lewis M. Alexander, ed., *The Law of the Sea: National Policy Recommendations,* Proceedings of the Fourth Annual Conference of the Law of the Sea Institute, June 1969 (Kingston, R.I.: University of Rhode Island, 1970), p. 371.

9. Statement of the Hon. Donald L. McKernan, in Lewis M. Alexander, ed., *The Law of the Sea: The Future of the Sea's Resources,* Second Annual Conference of the Law of the Sea Institute, June 1967 (Kingston, R.I.: University of Rhode Island, 1968), pp. 118–19.

10. Michael Redfield, "The Legal Framework for Oceanic Research," in Wooster, ed., p. 62.

11. Absolute freedom of mobility for scientists is the predominant theme of National Academy of Sciences, *International Marine Science Affairs,* a report by the International Marine Science Affairs Policy Panel of the Committee on Oceanography, Washington, D.C., 1972.

12. Franssen, p. 157, makes this distinction.

13. Statement of John A. Knauss, in *The Law of the Sea: National Policy Recommendations* (1969), p. 400.

14. Remarks of Dale C. Krause, in ibid., p. 393; see also Franssen, pp. 158–59.

15. Cited by Franssen, p. 158.

16. Franssen, p. 157.

17. See William T. Burke, *Marine Science Research and International Law,* Occasional Paper No. 8, University of Rhode Island Law of the Sea Institute (1970), pp. 28–29.

18. Franssen, pp. 170–71.

19. E. D. Brown, "Freedom of Scientific Research and the Legal Regime of Hydrospace," *Indian Journal of International Law* 9 (1969):347.

20. Convention on the Continental Shelf, art. 5, sec. 8.

21. Alexander and Hodgson, (1975) p. 589.

22. Redfield, p. 57.

23. See the Resolution of the Latin American Meeting on Aspects of the Law of the Sea, done at Lima, August 4–8, 1970, reprinted in Eduardo Ferrero, "The Latin American Position on Legal Aspects of Maritime Jurisdiction and Oceanic Research," in Wooster, ed., pp. 104, 99–107.

24. See Burke, pp. 2–10; National Academy of Sciences (1972), p. 62.

25. Judith A. Tegger Kildow, "Nature of the Present Restrictions on Oceanic Research," in Wooster, ed., p. 13.

26. Ibid.

27. Ibid., pp. 14–18.

28. Maureen N. Franssen, "Oceanic Research and the Developing Nation Perspective," in Wooster, ed., pp. 186–93.

29. See J. Hirshleifer, "The Private and Social Value of Information and the Reward to Inventive Activity," *American Economic Review* 61 (1971):561−74; and John M. Marshall, "Private Incentives and Public Information," ibid. 64 (1974):373−90.

30. Hirshleifer, p. 568.

31. Marshall, pp. 377, 385, 389.

32. Ibid., p. 380.

33. James L. Johnston (1976b), pp. 184−85.

34. It is possible that Brazil is in this category, in spite of its heavy restrictions on almost all types of scientific effort in its EEZ—note that the comment quoted earlier was of a Brazilian diplomat—for it has permitted, and even encouraged in some cases, extensive exploration of the crust of its continental shelf area. Scientists seeking basic information about the geology of this area have been granted access by Brazil under the condition that they do more detailed work that would be usable for oil exploration by the Brazilian national petroleum organization. Brazil has also permitted research into horizontal currents in its EEZ which of course would be useful for later construction and positioning of offshore oil drilling rigs. See Maureen N. Franssen, pp. 192−93.

35. Aside from the U.S.S.R., the People's Republic of China, North Korea, and Vietnam, this category includes Burma, Turkey, and several Middle Eastern states. See Maureen Franssen and Judith Kildow.

36. National Academy of Sciences (1972), p. 66.

37. This was proposed by Osgood et al., *Toward a National Ocean Policy: 1976 and Beyond*, p. 190.

38. National Academy of Sciences (1972), pp. 76−78. This has also been recommended by Burke, p. 22, and by Brown, p. 368.

39. National Academy of Sciences (1972), pp. 63−70.

40. Ibid., pp. 64−66.

41. At least one U.S. oceanographic organization engages in exchanges of this sort with a Latin American nation and appears to be given regular access to its coastal areas. Herman Franssen, pp. 170−72.

42. Friedheim and Kadane, "Ocean Science in the U.N. Political Arena," p. 501.

Chapter 8

Deep-Sea Mineral Resources*

In December 1872, H.M.S. *Challenger*, a wooden steamship, set out on an epic scientific exploration of the oceans. During the following five and a half years it circumnavigated the planet and took measurements of depths, temperatures, currents, and contours as well as samples of flora, fauna, and sediments in every major ocean. The charts and surveys amassed by the *Challenger* expedition were eventually published in a series of fifty volumes which mark the beginning of oceanography as a separate field of systematic inquiry.

One of the major discoveries of the *Challenger* was that nodules of rocklike materials, often the size and shape of potatoes, lay on the deepest bottoms of the Atlantic, the Indian, and particularly the Pacific oceans. The nodules were recognized then to be rich in several minerals but they remained a scientific curiosity until the 1950s. Rising prices of metals and advances in technology have recently generated great interest in these resources and have raised the possibility that they can be exploited commercially.

There is, however, substantial controversy over the manner in which they should be exploited. In particular, the possibility of unregulated competition among private firms to mine the seabeds has met with widespread concern. Leaders of major powers are fearful that unregulated competition for nodules could lead to international instability or even conflict. Leaders of poorer nations presently without the technology to exploit believe that these mineral riches should be the "common heritage of mankind" and should be mined by an international organization mainly for the benefit of states that are at a disadvantage in wealth or geography. Some economists have argued that exploitation would be inefficient without regulations that create exclusive property rights to unmined deposits. The ocean miners, for their part, are of two minds on the prospective benefits of regulation. On the one hand, they are concerned that the creation of a strong international regime to control all access to the deep seabeds would attempt to protect land-based minerals producers and possibly discrimi-

---

*Portions of this chapter have been drawn from Eckert (1974).

nate against private enterprise miners. But some miners also maintain that bankers are generally unwilling to extend vast loans without settled seabed property rights that would indicate security of tenure and reduce the possibilities of claim jumping. The continued uncertainty about an international agreement that might call for restrictions in seabed production by private miners or subject them to onerous taxes and royalties has, according to the miners, caused them to postpone investments and has raised the total cost of their activities. For all these reasons, ocean mining and possibly an international authority to regulate it have become one of the thorniest issues at the Law of the Sea Conference.

The purpose here is to apply economic analysis to available information on the nature and mining of nodules to determine (1) whether regulation of some sort would tend to avoid their economically inefficient exploitation, and (2) if so, what powers the regulatory authority should possess. This analysis is preceded by a discussion of the characteristics of nodules and the various exploitation technologies and a description of the structure of the incipient ocean mining industry and the possible impacts of its activities.

1. CHARACTERISTICS OF MANGANESE NODULES AND TECHNOLOGIES FOR EXPLOITATION

Nodules consist mainly of iron and manganese but they also contain smaller amounts of more valuable metals such as nickel, copper, and cobalt plus traces of about twenty other elements. They vary in size from 0.5 to 15 centimeters in diameter and can be shaped like small pellets or softballs. Their structure is honeycombed and highly porous, making them light and very fragile when dry. Deep-water photography and sampling indicate that nodules either form in clusters like oversized table grapes or are strewn one layer thick in fields resembling an extraordinary mosaic of cannon-ball or potato-shaped forms, partly embedded in a smooth carpet of mud (see Fig. 20). Because of the vastness of ocean space, estimates of their total weight can only be speculative, but one scientist estimated in 1965 that the Pacific Ocean alone contained over one trillion tons of these nodules.[1] Extending this estimate to take into account other deep ocean areas probably makes nodules "the largest mineral deposit on this planet."[2]

Nodules appear to be formed by the gradual accretion of metallic ions to hard nucleii of small volcanic rocks or such calcium compounds as the teeth of sharks or the earbones of whales. Their growth is not well understood by scientists but is believed to be "one of the slowest chemical reactions in nature, rates of accumulation being atomic layers per day."[3] One theory is that metals that are introduced to the oceans by submarine springs, volcanic emanations, and land-based runoff eventually precipitate to the great depths, and there the "rain"

FIG. 20.   A dense field of manganese nodules.

SOURCE: National Science Foundation, International Decade of Ocean Exploration, *Inter-University Program of Research on Ferromanganese Deposits of the Ocean Floor*, Phase I Report (Washington, D.C., April 1973).

of ions very slowly coats the nodule's nucleus, layer by layer, much like the structure of an onion, giving nodules their roughly concentric shape.[4] Nodules can flourish only in the areas where bottom disturbances are rare and where sediments are growing at a rate equal to or less than the rate of growth of nodules, which is about two to four millimeters in a million years, or one one-thousandth of the average rate of accumulation of the mud and clay that form abyssal muds.[5] What keeps these geologically ancient materials, which always are observed on the surface of the ocean floor, from being buried by rising sediments remains a mystery.[6]

Manganese nodules have been found at the bottom of all deep oceans and even the Great Lakes, but the deposits richest in minerals appear to be those that lie in the Pacific Ocean at depths of between 3,000 and 5,000 meters where waters are rich in nutrients and oxygen and sedimentation rates are very low. So far, the most promising region appears to be the Northeastern Pacific bounded roughly by the 6° and 20° North parallels of latitude and the 110° and 180° West meridians of longitude, in a band of sea 200 kilometers wide and 1,500 kilometers long stretching between the Hawaiian Islands and Central America (see Fig. 21.).[7]

Before minerals can be sold, the nodules must be found, dredged, and processed. Although their general location is known, extensive search and discovery effort is required to determine whether a particular deposit can be economically mined with given equipment over a certain period of time. This is determined by: the grade of ore; the size of the area of the deposit; the size, uniformity, and concentration of nodules; the depth, topography and sediment conditions of the ocean floor; the weather conditions on the surface of the ocean; the distance of the mine site from processing plants; and the nature of the rights a miner is given or the regulations under which he is made to work.

The physical characteristics of nodule deposits are highly variable.[8] Deposits usually occur in irregular patches rather than in broad, continuous fields, and the concentration of nodules within one patch can change significantly over distances as short as a mile; thus, detailed topographic charts and multiple samples are necessary to determine the value of a deposit.[9] The richest deposits apparently are not found on the spacious, smooth provinces of the ocean floor that would be most efficient for dredging, but in regions having continuous canyons and hills of changing slope and undulation where some dredges could not operate without risk.[10] For example, one firm has identified high-assay deposits in an area of the Pacific Ocean basin that is hilly throughout, having mountain peaks that vary in height by a factor of ten. Central Pacific hills tend to be circular and lack any definite trend, but in the eastern Pacific there are long north-south ridges with slopes of between 10 and 60 degrees. The area has many obstructions, including escarpments, outcrops, and boulders, which make as much as one-quarter of the mine site inaccessible. Smooth sea floors in broad abyssal plains contain fewer

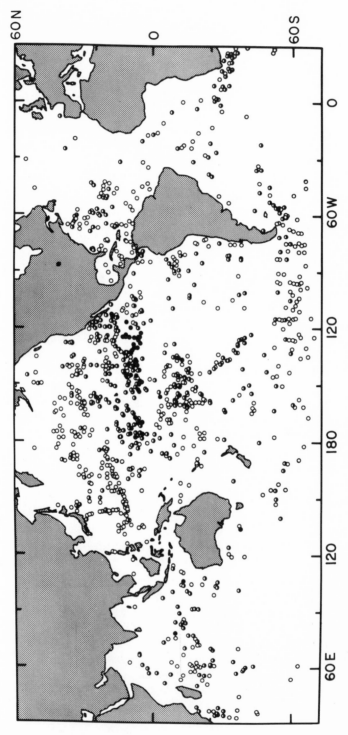

FIG. 21. Worldwide distribution of manganese nodules. The most extensive and the highest-grade deposits lie in the north-central South Pacific and North Pacific oceans. (Half-filled circles are analyzed nodules containing less than 1% copper, filled circles are analyzed nodules containing more than 1% copper, and open circles represent nodules for which analyses are not available.)

SOURCE: G. Ross Heath, "Deep-Sea Manganese Nodules," *Oceanus*, 21 (Winter 1978), p. 62.

nodules of high quality, presumably because of their higher rates of sediment deposition.[11]

Nodule assays also vary. A typical high-grade deposit contains 27 to 30 percent manganese, 1.1 to 1.4 percent nickel, 1.0 to 1.3 percent copper, and 0.2 to 0.4 percent cobalt.[12] The minimum assay for commercial mining of each metal separately appears to be 20 percent for manganese, 1.0 percent for nickel, 0.8 percent for copper, and 0.2 percent for cobalt provided that the nickel and copper assays together equal at least 2.0 percent.[13] However, assays can differ by as much as a factor of two within a given deposit so that a significant portion of the ore may be below the commercial grade. Also, nodules having high copper and low nickel assays can be found adjacent to nodules having low copper and high nickel assays.[14] Recent research suggests that nodule assays may be inversely correlated with the abundance (pounds per square foot) contained in a particular deposit.[15]

Because of differences in nodule qualities, quantities, and costs of extraction, prospective ocean miners will probably want to explore, sample, and map in some detail the bottom conditions of a relatively large number of deposits before selecting a few sites for extensive dredging. The seismic technologies used to locate oil and gas deposits are of little use in locating nodules, which requires ships having sophisticated capabilities for pinpoint navigation, photography, acoustics, closed-circuit television, grab-dredging, assaying and coring. These resources can cost up to $5,000 per day excluding scientific personnel.[16] Clearly the information gathered by this laborious and time-consuming search process is a valuable proprietary input into the entire process of ocean mining.

The mining of nodules requires the development of entirely new deep-ocean technologies. Efficiencies are uncertain since there is no previous experience with comparable systems. Reliable methods must be developed for a variety of difficult tasks: surveying areas by remote sensors and evaluating samples having high moisture content; collecting deposits from the ocean floor on a continuing basis at depths of up to three miles and lifting them to the surface; developing viewing systems that permit the mining machinery to be observed in operation and reveal any obstacles lying in the paths of dredge sweeps; developing structural materials that are resistant to corrosion and fatigue; eliminating waste materials such as silt and soil from the nodules at sea before ores are transported to shore for processing; and extracting metals without the use of conventional processes.

Currently there is experimentation with three patented methods for dredging.[17] Two of these involve continuous path dredging. A dredgehead is connected by conduit to a ship and movement of the head directly above the ocean floor accompanies the movement of the ship and pipe across the target in wide sweeping patterns. Apparently little lateral movement is possible, and the technical efficiency of the system is reduced by the difficulty, at a distance of three miles, of "plowing perfect rows" by the television or sonar.[18] In one variant of this system, nodules are lifted to the surface by huge hydraulic pumps, much larger than those used for water in coal mining or for mud in oil drilling. This approach is favored by the consortium organized by the Kennecott Copper Corporation. A second variant of the system raises the mixture of nodules, water, and soil to the surface by air lift much like an enormous tank-type vacuum cleaner. This system (see Fig. 22) avoids pumps and other machinery that could malfunction, but it offers difficulties in maintaining the appropriate vacuum pressure in the lengthy conduit. The dredgehead must be designed to filter out large nodules that could clog the conduit. This technology was developed by Deepsea Ventures, once a subsidiary of Tenneco, Inc., and now owned by the Ocean Mining Associates consortium (U.S. Steel, Sun Oil Company, and Union Minière of Belgium).

A third method is that of continuous line bucket dredging. This technology employs a rope to which specially designed dredge buckets are attached at given intervals. The rope forms a loop that passes through the ship's bow and stern, with the bottom end of the loop touching the ocean floor. By rotating the rope through the loop and moving the ship at right angles to the plane of the rotating loop, the buckets are dragged across the bottom and ore is gathered in a path that is traced by the movement of the ship and is as wide as the ship's length. This system, somewhat like an oversized bucket conveyor belt at a cement plant, is simple in conception; it operates mechanically without the aid of air or water pumps, and probably has the lowest engineering cost, but it may be inefficient since there is no way to control the movement of the buckets on the ocean bottom so as to avoid obstructions (parts of the rope may also be susceptible to tangles) or to limit the amount of mud and silt that is scooped up along with the nodules. This technology is controlled by the CLB Group, a mining consortium organized by Ocean Resources, Inc. The basic principles of operation of the CLB system are illustrated in Figure 23, which may be modified by using two ships working in tandem to complete the loop rather than a single ship working alone.[19]

A fourth technology, called fixed area dredging, has also been talked of. A patent for this procedure was established in 1966 by Global Marine, Inc., and was believed to be under development in conjunction with a 36,000-ton, 618-foot "mining ship," the *Glomar Explorer* (see Fig. 24), commissioned and operated by the Summa Corporation (owned by Howard R. Hughes). Although the details of this dredging technology were never clear, it was thought to be the most expensive and sophisticated of them all.[20] It appeared to employ a stationary surface ship, a collection device having a central base that would remain stationary on the ocean floor, and a rotating arm attached to the base with a movable carriage which, moving in and out along the arm, would act as the dredgehead. Nodules would be crushed within the base and then pumped by water up the conduit to a barge that would lie submerged beneath the ship. When most of the nodules lying within the radius of the base had been collected, the

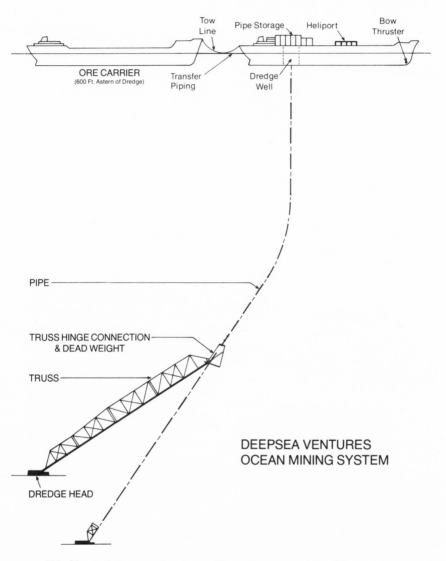

FIG. 22.   Artist's conception of one of the systems proposed for mining nodules.

SOURCE: UN, *Economic Implications of Sea-Bed Mineral Development in the International Area: Report of the Secretary General*, Doc. A/CONF.62/25 (May 22, 1974), p. 18. (Figure supplied to UN courtesy of Deepsea Ventures, Inc.)

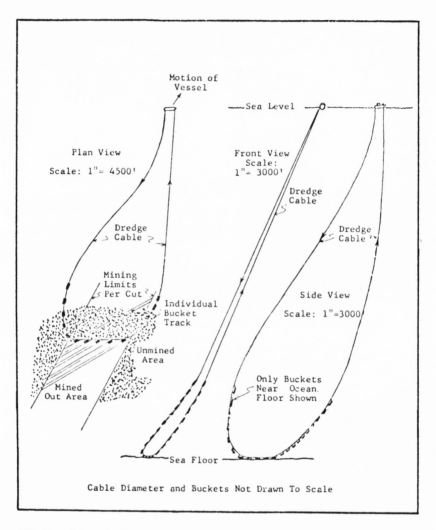

FIG. 23. Schematic drawing illustrating the design and operation of the Continuous Line Bucket System for mining deep ocean nodule deposits as proposed by Y. Masuda. A successful pilot test of this system was conducted in over 12,000 feet (3,650 meters) of water north of Tahiti in the summer of 1970.

SOURCE: John L. Mero, "Potential Economic Value of Ocean-Floor Manganese Nodule Deposits," in David R. Horn, ed., *Ferromanganese Deposits on the Ocean Floor* (National Science Foundation, International Decade of Ocean Exploration, Washington, D.C.: 1972), p. 199; reprinted in James E. Mielke, *Ocean Manganese Nodules,* prepared at the request of Henry M. Jackson, chairman, U.S. Senate Committee on Interior and Insular Affairs, 94th Cong., 1st Sess., June 1975, p. 19.

FIG.24. *Glomar Explorer*, Port of Long Beach, 1973.

SOURCE: Photograph by Chester H. Eckert.

entire system would be relocated. (It could probably be adapted to a different type of collection device, such as a tracked crawler that could gather nodules by moving along the ocean floor like a piece of earthmoving equipment.) The 324-foot barge, designed and constructed by Lockheed Missiles and Space Company, was believed to serve both as a carrying device for the collection vehicle (which was too large to be lowered through the pipe-handling well in the hull of the ship) and as a temporary storage facility for the crushed nodules.

As it turned out, the actual purpose of these devices had little to do with ocean mining. The stated purpose of the ship and barge was part of an elaborate and extraordinary cover to conceal the true mission as part of "Operation Jennifer." This was the attempt by U.S. military and intelligence agencies to raise a 320-foot Russian submarine that had exploded and sunk in 1968 in waters 5,000 meters deep some 750 miles northwest of Hawaii.[21]

Whether the *Glomar Explorer* had been designed for mining and diverted to intelligence activities or whether it had been intended for the latter purpose all along is still not known, but the possibilities of using the ship for mining were clear. As James L. Mielke described it: "the fact that Global Marine has a patent for a deep seabed nodule mining system filed as early as December 1966 that appears to be compatible with the ship and barge system actually constructed, would suggest that the basic technology developed for retrieval of the submarine . . . could readily be transferred to nodule mining. The claw arrangement described in the press for grappling the submarine could be replaced by the mining head described in [the] patent.''[22] Although the United States government, which apparently owns the ship, for some time had difficulty leasing it for mining purposes, in January 1978 a short-term lease was taken out by Global Marine Development, Inc.[23] This firm will operate the ship for Ocean Minerals Company, a consortium between Lockheed Missiles and Space Company (which developed a part of the Hughes technology), Standard Oil Company of Indiana, and several European firms including Royal-Dutch Shell. Evidently the technology that is being used is not fixed area dredging but an air-lift system coupled with a mobile collection device that rests on the ocean floor.

The nature of the technologies so far suggested will greatly affect the economics of nodule mining. It is understood that it is impossible to mine 100 percent of the nodules in a deposit. Some nodules will float away when the bottom is disturbed since their weight is usually only twice that of water. Others will be missed by sweeping patterns or locations of dredges. Still more lie in inaccessible locations or will have assays beneath the minimum cutoff grade. At best, it is likely that only 50 percent of the nodules in a field will be harvested, and collections may average at 25 percent.[24] There is, furthermore, an important relationship between, on the one hand, the type of nodule to be mined and the hardness and typography of the ocean bottom where the deposit lies, and, on the other, the type of dredging system used. Since nodules vary so greatly in size and location, dredging equipment has to be tailored to suit the specific characteristics of a deposit—or, alternatively, deposits have to be chosen to suit the equipment.[25] The continuous path dredge, for example, cannot easily mine areas where nodules are large and highly concentrated or are located in narrow canyons or on escarpments.[26] The fixed-area dredge would require an ocean floor of sufficient hardness to support a heavy engineering device. The continuous line bucket may be the most efficient on a flat or slowly undulating bottom free of potential snags. Whether or not greater flexibility can be introduced into these technologies, and what the cost of doing so will be, remains to be seen, but for the present it seems that the same mine site can be profitably mined by two different miners only if they have nearly identical technologies and identical information about the nature of the deposit and the accompanying bottom terrain.

In order to increase the likelihood that miners will find suitable bottom conditions, types of nodules, and quantities of nodules, industry sources have argued that firms must be given rights to deposits, which may extend over large areas. Deepsea Ventures has suggested that specific claims to areas of deposits be made in one or more blocks of 22,000 square kilometers (or about 8,500 square miles) each, an area probably large enough to provide a 40-year supply of satisfactory nodules for an extraction plant designed to process at least 1,000,000 tons of nodules per year.[27]

There are also uncertainties in the technologies for processing nodules to extract metals. Because of the unique minerology of nodules, entirely new processing techniques are demanded. Five techniques are under consideration and two are undergoing extensive tests, but the results so far are not decisive either in cost or in technical efficiency.[28] Although the details are proprietary, it is clear that the extraction process must also to some extent be tailored to the nature of the deposits and vice versa. One of these methods would produce only the three highest priced metals from the nodules—nickel, copper and cobalt. Large tonnages of nodules are required to obtain enough of these metals for profitable operation, so the dredging system must be able to sustain a relatively high rate of output. Another process would also produce manganese, which is plentiful in nodules. This processing system would require smaller volumes of ore to yield commercial quantities of metals and could be less selective among nodule deposits on the basis of nickel and copper assays. Thus the metallurgical systems must also be designed with the nature of the nodule deposits in mind, which further increases the degree of specialization between the mine site and the means for exploiting it.

Significant attempts have already been made to assess the probable environmental impact of ocean mining. The conclusions so far indicate that the impact will be very minor.[29] Ocean bottoms at abyssal depths are biologically barren, with few living organisms. Dredging will stir bottom sediments up to 20 centimeters below the sea floor and will distribute these materials in the lower 100 or so meters of the water column.[30] Agitation in the path of the dredge may kill some benthic (bottom-living) organisms, especially those with slow rates of reproduction. Others may be smothered when these materials again settle to the bottom. It is certain, however, that mining will for some time be confined to relatively few sites and that within these less than half of the ocean bottom will be disturbed by the action of the dredge. Agitation may transport spores that are dormant in one area of the ocean to other areas where they may be reactivated, but exchanges of this sort caused by mining are minor compared with those caused by natural processes.[31] Nutrient-rich bottom materials and water will be distributed throughout the water column as nodule miners attempt to separate as much silt and mud from the nodules as is possible at the surface before loading ore on barges for shipment to processing plants. The effect of contaminating surface waters with bottom materials is uncertain: phytoplankton growths could be stimulated owing to the elevation of levels of nutrients, or could be limited by the increase in the turbidity in the euphotic zone.[32] Again, the full effects in either direction are likely to be small owing to the relative insignificance of the areas being worked in comparison with the full ocean. It is possible that processing nodules at sea could have harmful environmental consequences if the chemicals used to separate minerals were dumped into the sea without being treated or neutralized. Transportation costs for such processing materials would be much higher than costs for shipping nodules to factories on land,[33] however, and processing at sea could also pose hazards for mining crews, so it is unlikely that it will be done. There would certainly be fewer environmental objections to land processing, since nodules, unlike many land-based ores, are not embedded in sulfuric compounds.[34]

2. ORGANIZATION OF OCEAN MINING

Metals Produced

Ocean mining, if it ever develops into a full-fledged operating industry, will have been largely a response to more than two decades of rising prices of metals. The industry would offer sources of mineral supplies that are substitutes either for land-based deposits or for recycling during an era in which metal prices are expected to rise even faster than previously (see Fig. 25).[35] Extraction costs have been rising for terrestrial ores in the United States owing to environmental constraints, in foreign countries owing to political instability, and in general because of declining assays. Whereas the grade of nickel output in 1890 was about 9 percent, today it is only 2.3 percent; the average content of U.S. and Canadian copper has declined from 0.82 to 0.71 percent.[36] Merely the knowledge that the oceans contain vast resources of minerals seems to be acting as a brake on the prices of terrestrial deposits, and the faster these prices rise the more economical future seabed production becomes. The greater the total future supplies of metals from land and sea, the lower the prices to producers and consumers of countless intermediate and final goods that are high in metal content. Furthermore, the apprehensions that terrestrial mineral sources could be cartelized successfully much like oil supplies (this possibility is discussed in Chapter 9) or that their future prices may begin to fluctuate widely in the way that food prices do give an additional incentive for finding new substitute sources of supply at sea. An ocean mining industry that has nominal spillover effects on the environment and is free of both political interference and restraints on production offers obvious attractions.

The four major minerals that nodules contain are used for a variety of purposes. Manganese is a constituent of dry cell batteries, but its main use is in steelmaking where, depending upon the particular process, it either adds strength or acts as a "scavenger" to remove sulfur and other impurities. Terrestrial manganese ores are widely distributed throughout the globe and for some purposes are superior to the manganese metal that nodules contain. Nickel also is used in steelmaking for its strength and resistance to corrosion. Steel alloys, especially the popular stainless products, are used in many consumer goods

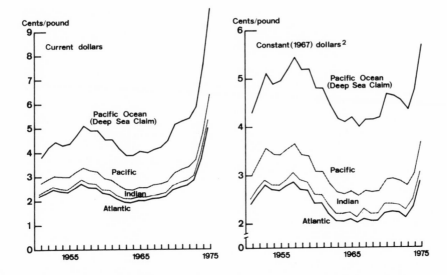

FIG. 25. Gross value during the period 1960−75 of the metals that manganese nodules contain, by location of deposit, in cents per pound.[1]

[1]Weighted sum of the annual average prices of copper, nickel, cobalt, and manganese, where the weights reflect the mineral content of a typical nodule from each ocean.

[2]Deflated by the wholesale-price index.

SOURCE: Michael Gorham, "Dividing Up the Minerals of the Deep Seabed," *Federal Reserve Bank of San Francisco Economic Review*, Winter 1978, p. 9.

industries as well as in the production of such capital goods as jet airplanes and their engines, pollution control equipment, and petroleum refining. Nearly half the supply of nickel is mined in Canada, but the deposits there are apparently giving out and the best ones are now about equal in assay to the average nickel content of nodules. Copper is widely used for electrical conductivity and resistance to corrosion. The United States is the world's major producer of copper, the only metal of the four for which it has important domestic sources. Copper also has the largest world market, about fourteen times the size of the 1976 market for nickel. Both copper and nickel can be extensively recycled, though at great cost. The fourth metal, cobalt, is often obtained as a byproduct of processing nickel and copper ores. Cobalt now has the highest price of the four, but the quantity used is less than one percent of that of copper.[37] Its uses include the manufacture of permanent magnets and steel alloys, where it adds resistance to high temperatures and often can substitute for nickel in resisting corrosion. The distribution of the value of production for these four metals between developed and developing countries in 1971 is shown in Table 39, and the share of each that the United States imports is shown in Table 40. All told, about a

TABLE 39

APPROXIMATE 1971 VALUE OF MINERAL PRODUCTION DIVIDED BETWEEN
DEVELOPED COUNTRIES AND DEVELOPING COUNTRIES

(millions of 1971 dollars)

	Cobalt	Copper	Manganese	Nickel	Total	Percent of World Output
I. TOTAL	$115	$6,125	$223	$445	$6,908	100%
II. Developing Countries	88	2,602	94*	45	2,829*	41
III. Developed Countries	27	3,523	125	395*	4,070*	59
Developed countries						
United States	–	1,522	–	9	1,531	22.2
Canada	11	720	–	186	917	13.3
U.S.S.R.	8	680	76	80	844	12.2
Australia	2	195	11	22	230	3.3
South Africa	–	174	36	9	219	3.2
Japan	–	133	2	–	135	2.0
Poland	–	99	–	–	99	1.4
France	–	–	–	71	71	1.0
Rhodesia	–	–	–	9	9	0.1
Finland	6	–	–	–	6	0.1
Greece	–	–	–	9	9	0.1
Developing countries						
Chile	–	790	–	–	790	11.4
Zambia	10	718	–	–	728	10.5
Zaire	65	449	4	–	518	7.5
Peru	–	235	–	–	235	3.4
Philippines	–	230	–	–	230	3.3
China	–	110	12	–	122	1.8
Mexico	–	70	2	–	72	1.0
Cuba	8	–	–	27	35	0.5
Brazil	–	–	29	–	29	0.4
Gabon	–	–	20	–	20	0.3
India	–	–	20	–	20	0.3
Indonesia	–	–	–	18	18	0.3
Morocco	5	–	–	–	5	0.1
Ghana	–	–	7	–	7	0.1

NOTE: Countries are listed in ranking order of the value of the four metals combined. Each of the countries listed produces at least one percent of the world production of one of the four metals. An * indicates an adjustment has been made owing to an error in the original source.

SOURCE: *U.S. Working Paper on the Economic Effects of Deep Seabed Exploitation,* UN Doc. A/CONF.62/ C.1/L.5 (July 31, 1974), p. 11. Data were taken from UNCTAD documents TD/B/449/Add. 1; TD/B/484; TD/B/483; TD/113/Sup.4; UN Doc. A/CONF.62/25; and U.S. Department of the Interior, 1971 *Minerals Yearbook.*

TABLE 40

IMPORTANT METALLIC CONSTITUENTS OF MANGANESE NODULES
IN RELATION TO U.S. METAL IMPORTS

Metal	Main Land-Based Producers	Fraction of U.S. Needs Imported	Sources of U.S. Imports	Main Uses	Potential Land-Based Sources
Nickel	Canada (37%) U.S.S.R. (21%) New Caledonia (16%) (3 firms dominate)	60-65%	Canada (66%)	Steel*	Canada, U.S., Guatemala, Colombia
Manga-nese	U.S.S.R. (40%) South Africa (15%) Gabon (12%) Brazil (10%) Australia (7%) India (6%)	100%	Gabon Brazil	Steel†	Many
Cobalt	Zaire (60-65%) Zambia (10%) Canada (9%)	100%	Zaire (80%) Norway (8%) Canada (6%)	Steel*	New Caledonia, Australia Many
Copper	U.S., Canada CIPEC‡	10%	CIPEC Canada	Electrical equipment	Numerous

*As a constituent of alloys.
†As a deoxidizing and desulfurizing agent, and as a constituent of alloys.
‡Council of Copper Exporting Countries (Australia, Chile, Indonesia, Papua-New Guinea, Peru, Zaire, and Zambia).

SOURCE: U.S. Council on International Economic Policy, *Critical Imported Materials,* special report, December 1974, reprinted in Basil N. Petrou and R. David Ranson, "Resources from the World's Deep Seabeds: The Law and Economics of an Unborn Industry" (Washington, D.C., draft mimeo, 1975).

dozen developing countries produce one or more of the four metals that nodules contain, but only four of these (Chile, Gabon, Zaire, and Zambia) derive a significant fraction of their total foreign exchange earnings from minerals.[38]

The U.S. Department of the Interior has estimated that nickel will be the most profitable metal from ocean mining and will contribute about 70 percent of the industry's total revenues through the 1980s.[39] Although world demand for nickel is anticipated to rise by only 3 percent,[40] higher nickel prices should stimulate new investments in land and seabed mining, with ocean mine sites having operating costs that are similar but investment costs that are lower.[41]

Table 41 shows that nodules contain the four metals in proportions that differ significantly from the relative quantities that are demanded in world markets. Because of the given proportions between metal quantities that a given batch of nodules will contain, it would be difficult to produce just one metal without getting a certain output of other ores or metals as byproducts. (The same situation

TABLE 41

PROPORTIONS OF METALS TYPICALLY CONTAINED IN NODULES RELATIVE TO THE
PROPORTIONS OF WORLD MARKET DEMANDS

Metal	Proportion in Typical Nodules	Proportion of Quantities Demanded in World Markets
Manganese	90.0	56.0
Copper	4.5	40.0
Nickel	4.6	4.0
Cobalt	0.9	0.15
	100.0%	ca. 100.00%

SOURCE: Robert E. Osgood, Ann L. Hollick, Charles S. Pearson, and James C. Orr, *Toward a National Ocean Policy: 1976 and Beyond* (Washington, D.C.: National Science Foundation, 1975), p. 165.

is found in terrestrial mining, where cobalt or nickel can be relatively inexpensive byproducts of copper, and in a variety of other joint products such as beef and hides or blood and blood plasma.) The scale of nodule processing suggests that each complete mining operation will supply trivial quantities of copper and nickel relative to their world demands, but significant amounts of manganese and cobalt.

The potential versatility in the production of different metals from nodules is one of the industry's main attractions. Though there might be a significant increase in demand for only one of the metals—nickel, shall we say—the lack of increased demand for the other three would not necessarily deter the future development of the whole industry.[42] Since one nodule contains some portions of all four metals, the additional materials produced as byproducts of nickel, for example, may be sold profitably as long as the price each one brings exceeds the costs of extracting and processing it. In other words, once a nodule mining and processing system had been constructed and nodules harvested, the marginal costs of producing salable metals other than nickel might well turn out to be relatively low compared with the gains. Not only could the four major metals be produced, but other minor metals that nodules contain—such as molybdenum, vanadium, silver, and zinc—could become byproducts if individual prices exceeded the extra costs of production.

The ocean miner's choice of which materials to produce from nodules depends on the same kind of analysis that is involved in the classic problem of joint products in economics—that is, whether the cattle rancher should produce only the beef from his steers or their beef and hides together. The rancher will make a profit if the beef brings a price of, say, $750 and it costs only $600 to raise and slaughter each steer. If it costs more to process the hide than it will bring in the leather market, then the hide will be discarded along with other waste portions of the animal. If the marginal cost of tanning and processing the hide as a byproduct is $100 and the marginal revenue from the sale of each hide is $150, then obviously the hide will not be discarded if the rancher seeks to increase his profits. The ranching operation that had $150 profit per steer when beef alone was being produced would have 33 percent additional profit if the price of hides exceeded their marginal costs by $50. The importance of the hides takes on different proportions if different assumptions are made about the price and cost of beef. For example, if the cost of raising a steer increases to $800 and the other elements of the problem are unchanged, then producing the hide along with the beef will be essential to the continued profitability of the enterprise as a whole. Although the firm's "beef division" may incur accounting losses, the costs of the beef division and the "hides division" may be exceeded by their combined revenues. The rancher will also produce both beef and hides if in the original case the demand for beef falls so that each steer now fetches only $575 in the beef market. In this case the rancher will have to cease production altogether unless the revenue from hides exceeds the costs by at least $26.

The essential economic principle in each of these examples is that the gross profitability of the entire ranching operation will be determined by the algebraic sum of the subprofitabilities of each individual division (beef, hides, meal made from the bones of the steer, and so on), and will not be geared strictly to the price of beef alone. The hides and other products of cattle raising are analogous to the cobalt, manganese, and possibly other materials that will become the joint products of nodules. Mine sites may be chosen now mainly for their relative content of nickel if its demand presently is rising fastest, just as steers may be bred more (but not solely) for their quality of beef rather than for hides if the value of the beef happens to be proportionately large. But there will probably be opportunities for additional profit through the sale of byproducts, and ocean miners can be expected to take advantage of them. (Changes in the relative prices of nickel and cobalt or nickel and manganese may still present profit opportunities for miners since the processing of nodules for nickel and copper yields these materials anyway.) The selection of particular mine sites for dredging will, of course, be made on the basis of their overall net profitability as determined by world demand for these metals and marginal costs of processing.

Potential Economic Rents

Projections of future product demands and prices are almost always a hazardous undertaking because there are so many variables that can affect the result. In the case of metals, increased demands depend not only on increases in population and world income but also on changes in the prices of other metals that can be substitutes for these metals in the production of final goods and on inputs that are complementary in production. Increased supplies of cobalt as a

TABLE 42

PROSPECTIVE DEEP-SEA PRODUCTION OF SELECTED MINERALS RELATIVE TO TOTAL
U.S. DEMAND, U.S. IMPORT DEMAND, AND WORLD DEMAND FOR THESE
MINERALS IN 1985 AND 2000

(in percent)

Mineral	1985			2000		
	Total U.S. Demand	U.S. Import Demand	World Demand	Total U.S. Demand	U.S. Import Demand	World Demand
Manganese	85.0	85.0	9.0	636.0	636.0	49.0
Copper	6.0	18.0	1.0	17.0	30.0	3.0
Cobalt	398.0	398.0	83.0	1,600.0	1,600.0	215.0
Nickel	85.0	97.0	20.0	273.0	307.0	48.0

SOURCE: David B. Johnson and Dennis E. Logue, "U.S. Economic Interests in Law of the Sea Issues," in Ryan C. Amacher and Richard James Sweeney, eds., *The Law of the Sea: U.S. Interests and Alternatives* (Washington, D.C.: American Enterprise Institute for Public Policy Research, 1976), p. 45.

result of nodule production will, for example, have some effect upon the market for nickel because one can be substituted for the other in the production of steel alloys, but the effect will necessarily be slight simply because the total volume of cobalt production will still be much less than that of nickel even after nodule production begins. It is likely, too, that the prices of manganese and cobalt will decline, since the expected ocean supplies of these metals will be larger than present terrestrial supplies. One should expect, however, that the discovery of new and possibly exotic uses of these metals will be stimulated if prices fall sharply.[43]

Some of the difficulties of projection were taken into account by David B. Johnson and Dennis E. Logue in their analysis of various estimates of the supplies of each metal relative to world and U.S. demands.[44] Their data are shown in Table 42. They assumed that six firms would be in operation by 1985, of which three would be U.S. firms, and that thirty firms would begin operation by 2000.[45] Their data suggest that a significant portion of U.S. demand and imports can be supplied by deep-sea sources in 1985 and even more by 2000. The effect on U.S. imports is especially great since nodules are expected to offer ores at prices that are less than the cost of extracting metals from U.S. domestic deposits.

An estimate of the value of nodule production to the U.S. was made by Robert R. Nathan and Associates.[46] They assumed that by 1985 some 7,000,000 tons of nodules per year would be produced by three U.S. firms. Their results, valued at 1973 prices of the four major metals, are presented in Table 43. Their conclusions were:

the total value of manganese nodule mining activity around 1985 could be projected at about $534 million at 1973 prices. Roughly one-third of this, or about $180 million, could be attributed to marine mining activity, the balance being value added in onshore processing. In actuality . . . the indicated volume of metal production, compared with demand, is likely to have a depressing effect on the market prices for both cobalt and manganese. Only in a commercial sense, however, would this reduce the value of the marine output. In an economic, or "opportunity cost," sense, the value of the marine-source manganese and cobalt would include the saving achieved by not having to use metal from the displaced terrestrial sources. In other words, the substitute manganese and cobalt from the ocean would be worth at least the value of the terrestrial manganese and cobalt which they replaced—or even more if the lower prices were to permit increased consumption.[47]

Estimating future demands and prices in terms of 1973 dollars, they calculated that the value to the United States of nodule production by U.S. firms would be

TABLE 43

ESTIMATED 1985 RECOVERY OF METALS BY U.S. DEEP-OCEAN MINING
ENTERPRISES, AND VALUE AT 1973 PRICES

Item	Nickel	Copper	Cobalt	Manganese
Approximate average content in initially mined ore (%)	1.25	1.15	0.25	28
Deepsea Ventures–1 million tons of ore:				
Recoverable metal (tons) per 100 tons of ore at 95% recovery rate	1.2	1.1	.24	27
Tons of metal recovered (thousands)	12	11	2.4	270
Other operations–6 million tons of ore:*				
Percent of metal recovered	80	80	50	–
Recoverable metal (tons) per 100 tons of ore	1.00	.92	.12	–
Tons of metal recovered (thousands)	60	55	7.2	–
Total tons of metal recovered (thousands)	72	66	9.6	270
Price per ton (dollars) (1973)[†]	3,050	1,200	5,740	660
Gross value at 1973 prices (millions of dollars)	220	79	55	180

*Original data from Hammond (II), pp. 644–46.
†U.S. Bureau of Mines, Commodity Data Summaries, 1974.
SOURCE: *Economic Value of Ocean Resources to the United States*, p. 21.

$129 million in 1985 and $278 million in 2000. These results are shown in Table 44. Most of this value is accounted for by reduced imports and increased security of supply. But these gains would decline if an international authority were created to regulate nodule production and if it levied royalties on mining or enacted regulations that discriminated against U.S. firms.[48]

The economic rents to the U.S. from nodule production depend upon the reduction in prices of the four major metals rather than upon savings in foreign exchange (which are simply a gain to the U.S. at the expense of the particular mineral-exporting country). This rent would amount to the difference between the price of terrestrial metals that the U.S. would potentially import and the price of these metals when extracted from nodules. This difference would be captured by the U.S. at large regardless of whether or not the nodules were produced by U.S. firms. Assuming that only the price of cobalt declined, the Robert R. Nathan report estimated economic rents to the U.S. of about $33 million in 1985 and $65 million in 2000; if byproducts of cobalt also displaced U.S. imports, the rents could rise to $51 million in 1985 and $95 million in 2000 (see Table 8).[49] These estimates of rent, however, appear low when compared to the number of ocean mining consortia that have been formed and the huge investments that they are now contemplating. The estimates may also be low since the production of copper and nickel from nodules is likely to prevent the prices of terrestrial deposits of these metals from rising as fast as they would if there were no ocean mining. On the other hand, the rents could be reduced drastically if a prospective international authority were able to control the price of cobalt without eliminating the production of other metals—as it could surely do if it were the exclusive producer of metals from nodules, and could probably do even if it allowed private firms access to ocean deposits, since cobalt would have the least value of the four metals. United States consumers of metals would still gain the increased value of import substitution even if the international authority discriminated against U.S. firms as long as it did not attempt to monopolize nodule production or otherwise tamper with market prices. The more extensive international regulation becomes, the more uncertain future rents become.

Impact on Terrestrial Producers

Tables 39 and 45 together provide a rough indication of the impact of nodule production on various terrestrial producers of the four metals. These data, assembled from United Nations studies and contained in a Working Paper by the United States delegation which was presented to the 1974 session of UNCLOS at Caracas, suggest order-of-magnitude estimates for the value of metal production based on 1971 prices.[50] For copper, the value of production is, from Table 39, nearly eight times as large as the values of production for the other three metals

TABLE 44

Projected Total Revenue from Aggregate U.S. Production of the Four
Metals That Nodules Contain and the Portion of Revenue That Is
Attributable to Ocean Mining, Estimated for 1985 and 2000

(in 1973 dollars)

Metals	1985			2000		
	Output (thousand short tons)	Price (per ton)	Total Revenue (millions)	Output (thousand short tons)	Price (per ton)	Total Revenue (millions)
Manganese	270.0	$ 200	$ 54	540.0	$ 200	$108
Cobalt	9.6	1,500	14	19.2	1,500	28
Nickel	72.0	2,900	209	144.0	3,040	438
Copper	66.0	1,660	110	132.0	1,980	261
Total			387			835
Approximate amount attributable to ocean mining			129			278

Source: *Economic Value of Ocean Resources to the United States,* p. 26.

combined. In 1971, developed countries generated 57.5 percent of the world's terrestrial copper, 56.0 percent of the manganese, and 89.9 percent of the nickel. Only cobalt was produced more by developing countries, with developed countries producing only 23.5 percent of the world supply. It is also clear from Table 39 that most countries produce at least one metal as a byproduct of another. Zaire, the world's largest producer of cobalt, retrieves this metal as a byproduct of copper, the value of production of which was more than seven times greater than that of cobalt. It follows that if Zaire were harmed by a drastic decline in the price of cobalt owing to the nodules, it would still benefit from the anticipated increase in the demand for copper, of which it is the sixth largest producer in the world. Among the three other developing-country producers of cobalt, Zambia and Cuba, like Zaire, generate cobalt as a byproduct of either nickel or copper. Only Morocco, the world's smallest producer of cobalt (and also Finland among the developed countries), has ores that yield cobalt as a primary product rather than a byproduct.

Table 45 contains the U.S. delegation's 1971 estimates of future production of the four metals from seabeds, from terrestrial sources, and from all sources combined. Assuming that the division of terrestrial production between developing and developed countries will remain about the same, the delegation concluded that the projected income of terrestrial producers will increase by more than 50 percent by 1980 even with the advent of seabed production.

TABLE 45

FUTURE VALUE OF MINERAL PRODUCTION, TERRESTRIAL AND OCEAN,
DIVIDED BETWEEN DEVELOPED COUNTRIES AND DEVELOPING COUNTRIES, AS
ESTIMATED IN 1971 BY THE U.S. DELEGATION TO UNCLOS

(millions of 1971 dollars)

	Cobalt	Copper	Manganese	Nickel	Total
Landbased					
Developing countries					
1971	88	2,602	94	45	2,829
1980	99	4,036	110	131	4,376
1985	106	5,214	150	175	5,645
Developed countries					
1971	27	3,523	125	395	4,070
1980	31	5,346	200	486	6,063
1985	34	6,755	213	650	7,652
Seabeds					
1971	0	0	0	0	0
1980	70	123	12	135	340
1985	120	158	33	181	492
Total					
1971	115	6,125	219	440	6,899
1980	200	9,505	322	752	10,779
1985	260	12,127	396	1,006	13,789

SOURCE: See Table 39.

Costs, Rates of Entry, and Claims

It has been estimated that the total costs over a five-to-ten-year period to explore a mine site and construct enough dredging equipment and processing plants to handle about 3,000,000 tons of dry nodules per year would amount to $300-500 million (1975).[51] The principal economy of scale in ocean mining appears to lie in processing, so two or three separate dredging operations may be required for each processing plant.[52] Only 3-10 percent of the total cost is estimated to be due to prospecting and exploring a mine site.[53] These cost conditions and the combined uncertainties of locating, dredging, and extracting metals from nodules suggest that the industry will for some time have relatively few firms and low rates of entry. Consortia, such as the four that are presently in existence, offer obvious advantages, not only of spreading the risk and drawing wider support for ocean mining among various governments, but also of direct financing as opposed to loans, since bankers have for the most part been skeptical of deep-sea mining. More than 100 separate firms (either private or national) around the globe are now involved in the industry in some way,[54] and the abundance of mining sites at sea makes the likelihood of monopoly elements extremely small.

It is now generally anticipated that there will be as many as six actual mining operations by 1985.[55] From the start, however, the industry has tended to be overoptimistic about its prospects, and one must bear in mind that the possibilities of high-quality mine sites will probably exceed by far their real exploitation for many years to come.[56] Between 180 and 460 commercially workable sites are believed to exist, of which between 80 and 190 are prime sites located in the area of the northeastern Pacific Ocean noted earlier. Thus the number of mine sites of the best quality is likely to be at least four times and perhaps as much as twenty times the number of miners by the year 2000.[57]

Ocean miners complain that the activity of the industry has been stymied both by the absence of a firm United States policy and by the slow deliberations at UNCLOS. All the important technical barriers to the recovery and processing of manganese nodules have been solved, they say, but the construction of expensive dredging and processing systems for regular operation cannot proceed until political and legal uncertainties have been removed. In the words of one prominent representative of a mining firm, "there is no longer any doubt [in 1975] about the technical and economic feasibility of ocean mining. The technology is ready; the investment climate is not."[58]

These uncertainties appear to be of two kinds.[59] First, miners and their bankers seek some sort of legal assurances that mine sites which they have prospected and explored, at considerable expense, will not be usurped by rival mining firms or interfered with during dredging operations by foreign governments. So far, miners have no recourse against such actions in international courts, nor have ocean mining investments been licensed in any way by United States policy or legislation. Furthermore, there is a distinct possibility that UNCLOS may produce a treaty that is unfavorable to mining by private firms. A treaty that established substantial royalties or taxes on ocean mining, or retroactively modified boundaries of mine sites, or created international institutions to govern ocean mining in the name of all mankind could very well be prejudicial to the economic interests of these largely American-led consortia and could reduce the economic rents that they would otherwise collect. Ocean miners are understandably reluctant to enter into the most expensive and risky phase of their activities, making financial commitments perhaps in excess of a half-billion dollars, without "deeds" to mine sites from some governmental authority or else assurances from their own government that a treaty which is unfavorable to ocean mining will not be negotiated without indemnifying their previous investments.

One indication of the seriousness of the concerns of ocean miners was the filing of a claim by Deepsea Ventures, Inc. in 1974 with the U.S. Secretary of

State to an area in the northeast Pacific Ocean.[60] The mine site (Fig. 26), which Deepsea says it discovered in August 1969, amounts to 60,000 square kilometers (an area more than twice the size of Ireland). The nodules lie in depths of between 2,300 and 5,000 meters, more than 1,000 kilometers from the nearest island, and more than 1,300 kilometers seaward of the outer edge of the nearest continental margin. Thus the area claimed lies beyond the limits of jurisdiction presently set by any coastal nation. The Deepsea claim states that "it has discovered and taken possession of, and is now engaged in developing and evaluating [the deposit], as the first stage of mining," and that it asserts "the exclusive rights to develop, evaluate and mine the Deposit and to take, use, and sell all of the manganese nodules in, and the minerals and metals derived therefrom."[61] On the basis of an elaborate legal argument which it submitted justifying the validity of the claim under international law, Deepsea requested "the diplomatic protection of the United States Government with respect to the exclusive mining rights described and asserted in the foregoing Claim, and any other rights which may hereafter accrue to Deepsea as a result of its activities at the site of the Deposit, and similar protection of the integrity of its investments heretofore made and now being undertaken, and to be undertaken in the future."[62]

This presentation has so far received no official support from the U.S. Department of State; its response did not go beyond emphasizing that ocean mining is a high seas freedom, and thus the matter is still quite unresolved. The question of what sort of property system would be necessary for exclusive rights to deep-sea mine sites is of great interest, however. In Section 3 I shall discuss this. Section 4 will analyze several arguments to determine whether economic inefficiency could be avoided without the creation of property rights or international regulatory arrangements, and Section 5 will analyze the question of whether economic inefficiency could be avoided with them.

3. BASIC FEATURES OF A PROPERTY SYSTEM[63]

A property system contains four components: (1) an unambiguous description of the resource, or in the case of land, well-defined procedures for delimiting boundaries; (2) exclusivity in capturing the benefits of its use; (3) enforcement at low cost against unauthorized use; and (4) procedures for registering claims and allowing transfers among economic agents (such as a tract index in the case of land). The importance of each point is best seen by its absence. Ambiguity in the definition of rights raises negotiation or litigation costs and thus restricts exchanges. Nonexclusivity of rights reduces the incentives to acquire the economically efficient quantity of information on the value of the resource in different uses and to devote the resource to its highest valued use. The results

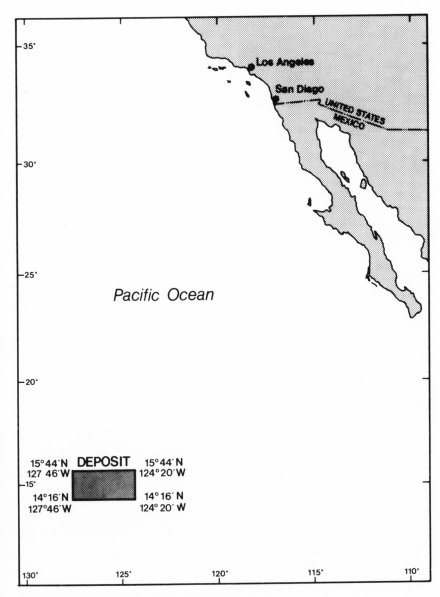

FIG. 26.   Mine Site in Northeastern Pacific Ocean Claimed by Deepsea Ventures, Inc.
on November 15, 1974.

SOURCE: Deepsea Ventures, Inc., *Notice of Discovery and Claim of Exclusive Mining Rights, and Request for Diplomatic Protection and Protection of Investment,* filed with the U.S. Secretary of State, Washington, D.C., November 15, 1974.

are the same if there are relatively high costs of enforcing against trespass. Restraints or other legal rules that increase the cost of exchange diminish incentives for allocating rights to more productive uses. If exchange costs are low, such features of rights packages as the size of tracts need not be optimal at the start since subsequent transactions will gradually rearrange the tracts into efficient configurations.[64] Wherever practical, competitive bidding at auctions is one of the possible low-cost methods for assigning initial rights bundles among potential users. Auction bidding lessens the opportunity for making assignments on the basis of influence or favors, and it enhances the likelihood that the rights will be acquired by the most efficient users.

Property rights should not be established, however, for reasons of economic efficiency, when any of four conditions occurs.

First, it would be unnecessary to create rights to "free" goods—that is, commodities that no one would pay to obtain more of and hence do not command prices. But nodules are not free goods, even though no one presently owns them. The nonuniformity of nodule location and quality makes it necessary that costs be incurred to find and mine deposits. Scientists have speculated that the world's total supply of nodules may be greater than could ever be used: its absolute rate of accumulation is enormous even though its percentage rate of accumulation is small.[65] But it is unlikely that nodules of the best qualities and locations are growing at the fastest rates. It is more plausible that the wide variability that characterizes known deposits will apply also to newly discovered deposits.

Second, property rights should not be created when the cost of assigning or enforcing them through markets exceeds their value. In these cases zero-priced resources can be consistent with avoiding economic inefficiency. This situation applied to most ocean resources during the era of unrestricted high seas freedoms before World War II. The lack of congestion made it unnecessary to ration available ocean space among competing uses or claimants. Since the number of ocean miners is for some time likely to be small relative to the number of high-quality mine sites, a complex property system for nodules may be avoidable at least until congestion causes scarcity in the selection and dredging of deposits.

Third, regulatory authorities do not always have uniform incentives to avoid economic inefficiency. Although the creation of a regulatory body may improve resource allocation by eliminating some inefficiencies, it may create significant new inefficiencies which will make it impossible for all the benefits from regulation to exceed its total costs. Studies of regulated industries of various kinds in the United States have revealed inefficiency losses that can be attributed directly to regulation, and therefore call into question its overall economic desirability. A decision for or against regulation—creating and enforcing a property system—on economic grounds must include some a priori assessment of the total costs and gains of each major regulatory alternative.

Fourth, regulation should be imposed on an industry only at the moment when enough information is available to indicate that all the expected gains from regulation would exceed all the expected costs. Recent attempts to deregulate several industries in the United States suggest that inappropriate regulations, once in place, are expensive to change, if not irreversible, since the beneficiaries of regulation oppose reforms.

4. ECONOMIC RATIONALE FOR REGULATING OCEAN MINING

The legal principle currently governing ocean mining is that of "open access," meaning that any miner may dredge as he pleases in international waters under traditional high seas rights.[66] Existing law gives the miner secure ownership of his dredges, ships, and shore-based processing facilities—all the resources used in mining except the nodules lying on the ocean floor. Without new regulations, no miner will have exclusive rights to unmined nodules until he has got them aboard ship, and he will certainly not have permanent rights to unmined deposits on the ocean bottom where harvesting occurs. The two economic arguments favoring regulation hinge on the absence of exclusive property rights to unmined deposits and whether this absence will lead to economically optimal investment decisions. The first argument claims that nodule exploitation would tend to be too low because of the "free-rider" problem, and the second claims that investment would be too great because of the "common pool" problem. The suggested solution in each case of inefficiency is to create a property system to remove the inefficiency.

The Free-Rider Problem

One argument for regulating the exploitation of nodules is that the absence of property rights in unmined deposits would inhibit a miner's incentives to engage in the optimal degree of searching and dredging since the benefits of these investments would not return to him exclusively—other miners who did not search for deposits would inevitably gain from the first miner's searches.[67]

To take an example, assume that one miner begins to dredge a mine site after completing a five-year program of exploration and investment in mining and processing facilities. A second miner has incurred the same costs as the first except for the costs of search. Rather than search independently for his own mine site, the second miner decides to dredge strictly on the basis of what he can ascertain of the first miner's knowledge of the deposit. By means of radar or visual sightings, the second miner follows along after the first, taking care to avoid the same tracks that he has dredged because of the unlikelihood of finding suitable concentrations of nodules there, and also being careful not to foul his dredging gear in the other's since this would impose costs on them both. The second miner, in other words, becomes a poacher or a free-rider on his competitor's investment in search. If the free-rider's dredging is almost as efficient as the searcher's dredging, his overall rate of return will be greater than the searcher's, simply because he has had no searching costs. According to this argument, then, unless search efforts are given legal protection against poaching, no miner will have economic incentives to play the role of the searcher. And therefore, since no miner can have the exclusive benefits of search, the amount of search and investment in the industry will be inefficiently low, and the final prices of metals will be higher than otherwise. The solution to the resulting economic inefficiency of too little investment would appear to be to give searchers protection against free-riders by creating exclusive rights to unmined deposits.

The basic premise of the free-rider argument is that the expensive search activities of the exploratory miners in finding valuable and technically suitable deposits would become public knowledge once their initial dredging began. The validity of the free-rider argument hinges on the cost to searchers of keeping their information on nodule deposits private and confidential. These data include maps of bottom terrain, samples of ores, and bottom sightings with sonar and closed-circuit television. This information is valuable since detailed searching would usually generate a higher rate of return than random dredging without search. But there are also several economic forces that would inhibit incentives for free-riding by preventing these trade secrets from automatically becoming public knowledge once the exploratory miner starts to dredge.

First, only in a world of zero information and adjustment costs would each miner have identical information on the location of the most profitable nodule deposits. The number of deposits of prime quality appears to be large, and the number of minimum quality is even larger, relative to the likely number of miners over the next twenty or thirty years. Different miners will have differing beliefs about the the profitability of various deposits, and it is this distribution of beliefs together with the large number of deposits that will induce miners usually to spread out for dredging rather than to cluster.

Second, free-riders would give up the opportunity cost of independent search which might perhaps reveal deposits of even greater value than they would find by shadowing the searching miner.

Third, the searcher's dredging activity tells the potential free-rider only that he has found a deposit of minimum quality which fits his dredging and processing technologies. The free-rider who observes or imitates the dredging activities of another miner does not necessarily obtain reliable maps or other information about the extent of the field, its average assay of ore, the bottom terrains and sediments three miles down, or the most efficient sweeping patterns for this area.

If free-riding yields only a slight amount of information, miners would not forego investment in search out of a fear of free-riding, provided that is, that their accurate data could be kept exclusive and confidential even though rights to unmined deposits were not exclusive under an open-access policy for ocean mining.[68] As long as the searcher's costs are substantial and his work cannot be duplicated cheaply by free-riders unless sold or publicly disseminated, the searcher's investment will be protected even in the absence of legal rights to the deposit.[69] Indeed, rather than free-riding, it would usually be in the interest of new miners to purchase data from searchers, or buy an equity in them, or hire away their employees, or search independently.

Fourth, the dredging technologies and the processing technologies of the searcher and the free-rider may have important differences. Evidently the entire mining system must be carefully tailored to the conditions of the particular mine site, taking into account variations in depth, bottom conditions, and size and concentration of nodules. This implies that a mine site that fits the searcher's system may not fit the free-rider's. Their dredgers may differ in a variety of features—the required strength of bottom sediments, flexibility in accommodating risky and variable bottom terrain, tolerances for nodules of certain types and concentrations, and the cost of processing batches having significantly different assays. The greater these differences are, the greater the incentives of most miners to spread out rather than to cluster. And of course free-riders, having no detailed data as the result of search, cannot choose their sites to suit their equipment.

Fifth, the incentives for free-riding would be reduced if it were inexpensive for miners to reach an agreement on the exclusive use of a particular mine site by just one of them. The extra gain derived from exclusiveness would be the maximum that either miner would pay the other in a bargain for sole use. Assume that this extra gain is greatest for the searcher and also that the costs of obtaining information, making, and enforcing exchanges are negligible. If the searcher. could have legal protection against free-riding, he would retain exclusive use since the amount that the second miner would pay for the deposit would be less than its value to the searcher. If it were not, the searcher would sell. But even if the searcher did not have legal protection—which is in fact the situation at present—he would still retain exclusive use since he would pay the second miner an amount that was less than the maximum value of the deposit to him but at least one dollar greater than the cost to the second miner of shifting to the next-best deposit. As long as transactions costs are trivial, the allocation of resources—the exploitation of the deposit by the highest valued user—would not be influenced by the assignment of property rights.[70]

The incentives of miners to divide deposits formally, or even to agree tacitly to avoid one another's area of search, would depend upon the level of transactions and enforcement costs. These would vary according to the number, size, and value of deposits, the number of miners, and monitoring technologies. The cost of making agreements of this kind between two or more ocean miners is likely to be relatively low for the foreseeable future since the number of miners is likely to be small relative to the number of profitable deposits. These costs could be even smaller if the developers of mining technologies were able to lease their dredges with territorial restrictions, taking their profits partly in the form of production royalties or some other tie-in arrangement.

In sum, the cost advantages of free-riding are doubtful because of the cost of obtaining reliable information without purchasing it or searching independently, the opportunity costs of forgoing independent search, differences between miners' technologies and the physical characteristics of mine sites, and the possibility of de facto agreements to divide deposits. Judging strictly on an a priori analysis, one cannot say definitely that investment would be suboptimal without regulations creating exclusive property rights, and it appears that arguments to this effect by the proponents of regulation of ocean mining are not persuasive.

The Common Pool Problem

The inefficiencies of common pool situations should not be found in ocean mining because nodules lack the fugitive characteristics of fish or underground fluids: they do not wander or flow markedly. Unlike the competitive drilling of oil from a common reservoir, dredging nodules at one location should not affect the cost of dredging elsewhere. Therefore, an ocean miner would not have incentives to hasten dredging out of a concern that the nodules in a particular deposit will not stay put. Unlike fish, nodules do not reproduce or grow at rates that significantly affect the present value of the current stock. The absolute rate of growth from the existing stock of nodules is large in tonnage because the stock is large, even though each nodule may acquire only a few layers of atoms per year. But the percentage rate of growth of the stock is trivial and, unlike fish, can for all practical purposes be ignored.[71] Hence, regulations designed to reduce the extraction rates for fish and oil because of their physical characteristics should not be necessary in order for nodules to be extracted at the economically efficient rate.

It is also unlikely that there would be a competitive race to dredge unowned deposits out of a fear that other miners would get them first. Ocean miners would not have incentives to dredge at greater-than-optimal rates if: (1) detailed searching and mapping generated a higher rate of return than random dredging without search; and (2) information on deposits were available only at significant cost and could be kept confidential. Exclusive rights to unmined deposits would not be required to bring forth the optimal rate of exploitation provided expensive search information could be maintained as a trade secret. This applies a fortiori if deposits must be tailored to particular dredging technologies, or vice versa.[72]

It is possible, however, that there may be too much search to locate profitable deposits, like a land rush, in which there may be personal benefits to the individual who arrives on the scene five minutes ahead of his competitors but at the same time, from society's point of view, wastes resources. The total cost of search would be lower if individuals had exclusive, nonoverlapping rights to evaluate and select parcels of land in different regions. The problem lies not in the absence of exclusive ownership rights to unmined deposits but in the absence of exclusive rights to search. Overinvestment in competitive search effort is found in a multitude of markets for resources that are exclusively owned, such as jobs and common stocks, as well as in markets for resources that are not exclusively owned, such as oil and fish, as was seen in Chapters 4 and 5. There is no reason to suspect that the inefficiency caused by common pool ownership of search rights would be greater for nodules than for other resources on land or sea.

On the basis of the foregoing economic analysis, one cannot give a decisive answer to the claims that the search, investment, and production of nodules would be nonoptimal without exclusive and enforced rights to unmined deposits. But it does suggest that a policy favoring regulation cannot be supported on economic grounds until more is known about the industry's costs, technologies, operating conditions, and incentives. It is possible that the gains from search and investment even in the absence of legal protection may be sufficiently large to avoid inefficient resource allocation, thus enabling a regulatory apparatus to be avoided. Even if there were incentives to overinvest or underinvest, the pertinent question becomes whether the extent of resource misallocation due to the unregulated nonoptimal level of investment is greater than the expected level of resource misallocation due to imposition of the regulatory mechanism.

5. ALTERNATIVE REGULATORY MECHANISMS

The principal controversy concerning the deep seabed minerals at UNCLOS has not been over whether there should be regulation but rather over how much there should be. The main reason at UNCLOS for regulating ocean mining has been to redistribute the world's wealth; avoiding inefficient resource use has been only a minor concern. Three international regulatory alternatives—a registry office, a licensing authority, and an operating authority—have been proposed. They will be evaluated here for their impact on efficiency. The question of distribution will be treated in Chapter 9.

International Registry Office

Of the three proposed regulatory mechanisms, a registry clearing house would be the weakest. It would involve the establishing of an international agency to which participating nations would bring claims in behalf of their citizens to explore and exploit a certain portion of the seabed. Claims would be recorded on a first-come, first-served basis. The initiative in recording claims would lie in the participating nations rather than in the agency itself, although the agency might share in tax revenues collected by the participating nation from ocean mining. The recording nations would license firms or individuals to mine the claims according to the applicable civil, criminal, tax, and other law of each nation. The registry would have no powers of enforcement or policing other than to inspect and would have practically no power to resolve disputes over competing first-in-time claims to particular sites among two or more recording nations or their miners.[73]

An institution of this type would have an adverse effect on efficient exploitation if registration were mandatory for dredging and if comprehensive data on the nature and location of the deposit had to be made public as a precondition for recording. Forcing the dissemination of confidential and valuable data could raise the gains from free-riding, which would reduce the returns from independent search.

International Licensing Authority

An international licensing authority would have jurisdiction over seabed use beyond the simple registration of claims. It would establish property arrangements designed to prevent the serious inefficiencies that are alleged to accompany open access in spite of the fact that such arrangements do not appear to be necessary. The nature of this regulatory alternative is best illustrated by the Draft Convention on the International Seabed Area and the proposal to create an International Seabed Resource Authority, which were submitted to UNCLOS in 1970 by the United States delegation.[74] This document has since been modified by the negotiating process. It is used here only to reveal one of the tangible regulatory options that is open to UNCLOS and to illustrate the policies that were at one time advocated by the nation most interested in ocean mining.

One of the most striking features of the U.S. proposal is the high transactions costs of decision making in the seabed authority. An assembly composed of all nations that ratified the treaty would vest administrative functions in a council of twenty-four states selected according to a complex formula in order to assure "balance" in terms of world wealth and geography. Specifically, of the twenty-four states, six would be the most industrially advanced members of the assembly measured by gross national product. At least twelve of the remaining eighteen would be developing countries, and at least two would be either land- or shelf-locked. An affirmative decision of the council would require a series of consents involving its entire membership and certain subgroups of states: a majority of at least thirteen of the total membership of twenty-four states; four of the six developed countries; and twelve of the other eighteen nations. Any three developed countries or nine other states could block action.[75] This division of authority between an assembly and a council is much like that of the United Nations itself, in which there is a General Assembly where each nation has one vote and a Security Council where voting is weighted. A seabed authority organized according to the UN model would be unlikely to gain fame for its decisiveness.

If the U.S. Draft Convention were adopted and enforced, its net impact on economic efficiency would be unclear simply because it is difficult to confine any governmental organization to measures that will clearly avoid inefficiency. For example, the U.S. proposal would permit the authority to impose certain regulations that are likely to promote efficiency. These include exclusive and transferable blocks (area rights) for exploration and exploitation, competitive bidding for blocks, and strict liability for environmental damage. But the U.S. proposal goes beyond this in giving the authority power to impose several other regulations, including work requirements, the nature of rights to area blocks, and taxes on nodule output, which would clearly promote inefficiency.[76]

To take these in order: enforced work requirements would compel miners to spend a certain amount of their resources each year as a condition of retaining their exploitation rights. This requirement has been analyzed by Kenneth W. Clarkson and his results were similar to those of Kenneth Dam's analysis of work requirements for North Sea oil exploitation, which were described in Chapter 4 (pp. 105−07).[77] Clarkson has shown that work requirements would raise entry costs by accelerating investments beyond the optimal (unconstrained) amount of investment. This would reduce the number of firms bidding for blocks (and incidentally would therefore raise the prospects for successful collusion in bidding) and make the production of seabed minerals less competitive than otherwise. In the case of blocks which would be only marginally profitable without regulations, enforced work requirements that exceeded unconstrained optimal investments would make exploitation of these blocks unprofitable until some time had passed and metal prices had increased. Inefficiency would result because production from blocks that would have been barely profitable at lower prices would be postponed. In blocks that would still be profitable with work requirements (but less profitable than in their absence), a variety of inefficiencies would result. Extraction would begin too soon at rates that would be too high. Production costs would rise since the use of capital-intensive technologies (and especially capital in less expensive, highly depreciable forms) would be rewarded. Wasteful activities would occur since firms would attempt to avoid work requirements (by putting more into off-site investments than into on-site investments, for example). Not only would resources be wasted if the cost of enforcing work requirements were zero, but additional resources would be dissipated because of the miners' incentives to evade regulations and the incentives of the authority to attempt to enforce them.

A second inefficient element of the U.S. Draft Convention lies in the requirement that miners return to the authority three-fourths of their block "when production begins." This provision, called fractional relinquishment, would give the ocean miner incentives to explore at too great a rate so that he could relinquish the least valuable portion of the block to the authority and retain the most valuable portion for exploitation. Since exploration would be hastened to an inefficient degree, exploitation would also be inefficient.

Third, distortions would arise from the size of blocks and nature of rights to their use. The U.S. Draft Convention proposes that blocks be approximately 40,000 square kilometers. Each exploitation license would apply to one block only, but exploitation licenses to a rectangle containing as many as four contiguous blocks could be taken out under one certificate and reduced to a single block when production began. Unless the size and number of blocks that could be held were reasonably close to the optimal areas for exploration and exploitation, some inefficiency would result.[78] Resource allocation would be distorted if the postrelinquishment rectangle, containing no more than four contiguous blocks each having a maximum size of 10,000 square kilometers, proved too small for optimal exploitation, and inefficiency would also occur if the postrelinquishment rectangle proved too large for optimal resource exploitation, since blocks could not be subdivided into smaller production units.[79] It has been stressed throughout this book that economic efficiency in ocean resource use can be obtained regardless of the initial distribution and configuration of rights provided that rights can be exchanged and rearranged at low cost.[80] But to set a seemingly arbitrary ceiling on block size and to prevent subdivision of blocks is bound to create some degree of regulatory-induced inefficiency.

Fourth, the Draft Convention would tax ocean mining to generate the revenues to support the seabed authority. It proposes auctions and one-time license fees that would promote efficiency by capturing for the authority a portion of the economic rents attributable to ocean mining. But it also proposes royalty taxation that would tend to reduce output and raise mineral prices in a manner analogous to the royalty taxation of offshore hydrocarbons that was described in Chapter 4 (see pp. 107–08). Thus, the authority would probably employ a mixture of economically efficient and economically inefficient taxes which together would have an uncertain impact on resource allocation.

Fifth, it is unrealistic to assume that the decision makers of the authority would pursue the objective of economic efficiency only. They would also be likely to take into account the implications of their actions on the revenue that the authority could capture as well as the political consequences of various moves. For example, reducing the number of licenses offered for sale each year would raise the prices of metals and encourage inefficiency. But this step could also accomplish the dual purpose of increasing the wealth of the authority while protecting land-based mineral producers from sea-based competition. Since any three of the six developed countries on the council or any nine other members could block action, it is inevitable that some of the authority's major policies would be inconsistent with the competing goal of avoiding the waste of resources.

International Operating Authority

The third regulatory alternative under consideration at UNCLOS, the international operating authority, would have substantially broader powers than the licensing and regulatory authority proposed by the United States. This alternative—termed "Enterprise"—would be granted a "monopoly of exploiting the resources of the [deep sea] area." It would also undertake "all activities relating to production, processing and marketing" of all the nodules extracted in ocean areas beyond the limits of national jurisdiction. The Enterprise concept was originally proposed in 1971 by thirteen Latin American nations,[81] and judging by the number of nations that support it, it has become the most popular scheme for regulating ocean mining that UNCLOS has considered. The concept has been modified and refined to the point where it includes many provisions that are favorable to the developing countries that would not otherwise be among the first-generation ocean miners. For example, as this proposal evolved through 1973, Enterprise would be prevented from subcontracting exploitation exclusively to developed-country mining firms; it would also be required to fix prices or take other necessary steps to protect developing-country terrestrial producers of metals, to give priority to developing countries in hiring personnel and in locating nodule processing plants, and to create "reserve" ocean areas in which developing countries could be given exploitation rights on preferential terms.[82] Developed countries and their ocean miners have quite naturally strongly opposed the Enterprise concept in this extreme form, and during the 1975 and 1976 sessions of UNCLOS debate on the matter became so acrimonious that it nearly wrecked the entire conference.

From the standpoint of economic efficiency, a seabed authority and Enterprise organized along these lines would be even less desirable than one organized according to the 1970 United States proposal. The waste of resources that would be possible under the U.S. scheme would be as nothing alongside the inefficiencies that would certainly accompany Enterprise. Enterprise would, in short, constitute a monopoly of ocean mining geared to protecting the interests of a group of terrestrial metal-producing states that were neither among the world's lowest-cost producers of metals nor its main consumers of metals. Whether Enterprise restricted ocean mining output to generate a monopoly gain that could be redistributed to poorer countries or restricted it to protect terrestrial metal producers, the effect would be the same: to raise metal prices above the level that would be reached under an open access regime and to harm consumers of metals in developed and developing countries alike. Exploitation would be delayed beyond the time when it was economic, and it is doubtful that low-cost miners would be given access on a par with producers of other nations or would even be given access at all. And if the subsoil of the deep seabeds were also found to contain economically exploitable deposits of hydrocarbons, the inefficiencies brought about by Enterprise in the metal markets would be compounded in markets for petroleum products.

6. CONCLUSIONS

As with other ocean resources, the central economic question to be raised for ocean mining is: Which structure of property rights in the deep seabeds will avoid inefficient uses of these minerals and the allied resources required to harvest and process them?

Whichever structure of property rights may be selected, at least a portion of the economic rents will be dissipated through competition. The extent of dissipation depends upon the related competitive processes and the associated transactions costs. If transactions and entry costs are low then most of the rents may be obtained; at the limit, all rents would be obtained if these costs were zero. The amount of rent that remains will vary according to different property arrangements and systems of resource allocation. For example, the absence of property rights (or regulations accomplishing the same purpose) in uncaught fish plus the relatively low entry costs that are common to fishing industries have generally led to the dissipation of most of the economic rents to fisheries. On the other hand, property rights in unextracted hydrocarbon resources along the U.S. Outer Continental Shelf and in the North Sea have doubtless created economic rents, a fraction of which have been dissipated through various associated processes of competition—such as royalty taxes, auction bids, and work requirements. Some of the rents will be dissipated even in the effort to create the legal system or regulations governing resource allocation, as is now happening in the time-consuming debate at UNCLOS over the nature and extent of a regulatory regime for ocean mining.

This chapter has described two possible allocation systems for deep-sea minerals, one of strictly open access, the other of property titles to particular mine sites along with certain kinds of controls. Under the open access system some of the rents to ocean minerals would be dissipated through competitive search and discovery effort—hiring the most competent searchers and attempting to keep their discoveries confidential as trade secrets. The second system would create property titles in the deep seabeds, possibly enforce them in some manner, tax them, govern their exchange, and, depending on particular schemes, involve an international organization in production and marketing decisions. Under this system rents would be dissipated through competition for the titles themselves, tax payments, and the organizing of productive efforts in a higher-cost fashion which catered to the wishes of the regulators themselves. Viewing the problem in this way, a more accurate construction of the question raised earlier would be: Which allocation system and its associated competitive processes would leave the greater residual rents to ocean minerals?[84]

The literature on ocean mining is nearly unanimous in recommending international regulation of some kind before exploitation begins in order to maximize deep-sea rents. I have argued that this unanimity of opinion is surprising in view of the present lack of information about technological efficiencies and the incentives for economic inefficiencies, especially given the mixture of gains and costs that is likely to characterize the achieving and enforcing of international property arrangements. This argument has led me to the conclusion that inefficiency in ocean mining is least likely to occur *without* the property arrangements that appear to promote efficiency for the ocean resources discussed in earlier chapters. The gains from search activities in ocean mining may be sufficiently large and may be obtained by miners at sufficiently low cost to avoid either the underinvestment typical of free-rider situations or the excessive investment which is typical of rent-dissipated common pools. Simply put, a priori economic analysis cannot support a decision to regulate ocean mining at this time, assuming that the overriding policy purpose is to avoid economic inefficiency.

Perhaps the most striking feature of this conclusion is that deep-sea nodules appear to represent an exception to the general argument of this book in favoring the creation of property arrangements for ocean resources as a device for avoiding inefficient outcomes. Unlike fish, oil, navigation, and water quality, nodules do not appear a priori to fit Demsetz's theory of the emergence of private rights in what were previously communal resources. Nodules are so plentiful as compared with the number of firms that are likely to mine them that congestion in ocean mining is unlikely to develop for some time (as was true of other ocean resources before 1945). The development of property systems to govern their allocation would probably cost more than they would be worth. Creating detailed property and allocation systems at this time would therefore be inefficient. It is true that my conclusion stresses the cost of taking some positive regulatory action, including the possibility that regulators would raise costs because of monopoly or other inefficiencies inherent in any regulatory system. But the conclusion follows from economic analysis which implies that the smallest value of economic rents would probably be associated with the pro-regulatory policy. In this case it would appear that the most cautious policy is also the wisest economically, in that it would yield the greatest wealth to the world as a whole.

A decision to regulate can, of course, be made at a later time if inefficiencies develop in connection with an open access regime, and experience during the intervening period would suggest the particular institutional arrangements that would be most likely to generate more benefits than costs. If congestion and disputes arise, they could probably be removed at least cost by creating joint

ventures or consortia among those miners and states having the necessary technologies and the resources to exploit. Their number would be small and their
national interests in the oceans would be similar, which would reduce the
desirability of weighted voting or other decision-making procedures that had
relatively high transactions costs. Oceans could be divided among these states for
the limited purpose of creating exclusive mining areas, or certain common rules
of exploitation could be reached to control activities in all areas. A one-time
negotiation would probably be least expensive, but it should take place only
when the technologies have been worked out sufficiently to indicate clearly the
number of nations having interests in ocean mining. Until a single technology
becomes dominant or disputes arise, even consortium agreements are inferior on
economic grounds to the maintenance of an open access regime, at least for the
present.

Notes

1. John L. Mero, *The Mineral Resources of the Sea* (Amsterdam, London, and New
York: Elsevier Publishing Co., 1965), pp. 121–241.

2. Bruce C. Heezen and Charles D. Hollister, *The Face of the Deep* (New York:
Oxford University Press, 1971), p. 423.

3. Ibid.

4. Mero, pp. 135–37, 145–46; Heezen and Hollister, pp. 440–42; Allen L. Hammond, "Manganese Nodules (I): Mineral Resources on the Deep Seabed," *Science* 183
(1974):502–3.

5. Mero, pp. 118, 139–40; Heezen and Hollister, pp. 438–41; Hammond (I), p.
503. Another source places the rate of growth at one millimeter per one thousand years.
See Enrico Bonatti, "The Origin of Metal Deposits in the Oceanic Lithosphere," *Scientific American*, February 1978, pp. 54–61.

6. It was thought for some time that the nucleii attracted the colloidal particles from
the surrounding saltwater and that deep-water currents were instrumental both in bringing
fresh supplies of ions and in sweeping away sediments that would bury the nodules and
halt their growth, somehow rolling them about the ocean floor, gently and slowly, to
expose all surfaces to the rain of manganese and other elements. More recently it has
been argued that nodules acquire metals through the underlying bottom sediments rather
than from the adjacent waters. Some nodules that are rich in nickel content have been
found in sediments that contain little of that metal. Another theory alleges that nodules,
like coral, grow with the effort of microorganisms. Small tubular forms of life composed
of ferromanganese materials have been found to inhabit nodules. These organisms may

be responsible for buoying and agitating them on the surface of sediments. See Hammond (I), p. 503; Werner Raab, "Physical and Chemical Features of Pacific Deep Sea Manganese Nodules and Their Implications to the Genesis of Nodules," in David R. Horn, ed., *Ferromanganese Deposits on the Ocean Floor* (Washington, D.C.: National Science Foundation, International Decade of Ocean Exploration, 1972), pp. 31−49; Henry L. Ehrlich, "The Role of Microbes in Manganese Nodule Genesis," in ibid., pp. 63−69.

7. D. R. Horn, B. M. Horn and M. N. Delach, *Metal Content of Ferromanganese Deposits of the Oceans* (Tech. Rep. No. 3, NSF GX 33616, National Science Foundation, International Decade of Ocean Exploration, 1973).

8. This is stressed in almost every technical source. See Cmdr. Wayne J. Smith, U.S. Navy, "An Assessment of Deep-Sea Manganese Nodule Exploitation Technology" (mimeo. draft, Virginia Beach, Va., 1972), pp. 2−7; Allen L. Hammond, "Manganese Nodules (II): Prospects for Deep Sea Mining," *Science* 183 (1974):644−46; John L. Mero, "A Legal Regime for Deep Sea Mining," *San Diego Law Review* 7 (1970):488−503; M. D. Hassialis, "Preliminary Economic Evaluation of a Ferromanganese Deposit," in *Inter-University Program of Research on Ferromanganese Deposits of the Ocean Floor* (Washington, D.C.; National Science Foundation, International Decade of Ocean Exploration, Phase I Report, April 1973), pp. 353−58; James E. Mielke, *Ocean Manganese Nodules,* prepared by the Congressional Research Service at the request of the U.S. Senate Committee on Interior and Insular Affairs (Washington, D.C.; June 1975), pp. 3−13; W. D. Siapno, "Exploration Technology and Ocean Mining Parameters," presented at the 1975 Convention of the American Mining Congress, San Francisco, reprinted in *Current Developments in Deep Seabed Mining,* Hearing before the Subcommittee on Minerals, Materials, and Fuels of the U.S. Senate Committee on Interior and Insular Affairs, 94th Cong., 1st Sess., pt. 1, November 7, 1975, pp. 207−45; J. E. Flipse, M. A. Dubs, and R. J. Greenwald, *Pre-Production Manganese Nodule Mining Activities and Requirements; Background Information to Describe Typical Phases and Activities of a Commercial Ocean Mining Development Program Including Equipment, Cost, Time and Resource Requirements* (Deepsea Ventures and Kennecott Copper Corp., mimeo, March 15, 1973); reprinted in *Mineral Resources of the Deep Seabed,* pt. 1, pp. 602−700.

9. Flipse, Dubs, and Greenwald, pp. 20, 30−34.

10. Ibid., pp. 21−24, 45.

11. Siapno, pp. 229−32.

12. Hammond (II), p. 644.

13. Siapno, p. 237.

14. Flipse, Dubs, and Greenwald, pp. 34−41.

15. H. W. Menard and J. Z. Frazer, "Manganese Nodules on the Sea Floor: Inverse Correlation Between Grade and Abundance," *Science* 199 (1978):969−70.

16. Flipse, Dubs, and Greenwald, pp. 17 and 82.

17. Most of the detailed information concerning these technologies is still proprietary and closely guarded. The available public information is very generally stated and must be interpreted with some caution. See Smith, pp. 8−14; Flipse, Dubs, and Greenwald, pp. 41−45; Mielke, pp. 13−20; Hammond (II), p. 644; UN, *Economic Implications of*

Sea-Bed Mineral Development in the International Area: Report of the Secretary General,
A/CONF.62/25, May 22, 1974, pp. 15–22.

18. "Given the currents throughout the water column, even with the precise steering
of the mine ship to a course exactly 15 meters [the likely width of the dredgehead]
parallel to the previous run, the mine head at the bottom could be sweeping a new row
anywhere within a 150 meters path. One mining company, after several computer simu-
lation exercises, was forced to conclude that the best procedure would be to simply sweep
the mine site at random." UN, A/CONF.62/25, p. 92.

19. Ibid., p. 19.

20. This paragraph is based on technical reports written before the true purpose of the
ship and the barge were known publicly and before Mr. Hughes's death.

21. See Mielke, pp. 32–35; Jerry Cohen and George Reasons, "CIA Recovers Part of
Russian Sub," *Los Angeles Times,* Mar. 16, 1975.

22. Mielke, p. 33.

23. See two articles in the *Los Angeles Times*; "Glomar Up for Lease after U.S. Agencies Turn It Down," Feb. 27, 1976, and "Glomar Explorer Leased for Sea Mining,"
Jan. 28, 1978.

24. Flipse, Dubs, and Greenwald, pp. 25, 74–75; Mielke, pp. 14–15.

25. Flipse, Dubs, and Greenwald, p. 20.

26. For example, one extensively sampled 225-square-mile deposit had a mean
concentration of nodules of about 2 lb. per square foot with a standard deviation of 0.76
for adjacent sampling stations and 0.58 for stations one mile apart. Evidently Deepsea
Ventures' dredging technology operates most efficiently in concentrations of about
1.5 lb. per square foot. Ibid., pp. 30–34.

27. Ibid., pp. 74–75.

28. See Hammond (II), pp. 645–46; Mielke, pp. 20–25; Smith, pp. 14–22; UN,
A/CONF.62/25, pp. 22–25.

29. This is the conclusion of Richard A. Frank, administrator, U.S. National Ocean
and Atmospheric Administration, Department of Commerce, in "The Promise of Deep
Seabed Mining," *Congressional Record—Senate,* vol. 124, no. 35, March 13, 1978,
pp. S.3492–93. See also Hammond (II), p. 646; Mielke, pp. 27–30; National Academy
of Sciences, National Research Council, Marine Board, Panel on Operational Safety
in Marine Mining, *Mining in the Outer Continental Shelf and in the Deep Ocean*
(Washington, D.C.: 1975).

30. National Academy of Sciences (1975), p. 90.

31. Mielke, p. 28.

32. Ibid.

33. National Academy of Sciences (1975), p. 92.

34. Mielke, p. 30.

35. See U.S. National Commission on Materials Policy, *Towards a National Materials Policy: Basic Data and Issues: Interim Report* (Washington, D.C., 1972), pp. 16,
18–20, 26; Wayne J. Smith, "International Control of Deep Sea Mineral Resources,"
Naval War College Review, June 1972, pp. 82–90; "Economic Considerations of Deep

Sea Mineral Resources'' (mimeo draft, Virginia Beach, Va., October 1972); Edmund Faltermayer, ''Metals: The Warning Signals Are Up,'' *Fortune,* October 1972, p. 109; Mielke, pp. 41–59; Conrad G. Welling, ''Ocean Mining Systems,'' paper presented at the annual convention of the American Mining Congress, San Francisco, September 28– October 1, 1975, reprinted in *Current Developments in Deep Seabed Mining,* pt. 1, pp. 194–206.

36. Michael Gorham, ''Dividing Up the Minerals of the Deep Seabed,'' *Federal Reserve Bank of San Francisco Economic Review,* Winter 1978, p. 10.

37. For the prices of the four metals see Table 43 below.

38. Danny M. Leipziger and James L. Mudge, *Seabed Mineral Resources and the Economic Interests of Developing Countries* (Cambridge, Mass.: Ballinger Publishing Co., 1976), p. 138.

39. Rebecca L. Wright, *Ocean Mining: An Economic Evaluation* (Washington, D.C.: U.S. Department of the Interior, Ocean Mining Administration, May 1976).

40. U.S. Department of the Interior, Bureau of Mines, *Mineral Facts and Problems,* 1975 ed. (Washington, D.C.: Bureau of Mines Bulletin 667, 1976), p. 745.

41. See Wright.

42. For a different view, see ibid., passim.

43. One example is the substitution of manganese for lead in the production of tetraethyl gasoline. However, in 1977 Congress heard legislation that would ban such additives on the grounds that they would reduce the efficiency of catalytic converters. ''Conferees Barring a Gasoline Additive, MMT, Provisionally,'' *Wall Street Journal,* July 29, 1977.

44. David B. Johnson and Dennis E. Logue, ''U.S. Economic Interests in Law of the Sea Issues,'' in Ryan C. Amacher and Richard James Sweeney, eds., *The Law of the Sea: U.S. Interests and Alternatives,* p. 45.

45. It should be noted that the predictions of Johnson and Logue, as well as those of Nathan Associates referred to below, were based on the assumption that the Summa Corporation would be one of the three major U.S. processors. This assumption may still be valid since the gap left by Summa Corporation is apparently being filled by Ocean Minerals Company (the Lockheed consortium).

46. *The Economic Value of Ocean Resources to the United States,* pp. 18–19.

47. Ibid., p. 22.

48. Ibid., p. 27.

49. Ibid.

50. UN, *United States Working Paper on the Economic Effects of Deep Seabed Exploitation,* A/CONF.62/C.1/L.5, July 31, 1974, p. 6.

51. Mielke, p. xiii.

52. Ibid., p. 38.

53. Flipse, Dubs, and Greenwald, pp. 1, 17, 82; interview by telephone with Ray Kaufman, Deepsea Ventures, Inc., Gloucester, Va., August 8, 1973.

54. Mielke, pp. 35–36.

55. Johnson and Logue, p. 44.

56. In 1970, for example, John L. Mero of Ocean Resources, Inc., La Jolla, California, one of the principal firms involved in the CLB system, estimated that there would be five active nodule operations by 1975 and perhaps 50 by the year 2000. See Mero (1970), p. 500.

57. See Alexander F. Holser, *Manganese Nodule Resources and Mine Site Availability* (Washington, D.C.: U.S. Department of the Interior, Ocean Mining Administration, August 1976). Menard and Fraser, pp. 969–71, argue that this conclusion is faulty and that the actual number of workable mine sites is far smaller.

58. See statement of Marne Dubs, in *Current Developments in Deep Seabed Mining,* pt. 1, p. 4. See also ibid., pp. 2–4.

59. This is a continuing theme of testimony before the Subcommittee on Minerals, Materials, and Fuels of the U.S. Senate Committee on Interior and Insular Affairs, in its series of hearings on developments in deep-sea mining. See statements of T. S. Ary, Union Carbide Exploration Corp., C. H. Burgess, Kennecott Copper Corp., and John E. Flipse, Deepsea Ventures, Inc., in *Development of Hard Mineral Resources of the Deep Seabed,* Hearings on S.2801 before the Subcommittee on Minerals, Materials, and Fuels of the Senate Comm. on Interior and Insular Affairs, 92nd Cong., 2d Sess., (June 2, 1972), pp. 25–44; statements of C. H. Burgess, M. A. Dubs, Kennecott Copper Corp., and T. S. Ary, in *Mineral Resources of the Deep Seabed,* pt. 1, pp. 96, 105, 124–25, 142, 145–46; statement of John L. Mero, in *Perspectives on Ocean Policy,* p. 314; Northcutt Ely, "Deep Seabed Minerals; Congress Steams to the Rescue," *Congressional Record* (April 14, 1976), p. 122; statements of M. A. Dubs, J. E. Flipse, Deepsea Ventures, Inc., James G. Wenzel, Lockheed Missiles and Space Co., Inc., and C. Thomas Houseman, Chase Manhattan Bank, N.A., in *Current Developments in Deep Seabed Mining,* pt. 1, pp. 2–26; Leigh S. Ratiner, U.S. Ocean Mining Administration, statement before the American Mining Congress, San Francisco, October 1, 1975, U.S. Department of the Interior News Release (Oct. 2, 1975).

60. Deepsea Ventures, Inc., *Notice of Discovery and Claim of Exclusive Mining Rights, and Request for Diplomatic Protection and Protection of Investment,* filed with the Secretary of State, November 15, 1974.

61. Ibid., pp. 1 and 3.

62. Ibid., p. 4. Opinion of the Law Offices of Northcutt Ely, *International Law Applicable to Deepsea Mining,* submitted to Deepsea Ventures, Inc., Washington, D.C., November 14, 1974, p. 4.

63. Most of this and the two sections that follow has been taken from Eckert (1974).

64. See Demsetz (1966), p. 66, and (1967), p. 357.

65. Heezen and Hollister, p. 423.

66. Professor Louis Henkin has stated that under current international law "Most [Western] lawyers, I believe, would conclude that—without claiming permanent rights in sea-bed—states (or their nationals) could lawfully exploit resources in the deep-sea bed and keep what they extract." Louis Henkin, "The Changing Law of Sea-Mining," in *Inter-University Program of Research on Ferromanganese Deposits of the Ocean Floor,* p. 340.

67. This argument has been advanced by Francis T. Christy, "Marigenous Min-

erals—Wealth, Regimes, and Factors of Decision,'' in *Symposium on the International Regime of the Sea-Bed: Proceedings* (Accademia Nazionale dei Lincei, 1970), p. 113; Orris C. Herfindahl, ''Some Problems in the Exploitation of Manganese Nodules,'' in Lewis M. Alexander, ed., *The Law of the Sea: Needs and Interests of Developing Nations*, Proceedings of the 7th Annual Conference of the Law of the Sea Institute (Kingston, R.I.: University of Rhode Island, 1973), pp. 36–38; David B. Brooks, ''Deep Sea Manganese Nodules: From Scientific Phenomenon to World Resource,'' in Lewis M. Alexander, ed., *The Law of the Sea: The Future of the Sea's Resources* (1968), pp. 37–38.

68. The miners themselves have taken pains to keep their exploration data proprietary and to ''restrict the flow [of information] as much as possible,'' including its use by the U.S. government. See testimony of American Mining Congress, M. A. Dubs, and J. E. Flipse, in *Mineral Resources of the Deep Seabed*, pt. 1, pp. 149, 153; pt. 2, pp. 1022, 1030, 1042.

69. Under certain circumstances it may be more profitable for the discoverer deliberately to disseminate his valuable information if he has first invested in the equities that are likely to rise in value because of his discovery. Others would perform the actual exploitation or production, but the discoverer (or the inventor) still captures sufficient wealth to have made his search efforts worthwhile. This argument was first applied to the question of patents, where legal protection of ideas was thought to be required to give inventors sufficient incentive to engage in discovery effort. The demonstration that investment in equities was an alternative to protecting the inventor through legal patents was a major revision to the theory of inventive activity. See J. Hirshleifer, ''The Private and Social Value of Information and the Reward to Inventive Activity,'' *American Economic Review* 61 (1971):570–72.

70. R. H. Coase, ''The Problem of Social Cost,'' *Journal of Law and Economics* 3 (1960). This application of the Coase Theorem is identical to the problem of pollution discussed in Chapter 6.

71. This is true because it takes so many centuries for perceptible growth to occur. At a 4 percent rate of discount, for example, the present value of one dollar's growth in nodules available in 100 years is less than two cents. Although mining nodules at one location may increase the rate of growth of nodules elsewhere, since removing some deposits may reduce the number of objects on the ocean floor to which metallic ions can adhere, the present value of this growth is so small that society should disregard it.

72. For an argument that common pool problems would be typical of nodule exploitation see Brooks, p. 38; Francis T. Christy, Jr. (1970), pp. 138–41, 150, and also by Christy, ''Economic Criteria for Deep Sea Minerals,'' *International Lawyer* 2 (1968): 224–42.

73. For a discussion of various registry proposals see Robert L. Friedheim, *Understanding the Debate on Ocean Resources*, in University of Denver Monograph Series in World Affairs, monograph no. 3, 1968–69 (1969), pp. 17–21; U.S. Commission on Marine Science, Engineering, and Resources (the Stratton Commission), *Our Nation and the Sea: A Plan for National Action* (Washington, D.C., 1969), pp. 147–51. There are a variety of proposals for registries, but those discussed here would only have recording functions and no enforcement powers.

74. "Draft United Nations Convention on the International Seabed Area," apps. A & B, UN Doc. A/AC. 138/25 (August 3, 1970), *International Legal Materials* 9 (1970): 1046—80, also reprinted in Leigh S. Ratiner, "United States Oceans Policy: An Analysis," *Journal of Maritime Law and Commerce* 2 (1971):451—80.

75. Ratiner, pp. 251—52. The proposals advanced by other nations for the structure of the council and assembly are described in Lewis B. Sohn, "The Council of an International Sea-Bed Authority," *San Diego Law Review* 9 (1972): 414—21.

76. Johnson and Logue, p. 47, advocate the creation of a registry as being the least expensive regulatory institution, but in doing so they are ignoring the difficulty of binding an institution constitutionally to confine its regulations only to those that promote efficiency and to avoid making regulations that attenuate efficiency.

77. Kenneth W. Clarkson, "Economic Effects of Work Requirements in Leases to Develop Seabed Resources," *Virginia Journal of International Law* 15 (1975): 795— 814.

78. See also UN A/CONF.62/25, p. 88.

79. Ibid.

80. Coase (1960); Demsetz (1966) and (1967).

81. UN, "Working Paper on the Regime for the Sea Bed and Ocean Floor and Its Subsoil Beyond the Limits of National Jurisdiction," submitted by Chile, Columbia, Ecuador, El Salvador, Guatemala, Guyana, Jamaica, Mexico, Panama, Peru, Trinidad and Tobago, Uruguay, Venezuela, UN Doc. A/AC.138/49 (August 4, 1971), art. 14, p. 3.

82. UN, *Report by the Chairman of Working Group I (Mr. Pinto)*, UN Doc. A/AC. 138/SC.1/SR.70 (July 1, 1973), p. 9.

83. The view of American ocean miners in opposition to a seabed monopoly regime are plainly stated in *Mineral Resources of the Deep Seabed*, pt. 1, pp. 94, 105, 148—49, 153.

84. I am indebted to Professor Yoram Barzel for several conversations that led to forming this argument. See also Steven N.S. Cheung, "The Structure of a Contract and the Theory of a Non-Exclusive Resource," *Journal of Law and Economics* 13 (1970):53, 64.

PART TWO

Policy Evaluations

CHAPTER 9

UNCLOS: The Making of an Ocean Treaty

Since 1967, two distinct, evolutionary, and often competing processes of international law making have attempted to forge new property arrangements in the oceans. Neither process had been completed by the end of 1978, but the general direction, central ingredients, and economic implications of each had become relatively clear. The enclosure movement of the oceans is the older and more decentralized process of the two. The second process is the Third United Nations Conference on the Law of the Sea (UNCLOS), begun in 1967 as a response to twenty years of experience with enclosure. UNCLOS is a highly centralized, essentially political, and quasi-parliamentary activity that is intended to vote a basic ocean treaty to become new international law.

UNCLOS is more comprehensive than the enclosure movement in four ways. First, participation is not confined to coastal states. UNCLOS potentially includes almost every nation-state in the world as well as various religious organizations and liberation movements which participate usually without voting. Adoption of a comprehensive treaty requires the votes of two-thirds of the participating states.[1] Second, UNCLOS would establish property rights to deep-sea nodules in addition to the five relatively coastal resources that were described in Chapters 3–7. In contrast, the enclosure movement has largely been confined to these five coastal resources. Third, UNCLOS could establish United Nations ownership of the "international area" beyond the limits of national jurisdiction at the time the treaty is ratified as well as of the resources contained in the area, whereas most enclosures established claims to resources only and not to the ocean territory or the water column per se.[2] Fourth, some of the nations participating in the UNCLOS process have sought to make this international area as large as possible by halting or reversing the momentum toward larger and increasingly frequent enclosures. As with the enclosure movement, the UNCLOS process has been shaped by the distributional aims of individual countries or blocs of countries. However, the two processes appear to produce some resource-use outcomes that diverge in their impact on both the distribution of world wealth and on economic efficiency.

When UNCLOS began, expectations ran high. The conference was supposed "to write a constitution for 70 percent of the world"[3]—a "comprehensive and widely accepted" treaty which, in addition to being suited to the new era of increasing and changing ocean uses, would halt the process of enclosure, demilitarize the seabeds, and redirect ocean wealth toward the developing countries. After six years of preparatory effort and five years of negotiations, relatively few of these goals have been met. By 1978 it appeared that UNCLOS either will yield a treaty that reinforces the enclosure movement rather than reverses it or else will yield no treaty at all.

The purpose of this chapter is to discuss some of the opportunities that UNCLOS offers for avoiding inefficient use of ocean resources. There being no treaty as yet, I shall evaluate the UNCLOS achievements to date in terms of certain treaty texts which have the status of working papers. These have been widely circulated and discussed among delegations during the conference sessions of 1975—78, and in the view of many observers some combination of the two most recent texts may be taken as representing approximately the treaty that the largest number of nations could endorse.

To understand the efficiency implications of UNCLOS outcomes, or for some resources the lack of UNCLOS outcomes, it is first necessary to understand the UNCLOS process itself, since the procedures for reaching decisions at UNCLOS appear to have exerted a strong influence on the substantive decisions that the conference has reached or is attempting to reach. Section 1 will discuss what I call the transactional structure of the UNCLOS process. Section 2 deals with the conference progress to date. Section 3 analyzes the treaty texts for efficiency impacts.

1. THE TRANSACTIONAL STRUCTURE
OF UNCLOS

Economists and political scientists over the past twenty years have developed the elements of a theory of group behavior or collective choice. This body of knowledge, usually called the theory of social choice, is essentially a theory of voting. One of its most important theorems tells us that there is probably no single method of expressing the aggregated preference of a group that "best" reflects the group's "will." Instead, for a given attempt at group decision making, the ultimate outcome depends to an important extent upon the given procedure employed to aggregate the preferences of individuals into the "preference of the group."[4] Indeed, the logical connection between the ultimate social choice and the process by which this choice is made is so tight, at least in this body of theory, that the two are almost inseparable. For example, the outcome of presidential elections in the United States might be drastically changed if the constitutional rules were different—such as requiring a two-thirds rather than a simple majority in the Electoral College, or abolishing the Electoral College, or replacing the complex system of presidential preferential primary elections within the various states with a single nationwide presidential primary election. In each of these hypothetical cases it would be correct, as a matter of social choice theory, to say that the change in the group decision rule was itself the change in the group decision.

Recently this same theoretical analysis was extended to legislative and judicial processes. The tentative results of this investigation have been to call into question the "fairness" of procedures whose consistency and neutrality had once been unquestioned. Michael E. Levine and Charles R. Plott have argued:

> If the legitimacy of legal procedures depends even in part on the premise that procedure is a neutral midwife to the genesis of an institution's substantive decisions, then the specification of important, even determinative, procedural influences on outcomes may be of considerable practical . . . importance. While the assumption that procedures can influence outcomes will certainly not shock any reasonably sophisticated legal observer or participant, the degree of procedural influence posited by the social choice literature and the predicted difficulty of neutralizing it might well come as something of a surprise even to the sophisticated advocate of "fair" procedures.[5]

This brief sketch of just one element of the theory of social choice scarcely does justice to the importance and richness of its implications. But I have raised the issue only to show that there is ample precedent in the theory of group decision making among individuals for the argument that I am about to make concerning group decision making among nations.[6] My hypothesis is that the transactional structure of UNCLOS has influenced the conference's substantive outcomes, and in some cases the lack of them. The UNCLOS *process* is not a "neutral midwife." Rather, this structure, which itself was the result of certain key decisions taken before substantive negotiations actually began, has to a certain extent biased voting systematically in favor of certain countries or groups of countries, chiefly the younger, economically developing countries which were carved out of the imperial systems that began to decay shortly after the end of World War II. This transactional structure also appears to be responsible for the seemingly interminable delays that UNCLOS has experienced, its verbosity, and the deep conflict between the two major groups of voting countries, one faction having numerical strength and the other having few votes but military and economic strength. This conflict began in 1967 when UNCLOS began and became widely known in 1975 when a stalemate was reached over important issues. Thus, the UNCLOS "process" is, to an important degree, the actual UNCLOS outcome.

Number and Diversity of Participants

The preparatory work for UNCLOS began in 1968 with an ad hoc Seabed Committee of the UN General Assembly. This committee started with 35 member nations, and in 1970 and 1971 it was expanded to 91 nations and given the status of a permanent committee.[7] By July 1974, when substantive negotiations began, the number of nations (and other political entities) invited to participate had been increased to 149. Of these, 137 nations plus the Holy See actually attended,[8] and the number of individuals holding credentials from these governments was about 1,450.[9] In addition, there were 12 nonvoting delegations representing "people's movements" or "liberation fronts," 20 groups of nonvoting observers from official UN or other governmental organizations, and 33 groups of observers reflecting the interests of consumers, environmentalists, internationalists, labor, airlines, students, and so on.[10] Including journalists, the total number of credentialed participants and observers was nearly 5,000. For the most part, nongovernmental observers were allowed access to the floor for conference debates and were expected to lobby for their particular interests among the delegates. One group was bold enough to submit a proposal to the conference, a right usually reserved for the delegations of voting nation-states.[11]

There are two reasons for this steady increase in the size of UNCLOS. First, its chief purpose is to produce a binding set of "new constitutional rules" for the use of the oceans, and since nations usually cannot be bound to rules to which they have not given their sovereign consent, most countries have insisted on participating in the process by which the new constitutional rules are promulgated.[12] The second reason is political. Groups of countries that for various reasons were, as they think, "left out" of the process that created the "old" law of the sea want to participate in changing it. These include the young countries created in the 1950s and 1960s plus the landlocked countries that played only a minor role in the First and Second UNCLOS owing to their geographically related interests and lack of naval forces. The expansion of the original General Assembly Seabed Committee from 35 to 86 and eventually to 91 members in 1971 was done in consultation with regional groupings and with a view to giving the committee a widespread geographical representation.[13] From there it was a relatively simple step to make participation universal.

It is obvious that under the United Nations system it is difficult, if not impossible, to confine participation to a small or moderately sized subgroup of countries. In this case, decisions put to the vote according to the rule of one-nation, one-vote may jeopardize the interests of the "traditional" law-of-the-sea countries since they are relatively few in number. Clearly, if these traditional countries hoped to develop the new law of the sea in favor of the same naval and maritime interests that were reflected in the old law, they should have selected some forum outside the United Nations system.

Among the voting participants at UNCLOS, there are three main points of division: income or wealth, political geography, and land versus ocean mining. Of the total of 149 participants, only 29 can be called economically developed, but within the two groups of developed and developing countries there is a tremendous diversity in national economic interests and in oceans interests. Most of the developed states have interests in commercial navigation, but only a few of them have strong naval interests. Among the developing countries, the differences are vast. Compare, as an extreme example, the People's Republic of China and Nauru. Both are "developing" countries, each with an equal vote, but China has over 800 million people and appears to have extensive offshore hydrocarbon resources, and Nauru is a small Pacific island with only 6,500 people but high per capita incomes and relatively few offshore resources. The growth in the number of small, developing countries that have joined the United Nations system within the past two decades has been so great that "Theoretically, it would [have been] possible to assemble a majority in the General Assembly that would represent as little as 4.7 percent of the world's population [and] 1.3 percent of gross world product."[14]

The division in political geography is also complex. By coincidence, the breakdown in numbers of coastal countries and landlocked countries in 1974 was exactly the same as that of developing and developed countries—120 and 29 (see Table 7). Of the 25 major states in the landlocked group (not counting Andorra, Liechtenstein, San Marino, and Vatican City), 13 are in Africa, 5 are in Asia, 5 are in Europe, and 2 are in Latin America. Among the coastal states there are sharp differences in the length and nature of coastlines. For example, over one-third (48) have continental margins that extend beyond 200 miles.[15] The other two-thirds include about 20 countries that either have narrow shelves or are "shelf-locked" in the sense that they lack direct access to the high seas without crossing the continental shelf areas of other countries (for example, the Federal Republic of Germany, Iraq, Singapore, and Zaire). Something like 111 states have strong geographical interests of one extreme or another—59 broad-shelf countries and about 52 countries that are geographically disadvantaged in that they are landlocked, shelf-locked, or narrow-shelved. Either of the two groups is large enough to constitute a "blocking third" against UNCLOS treaty articles that do not conform to their interests, assuming that this issue is sufficiently important to lead them to vote on shelf-related issues as opposing factions. Other geographical subdivisions in which interests may conflict could be drawn between nations that border straits and those with commercial maritime interests that do not; between coastal fishing countries and distant-water fishing countries; between archipelago states, island states, and countries with island possessions, and all the others.[16] Even more subdivisions could be formed by culling out regional groupings such as the North Sea or Caribbean countries.

The third main division, between ocean mining and land-based mining countries, is somewhat more clear cut in that the potential ocean mining nations number fewer than one dozen, including Australia, Belgium, Canada, France, the Federal Republic of Germany, Japan, the United Kingdom, the United States, and the U.S.S.R. In general, their interests are opposite to those of the twenty-five or so land-based mineral extractors; these include about fourteen developing nations, but of the eleven others, about half are likely to be ocean miners at some future time (see Table 39).

At the opening of the Caracas negotiating session, UN Secretary General Kurt Waldheim stated that UNCLOS "is hard to parallel in complexity and in the very concrete nature of the national and international interests at stake."[17] This assessment is undoubtedly correct. It may also be an understatement in that the transactions costs of UNCLOS are so large that its effectiveness will probably be small. Sizable transactional resources are eaten up as 138 delegations and 1,450 individuals simply attempt to learn one another's positions on a variety of issues and then negotiate a mutually agreeable position. Quite apart from the time spent in obtaining space, learning names and telephone numbers, and locating the people with whom one hopes to negotiate, there is the often considerable time spent in debating issues and making speeches, since each of the 138 delegations must have its chance to demonstrate its familiarity with the complex issues involved.

Beyond all this, however, is the problem of the great diversity of national interests, which makes it nearly inevitable that some countries will seek treaty outcomes that others will strongly oppose. As Robert L. Friedheim has pointed out, UNCLOS is not like the typical meeting of a club, a township, or even a political convention, for which there has been a prior culling so that there are some common interests in an avocation, residential location preferences, or political beliefs.[18] On the contrary, UNCLOS has been organized quite as much with respect to differences in national interests as to similarities in interest— landlocked countries, for example, as opposed to broad-margin coastal states with aims that are in some instances diametrically different when it comes to treaty proposals, or countries with land-based mining interests as opposed to those with ocean mining interests. Differences such as these may be extremely expensive to resolve in terms of the time, effort, and other transactional resources that are required, and some differences may be so expensive to settle that costs outweigh gains. As a result, it would not be surprising if UNCLOS produced either (1) vague treaty articles that skirted the central issues, (2) no treaty articles at all on certain important subjects (amounting to an agreement to disagree), or (3) a relatively narrow treaty handed down by a determined majority of countries that could not be universally accepted. And any of these outcomes would be a "failure" in terms of the criteria for success that UNCLOS adopted.

Agenda Issues

Ann L. Hollick, commenting on the work of the 90-odd-member Seabed Committee in preparation for the Caracas negotiating session, noted wryly that "its most notable accomplishment in six years of meetings was the preparation of the agenda."[19] This List of Subjects and Issues, shown in Table 46, contains a total of 105 items—25 principal issues, broken down into 61 sub-items and 19 sub-sub-items.[20] This list has served as an agenda for debate and could become an agenda for voting if a simple majority of the participating states agreed.

Several features of the List of Subjects and Issues deserve emphasis. First, it was prepared and sponsored by 56 countries, all but two of which (Romania and Spain) were developing countries. Second, it appears to be laden with issues that are of special importance to certain blocs of nations noted earlier (although each state within its group may value various items differently). For example, the interests of developing countries are recognized in item no. 14 (with its one sub-item and three sub-sub-items) on the development and transfer of technology. The same applies to item no. 1 (and in at least two of its six sub-items) concerning the creation of an international regime for the seabed and the ocean floor and the sharing of its revenues with developing countries. This item is not only at the head of the list but it appears to be one of the most important issues at UNCLOS since disagreements over these matters nearly brought an end to the conference during its 1975 session and have slowed down the progress of all sessions since then.

The *rights* of coastal countries are emphasized in item no. 2 (and in at least three of its five sub-items and two sub-sub-items) concerning the territorial sea; in item no. 3 (and its three sub-items) concerning the contiguous zone; in item no. 5 (and nearly all of its six sub-items) concerning the sovereign resources of the continental shelf; and in item no. 6 (including many of its nine sub-items and ten sub-sub-items) concerning the exclusive economic zone beyond the territorial sea. The *duties* of coastal states are given much less attention. They are mentioned almost in passing in sub-items no. 5.1 (the continental shelf) and no. 6.1 (the EEZ), but are raised implicitly in item no. 7 (and most of its seven sub-items) concerning the preferential rights of coastal states in areas beyond the territorial sea in which they have nonexclusive jurisdiction.

The geographically disadvantaged states secured two principal items on the list that reflect their ocean interests. The interests of landlocked nations, including rights of transit to the sea and equality of treatment in ports, are dealt

TABLE 46

1. International régime for the sea-bed and the ocean floor beyond national jurisdiction

    1.1   Nature and characteristics

    1.2   International machinery: structure, functions, powers

    1.3   Economic implications

    1.4   Equitable sharing of benefits bearing in mind the special interests and needs of the developing countries, whether coastal or landlocked

    1.5   Definition and limits of the area

    1.6   Use exclusively for peaceful purposes

2. Territorial sea

    2.1   Nature and characteristics, including the question of the unity or plurality of régimes in the territorial sea

    2.2   Historic waters

    2.3   Limits

    2.3.1 Question of the delimitation of the territorial sea; various aspects involved

    2.3.2 Breadth of the territorial sea, global or regional criteria; open seas and oceans, semi-closed seas and enclosed seas

    2.4   Innocent passage in the territorial sea

    2.5   Freedom of navigation and overflight resulting from the question of plurality of régimes in the territorial sea

3. Contiguous zone

    3.1   Nature and characteristics

    3.2   Limits

    3.3   Rights of coastal states with regard to national security, customs and fiscal control, sanitation and immigration regulations

4. Straits used for international navigation

    4.1   Innocent passage

    4.2   Other related matters including the question of the right of transit

5. Continental shelf

    5.1   Nature and scope of the sovereign rights of coastal states over the continental shelf; duties of states

    5.2   Outer limit of the continental shelf: applicable criteria

    5.3   Question of the delimitation between states: various aspects involved

    5.4   Natural resources of the continental shelf

    5.5   Régime for waters superjacent to the continental shelf

    5.6   Scientific research

6. Exclusive economic zone beyond the territorial sea

    6.1   Nature and characteristics, including rights and jurisdiction of coastal states in relation to resources, pollution control and scientific research in the zone; duties of states

TABLE 46 (Cont.)

TABLE 46 (Cont.)

9.2   Rights and interests of land-locked countries

9.2.1 Free access to and from the sea: freedom of transit, means and facilities for transport and communications

9.2.2 Equality of treatment in the ports of transit states

9.2.3 Free access to the international sea-bed area beyond national jurisdiction

9.2.4 Participation in the international régime, including the machinery and the equitable sharing in the benefits of the area

9.3   Particular interests and needs of developing land-locked countries in the international régime

9.4   Rights and interests of land-locked countries in regard to living resources of the sea

10. Rights and interests of shelf-locked states and states with narrow shelves or short coastlines

    10.1 International régime

    10.2 Fisheries

    10.3 Special interests and needs of developing shelf-locked states and states with narrow shelves or short coastlines

    10.4 Free access to and from the high seas

11. Rights and interests of states with broad shelves

12. Preservation of the marine environment

    12.1 Sources of pollution and other hazards and measures to combat them

    12.2 Measures to preserve the ecological balance of the marine environment

    12.3 Responsibility and liability for damage to the marine environment and to the coastal state

    12.4 Rights and duties of coastal states

    12.5 International cooperation

13. Scientific research

    13.1 Nature, characteristics and objectives of scientific research of the oceans

    13.2 Access to scientific information

    13.3 International cooperation

14. Development and transfer of technology

    14.1 Development of technological capabilities of developing countries

    14.1.1 Sharing of knowledge and technology between developed and developing countries

    14.1.2 Training of personnel from developing countries

    14.1.3 Transfer of technology to developing countries

15. Regional arrangements

16. Archipelagos

17. Enclosed and semi-enclosed seas

18. Artificial islands and installations

TABLE 46 (Cont.)

19. Régime of islands:
    (a)   islands under colonial dependence or foreign domination or control;
    (b)   other related matters.

20. Responsibility and liability for damage resulting from the use of the marine environment

21. Settlement of disputes

22. Peaceful uses of the ocean space; zones of peace and security

23. Archaeological and historical treasures on the sea-bed and ocean floor beyond the limits of national jurisdiction

24. Transmission from the high seas

25. Enhancing the universal participation of states in multilateral conventions relating to the law of the sea.

SOURCE: UN Doc. A/AC.138/66/Rev.1 (August 16, 1972).

with in item no. 9 (including its four sub-items and four sub-sub-items). The interests of narrow-shelf states are recognized in item no. 10 (including its four sub-items).

In contrast, the list mentions relatively few issues about which the traditional law-of-the-sea countries feel most strongly. For example, the question of "free transit through international straits" has been strongly championed by both the United States and the Soviet Union, but it does not appear on the list in the form or wording that both countries have favored.[21] Sub-item no. 2.5 raises the question of "freedom of navigation and overflight" but only in relation to the "problems resulting from the question of plurality of regimes in the territorial sea." "Freedom" is mentioned in sub-item no. 8.3 concerning the high seas but only in relation to "freedoms of the high seas and their regulation." "Freedom of navigation and overflight" is raised in sub-item no. 6.3, but only in relation to the "exclusive economic zone beyond the territorial sea," and the phrase is omitted entirely from item no. 4 concerning "straits used for international navigation" in which connection both countries attached the greatest significance to free transit. Sub-item no. 4.2 raises the "question of the right of transit" in straits but only as part of "other related matters." The same point applies to item no. 13 concerning scientific research, which fails to mention the freedom to engage in these activities, another negotiating point that the U.S. and the U.S.S.R. sought to establish.[22]

In short, the ocean interests that were among the most important for the U.S. and the U.S.S.R. in 1972 do not appear to have been given the same priority on the List of Subjects and Issues as have the interests to which developing and landlocked countries then attached the greatest importance. The result is scarcely surprising, however, since, according to Richard N. Gardner, an "all-out battle [was] required to secure seats for the United States on the steering and drafting committees that [would] set the Caracas agenda."[23] Although in 1976 the United States eventually obtained draft treaty language stipulating its coveted right of transit through straits, it was only after intensive bargaining in which the U.S. sacrificed resource rights that were arguably of even greater value than the navigation rights obtained in exchange. After this experience it would be remarkable indeed if either the U.S. or the U.S.S.R. believed that the "procedural midwife" at UNCLOS was strictly neutral.

Rules for Voting

Deliberations at UNCLOS over the adoption of parliamentary rules of procedure consumed all of a special two-week "procedural" session held at the New York headquarters in December 1973, plus the first week of the first full negotiating session held at Caracas in 1974—altogether a fourth of the total time devoted to the first two conference sessions. Of the 66 different "Rules of Procedure"[24] adopted on July 12, 1974, the three most important pertain to the procedures for voting. These are Rules 37, 39, and 40 and the appendix incorporating the "Declaration of Gentleman's Agreement." The adoption of these rules became controversial owing to the desire of the developing countries to use the rules of procedure to gain an advantage over the developed countries, and vice versa.

The developed countries argued that the acceptance of new international law had to be broadly based to be effective, and therefore that a three-fourths voting rule, or perhaps one even closer to unanimity, should be required since the proposed treaty would create whole new divisions of property rights to ocean resources.[25] In particular, they believed that anything short of a broad consensus over the new treaty, and especially a simple paper majority composed of small and powerless states, would be meaningless. Their argument is strikingly similar to another major insight from the social choice literature that was put forward by James M. Buchanan and Gordon Tullock.[26] They analyzed the problem of under what conditions individuals who were voting in a democratic society would prefer certain choices to be made according to the rule of unanimity rather than the rule of simple majority. Buchanan and Tullock suggested that the rule of unanimity would be preferred for collective decisions affecting the overall structure of human or property rights where the group's choice would impose very great costs on particular individuals. For example, each individual might place a higher value upon the group being required constitutionally to obtain *his* consent before determining either the rules governing individual speech and expression or the rules for dividing activities between the public and private sectors. In contrast, many individuals might be satisfied with a constitutional rule of simple majority for such less important public choices as residential zoning or mosquito abatement. Carrying this analysis to the law of the sea, the problem of creating and dividing ocean property rights between the "international" and "national" sectors appears to have a logical structure that is similar to the intranational problem of dividing activities between the public and private sectors that Buchanan and Tullock studied. Therefore, the application of their theorem for individual decision making would appear to support the argument of the developed countries in favor of a three-fourths majority voting rule (or perhaps one even stronger). The bloc of developing countries, however, took the position that UNCLOS could not continue to debate every question until consensus was achieved, and that in the interests of expediency the conference ought to adopt the rule of simple majority.[27]

The negotiated compromise appeared to give both blocs something that they sought but in fact it advanced the interests of the developing countries more than those of the developed countries. Under the usual voting rule at the UN General Assembly, "important" issues are settled by a two-thirds majority of the states present and voting at a particular meeting. Abstentions and absences effectively count as partial votes since they do not make the achievement of the requisite majority more difficult. In this case, if 147 nations were represented at the General Assembly and 100 of them either abstained or were absent, a measure would pass if 32 states voted "yea" and 15 votes "nay." Under the UNCLOS compromise, Rule 39 permits a treaty to be adopted if it obtains two-thirds of the delegations "present and voting," provided also that it gets at least 74 votes—an absolute majority of the 147 countries that participate. Under Rule 40, "those present and voting" is determined by the number of countries in attendance at a given six- or eight-week session of UNCLOS rather than the number in attendance on a particular meeting day when votes occur. Thus the requisite majority of 74 votes is a binding constraint on UNCLOS decisions which is not affected either by absences or by abstentions.[28] For votes at meetings of the General Assembly, absences or abstentions do affect the requisite majority for the adoption of important measures, and therefore permit additional nuances in voting; this allows more opportunities for trading votes. The UNCLOS compromise therefore worked to the advantage of the developing countries not only by establishing a two-thirds rather than a three-fourths majority rule, but by defining "those present and voting" in a manner that reduced the opportunities for developed countries to vote strategically.[29]

The compromise on voting rules benefited the developed countries by establishing a gentleman's agreement that "the conference should make every effort to reach agreement on substantive matters by way of consensus and there should be no voting on such matters until all efforts at consensus have been exhausted." Rule 37 stipulates several rules for finding that "all efforts at reaching general agreement have been exhausted,'' permits voting delays for a ''10-day cooling-off period'' at the request of at least fifteen delegations, and allows a series of additional but minor delays in voting provided a simple majority of the conference agrees. In short, a vote can be taken only when a majority of states believe that further negotiations would be fruitless, which appears to protect at least some of the interests of the developed-country minority.

This ''victory'' for the developed countries came at a price, however. First, it opened the possibility of a series of procedural delays whenever fifteen delegations believed that delays would advance their national interests. In fact this has not proved to be a problem since the conference has rarely taken a vote. Otherwise the delays could be crippling since 400 different treaty articles have been under consideration. The inevitable delays brought about by attempting to reach consensus among so many delegations having different ocean interests appear to be an excellent illustration of the principle, first advanced in this context by Ronald H. Coase (1974), that transactions costs tend to increase the greater the number of countries involved in the negotiations.

Second, the voting rules at UNCLOS do not require that voting be limited to a single, all-encompassing treaty. The rules permit individual issues to be voted *seriatum* and could encourage serial voting since a pronounced advantage is given to the bloc of countries that is strong enough to determine the individual elements of the treaty and the sequence in which they are placed on the voting agenda. A numerical minority in a parliamentary situation will advance its interests usually in proportion to its ability to establish procedural rules that maximize the opportunities for ''strategic'' voting, that is, ''logrolling'' or vote trading. The operational equivalent of this proposition in the UNCLOS setting would be to vote, on a single occasion, the entire ocean treaty on a take-it-or-leave-it basis. This is because UNCLOS is not, or at least is not supposed to be, a continuing parliamentary body. Once its business is completed, the conference is expected to disband. Therefore, the opportunities for vote trading are limited mainly to the issues on the UNCLOS agenda. It would be risky for one country to trade its vote on an UNCLOS issue to which it attaches relatively little importance in exchange for another country's vote on an issue that the first country wanted at some future international conference that has yet to be convened or even at a future session of the UN General Assembly which has yet to organize its voting agenda. The cost to the first country of enforcing its exchange of votes with the second country would not be prohibitive since most countries probably want to avoid reputations for reneging; also, the General Assembly does meet at least once each year. Nevertheless, the enforcement costs would still be relatively high. In contrast, voting an omnibus treaty up or down on one occasion would make it relatively inexpensive for the minority-bloc countries to make sure that their ''trading partners'' had honored the voting promises that had been made to the minority countries on issues of great importance to them.

If voting in sequence on a large number of issues is allowed, then a strong advantage will probably be held by the bloc of nations that is able to determine the particular series of votes as well as the agenda. Robert L. Friedheim and James L. Johnston have argued that this type of voting procedure gives an overwhelming advantage to the group of developing countries at UNCLOS since the participation of a high fraction of this group is required to determine both the order of voting and whether substantive motions carry or fail.[30] The states that are able to place their favorite items high on the voting agenda would find it relatively inexpensive to abandon one-time pledges they may have made to countries outside this bloc concerning their votes on items that are placed low on the agenda and thus are low on the majority bloc's list of priorities. States that did not belong to this bloc, such as the United States or the Soviet Union, might find that their favorite issues were placed near the end of the voting agenda and that certain countries' votes that had been "promised" to them on these issues would fail to materialize when the tally was recorded.[31]

Levine and Plott have argued that the right to determine the agenda becomes all the more important as the size of the group increases. The agenda influences group choice in two ways.[32] First, it limits the information available to individual decision makers about the patterns of preferences in the group. The chief means of revealing preferences is by voting, and this is agenda-controlled. Verbal communication may exist but it is a poor substitute for "straw votes" when the size of the group is large. In effect, the large group raises the uncertainty for every option except those that appear on the agenda. Second, the agenda controls the ability to engage in strategic voting by limiting the available set of strategies to those contained in the agenda. It would be difficult to vote for "free transit through straits" or to organize a coalition that would favor it if "free transit through straits" does not appear on the agenda for discussion. "So, by reducing the influence of others' preferences and by determining the set of strategies available to him, the agenda effectively influences the voting pattern of each individual in the group. It thereby influences the choice made by the group."[33]

2. ACCOMPLISHMENTS OF UNCLOS THROUGH 1978

Until 1978, the public expressions of United States' delegates were full of hope that UNCLOS could produce a comprehensive and widely acceptable treaty, though they seem to have been most optimistic before the conference negotiations actually began. On March 1, 1973, during the preparatory work before the first negotiating session, Charles N. Brower, the acting legal adviser of the Department of State and the chairman of the U.S. Inter-Agency Task Force on the Law of the Sea (a body charged with coordinating U.S. policy between executive departments), wrote Senator Henry M. Jackson confidently: "We believe that there is reason to expect that the schedule for the Law of the Sea Conference outlined in the Conference Resolution just passed by the [United Nations] General Assembly will be adhered to. As previously indicated, the pre-amble of the Conference Resolution expressly states the expectation that the Conference will complete its work in 1974 or at the very latest in 1975."[34] Brower's successors continued to be more optimistic than not over the ensuing five years and six conference sessions. But in April 1978, during the seventh session, U.S. Ambassador-at-Large Elliot L. Richardson declared: "We have to recognize the possibility, indeed the probability, that we won't succeed. . . . When you say there is a one-in-three chance of success, you have to say there is a probability of failure under those circumstances."[35] In fact, optimism for the success of UNCLOS, expressed either in public or in private, had never been warranted. The high-cost transactional structure of the conference and its non-neutral procedures made the achievement of a comprehensive and widely accepted treaty from the outset a very difficult and perhaps a very remote possibility.

Procedural Defects

Between 1973 and the spring of 1978, UNCLOS convened for a total of 51 weeks: a two-week procedural session in New York in 1973 followed by six negotiating sessions consisting of ten weeks in Caracas in 1974, eight weeks in Geneva in 1975, eight weeks followed by seven weeks in New York during 1976, another eight weeks in New York in 1977, and most recently an eight-week session in Geneva beginning in April 1978. Counting the preparatory work and the intersessional business, UNCLOS since 1970 has been nearly a full-time occupation for the many delegates and their staffs. A prominent European delegate lamented to me in 1974 that he had not spent a summer with his family in five years. "The Law of the Sea," he told me, "is not so much an activity as a way of life." As discouraged as he was at the time, he might have been even more so had he known with certainty that at least another four summers of law-of-the-sea activity loomed ahead.

The work of the conference is divided among three substantive committees, each of which is supposed to develop draft treaty articles.[36] Committee I is charged with item no. 1 (see List of Subjects and Issues, Table 46) concern-ing the development of an international regime for the seabed and the ocean floor, and also with item no. 23 concerning archeological and historical treasures found on the seabed, beyond the limits of national jurisdiction. Committee II is charged with sixteen items consisting mostly of the traditional law-of-the-sea issues. These include the territorial sea and contiguous zone, straits, the continental shelf, coastal state rights beyond the territorial sea, and the high seas (items nos. 2 through 8); issues pertaining to geographically disadvantaged states (items nos. 9 and 10); broad-shelf states (item no. 11); archipelagic states (item no. 16); enclosed and semi-enclosed seas (item no. 17); artificial islands and installations (item no. 18); the status of islands (item no. 19); and radio transmission from the high seas (item no. 24). Committee III is charged with three items: the preservation of the marine environment (item no. 12); scientific research (item no. 13); and the transfer of technology (item no. 14). Four issues are to be considered by all three committees so far as each is germane to their particular mandates: regional arrangements (item no. 15); responsibility and liability for damage resulting from the use of the marine environment (item no. 20); machinery for the settlement of disputes (item no. 21); and the peaceful uses of ocean space (item no. 22). Two issues to be considered directly by the Plenary are item no. 22 and item no. 25, "enhancing the universal participation of states in multilateral conventions relating to the law of the sea."

The "agenda inherited from the United Nations Seabed Committee," Arvid Pardo observed in 1974, "contains serious omissions and duplications, a defective Conference structure in which closely related items are assigned to different committees and which encourages fragmented consideration of complex problems."[37] As for duplications, four agenda items were, as noted above, expressly assigned to each of the three committees so far as each item was germane to their mandates, but some other items implicitly overlap committee jurisdictions. The issue of scientific research in the coastal area, for example, is germane to the work of Committee III directly and Committee II indirectly since its mandate concerns both the continental shelf and the EEZ. The technology for exploiting the deep seabeds is held by relatively few countries, which makes the creation of an international regime to exploit these resources (the mandate of Committee I) partly dependent upon the transfer of technology (the mandate of Committee III). Also, the delimitation of the boundaries of the "international area" (the mandate of Committee I) would depend upon the seaward limit of the EEZ (the mandate of Committee II). Committee II itself contains a variety of contradictory mandates, such as the interests of broad-shelf states versus narrow-shelf states, coastal states versus geographically disadvantaged states, archipelagic states versus maritime states, and high seas fishing states versus preferential fishing rights for coastal states in areas beyond their territorial seas. As for important omissions or deletions from the List of Subjects and Issues, the most obvious is the delimitation by coastal states of the base lines from which the territorial sea and other jurisdictional zones are measured. The issue of base-line determination, which Pardo from the start has recognized as being almost essential to an attempt to halt or reverse the process of enclosure, is not mentioned directly in any of the 105 items, sub-items, or sub-sub-items on the agenda displayed in Table 46.[38]

In the first six sessions of UNCLOS, the Plenary held approximately 106 formal meetings through June 1978. Committee I held 44 formal meetings; Committee II held 56; and Committee III held 38. But these figures merely hint at the amount of actual work. Approximately 50 percent of these formal meetings were held at the Caracas session alone.[39] Since then, or midway through the 1975 Geneva session, work has been of a more informal sort, after it was realized that the three committees had produced few positive results not only because their mandates were confusing but because of size: every nation participating was a member of each committee as well as of the plenary. Thereafter, formal meetings were largely dispensed with in favor of smaller "working groups" of between twenty and forty geographically representative states in each committee. Of course, this did little to resolve the underlying divisiveness within the conference. Paul N. McCloskey, Jr., a member of the United States Congress (R.-Calif.) and also a member of the U.S. delegation to UNCLOS in 1976, watched what happened in Committee I:

> It was realized that negotiations could only go forward and compromises reached in a small group of perhaps 20 representatives. In organizing this small group, the Committee I chairman was first forced by the various regional organizations to expand the membership of the group to almost 30 to give each region some representation. He was then forced to choose two co-chairmen to please the advocates of the two main viewpoints. Finally, to please those who were left out, he made the decision to allow the group to be open-ended. This allowed the participation of all interested delegations so that they would be assured that nothing would happen behind their backs and that their interests would be represented. It was simply impossible for the chairman to form the small representative group necessary for effective negotiations.[40]

Perhaps the most obvious evidence of the transactional impediments at UNCLOS is its mass of verbiage. At Caracas, 90 mimeograph operators were reported to have worked around the clock on 27 machines to produce the 250,000 pages of daily documentation that were turned out by the delegates. The index alone for the Caracas documents was 160 pages long.[41] If the lifeless, repetitive character of the documents reflected the actual proceedings, it is scarcely surprising that some delegates reportedly "doodled" and roamed restlessly.[42]

Time was wasted in the conference meetings and agenda making, too. For example, the first six days of meetings at Caracas were set aside for opening "general statements."[43] An entire morning of "irrelevant grandiloquence" was devoted to praise of Simon Bolivar and there was an almost ritualistic expression of diplomatic condolences to Chile over a tanker accident off its coast which occurred during the meetings.[44] In March 1975, the conference's work at Geneva was suspended while 51 separate countries paid tribute to the late King Faisal, and at New York in September 1976, 35 countries expressed sympathy at the death of Chairman Mao.[45] Each event consumed an entire session of the Plenary. Some of these speeches could well have been given up if there had been a serious and widespread intention to complete a treaty expeditiously. After all, the prospect of the conference placed some countries in a prisoner's dilemma situation to make new enclosures or expand old claims before the treaty was adopted and ratified. Indeed, Secretary General Waldheim said that "Time is not on our side and delay would be perilous. We face the very real probability of increasing the causes of disputes between nations unless agreement is reached."[46]

Yet delay became UNCLOS's most notable feature, especially during the important, early sessions. Its inability to agree at Caracas on anything but the width of the EEZ, which had already been established by the enclosure movement, prompted scathing criticism from American newspapers. The *Washington Post* in 1972 called UNCLOS "a permanent floating oceanic crap game" which, the *Wall Street Journal* added later, is a "fiesta" that "floats from spa to shining spa."[47] Frivolous comments of this sort are hardly fair to the vast amount of time and resources that have been devoted to the conference effort, but they do get to the root of the weakness of its transactional framework: trying to form an agreement among a huge number of countries having widely differing ocean interests. Thus, the pace of the conference was set by groups of countries with interests in delaying an agreement.

The forces for delay were numerous. First, coastal states that had made enclosures had relatively little to gain from a treaty unless it would merely annoint the enclosures that they intended to enforce in any case, and they had reason to drag things out when it became clear that certain provisions of the draft treaty articles (to be noted later) could dilute the exclusivity of their coastal property rights. Second, the landlocked and geographically disadvantaged states had interests diametrically opposed to those of the coastal states and also had the votes to block a treaty that advanced coastal interests only. Third, some nations hedged because they simply failed to understand the complex issues at hand.[48] Fourth, the ocean mining countries stalled for a time when it appeared that the group would vote a treaty contrary to their interests. Later the land-based mining countries attempted to stall when it became clear that the ocean miners wanted a satisfactory treaty before beginning their dredging. Because several of these forces often worked simultaneously, delays were almost inevitable.

Characteristically, more time was wasted in a petty procedural dispute even during the seventh session at Geneva in April and May 1978. The diplomatic status of H. S. Amerasinghe, who had served as president of the conference since its inception, was placed in doubt when his home government (Sri Lanka) replaced him with a different delegate. The procedural question was whether someone who was not a representative could fill such an important post, and the debate droned on for ten days because of regional quarrels that are typical of UN decision making. (Certain coastal states thought Amerasinghe was too biased toward the landlocked and geographically disadvantaged countries.) The vote to keep Mr. Amerasinghe in this position in spite of his change of status is one of the few decisive actions that the conference has taken.[49]

Negotiations Other Than Ocean Mining

UNCLOS outcomes by June 1978 can be divided roughly into three very broad categories. The first category includes issues over which agreement has essentially been reached. Most of these issues include the outcomes of the enclosure movement which the conference has "ratified." The second category includes resource issues on which agreement has yet to be reached but for which the conference appears to be approaching agreement. Some of these apparent compromises tend to change from session to session. The third category includes the seabed issues, on which UNCLOS thus far has utterly failed to compromise.

The most notable achievement of the conference so far has been to agree on the 12-mile territorial sea and the additional 188-mile Exclusive Economic Zone which the enclosure movement had established. Aside from granting coastal states clear resource exploitation rights on the continental shelf and in the EEZ, maritime countries attempted to have the remainder of the zone characterized as "high seas" in which coastal states would have limited rights. The most that the maritime countries could get, however, was a middle position which described the EEZ as a zone *sui generis*—neither high seas nor a territorial sea but with protection for maritime rights of transit and overflight. The maritime countries also failed consistently to water down coastal restrictions on scientific research. Agreement was reached to grant coastal states control over land-based pollutants, ocean dumping, and continental shelf pollution.

The second category of issues—those over which UNCLOS may be moving toward agreements—includes jurisdiction over resources that involve either wealth redistribution or potentially extensive spillovers. Maritime states prevented coastal states from imposing "unreasonable" rules against vessel source pollution, but the resulting treaty articles on tanker construction and operating standards would have a weak effect at best on improving the ocean environment and would probably in the long run generate more economic costs than gains. Articles on migratory and anadromous fish would differ little from the enclosure movement in their impact on efficiency. The most bitter debates on issues in this category included revenue sharing from petroleum, the delimitation of the outer boundary of the continental shelf, the delimitation of EEZ boundaries between opposite and adjacent states, the division of fishing rights between coastal and either landlocked or geographically disadvantaged states, and granting landlocked states the right of access to the sea across lands of their adjacent coastal state neighbors. By June 1978 it appeared that at least some of these issues would have to be settled as a package, largely at the insistence of the landlocked and geographically disadvantaged countries.

In sum, issues over which UNCLOS by June 1978 either had reached agreement or appeared to be approaching an agreement were the subjects mandated to Committees II and III. Other than the agreement on a 12-mile territorial sea and a 188-mile EEZ, which came quickly and easily, most of the issues on which agreement is possible have been bargained over a four-year period (not counting the preparatory work between 1967 and 1973). At least some of this delay can be attributed to the conflicting mandates of Committee II and the inappropriate division of items on the List of Subjects and Issues between Committees II and III. Moreover, a few highly distributional issues remained unsettled. It is not even certain that the draft treaty articles represent a workable compromise of the various issues involved; this will only be learned if and when the treaty as a whole is brought to the vote.

Ocean Mining: The Intractable Issue

In March 1976, Bernardo Zuleta, the Colombian diplomat who serves as secretary general of UNCLOS, described metaphorically how the attempt had been made to assemble a compromise treaty that would be palatable to various nations: "The treaty has to be concocted like a paella to satisfy all tastes. One prepares the seafood, the meat, the chicken and the rice, but they are just an assortment of separate dishes until they are blended into perfect unity and the result is paella—or a treaty for all."[50] Kathleen Teltsch, a writer for the *New York Times*, described the process without the metaphor: "The strategy behind the single text is to allow margin for bargaining. A powerful seafaring country, in exchange for guarantees about passage through straits, would be expected to be more amenable to the poorer nations' demands for a more equitable sharing of the ocean resources."[51]

Whether or not this compromise treaty would be attractive to the maritime countries depended upon their relative evaluations of the value of military access rights as compared with resource access rights. In the case of the United States, naval access through straits has usually been its dominant policy objective in the law of the sea and its primary objective at UNCLOS. But resource access rights were also important to the United States. Gradually, as we shall see in Chapter 10, inflation and rising resource scarcities made these interests in some ways equal to the others, and in 1973 led to a dispute within the U.S. government between advocates of the two policy goals. As the UNCLOS minerals debate widened to include political and ideological issues as well as economic matters, it resulted in a clash between the younger developing countries and the older developed nations. The discord became so intense that the cost to the developed countries (which were also the prospective ocean miners) of obtaining their desired military access rights increased drastically in terms of the resource access rights that the developing countries demanded in exchange. As a result, the entire concept of a "paella—a treaty for all" was placed in serious doubt.

From the start the ocean mining debate had four main controversies:

1. Would the seabed be exploited by the private firms or state enterprises of individual countries probably subject to some form of international regulation, or would *all* exploitation be reserved for the international equivalent of a government monopoly?

2. Would the resource policy to guide exploitation be competitive or cartelizing by regulating production, dividing markets, and fixing prices?

3. Would the scope of the international regime include ownership of not only the minerals found on the seabed but also the seabed itself, all minerals and other objects found on or under it, the water column above it, and the right to control all scientific research in the international area beyond national jurisdiction?

4. Would the international authority reach decisions according to the rule of one-nation, one-vote as is characteristic of UNCLOS as a whole, or would voting be weighted to reflect the strengths and interests of the principal countries that would invest in, produce, and consume deepsea minerals?

The United States and other potential ocean mining countries preferred treaty articles creating an international regulatory or licensing regime similar to the 1970 U.S. proposal, the Draft Convention on the International Seabed Area. However, the power of this authority would be delimited carefully and its relationship with operators would be entirely contractual.[52] First, exploitation would be undertaken by private firms or state enterprises operating under international regulations, not by the international authority. The criteria for determining the rights of states or their nationals for access to ocean mining areas were to be absolutely uniform and nondiscriminatory between countries. Rights to ocean areas had to be exclusive and of a given size and known duration. The fees that could be charged for licenses, and the royalities that the authority could levy, had to be set in advance in the treaty. The proprietary data of mining companies had to be protected. Satisfactory procedures for the quick settlement of disputes, an absence of restraints on the transferability of licenses, and maximum limits on penalties for violations were essential. The authority would not be able to modify such rules at its sole discretion, and strictly bilateral questions such as the transfer of technology were to be negotiated by the countries directly involved. As the United States delegate to Committee I summarized it in 1974: "We cannot have the Authority deciding one day to make a particular kind of contract with a particular exploiter and then the very next day another contract with much more favorable conditions with his competitor. That breeds discrimination. Sovereign States have the right to discriminate, the Authority does not. A Sovereign State does not administer the Common Heritage of Mankind, the Authority does. Let us not draw too many analogies from our government practices."[53]

Second, the U.S. proposals would not have given the authority any power whatsoever to limit licenses or production for the purpose of supporting mineral prices. Third, the authority would not have either express or implied ownership of the seabed minerals, the seabed itself, or anything that might be found on or under it. The authority would not have express or implied power to control scientific research or to regulate navigation of any kind in the international area beyond national jurisdiction. Fourth, as an added assurance of impartiality and neutrality, the authority's procedures for voting would have to be weighted in favor of the ocean mining countries which could be outvoted so easily on a strict one-nation, one-vote system.

A completely different concept of the "common heritage of mankind" was offered by the developing countries. UNCLOS issues and personalities could not be separated entirely from other persistent issues on the agenda of the United Nations. Among these was the attempt of the Third World to create a "New International Economic Order" designed to redistribute world wealth in favor of poorer countries. These countries formed what came to be called the "Group of 77" in 1968 at the Algiers meeting of the United Nations Conference on Trade and Development (UNCTAD). By 1971, the group was 96-strong and had adopted an "Action Program" which stated, among other things, that developing countries should "encourage and promote appropriate commodity action, and particularly, the protection of the interests of primary producers . . . through intensive consultations among producer countries in order to encourage appropriate policies, leading to the establishment of producers' associations and understandings."[54] By 1974, the group had grown to 106 and was sufficiently united to demand, at the UN General Assembly session that focused on higher oil prices, a combination of commodity cartels, favorable trade agreements, more direct investment by developed countries, more grant aid, and more technology transfer.[55] Since 1970 the group has often been led by a coalition of Third World ideologues and by representatives of developing countries with a large stake in land-based mineral production.[56] Their approach to ocean mining, which reflects these larger, non-UNCLOS issues, was set forth in 1974 in eleven "Basic Conditions" which they believed should control exploitation in the international area. These were: (1) "The area and its resources being the common heritage of mankind . . . are vested in the Authority on behalf of mankind as a whole. These resources are not subject to alienation." (2) Title to these resources could not pass from the Authority "except in accordance with the rules and regulations laid down by the Authority and the terms and conditions of the relevant contracts, joint ventures, or any other such form of association entered into by it." (3) The Authority is to determine the timing and location of exploitation of the area. (4) The Authority may engage in mining operations itself or it "may . . . enter into contracts relating to one or more stages of operations with any person, natural or juridical . . . [including] scientific research, general survey, exploration, evaluation, feasibility study and construction of facilities, exploitation, processing, transportation and marketing." (5) The Authority shall select applications "on a competitive basis, taking into special account the need for the widest possible direct participation of developing countries, particularly the land-locked among them. The decision of the Authority in that regard shall be final and definitive." (6) The "rights and obligations arising out of a contract with the Authority shall not be transferred except with the consent of the Authority." (7) In all joint ventures and associations "the Authority shall have financial control through majority share and administrative control." (8) Contracts may be terminated by the Authority at its discretion. (9) All risks are to be borne by the entities that contract with the Authority. (10) Any individuals or firms that contract with or form joint ventures with the Authority are responsible for the transfer of "technology, know-how, and data relevant to the stage or stages of operation involved," and must also "undertake to provide at all levels training for personnel from developing countries particularly the land-locked among them, and employment, to the maximum extent possible, to qualified personnel from such countries." (11) The Authority has the right to limit seabed minerals production.[57]

Although the procedural rules at UNCLOS were supposed to require that every effort be made to find consensus on each issue before voting, and extraordinary efforts had in fact been made through 1978 concerning ocean mining, it was still not enough. Indeed, given the highly distributional and polemical nature of the debate, it is difficult to imagine how any compromise could have been reached on this issue that would have left the kernel of each side's position intact.

Each side of the debate found the other's position to be "unacceptable," and said so frankly even before negotiations began.[58] A. V. Lowe has shown that the basic divisions over ocean mining were obvious from the outset of discussions in the Ad Hoc General Assembly Seabed Committee in 1968 and have continued in essentially the same form through the preparatory work leading up to the UNCLOS negotiating sessions and subsequently in each of the six negotiating sessions themselves.[59] For example, during the two and a half years of preparatory work, the precursor of Committee I with jurisdiction over seabed issues was supposed to prepare drafts of twenty-one separate treaty articles concerning items nos. 1 and 23 of the List of Subjects and Issues. Of the twenty-one, the subcommittee was able to reach agreement on the "preambulatory principles" to only two relatively innocuous treaty articles: that the international area would "be open to use exclusively for peaceful purposes by all States, whether coastal or land-locked, without discrimination"; and that the activities undertaken there were to be in accord with the provisions of the forthcoming UNCLOS treaty and the United Nations Charter. In two and a half years practically no progress was made on the substantive questions of the organization and machinery of the regime and the limits of its operating authority.[60] Debate during this period on the key article concerning "Who will exploit the international area" was so divisive that four different "alternative texts" were drafted.[61]

In an attempt to break the impasse over ocean mining and several other issues that had developed during the preparatory work and at the 1974 Caracas negotiating session, the president of UNCLOS in 1975 asked the chairman of each committee to prepare an informal Single Negotiating Text. Each committee's text was supposed to reflect the limited number of agreements that had already been reached as well as the perceptions of each chairman of the preferences of a majority of states on those subjects where agreements had not been reached. The chairmen were free to include their own ideas on items that had not been discussed. The resulting documents would thus reflect to some degree not only the preferences of the three chairmen but also the preferences of the countries that had elected them as chairmen and had so far dominated the organization of the conference agenda in addition to much of its work. This may have looked a fair enough procedure, but it was in fact decidedly not neutral, because the formulation of the texts would be in the hands of the bloc of younger countries which had firm control over the agenda and over every other procedure.

Two of the texts that resulted clearly showed a certain bias in favor of these countries. The text for Committee II, prepared under the direction of its Latin American chairman, reflects the perspective of coastal states that wanted extensive enclosures and strong coastal state rights over living resources and scientific research. After four or five years of effort the conference has, as I mentioned earlier, moved toward agreement on many of the resource issues (although not on scientific research). In Committee I, Chairman Engo, a delegate of the Republic of Cameroon elected by a majority of the conference, produced a text that strongly reflected the views of the Group of 77. Indeed, his text was essentially the same as the "Basic Conditions" which the Group of 77 had demanded at the previous session of negotiations.

These treaty articles were just as objectionable to the advanced technology countries—and in particular the United States—in 1975 at Geneva as they had been in 1974 at Caracas. To improve its negotiating position, however, the United States in late 1975 began to offer the younger countries a curious combination of "carrots and sticks." By this time the U.S. policy apparently had been taken up personally by Secretary Kissinger.[62] Kissinger's "stick" was that the United States could not postpone unilateral seabed action much longer. At about this time the U.S. House of Representatives had passed a bill to create a 200-mile fisheries limit, and a bill to regulate U.S. exploitation of nodules in the "international area" was given an increasing possibility of passage in the Senate. It was widely predicted that passage before the conclusion of an UNCLOS treaty would infuriate the younger countries and might possibly ruin the entire UNCLOS effort.[63]

Kissinger's "carrots" amounted to concessions to the position of the Group of 77. In 1975 he offered to allow two "parallel access" systems of mining, whereby the international authority would mine on behalf of the developing countries and the ocean mining countries would concurrently mine for their own benefit, provided that the Authority's decision-making council was weighted in behalf of the advanced technology countries. The Group of 77 accepted Kissinger's offer and incorporated it in 1976 into the Revised Single Negotiating Text, but without incorporating the other changes that he wanted. So, in April 1976, Kissinger offered further concessions. First, the Authority could control the production of nodules during a "temporary" 25-year period. In effect, "production of the seabed minerals [would be] tied to the projected growth in the world nickel market, currently estimated to be about 6 percent per year."[64] Second, in what came to be called the "banking" system, U.S. ocean mining firms would be required to propose two fully explored mine sites to the Authority in return for the right to mine only one of them, with the other set aside for future mining by Enterprise. Third, Kissinger made vague suggestions that the U.S. would transfer ocean mining technologies to the developing countries. All these proposals were designed to reduce the rate of exploitation by the developed countries so that the developing countries would be assured of there being some nodules left for them to mine when (and if) they acquired the necessary technology. Such concessions produced little change in the stands of Committee I members, however; as Chairman Engo summarized the results of the next round of meetings, "It would clearly be less than candid to describe this as one of our more productive sessions."[65]

The Group of 77 may have been banking on a change in administrations with the 1976 U.S. presidential elections and possibly a better deal from President Ford's successor. Secretary Kissinger tried to dash these anticipations by saying that "there won't be a new administration" and that American policy would not change even if there were.[66] Then, as a final concession before the elections, he offered the developing countries U.S. financing of the initial operations of Enterprise so that it could begin operations concurrently with American firms. In return he demanded guaranteed access for American firms and weighted voting in the Authority's council.[67] But the only concrete result of these efforts was for the Group of 77 to agree to hold another session in 1977. Four weeks before the last 1976 session ended, one of the co-chairmen of the Committee I "working group," displaying the false optimism that had characterized UNCLOS from the start, asserted that "there was a general readiness . . . to engage in productive negotiations."[68] The plain fact was, however, that in the ocean mining debate, very little that was productive could be negotiated, and little that could be negotiated was productive.

To Engo, there had been a "climate of distrust and acrimony between opposing sides" for some time; failure was therefore "foreseeable and fore-seen."[69] For each side to dig in its heels, he said, was "a problem of the first magnitude"—

> a problem, in fact, that lies at the heart of our negotiation. It was a long, highly instructive and even necessary road we travelled these years since Caracas and indeed unknowingly continued to travel at this session. We all have to realize now that the journey is over and that we have arrived at the core of our prob-lem. . . . [The structure of the Authority] is the single most important decision that faces us in the First Committee, and I dare say, in the Conference as a whole. . . . We have now reached our valley of decision. We can proceed no further without a positive manifestation of political will that will enable us to adopt with confidence one or other of the . . . approaches that have been sug-gested during the Conference. With regard to these, there appears to be no indica-tion that the proponents of any will accept the others. We thus find ourselves in an impasse. There is little hope, I fear, that human ingenuity can find a way around. It can only be resolved through a change in the positions and attitudes that go to create this situation. This is the plain truth as I see it.[70]

This assessment of the ocean mining stalemate of 1976 was qualitatively almost identical to the assessment given back in 1974 by Christopher W. Pinto, the Sri Lanka delegate to Committee I and one of the most influential members of the Group of 77, when he declared that "progress had been made not in bringing the sides closer together but in clearly defining where they are farthest apart."[71]

The two sides were farthest apart in 1977. In an excellent illustration of UNCLOS' nonneutral procedures and the agenda power of the committee chairmen, Mr. Engo produced a new version of the seabed text which appeared to reflect strictly the views of his informal advisers of the Group of 77 and ignored the results of the preceding eight weeks of negotiations in New York.[72] These articles (1) weakened the system of parallel access that Kissinger had tried to establish; (2) expanded the Authority's discretion to allow it to require that, after 25 years, licenses held by private contractors would be transferred automatically to Enterprise, effectively to rule out private operations unless sought by the Authority as joint ventures; (3) extended the Authority's power over scientific research in the international area, arguably to the point of controlling it; (4) removed limits on the financial burdens which the Authority could impose on licensees and increased the number and types of possible burdens; (5) enhanced the Authority's power to restrict seabed production; and

(6) extended the Authority's power to include "all other minerals" such as hydrocarbons that might be found in the international area.[73] After Ambassador Richardson's firm rejection of this text, a few very minor improvements to it, from the standpoint of the U.S. and other ocean miners, were made at the seventh session of UNCLOS at Geneva in 1978. Successive sessions of the conference now appear to produce seabed treaty drafts that alternate between the Group of 77's "hard line" position, which is just about the "worst case" outcome from the standpoint of the ocean mining countries, and a slightly more yielding Group of 77 position which allows token concessions to the ocean miners.

It is difficult to see how the seabed provisions of the final treaty—if a treaty can be reached at all—can differ very much from the key elements of the position of the Group of 77. The United States delegation, in its summary report after the sixth session in 1977, was almost philosophical over the burdens it had to carry in Committee I and, implicitly, over the transactional structure of UNCLOS that put the U.S. at such an overall disadvantage:

> These difficulties are compounded by the fact that is is difficult to separate the seabeds negotiation into discreet [sic] elements which can be settled individually. Virtually every important issue—production controls, financial arrangements, nature of the International Seabed Authority, contract procedures, review, quota/antimonopoly provisions—relate to the core issue of access. In a sense, the negotiation is similar to playing a slot machine: all the cherries must be lined up in order to win. All of the issues noted above must be settled satisfactorily in order to achieve the objective of assuring nondiscriminatory access for States and their nationals. Thus, the package deal approach has characterized the negotiations to date and will continue to be necessary in future negotiating rounds.[74]

The analogy between Committee I procedures and a slot machine is perhaps more accurate than the U.S. delegation may have realized. The odds against the U.S. reaching a favorable (to its interests) and timely settlement of the several entwined issues in Committee I during any single round of negotiations are probably about equal to the odds against the slot player of lining up all three cherries on a single pull of the handle, simply because the procedures, agenda, and voting rules of UNCLOS have been twisted to give the Group of 77 a nonneutral advantage in constructing the negotiating package, much as the mechanism of the slot machine has been adjusted to tip the odds in favor of the house.

Which of the two sides would offer the "positive manifestation of political will" to make some agreement possible was difficult to foresee in 1978; after almost five years of hard bargaining, the "paella" had yet to be produced. Secretary Kissinger predicted the short-term course of U.S. policy correctly, however, for the Carter administration through mid-1978 was about as agreeable to the demands of the Group of 77 as the Ford administration had been. In 1978, as before, the easiest decision for UNCLOS to make was to hold more sessions.[75]

3. ECONOMIC IMPLICATIONS OF THE DRAFT TREATY TEXTS

The only substantial results of the sessions of UNCLOS between 1975 and 1978 have been the three successive draft texts of an ocean treaty. Each draft contains three relatively independent groups of articles that were prepared by each of the three cognizant committee chairmen following debate and discussion in their committees.[76] The most recent draft, the Informal Composite Negotiating Text, contains 303 articles in the body of the treaty (totaling 198 single-spaced pages) plus an additional 98 articles in seven annexes (and more amendments were introduced in following sessions). It is not my intention here to try and predict the content of the final treaty—that would in fact be something like trying to hit a moving target, for the texts have changed somewhat from session to session and further changes will undoubtedly be made. But I can evaluate the economic implications of the major alternative structures of resource rights that are contained in the two most recent versions of the treaty (the 1976 Revised Text and the 1977 Composite Text with the 1978 amendments) and see how they compare with the economic consequences of the enclosure movement that were detailed in Part One. (Table 47 gives a capsule summary of these comparisons.)

Enclosure

Both the 1976 and the 1977 texts "ratify" the enclosure movement with articles permitting straight base lines that incorporate most of the provisions of the Geneva Convention on the Territorial Sea and the Contiguous Zone, which in turn had incorporated very generous practices for determining base lines such as Norway's in the Barents Sea. But the two texts liberalize the Geneva provisions in three ways: (1) islands having atolls or fringing reefs may draw base lines from the low-water lines of the reef;[77] (2) coastal states "may determine baselines . . . by any of the methods provided . . . to suit different conditions";[78] (3) archipelagic states may draw base lines from outermost points provided that (*a*) the ratio of water area to the area of land and atolls is no more than nine to one, and (*b*) only 3 percent of segments exceed 100 miles, up to a maximum of 125.[79]

The 200-mile EEZ is, according to Committee II chairman Andres Aguilar, "neither the high seas nor the territorial sea. It is a zone *sui generis*."[80] In this view, all states would have equal rights of transit through the EEZ, and of communication by cables and pipelines. But coastal countries would be given all "sovereign rights for the purpose of exploring and exploiting, conserving and

TABLE 47

Probable Effect on Avoiding Economic Inefficiency of Two UNCLOS
Treaty Texts as Compared with the Enclosure Movement*

Category of Resource Rights	Revised Text of 1976	Composite Text of 1977-1978	Enclosure Movement
Drawing base lines and extent of EEZ	++	+	++
Navigation	++	++	++
Hydrocarbons	+	+	++
Fisheries			
Coastal	+	?	+
Migratory	0	0	+
Anadromous	+	+	+
Environment			

Where EEZs are large and
  pollution transport is not
  effective			

land-based	++	++	++
dumping	0	0	++
vessel-source	--	-	+

Where EEZs are small and
  pollution transport is
  effective			

land-based	+	+	+
dumping	0	0	0
vessel-source	-	-	--
Research	--	-	--
Deep-sea minerals	-	--	++

NOTE: (+) or (++) indicates that the particular resource rights would promote economic efficiency; (−) or (− −) indicates that the resource rights would promote economic inefficiency; (0) indicates that the resource rights would probably have a neutral impact on economic efficiency; and (?) indicates that the likely impacts are uncertain.

*These comparisons are based on the conceptual scheme of Chapter 2 and are relevant only across rows for the individual categories of resource rights.

managing the natural resources, whether living or nonliving, of the seabed and subsoil and the superjacent waters,"[81] and the coastal state would be entitled to enforce its rights by inspecting and boarding ships, making arrests, and imposing fines and other penalties.[82] The two texts diverge, however, in the assignment of resource rights within the EEZ which are not otherwise made explicit. Whereas the Revised Text gives residual rights to coastal states, the Composite Text resolves conflicts between coastal states and others "on the basis of equity and in light of all relevant circumstances, taking into account the respective importance of the interests involved to the parties as well as to the international community as a whole."[83] The Composite Text further emphasizes the EEZ rights of non-coastal states by declaring that "no state may validly purport to subject any part of the high seas to its sovereignty."[84] Provisions such as these would reduce exclusivity and raise transactions costs, and therefore lessen the likelihood of avoiding economic inefficiency.

Navigation

In general, both texts grant coastal states the right to control coastal navigation, although they place certain constraints on the exercise of that right. There is little evidence in either text to support the hypothesis that many coastal countries seek to curtail navigation extensively. Rather, these articles appear to be consistent with the argument outlined in Chapter 3 (pp. 74–79) that coastal states that engage in maritime trade, and in particular those that import oil, would not restrict navigation without taking into account spillover impacts. These texts also avoid the creation of new international organizations to regulate shipping.

The authority of coastal states to control navigation within the territorial sea is still limited by the 1958 Geneva rule of "innocent passage," but the definition of what transit is "prejudicial to the peace, good order, or security of the coastal state" has been broadened to include (1) "acts of willful and serious pollution," (2) "any act aimed at collecting information to the prejudice of the defense or security of the coastal state," (3) any fishing, and (4) "the carrying out of research or survey activities."[85] Both texts specifically extend recognition to the claims of coastal states to restrict passage in the territorial sea for the purposes of safety, conserving living resources, preserving the marine environment, and scientific research.[86] Sea-lanes and traffic-separation schemes are authorized, especially for "tankers and nuclear-powered ships and ships carrying nuclear or other inherently dangerous or noxious substances or materials," but the coastal states are also specifically instructed not to discriminate among ships of different nations or to adopt rules and practices that have discrimination as their practical effect.[87] The Geneva provisions permitting nondiscriminatory fees to be levied in exchange for services have not been modified, although more subtle fee schedules which could tie the right of passage to the purchase of bunker fuel or other goods and services have not been proscribed. (See Chap. 3, p. 78 above).

The rules for navigation through archipelagoes and straits are relatively congenial to the interests of maritime countries. All states enjoy a right of innocent passage through archipelagic territorial seas, and in the waters adjacent to the territorial sea archipelagic states may establish either sea-lanes of a minimum width or traffic-separating schemes (like those mentioned in Chapter 3) for passage between one area of the high seas or an EEZ to another area of high seas or EEZ; such routes must include routes and channels normally used for navigation or overflight.[88] "If an archipelagic State does not designate sea lanes or air routes, the right of archipelagic sea lanes passage may be exercised through the routes normally used for international navigation." In addition, an archipelagic state may not draw its base lines in a manner that would cut off from high seas or its EEZ the territorial sea of another state.[89]

For straits that are international waterways, the texts create a right of "transit passage," which straits states may not suspend, for ships engaged in "international navigation between one area of the high seas or an exclusive economic zone and another area of the high seas or an exclusive economic zone," although, the Composite Text adds, ships may not engage in scientific research activities during such trips without the permission of the straits state.[90] Straits states "may designate sea lanes and prescribe traffic separation schemes where necessary to promote the safe passage of ships."[91] Such plans must be submitted to the Inter-Governmental Maritime Consultative Organization (IMCO) "with a view to their adoption," but IMCO may not fail to adopt a plan to which the straits state(s) does not agree.[92] These articles indicate that the maritime states that were intent upon "free transit through straits" got most of what they wanted in the right of transit passage, and certainly more from their point of view than would have been implied by the rule of innocent passage.

Hydrocarbons

The continental shelf articles of the texts are generally consistent with avoiding inefficiency in mineral extraction. The "legal" shelf would extend out to 200 nautical miles or the edge of the margin, whichever is farthest.[93] Within the area the coastal state would exercise "sovereign rights" for exploration and exploitation that are "exclusive in the sense that if the coastal State does not explore the continental shelf or exploit its natural resources, no one may undertake these activities without [its] express consent."[94] This definition would eliminate both unowned areas and areas of shared ownership since the jurisdiction of the international authority would begin where the coastal state's ends.

However, the historic difficulty of nations in defining the limit of the shelf or margin has surfaced at the Third UNCLOS just as at previous meetings. UNCLOS has considered several relatively simple definitions of the margin, but has not yet been able to agree on one of them.[95] Moreover, the landlocked and geographically disadvantaged states are unwilling to agree to the definition of the margin until the questions of revenue sharing from shelf exploitation beyond 200 miles and of their fishing rights in the EEZs of neighboring coastal states are also settled. These tie-in arrangements have complicated the bargaining in a manner that is characteristic of UNCLOS and, of course, raise the possibility of inducing inefficiencies through extra taxes and nonexclusive ownership arrangements.

In the case of revenue sharing, developed coastal states would have to share with the international authority a portion of the revenues from exploitation beyond the 200-mile contour (which would exclude such vast deposits as those in the Persian Gulf, the Gulf of Mexico, and the North Sea). The extent of sharing is set tentatively at one percent of the value of well production beginning in the fifth year and increasing by one percent per year to the tenth year. Developing coastal states that are also net importers of minerals would be exempted.[96] Raising the taxes on marginal wells at greater depths (which would be the case beyond 200 miles from shore) means that some wells that would have been exploited without taxes may not become producers. Also, the tax rises over a period when reservoir pressures would normally decline, thus reducing the life of those wells at such depths that do produce. Thus, extra revenue-sharing obligations under an UNCLOS treaty will probably result in some inefficiency beyond what would occur under completely exclusive coastal enclosures.

Fisheries

The package of EEZ rights in each treaty text recognizes the tighter restrictions that some coastal states have imposed on the catch taken by foreign vessels; on certain species, gear, and seasons; and their enforcement through boarding, fines, and punishments. The texts are ambiguous, however, concerning the ideal rate of catch. In one set of articles they establish the criterion of "maximum sustainable yield, as qualified by relevant environmental and economic [as well as other] factors," and in another set they suggest that the rate of catch be limited to the "optimum utilization."[97] Either of these criteria would be an improvement over the straightforwardly inefficient criterion of maximum sustainable yield that was adopted in the 1958 Geneva Convention on Fishing and Living Resources. But the creation of economic rents in coastal species would also require that states limit entry by domestic fishermen.

Exclusivity of the rights of coastal states to exploit coastal fisheries is weakened somewhat owing to their distributional dispute with landlocked and geographically disadvantaged states. According to the 1978 amendments to the Composite Text, a coastal state is supposed to determine its capacity to harvest the living resources of its EEZ. Where the allowable catch exceeds this capacity, landlocked and geographically disadvantaged states "have the right to participate, on an equitable basis, in the exploitation of an appropriate part of the surplus . . . taking into account the relevant economic and geographical circumstances of all the States concerned."[98] Special consideration is supposed to be given to states that already participate in such fisheries through bilateral or regional arrangements as well as to the fishing interests and the nutritional needs of the coastal state. Where the harvesting capacity of the coastal state approaches the amount of the allowable catch of its EEZ, it must "operate in the establishment of equitable arrangements . . . as may be appropriate in the circumstances and on terms satisfactory to all parties."[99] However, *developed* landlocked and geographically disadvantaged states would be entitled to participate in fisheries in the EEZs of *developed* coastal states only.[100] Although these articles appear to reach a compromise on the conflicting distributional interests, they probably raise transactions costs as well by requiring "equitable" arrangements that are "satisfactory to all parties." Whether landlocked and geographically disadvantaged states pay coastal states for fishing rights or whether the latter pay to keep the former out is a distributional question beyond the limits of this study. But attempts to grant fishing rights in a single EEZ to every interested state probably reduce the possibilities for creating economic rents in fisheries.

The texts offer few possibilities for creating rents in migratory species owing to the higher transactions and enforcement costs involved. Articles that urge states to cooperate in achieving optimum utilization are no more likely to generate rents now than they have in the past under multilateral fisheries arrangements.[101] For this reason, 200-mile EEZs or special fisheries zones appear to offer a better opportunity (owing to smaller transacting costs) to create rents for the fraction of a species that each coastal state can enclose. Articles attempting to create rents for anadromous species by requiring that exploitation be confined to the EEZ of the home country[102] are essentially redundant on articles creating EEZs, and therefore would probably have no greater impact on efficient resource use than 200-mile enclosures.

Marine Environment

These articles recognize all four sources of pollution described in Chapter 6—land-based blowoff and runoff, seabed installations, dumping, and vessels—and the division of authority over them corresponds very roughly with the analysis of spillovers and transactions costs. However, the sanctions in each text against pollution of all types are very weak. This was to be expected for coastal state sources and is not unwarranted on the basis of economics, but it is neither necessary nor economically desirable for vessel sources if appropriate regulations can be put in place. Because some of these articles are not appropriate to the economics of vessel source pollution, they are likely to be a source of inefficiency to the extent they can be enforced.

The texts assign to nations "the obligation to protect and preserve the marine environment," to make resource exploitation rights contingent upon this duty, to internalize the full consequences of polluting activities that occur within their jurisdictions, and to require only that the "best practicable means" be used to reduce pollution.[103] Individual countries are thus left to decide whether it is economic to eliminate pollution and, if so, whether the appropriate action is unilateral or joint with other countries. Coastal states have jurisdiction over land-based sources as well as seabed installations.[104] Coastal states probably can enforce against such sources at lower cost than international bodies can, especially where coastal waters are not effective in transporting pollutants to other nations' EEZs, and regional cooperation is encouraged where spillovers are extensive. Developing countries are exempted from most of these provisions, however.[105]

The texts on dumping are consistent with the 1972 convention (see Chap. 6, pp. 175–76) in urging coastal states to establish antidumping domestic statutes and granting them exclusive jurisdiction over such activities within their EEZs, subject to appropriate regional coordination.[106] National standards against dumping are supposed to be no less effective than international standards.[107] This provision reflects the differences between abatement or spillover costs among nations and regions as well as the higher transactions costs of compen-sating those states that are subjected to what is for them an uneconomic international standard.

The texts on vessel pollution were designed to incorporate the standards for ballast discharge and for tanker design and construction of the 1973 IMCO Convention for the Prevention of Pollution from Ships as opposed to the system of strict liability described in Chapter 6 (pp. 184–91). As with the IMCO convention, the controversy between coastal states that sought firm pollution enforcement rights and the maritime states that sought relatively weak enforcement rights appears to have been resolved with treaty language that is favorable to the maritime states.[108]

Enforcement authority is divided between flag states, port states, and coastal states. Flag states are supposed to adopt laws and regulations that conform to international standards, to inspect vessels flying their flags and to prevent those that fail to meet standards from leaving home ports, and to enforce such rules effectively at the request of any state "irrespective of where the violation occurred."[109] This language is not related to the current international situation where many ships (and often those in poor condition) are registered in nations that they visit rarely and that are known to adopt registry standards that are widely considered as being lax.

The texts give coastal states the right to establish rules and regulations against pollution in their territorial sea, subject to the rules of innocent passage,[110] but provide weaker enforcement rights against violations in their EEZ. When a coastal state has clear grounds for believing that a violation of international standards has occurred in its territorial sea, it may inspect or if necessary arrest the vessel.[111] Within its EEZ, however, it may establish only those rules and regulations "conforming to and giving effect to generally accepted international rules and standards,"[112] and its enforcement of these rules may be limited to requiring that the vessel provide data on its identification, registry, and its last and next ports of call. These data, along with the details of the alleged violation, may be transferred to the port state to which the vessel is traveling or where it is already at dock. The port state is supposed to "endeavor to comply" with requests for investigations made by coastal states, but it is not compelled to investigate the incident, to enforce the international standard, or to transfer the proceedings back to the coastal state when it so requests.[113] In any case the port state would presumably discount the damage and abatement costs involved by more than would the coastal state that incurred them. The coastal state may directly enforce international standards within its EEZ in accordance with its own laws only when a vessel has "committed a flagrant or gross violation . . . resulting in discharge causing major damage or threat of major damage to the coastline or related interest of the coastal State, or to any resources of its territorial sea or economic zone."[114] But this provision must be waived if the flag state has already assumed liability or has otherwise bonded the vessel or provided for a compulsory insurance scheme, and vessels may not be prosecuted in two jurisdictions for the same alleged offense.[115]

Coastal states are granted special rights to establish and enforce nondiscriminatory laws and regulations for the prevention of pollution in ice-covered areas within their EEZs, which recognizes the special restrictions imposed by Canada in the Arctic Ocean, provided they are first submitted for IMCO's approval.[116]

In sum, neither text is likely to reduce vessel pollution to economically efficient levels. Each adopts the approach of internationally agreed vessel construction standards rather than strict liability for leaks and accidents, and each weakens coastal state enforcement relative to port states or international bodies which face different configurations of costs and rewards in addition to higher transactions costs. Some improvements to the Composite Text were in the offing during 1978. These amendments would have allowed coastal states to impose discharge standards exceeding international levels within the territorial sea, to establish other than monetary penalties for violations in the territorial sea, and to establish only "clear objective evidence" (rather than a "gross violation") before arresting polluting vessels in their EEZs.[117] However, these amendments had not been widely accepted through June 1978, and in any case would improve an economically unsatisfactory text only slightly.

Marine Scientific Research

Both texts retain important elements of the "consent regime" established in the 1958 Geneva Convention on the Continental Shelf, although the circumstances in which coastal states may legitimately withhold consent have been restricted. The essential purpose of the consent regime is to enable coastal states to distort marine research somewhat in favor of projects that benefit themselves and to maintain some degree of secrecy over research that contains military or commercial applications (see Chap. 7). Neither text distinguishes between fundamental and applied research, probably because of monitoring costs.[118]

The conduct of research in the territorial sea, the continental shelf, and the EEZ is subject to the permission of the coastal state in advance of the project. Coastal states may require that their personnel (a) participate in the voyage without contributing to the project's costs, (b) obtain preliminary and final reports of the research results, and (c) receive copies of all data and samples plus assistance in interpreting them.[119] The Composite Text, which is somewhat more favorable to research countries than is the Revised Text, provides that coastal consent will not be withheld "in normal circumstances" and that research projects will not be subjected to "unreasonable" delays or denials unless the project bears on the exploration or exploitation of resources, involves drilling or explosives, interferes with economic activities, or requires the construction of artificial islands or installations.[120] Tacit consent is assumed if a coastal state has not expressly denied an application for research within four months of receiving it.[121] From the point of view of research-oriented countries, these consent requirements, although strict, represent at least some improvement on the position taken by some coastal states at the Caracas session, which would have required their approval for research undertaken by satellites.[122]

One issue that remains to be settled is whether or not scientific results may be disclosed or published without the permission of the coastal state. The Revised Text contained a prohibition of this kind but the Composite Text deleted it.[123] Such a rule would reflect the high monitoring costs of applied versus basic research and the absence of a practical market in which the coastal state could hedge the adverse impact of unfavorable news upon its wealth (see Chap. 7, pp. 206–07). Thus, the Composite Text, if enforced, would have a slightly smaller negative impact on generating the economically efficient amount of new marine scientific information than either the Revised Text or the enclousre movement.

Deep Seabed Minerals

The seabed articles are unique within the texts in the degree to which they create institutions which promote economic inefficiency—almost as effectively as if that were the intended goal. These institutions bear little resemblance to the registry office or the licensing authority that were described in Chapter 8, which were weak forms of regulation that offered relatively mild impediments to efficiency, and they bear no resemblance whatsoever to the alternative that would maximize economic rents by postponing property rights altogether until crowding caused misallocations of either the free-rider or the common pool type. The principal difference between the seabed articles contained in successive treaty texts is that they alternate between creating a regime substantially more restrictive than was proposed by the United States in 1970 and a regime slightly less restrictive than the Basic Conditions demanded by the Group of 77 in 1974. The economic consequences would vary between, in the case of the former, a regime that would be hugely wasteful, or, in the case of the latter, something even worse.

Each text creates a highly bureaucratic Authority composed of three main organs. Superficially, this bears some resemblance to a system where powers are separated and each element has certain checks and balances over the other two, but in reality, all power flows from a legislative assembly that is composed of all treaty signatories, each having one vote, with voting rules identical to those of UNCLOS itself. The structure of the Authority contained in the Revised Text is shown in Figure 27. The executive body is the council, responsible for day-to-day business and for establishing general policies to govern the Enterprise. Its 36 seats are filled by the assembly upon nominations submitted by each signatory. Six of these are assigned to ocean-mining nations; another six are divided among mineral-exporting, landlocked, geographically disadvantaged, mineral-importing, large-population, and the least-developed countries. The other 24 are distributed to assure geographical balance.[124] The executive bureaucracy is enlarged by three specialized commissions. The technical commission would evaluate the engineering and environmental aspects of seabed license applications and exploitation techniques, scientific research, and the transfer of technology. The economic planning commission would set resource policy and determine the impact of seabed mining on the wealth of land-based mineral-exporting countries. The rules and regulations commission would assist the council in setting down procedures for seabed mining.[125] The assembly would appoint all eleven judges to the tribunal "with due regard to the principle of equitable geographical distribution and of assuring representation of the principal legal systems of the world." Judges would serve six-year terms, with reappointment possible, and would decide cases by a simple majority. Their orders would be "final and binding" and would be "enforceable in the territories of Members of the Authority in the same way as judgments or orders of the highest court of that Member State."[126] The tribunal would have jurisdiction over disputes between states or between a state (or its nationals) and either the Authority or the Enterprise, and the only law applicable to the resolution of such disputes would be the treaty itself plus the rules and regulations promulgated by the Authority.[127] Clearly this system of governance fails to protect the voting interests of ocean-mining countries, whose interests best approximate those of economic efficiency.

The same nonneutral UNCLOS procedures that have dominated its agenda and the structure of the Authority apparently also dominate its rules and practices. Although neither text is favorable to efficient resource use, the Composite Text is the worse of the two. There are fewer controls over scientific research in the international area in the Revised Text than in the Composite Text.[128] In the Revised Text the Authority must select among license applications on "a competitive basis" and can refuse to grant a contract on relatively narrow grounds.[129] The Composite Text removes these provisions and gives preference to applicants who are willing to form joint ventures with the Authority;[130] it also gives higher status to Enterprise than to the firms of member states.[131]

Each text claims that the Authority is supposed to avoid "discrimination" in the conduct of its affairs, but the opportunities for favoritism in such a

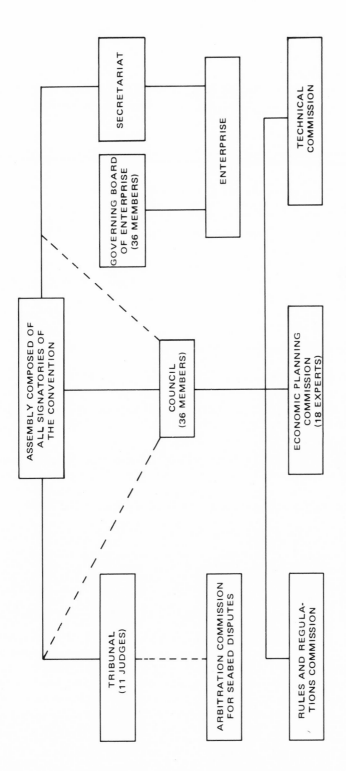

FIG. 27. Structure of proposed International Seabed Authority contained in the 1976 *Revised Single Negotiating Text*.

centralized organization are large and certain forms of discrimination are sanctioned. For example, giving "special consideration for developing countries . . . shall not be deemed to be discrimination."[132] Enterprise is authorized to sell "its products at lower prices [than the international market level] to developing countries, particularly the least developed among them,"[133] and to purchase materials and services from these countries so far as possible.[134] As Everett G. Martin of the *Wall Street Journal* put it, "supposedly politics wouldn't enter into the [Authority's] decision—just as there is no politics on the International Olympics Committee, for example."[135]

The extent to which the structure and powers of the Authority depart from the structure and power of present international organizations can best be seen by comparing it briefly with the International Telecommunications Union (ITU).[136] The ITU is the only specialized agency of the United Nations to deal with a particular resource, in this case the spectrum of electromagnetic frequencies. Its chief governing body is the Plenipotentiary Conference, consisting of all members, which meets about every five years and may revise all or any part of the ITU Convention by simple majority vote. Establishing "regulations" for the use of frequencies is done by an administrative council of 29 states elected by the Plenipotentiary Conference. An International Frequency Registration Board maintains a list of the frequencies used by individual countries, rights to which are usually established by first-in-time claims. The board is much like the registry clearinghouse model described in Chapter 8 (pp. 245–46). Its powers are limited to publishing notices stating the plans of individual countries to use frequencies and collecting objections to such plans by other countries. It has no power to reject applications even when it suspects that harmful interference will result; such disputes are always settled bilaterally by the countries involved. It also lacks power to monitor interference levels, and "it is firmly established that the union should not be an operating agency."[137] Countries in the ITU attempt to make decisions by unanimity, but failing that, by a two-thirds majority. Financial contributions are voluntary in occurrence and in amount. Hence, the structure, operational powers, and financing of the ITU are almost the antithesis of the proposed International Seabed Authority.

Both texts show that UNCLOS intends to reduce seabed minerals production for "the protection of developing countries from adverse effects on their economies or on their earnings."[138] Thus, the Authority may facilitate "through existing forums or such new arrangements or agreements as may be appropriate and in which all affected parties participate, . . . the growth, efficiency and stability of markets for commodities produced from the resources of the Area, at prices remunerative to producers and fair to consumers . . . The Authority shall have the right to become a party to any such arrangements or agreements resulting from such conferences."[139] Of course, both texts enjoin the Authority to limit the annual production of seabed minerals to a particular formula (which is different in each text) based on rates of increase in the world consumption of nickel.[140] Other than these express powers to control production, the Authority's power to determine the areas and minerals to be mined, the duration of contracts and limitations on renewals, and the degree of taxation and profit sharing (none of which is limited in either text) could accomplish the same result indirectly.[141]

The "parallel system" contained in the Revised Text, whereby private ocean miners would operate contractually with the Authority's permission while Enterprise mined different areas independently for the Authority's exclusive benefit, is much less inferior in efficiency terms to the "unitary system" of the Composite Text, whereby all exploitation was done either by Enterprise or by contractors in joint ventures with Enterprise. According to the so-called "banking system," which would require prior adoption of the parallel system, a private miner could propose two mine sites of equal area which he had explored in detail as part of the license application but would be granted rights to exploit only one of them. The other would be set aside by the Authority for its own immediate or future exploitation.[142] This scheme would thus in a sense promote efficiency, if only by limiting the most inefficient arrangements (those of Enterprise) to a number of mine sites no greater than those of the private miners, but it would at the same time double the cost of exploration and prospecting by private miners and would make it less easy, as explained in Chapter 8, to adapt particular seabed areas to specialized technologies. The arrangements contained in the Revised Text are thus superior to the Composite Text but are inferior to no text at all.

UNCLOS also appears to be biased against seabed production by countries with low-cost exploitation technologies. The conference has accepted in principle, as suggested by developing and developed countries alike, the establishment of a "quota or antimonopoly provision" to prevent a single country—presumably the United States—from exploiting more than a certain percent of the international area.[143] Moreover, once a treaty has been signed, it may provide for a review conference in twenty to twenty-five years to assure that past exploitation has taken place for the "common benefit of mankind" and without monopolization by a particular country.[144] Failure of the review conference to reach agreement could lead either to cancellation of private contracts under the parallel system, with reversion to the unitary system of exploitation by Enterprise alone, or to a moratorium on the approval of new contracts or new plans of work by private ocean miners.[145]

Creation of the international seabed authority is probably a necessary condition for a successful worldwide minerals cartel, which appears to be the objective at UNCLOS of the terrestrial mineral-producing nations. In this sense, seabed production, no matter how many countries engage in it, will be a force for competition rather than for monopoly of minerals. Restricting the entry of new seabed miners is not likely to be a sufficient condition for successful cartelization because the Authority would not automatically control production within the 200-mile EEZs of individual states.[146] But a treaty with restrictions on entry would facilitate cartelization in two ways: first, it would require smaller reductions in the quotas of land-based producers, hence placing fewer internal strains on the cartel and reducing the incentives of its members to shave prices;[147] second, signatures on the treaty of mineral-importing countries would bind them to prohibit imports at lower prices or in greater quantities than the Authority had decided upon.[148]

4. WHAT IF UNCLOS WERE TO VOTE?

In spite of the huge majority held by the younger countries, their skill in organizing an agenda that serves their own interest, and the almost inevitable difficulties faced by the developed countries in attempting to influence this powerful majority, only a few matters have actually come to a vote at UNCLOS in all its sessions. The transactional structure of the conference makes it extremely difficult to predict voting outcomes. The number of decision makers is large, and so is the number and complexity of issues. If all 149 countries had to decide on each of the 400 treaty articles under consideration in 1978, the decision matrix required to produce a final treaty would contain 59,600 cells! If only one-fourth of these articles were substantive issues, something on the order of 14,900 relatively important decisions would still be required. Thus, because of these costs in time alone, it seems probable that when and if negotiations are ever completed, the treaty will be approved, or rejected, as a whole after a single call of the roll of nations. To have a separate vote on every article in the treaty, and to allow nations that had objections to any article to state them one by one, could consume months of effort. Realizing this, the member nations have bargained intensively over the contents of successive treaty texts, for both sides are well aware of the importance of influencing the treaty package for a probable one-time vote.

An attempt to model UNCLOS voting has been made by Robert L. Friedheim and William J. Durch.[149] Their model predicts the votes of countries based on what their representatives have said at meetings of the UNCLOS Plenary and committees. From these speeches, certain "themes" are extracted to stand for national preferences on the substantive or procedural questions under discussion. Data for the model, therefore, constitute what states publicly claim their interests to be. For a particular issue, themes are arrayed along a spectrum between the polar extremes of offers and counteroffers. For example, the three-mile territorial sea is the strongest United States preference for territorial limits, to which the 200-mile territorial sea is the strongest counteroffer favored by certain Latin American nations. (The 50-mile territorial sea and the 200-mile EEZ would represent intermediate and possibly "compromise" positions.) Each position is ranked ordinally and then weighted by the number of times that the theme-position is repeated in speeches by each country. More than 40,000 observations were made for UNCLOS sessions between 1967 and 1975 for about 1,500 themes. Computer operations permit a variety of comparisons for individual countries, groups of countries, and changes in their positions. Predictions of preferences of countries that have not publicly declared their positions are estimated on the basis of the known positions of countries that have spoken and that have similar geographical or other oceans interests.

Figures 28 and 29 illustrate the model's predictions for preferred outcomes (votes if they were taken) on three UNCLOS issues: (1) who may exploit the international area, (2) the breadth of the EEZ, and (3) the strength of the coastal state's jurisdiction—its rights and duties—within the EEZ. Countries are divided according to two sets of interest groups. Geographical groups, subdivided according to length of coastline, are shown in the three graphs on the right-hand side of each chart. The division between the older-and-richer versus the younger-and-poorer nations—which political scientists refer to as the North-South split—is shown in each of the three graphs on the left-hand side of each chart. Figure 28 shows the predictions for the mean position of each of the two groups, and Figure 29 shows the standard deviations. As one moves up the Y-axis from the origin in each of the three pairs of graphs in either figure, one encounters, respectively, proposals for (1) increasingly exclusive exploitation of the deep seabeds by an international regime (graphs *a* and *b* in each figure); (2) increasingly broad EEZs (graphs *c* and *d* in each figure); or (3) increasingly exclusive coastal state jurisdiction over activities within the EEZ (graphs *e* and *f* in each figure).

The results that Friedheim and Durch found suggest that economic interests explain a great deal of the predicted voting at UNCLOS. As one might have expected, the North-South cleavage is more important than are geographical interests for the debate over the international seabed regime, whereas geographical interests—which can probably be taken to stand for geographically based economic interests—appear to dominate the debate over the extent and degree of coastal state jurisdiction.

In the debate over the international seabed regime, Figure 28 shows that the split between the rich and poor countries grew over the period 1971−75 (panel *a*) whereas there is no clear pattern for the group means for countries classified according to geography (panel *b*). Figure 29 shows that the standard deviations for the North-South groups declined over time (panel *a*), suggesting that opinion on this issue has solidified, especially for the Group of 77 states. Again, there is no pattern to the changes over time for the geographical groups (panel *b*).

In the debate over the breadth of the EEZ, Figure 28 shows that both Northern and Southern groups have tended over time to reach a single unified position (panel *c*) which in this case is equal to an EEZ of 200 miles. The broad-shelf

WHO MAY EXPLOIT THE AREA

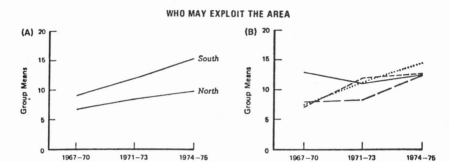

ECONOMIC ZONE DELIMITATION

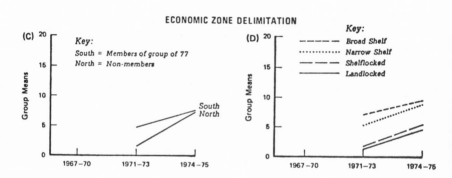

ECONOMIC ZONE JURISDICTION

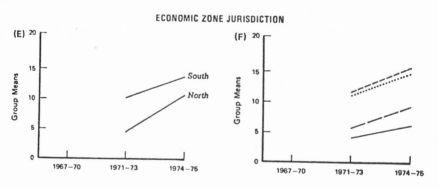

FIG. 28.   Trend in mean positions of several groups of countries on three law-of-the-sea
issues based on speeches delivered at UNCLOS.

SOURCE: Robert L. Friedheim and William J. Durch, "The International Seabed Resources Agency
Negotiations and the New International Economic Order," *International Organization* 31 (1977):
372. Copyright © 1977 by the Board of Regents of the University of Wisconsin System.

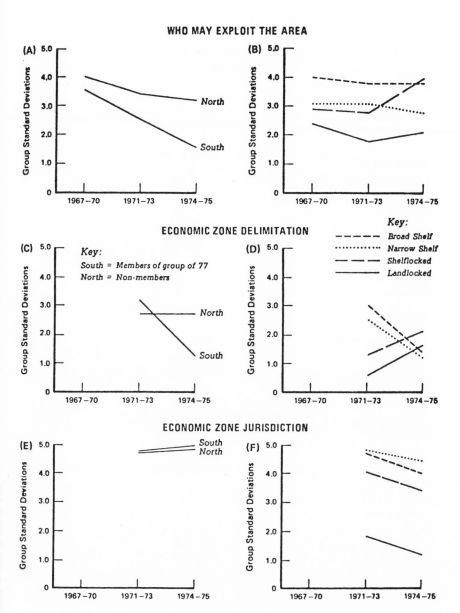

FIG. 29.   Trend in standard deviation of positions of several groups of countries on three law-of-the-sea issues based on speeches at UNCLOS.

SOURCE: Robert L. Friedheim and William J. Durch, "The International Seabed Resources Agency Negotiations and the New International Economic Order," *International Organization* 31 (1977): p. 373. Copyright © 1977 by the Board of Regents of the University of Wisconsin System.

countries' support for the 200-mile EEZ has been greatest and the landlocked countries' support has been least, with these differences being maintained over the sample interval (panel *d*). Figure 29 shows that the standard deviations for the Southern countries declined over time (panel *c*) which is consistent with the Group of 77's strong support for the 200-mile EEZ in spite of little support from the landlocked and shelf-locked groups. But there was no convergence between the deviations of the different geographical groupings (panel *d*). The results graphed in panels *c* and *d* show some of the difficulties that nations encounter when they attempt to bargain as a bloc in spite of certain differences in interests. Although the landlocked and shelf-locked countries agreed to the 200-mile EEZ in exchange for support on the issue of the seabed regime, they did not obtain from coastal states by 1975 either the fishing rights or the veto power over the nature of the international regime which they had also demanded.

In the debate over the degree of coastal state jurisdiction within the 200-mile zone, Figure 28 shows rising acceptance of coastal state controls for each of the geographical groups (panel *f*), although less so for the landlocked. Figure 29 supports this finding for the geographical groups, each of which had a falling standard deviation over the sample interval (panel *f*). Both means and standard deviations among different geographical groups are diverse, however, reflecting the differential importance that states assign to this issue depending upon their geographical-economic interests. Although Figure 28 appears to show that the North-South groups are converging on this issue (panel *e*), Figure 29 shows that the divergence in opinion remains high and actually increased over time (panel *e*). This suggests that the rich-poor dichotomy is a relatively unimportant factor in the debate over the degree of coastal state jurisdiction within the EEZ.

In sum, both for the breadth of the EEZ and for the degree of coastal state authority within it, geographic-economic interests appear to be a relatively strong factor in determining preference outcomes of individual countries at UNCLOS. This is consistent with my argument in Chapter 2 about the sources and the causes of the enclosure movement of the oceans.

Friedheim and Durch have also monitored the steady movement of opinion in favor of the highly centralized seabed authority and operating Enterprise. A licensing authority along the lines proposed by the United States in 1970 was favored in 1975 by fewer than one-third of participating states, too few even to block the centralized regime. The number of states speaking in favor of the Enterprise option grew fourfold between 1967 and 1975.[150] The treaty article favoring strong production controls would have received a two-thirds majority if it had been voted in 1976. The only countries to oppose commodity controls openly were the United Kingdom, the United States, and Japan. The one-nation, one-vote structure of the council of the Authority has been favored by all but fifteen countries since 1971.

Different outcomes could occur if single issues were not voted separately but were assembled into a treaty "package" that would be adopted or rejected on an all-or-nothing basis. Friedheim and Durch constructed two experimental "caucuses" in which different treaty packages were matched. First, a package hypothetically prepared by the Group of 77, containing its maximum demands on the seabed but compromise positions on non-seabed issues was matched against a package prepared by the developed states containing their most favored position on the deep seabeds (roughly comparable to the U.S. 1970 Draft Convention) and their compromise positions on non-seabed issues.[151] In this vote, more than 100 countries would have preferred the Group of 77's package, with the developed country package supported only by the United States, the U.S.S.R., Japan, and the EEC. For a second experiment, the developed countries' positions on the deep seabed were compromised into the "parallel-access-with-production-controls" regime which Secretary Kissinger proposed in 1976, with all the other elements of the first pair of packages held constant. Here the developed country package gains significant support but still falls short of the necessary two-thirds majority. This suggests that the conference will continue to be at a stalemate until some major change in opinion occurs.

5. CONCLUSIONS

To the extent that an individual country's choice between the two processes for making laws to govern the use of the oceans was influenced by the resulting changes in its wealth, it would make this decision on the basis of the greater economic rents net of the costs both of exploiting the resources and of acquiring a favorable structure and distribution of resource rights. For example, the offer prices that a coastal nation would be willing to "pay" in terms of bargaining concessions through UNCLOS for favorable property rights would be limited to the cost of obtaining rights to economic rents of about the same value through the enforcement of unilateral claims. The reverse also applies. The coastal nation would not devote resources to enforcing enclosures that exceeded what it would have to pay to obtain the same economic rents through UNCLOS. In each instance, the *net* value of the economic rents associated with UNCLOS, the political process, sets an upper limit to the frequency and extent of unilateral actions, just as enclosure, the economic process, would be shunned if the same value of rents could be achieved more cheaply through UNCLOS. If either law-making process becomes "too expensive" in terms of the resources sacrificed to obtain a given value of economic rents, a shift to the substitute process will occur.

The hard economic data required to make a net assessment of the economic rents associated with each process are not available at this writing and may not be until well after each process has run its course. Even so, a very rough comparison may be useful since it is likely that some countries will have to choose between the two before all the relevant data are in, and some of these choices may be irreversible. My analysis, summarized in Table 47, suggests that the enclosure movement is superior to either the 1976 or the 1977 draft UNCLOS treaty text for most resource categories and no worse for others. The two categories of resource uses for which enclosure appears to yield outcomes that are worse than at least one of the treaty texts are scientific research and vessel source pollution. In the case of the latter, the treaty texts rely on construction standards that would almost surely be less efficient than a system of tanker liability if information and enforcement costs were nil, and may still be inefficient given present levels of costs. The UNCLOS solution to the problem of vessel source pollution is more attractive than the enclosure movement only under two conditions: (*a*) where the mixing and transport of pollutants through the deep seas to coastal areas is effective, and (*b*) where the costs of detecting pollution from particular ships and enforcing against it are extremely high. For the deep seabeds, of course, the treaty arrangements that UNCLOS is most likely to yield offer economic rents that are smaller than anything short of a permanent moratorium on exploitation. In summary, UNCLOS offers the possibility of achieving a less inefficient degree of pollution from vessels at the cost of distorting possibly every other ocean resource use. Unless the cost of higher levels of vessel pollution is overwhelming, UNCLOS thus appears to be less attractive on economic grounds than enclosure. At the very least, a strong economic argument can be made for confining UNCLOS to vessel pollution problems alone.

The UNCLOS process also appears to be associated with higher costs of competition to acquire exploitation rights. The economic rents that are created either by UNCLOS or by enclosure will be dissipated both in actual resource exploitation and in prior competition among nations to adjust the structure and the initial distribution of property rights favorably to their individual wealths. In the case of enclosure, rents are dissipated as costs are incurred to enforce claims. In the case of UNCLOS, rents are dissipated in the bargaining costs, the enforcement costs that nations incur when international enforcement is weak, and in the prices that are offered to other countries for favorable property rights. Not only are transactions costs relatively high within the UNCLOS process, but total enforcement costs are also likely to be greater, for the reason that coastal states having valuable EEZ resources are likely to incur enforcement costs with or without a treaty. Furthermore, there is little reason to expect that the conflicts between states over the ambiguous rights and duties that UNCLOS creates will be less frequent or more easily resolved than the conflicts that would occasionally arise from overlapping enclosures. As the costs of competition and the expected costs of enforcement within the UNCLOS process have continued to rise, the attractions to nations of the enclosure process have become very strong—so strong that great parts of the UNCLOS treaty texts have aped the outcomes of enclosure. If the costs associated with UNCLOS continue to rise in the future, the attractions and the relative advantages of the remaining elements of the enclosure movement should become even stronger.

Notes

1. Beyond this the treaty would have to be ratified by the legislative or other procedures of each country.

2. The 200-mile territorial, categoric enclosures of nine Latin American and African countries are an exception.

3. Remarks of U.S. ambassador to UNCLOS, John R. Stevenson, quoted by Don Shannon, "Conference on Law of the Sea Opens Next Week," *Los Angeles Times*, June 13, 1974.

4. This is emphasized by Charles R. Plott, "Axiomatic Social Choice Theory: An Overview and Interpretation," *American Journal of Political Science* 20 (1976):520−23, 548−54, 567−75. See also Kenneth J. Arrow, *Social Choice and Individual Values*, 2d ed. (New York: John Wiley & Sons, 1963); James M. Buchanan and Gordon Tullock, *The Calculus of Consent*, passim.

5. Michael E. Levine and Charles R. Plott, "Agenda Influence and Its Implications," *Virginia Law Review* 63 (1977):563.

6. The assumption of wealth maximization in the theory of individual voting behavior must be dropped when this theory is extended to the behavior of nations.

7. U.S. Senate, Committee on Commerce and National Ocean Policy Study, *The Third U.N. Law of the Sea Conference*, prepared at the request of Hon. Warren G. Magnuson and Hon. Ernest F. Hollings pursuant to S. Res. 222, 94th Cong., 1st Sess. (Washington, D.C., 1975), pp. 12−13; United Nations General Assembly Official Records, *Report of the Committee on the Peaceful Uses of the Seabed and the Ocean Floor Beyond the Limits of National Jurisdiction*, 26th Sess., Suppl. No. 21, Doc. A/8421 (1971), p. 1.

8. *The Third U.N. Law of the Sea Conference*, p. 20; U.S., Department of State, National Security Council Inter-Agency Task Force on the Law of the Sea, *Memorandum NSC D-LOS #223* (Washington, D.C., mimeo, November 11, 1974). The only country not invited to UNCLOS was Taiwan, done to assure the attendance of the People's Republic of China. "The Oceans: Wild West Scramble for Control," *Time*, July 29, 1974, p. 51.

9. Robert L. Friedheim, *Parliamentary Diplomacy—A Survey* (Arlington, Va.: Center for Naval Analyses, Memorandum CNA76-0046, January 8, 1976), p. 4; hereafter cited as Friedheim (1976).

10. *The Third U.N. Law of the Sea Conference*, p. 20.

11. Friedheim (1976), pp. 17−18.

12. Ibid., pp. 26−28.

13. *The Third U.N. Law of the Sea Conference*, pp. 12−13; UN General Assembly Official Records, 26th Sess., Suppl. No. 21, Doc. A/8421 (1971), pp. 3, 10−11.

14. Paul H. Weaver, "Making the UN Safe for Democracy," *Fortune*, November 1975, p. 194.

15. John Temple Swing, "Who Will Own the Oceans?" *Foreign Affairs* 54 (1976):529.

16. Inevitably, there is some overlapping. For example, the United Kingdom is both a maritime country and a straits state.

17. Stanley Meisler, "U.N. Sea Conference Pits Poor Against Rich, Aligns U.S. and Russia," *Los Angeles Times*, June 21, 1974.

18. "A Law of the Sea Conference—Who Needs It?" in Robert G. Wirsing, ed., *International Relations and the Future of Ocean Space* (Columbia, S.C.: University of South Carolina Press, Studies in International Affairs, no. 10, 1974), pp. 46−53; hereafter cited as Friedheim (1974).

19. Ann L. Hollick, "The Third U.N. Conference on the Law of the Sea: Caracas Review," in Ryan C. Amacher and Richard James Sweeney, eds., *The Law of the Sea: U.S. Interests and Alternatives*, p. 124; hereafter cited as Hollick (1976).

20. UN General Assembly, Committee on the Peaceful Uses of the Sea-Bed and the Ocean Floor Beyond the Limits of National Jurisdiction, *List of Subjects and Issues Relating to the Law of the Sea to be Submitted to the Conference on the Law of the Sea Sponsored by [various countries]*, Doc. A/AC.138/66/Rev.1 (August 16, 1972).

21. David P. Stang, "Ocean Polemics," *India Quarterly* 29 (1973):142−43, reprinted in *Status Report on Law of the Sea Conference*, pt. 1, pp. 797−98.

22. Ibid., pp. 143−44.

23. Richard N. Gardner, "Regulating Use of the Oceans—It Is Time to Consider the Fish's Point of View," *New York Times*, Dec. 30, 1973, reprinted in *Mineral Resources of the Deep Seabed*, pt. 2, p. 873.

24. UN, Third Conference on the Law of the Sea, *Rules of Procedure*, Doc. A/CONF.62/30/Rev.1 (July 16, 1974).

25. See statements of the delegates of the U.S. and the U.S.S.R. in UN, Third Conference on the Law of the Sea, 2d Sess., *Provisional Summary Record of the Eighteenth Meeting*, Doc. A/CONF.62/SR.18 (June 28, 1974), pp. 4−7, 12−13.

26. Buchanan and Tullock, chaps. 5−6.

27. See, e.g., UN Doc. A/CONF.62/SR.17 (July 1, 1974), pp. 7−9.

28. Technically, the binding constraint is 74 votes if 111 or fewer states are present and voting; when more than 111 states are present at a session of UNCLOS, the binding constraint becomes two-thirds of that number, which will exceed 74. Joseph B. Kadane, *Analysis of the Voting Rule Adopted for Law of the Sea* (Arlington, Va.: Center for Naval Analyses Memorandum CNA1223-74, July 29, 1974).

29. I must thank Robert L. Friedheim for his criticism of an earlier draft of this subsection.

30. See Friedheim (1974), pp. 54–62, and James L. Johnston (1976a), p. 494.

31. In 1976, the United States ambassador to UNCLOS, T. Vincent Learson, said: "The U.S. position is that we want to avoid voting at all costs on an article-by-article, even on a section-by-section, basis if possible. That is also the goal of the management of the conference. We hope to arrive at a consensus." *Status Report on Law of the Sea Conference*, pt. 5, p. 1658.

32. Charles R. Plott and Michael E. Levine, "A Model of Agenda Influence on Committee Decisions," *American Economic Review* 68 (1978):146–60.

33. Ibid., p. 148.

34. *Mineral Resources of the Deep Seabed*, pt. 1, p. 18.

35. Quoted by William Claiborne, "U.S. Ambassador Pessimistic About Agreement on Seas," *Washington Post*, Apr. 14, 1978.

36. UN, Third Conference on the Law of the Sea, 2d Sess., *Organization of the Second Session of the Conference and Allocation of Items*, Doc. A/CONF.62/28 (June 20, 1974); Doc. A/CONF.62/29 (July 2, 1974).

37. Pardo (1975), pp. 397–98.

38. See Arvid Pardo, "Commentary," in Amacher and Sweeney, eds., pp. 162–63.

39. The approximate number of Plenary meetings at Caracas was 49. Committee I met 16 times, Committee II met 43 times, and Committee III met 15 times.

40. U.S., *Congressional Record (Extension of Remarks)*, vol. 122, October 26, 1976, p. E5754.

41. Barry Newman, "The 'Law of the Sea' Is Still Unwritten," *Wall Street Journal*, Aug. 27, 1974.

42. Kathleen Teltsch, "Delegates Doodle as Procedural Details Slow Down Progress at U.N.'s Law of the Sea Conference," *New York Times*, Mar. 28, 1976.

43. UN Doc. A/CONF.62/29 (July 2, 1974), p. 1.

44. Newman, p. 1.

45. See UN, "Law of the Sea Conference Pays Tribute to King Faisal of Saudi Arabia," United Nations Press Release SEA/21, March 27, 1975, and UN Doc. A/CONF.62/SR.73 (September 15, 1976).

46. Kathleen Teltsch, "Third U.N. Parley on Sea Law Opens," *New York Times*, Dec. 4, 1973.

47. *Washington Post* editorial, "A Permanent Floating Oceanic Crap Game," Dec. 11, 1972; *Wall Street Journal* editorial, "On to Calcutta," Aug. 29, 1974. Only the *New York Times* seized the fact that the conference had been able to issue a series of three postage stamps to commemorate its accomplishments in promoting "international cooperation." See Samuel A. Tower, "Stamps: 'Law of the Sea' Is U.N. Theme," *New York Times*, Nov. 10, 1974.

48. Evidently certain small countries "hired experts from Europe or the U.S. to help pull them through" and learn the issues. Newman, p. 15.

49. "UN Sea-Law Meeting Begins Seventh Session after 10-Day Dispute," *Wall Street Journal*, Apr. 7. 1978.

50. Quoted in Teltsch, "Delegates Doodle."

51. Ibid.

52. UN, *United States, Draft Appendix to the Law of the Sea Treaty Concerning Mineral Resource Development in the International Seabed Area*, Doc. A/CONF.62/C.1/L.6 (August 13, 1974). Similar proposals were made by other prospective ocean-mining countries: Japan, the U.S.S.R., and the eight nations of the European Economic Community. See *Status Report on Law of the Sea Conference*, pt. 2, pp. 858–59.

53. Reconstructed Extemporaneous Statement of Leigh S. Ratiner, alternate U.S. Representative, before Committee I of UNCLOS, August 9, 1974, reprinted in U.S. Senators Claiborne Pell, Edmund Muskie, Clifford Case, and Ted Stevens, *The Third U.N. Law of the Sea Conference: Report to the Senate*, 94th Cong., 1st Sess., February 5, 1975, p. 36.

54. See Daniel P. Moynihan, "The United States in Opposition," *Commentary*, March, 1979, p. 35.

55. See Roger D. Hansen, "The North-South Split and the Law of the Sea Debate," in *Perspectives on Ocean Policy*, pp. 122–23.

56. James L. Johnston (1976a), p. 496.

57. *Status Report on Law of the Sea Conference*, pt. 2, pp. 837–38.

58. See the statement of Ambassador Stevenson before the U.S. Senate, in ibid., p. 858.

59. "The International Seabed and the Single Negotiating Text," *San Diego Law Review* 13 (1976):490–506.

60. See Stang, pp. 138–41, and other testimony in *Mineral Resources of the Deep Seabed*, pt. 1, pp. 292–93, 299–302.

61. Stang, p. 140.

62. Henry A. Kissinger, "International Law, World Order, and Human Progress," a speech to the American Bar Association at Montreal, August 11, 1975, reprinted in *Status Report on Law of the Sea Conference*, pt. 4, pp. 1430–36; see also Murrey Marder, "Action Urged on Sea Law by Kissinger," *Washington Post*, Aug. 12, 1975.

63. This was emphasized in a speech by UNCLOS President Amerasinghe in United Nations Information Service, "Law of Sea Conference Ends Geneva Session After Appeal by Its President to Avoid Unilateral Action that Might Jeopardize Sea Law Convention," Press Release SEA/40, May 9, 1975, p. 3; reprinted in *Status Report on Law of the Sea Conference*, pt. 3, pp. 1399–1401.

64. Henry A. Kissinger, "The Law of the Sea: A Test of International Coopera-tion," a speech to the UN Association of the U.S., New York, April 8, 1976, reprinted in *Status Report on Law of the Sea Conference*, pt. 5, pp. 1940–49; see also Murrey Marder, "Kissinger Offers Compromise on Mining Ocean Minerals," *Washington Post*, Apr. 9, 1976.

65. UN, Third Conference on the Law of the Sea, *Report by Mr. Paul Bamela Engo, Chairman of the First Committee on the Work of the Committee at the Fifth Session of*

the Conference, Doc. A/CONF.62/L.16 (September 16, 1976), p. 3.

66. See "U.S. Pledges Sea-Mining Funds," *Washington Post*, Sept. 2, 1976; Associated Press dispatch, "Kissinger Tries to Save Law of Sea Conference," *Los Angeles Times*, Sept. 2, 1976; "Sea Law Session Ends with No Minerals Accord," *Washington Post*, Sept. 18, 1976.

67. Remarks by the Hon. Henry A. Kissinger, reprinted in *Congressional Record— Senate*, vol. 122, no. 149, September 29, 1976.

68. UN, Third Conference on the Law of the Sea, First Committee, *Weekly Report by the Co-Chairmen on the Activities of the Workshop*, Doc. A/CONF.62/C.1/WR.2 (August 20, 1976), p. 3.

69. UN Doc. A/CONF.62/L.16 (September 16, 1976), pp. 1, 4.

70. Ibid., pp. 4–5.

71. Newman, p. 1.

72. For some details of the seabed controversy during the 1977 session see "U.N. Sea Law Session Damages Prospects for Ocean Mining Pact, U.S. Aide Says," *Wall Street Journal*, July 21, 1977; "U.S. Envoy Calls Proposed Regulations on Ocean Mining Unacceptable," *New York Times*, July 21, 1977; William Claiborne, "High-Stakes Seabed Fight," *Washington Post*, Aug. 14, 1977; Frank Del Olmo, "Richardson Warns on Law of Sea Talks," *Los Angeles Times*, Oct. 18, 1977.

73. Statement of Ambassador Richardson, in *Status Report on Law of the Sea Conference*, pt. 6, p. 1964.

74. U.S. Delegation to UNCLOS, *Unclassified Report* on the Sixth Session of the Third United Nations Conference on the Law of the Sea, May 23–July 15, 1977 (mimeo, no date), p. 11; reprinted in ibid., p. 1977.

75. "Conference on Sea Law Makes Some Progress; Success Is in Doubt," *Wall Street Journal*, May 18, 1978.

76. UN, Third Conference on the Law of the Sea, *Informal Single Negotiating Text*, Doc. A/CONF.62/WP.8 (May 7, 1975), reprinted in *Status Report on Law of the Sea Conference*, pt. 3, pp. 1278–1395; *Revised Single Negotiating Text*, Doc. A/CONF.62/ WP.8/Rev.1 (May 6, 1976), reprinted in ibid., pt. 5, pp. 1671–1909; *Informal Composite Negotiating Text*, Doc. A/CONF.62/WP.10 (July 15, 1977); and *Reports of the Committees and Negotiating Groups on Negotiations at the Seventh Session* (Geneva, May 19, 1978), in the nature of amendments to the Informal Composite Negotiating Text (hereafter cited as Composite Text, Amendments of May 1978).

77. Revised Text, pt. II, art. 5; Composite Text, art. 6.

78. Rev. Text, pt. II, art. 13; Comp. Text, art. 14.

79. Rev. Text, pt. II, art. 119; Comp. Text, art. 47.

80. Andres Aguilar, "Committee II Chairman's Note," A/CONF.62/WP.8/Rev.1 (May 8, 1976), p. 4.

81. Rev. Text, pt. II, art. 44(1)(a), to be read in conjunction with arts. 46 and 47; Comp. Text, art. 56(1)(a), to be read in conjunction with arts. 58 and 59.

82. Rev. Text, pt. II, art. 61(1); Comp. Text, art. 73. Both texts grant the same bundle of rights to islands—Rev. Text, pt. II, art. 128(2); Comp. Text, art. 121(2)—and

to territories that have yet to gain full independence, in which case resource rights are vested in the people directly rather than in the metropolitan nation or UN organization acting as trustee. See Rev. Text, pt. II, p. 59; Comp. Text, p. 153.

83. Aguilar, p. 4; Comp. Text, art. 59.

84. Comp. Text, art. 89.

85. Rev. Text, pt. II, art. 18; Comp. Text, art. 19.

86. Rev. Text, pt. II, art. 20; Comp. Text, art. 21.

87. Rev. Text, pt. II, arts. 21(2) and 25(2); Comp. Text, arts. 22(2) and 26(2).

88. Rev. Text, pt. II, arts. 124 and 125(1), (4); Comp. Text, arts. 52 and 53(1), (4).

89. Rev. Text, pt. II, art. 125(12); Comp. Text, art. 53(12).

90. Rev. Text, pt. II, art. 37(2); Comp. Text, art. 38(2) and art. 40.

91. Rev. Text, pt. II, art. 39(1); Comp. Text, art. 41(1).

92. Rev. Text, pt. II, art. 39(4); Comp. Text, art. 41(4).

93. Rev. Text, pt. II, art. 64; Comp. Text, art. 76.

94. Rev. Text, pt. II, art. 65(2); Comp. Text, art. 77(2).

95. The four alternatives are (1) the 500-meter isobath beyond 200 miles; (2) the edge of the margin, apparently defined on the basis of an unspecified gradient limitation; (3) the U.S.S.R.'s suggestion of a 300-mile delimitation; and (4) the Irish suggestion of the base of the continental slope—which often is easier to determine than is the outer edge of the margin (see Hollis D. Hedberg in *Ocean Management*, 1973)—plus a maximum of 60 miles or, alternatively, to where the depth of sediments is at least one percent between that point and the foot of the slope. See U.S. Delegation to UNCLOS, *Unclassified Report* on the Seventh Session of the Third United Nations Conference on the Law of the Sea, March 28–May 19, 1978 (mimeo), p. 24.

96. Comp. Text, art. 82.

97. Rev. Text, pt. II, arts. 50(3) and 51(1); Comp. Text, arts. 61(3) and 62(1).

98. Comp. Text, Amendments of May 1978, "Compromise Suggestions by the Chairman of Negotiating Group 4," NG4/9/Rev.1, arts. 69(1) and 70(1).

99. Ibid., arts. 69(3) and 70(4).

100. Ibid., arts. 69(4) and 70(5). See also Rev. Text, pt. II, arts. 51, 58, and 59.

101. See Rev. Text, pt. II, art. 53(1), and Comp. Text, art. 64(1).

102. Rev. Text, pt. II, art. 55(3); Comp. Text, art. 66(3).

103. Rev. Text, pt. III, arts. 2, 3, 4(2), and 4(1); Comp. Text, arts. 193, 194, 195(2), and 195(1).

104. Rev. Text, pt. III, arts. 17(1) and 18(1); Comp. Text, arts. 208(1) and 209(1).

105. Rev. Text, pt. III, art. 17(4); Comp. Text, art. 208(4).

106. Rev. Text, pt. III, art. 20(1),(5); Comp. Text, art. 211(1),(5).

107. Rev. Text, pt. III, art. 20(6); Comp. Text, art. 211(6).

108. See Chapter 6, pp. 183–84. All warships are given immunity from such regulations. Rev. Text, pt. III, art. 45; Comp. Text, art. 237.

109. Rev. Text, pt. III, art. 27; Comp. Text, art. 218(1).

110. Rev. Text, pt. III, art. 21(3); Comp. Text, art. 212(3).

111. Rev. Text, pt. III, art. 30(2); Comp. Text, art. 221(2).

112. Rev. Text, pt. III, art. 21(4); Comp. Text, art. 212(4).

113. Rev. Text, pt. III, art. 28(3),(4); Comp. Text, art. 219(3),(4).

114. Rev. Text, pt. III, art. 30(6); Comp. Text, art. 221(6).

115. Rev. Text, pt. III, arts. 30(7) and 38(1); Comp. Text, arts. 221(7) and 229(1).

116. Rev. Text, pt. III, art. 43 and art. 21(5); Comp. Text, art. 235 and art. 212(5).

117. Comp. Text, Amendments of May 1978, ''Report to the Plenary by the Chairman of the Third Committee,'' pp. 79−86; U.S. Delegation, *Unclassified Report* on the Seventh Session of UNCLOS, pp. 32−34.

118. Such a distinction was made in the precursor to the Revised Text, but was deleted in both the Revised Text and the Composite Text because of the practical difficulties of monitoring. U.S. Delegation, *Unclassified Report* on the Third United Nations Conference on the Law of the Sea, March 15−May 7, 1976, New York (mimeo, undated), p. 16; reprinted in *Status Report on Law of the Sea Conference*, pt. 5, p. 1633.

119. Rev. Text, pt. III, art. 59; Comp. Text, art. 250. Nearby landlocked and geographically disadvantaged states also must be advised of the project and be provided, at their request, the same relevant information and assistance as the cognizant coastal state receives. Rev. Text, pt. III, art. 66; Comp. Text, art. 255.

120. Rev. Text, pt. III, art. 60; Comp. Text, art. 247(4).

121. Rev. Text, pt. III, art. 64; Comp. Text, art. 253.

122. U.S. Delegation, *Unclassified Final Report on Caracas Session* (mimeo, September 9, 1974), p. 20; reprinted in *Status Report on Law of the Sea Conference*, pt. 2, p. 912.

123. Rev. Text, pt. III, art. 61.

124. Rev. Text, pt. I, arts. 25 and 26. The Composite Text, art. 159, would allocate four seats to the bloc of ocean-mining countries, four to the bloc of land-based mineral exporters, four to the bloc of mineral importers, six to the special-interest developing countries, and eighteen geographically. Decisions would require three-fourths majority.

125. Rev. Text, pt. I, arts. 30, 31, and 32.

126. Rev. Text, pt. I, arts. 32−37, Annex III.

127. The Composite Text, Annex V, would put 21 judges in the full tribunal.

128. Rev. Text, pt. I, art. 10; Comp. Text, arts. 143(2) and 151(7).

129. Rev. Text, pt. I, Annex I, para. 8.

130. Comp. Text, Annex II, para. 5(g).

131. Explanatory Memorandum by the President of UNCLOS to Accompany the Informal Composite Negotiating Text, A/CONF.62/WP.10/Add.1 (July 22, 1977), p. 6.

132. Rev. Text, pt. I, art. 23; Comp. Text, Amendments of May 1978, NG1/10/Rev. 1, Annex A, art. 150 ter.

133. Rev. Text, pt. I, Annex II, para. 7(e).

134. Comp. Text, Annex III, para. 11.

135. ''Bureaucrats' Dream: Ocean 'Enterprise','' *Wall Street Journal*, Nov. 8, 1976.

136. See Harold K. Jacobson, ''ITU: A Potpourri of Bureaucrats and Industrialists,''

in Robert W. Cox and Harold K. Jacobson, et al., *The Anatomy of Influence* (New Haven and London: Yale University Press, 1973), pp. 59–101.

137. Ibid., p. 84.

138. Rev. Text, pt. I, art. 9(4); Comp. Text, Amendments of May 1978, NG1/10/Rev.1, Annex A, art. 151(g).

139. Rev. Text, pt. I, art 9(4)(i); Comp. Text, Amendments of May 1978, NG1/10/Rev.1, Annex A, art. 150 bis.

140. Rev. Text, pt. I, art. 9(4)(ii); Comp. Text, Amendments of May 1978, NG1/10/Rev.1, Annex A, art. 150 bis; NG1/7, Annex B; NG1/9, Annex C; NG1/11, Annex D.

141. Rev. Text, pt. I, Annex I, para. 12; Comp. Text, Annex II, para. 11.

142. Rev. Text, pt. I, Annex I, para. 4(d).

143. Ibid., para. 8(e); Comp. Text, Annex II, para. 5(1). See also the statement of Ambassador Learson in *Status Report on the Law of the Sea Conference*, pt. 5, p. 1614.

144. Comp. Text, art. 153.

145. Ibid., and Amendments of May 1978, NG1/10/Rev.1, art. 153.

146. The UNCLOS Secretariat has expressed concern that a seabed cartel would be seriously incomplete without restrictions on these sources. UN, *Economic Implications of Seabed Mining in the International Area: Report by the Secretary-General*, Doc. A/CONF.62/37 (February 8, 1975), p. 14.

147. Ryan C. Amacher and Richard James Sweeney, "International Commodity Cartels and the Threat of New Entry; Implications of Ocean Mineral Resources," *Kyklos* 29 (1976):307.

148. Johnston (1976a), p. 489. Cartels in bananas, bauxite, coffee, copper, phosphate, and tin have been attempted in recent years, but only the petroleum cartel has had much success. See C. Fred Bergsten, "The Threat from the Third World," *Foreign Policy* 11 (1973):102–24; and Sanford Rose, "Third World 'Commodity Power' Is a Costly Illusion," *Fortune*, November 1976, pp. 147–60.

149. "The International Seabed Resources Agency Negotiations and the New International Economic Order," *International Organization* 31 (1977):348–84. This model was developed at the Center for Naval Analyses of the University of Rochester, Arlington, Va., under contract to the U.S. Department of Defense, and its results were available to the U.S. delegation to UNCLOS. I must thank Professor Friedheim for showing me some of his unpublished work on this subject and for giving me comments on an earlier draft of this section.

150. "International Seabed Resources Agency," p. 358.

151. There are subtle distinctions between the two "compromise" packages for non-seabed issues. For scientific research in the EEZ, for example, the position of the developed countries is that coastal states may require consent for "commercial" but not for "basic" research; the Group of 77's compromise position is that coastal state consent is required but should be given if certain established conditions are met. In the case of EEZ jurisdiction, the developed countries' compromise position is that coastal state resource jurisdiction should be limited by international agreement, whereas the Group of 77 compromise position is that there should be exclusive coastal state control over all activities in the EEZ. Ibid., pp. 379–82.

CHAPTER 10

United States: The Making of an Ocean Policy

Few countries have as many major domestic and international interests in the oceans as the United States. This country is one of the two naval powers in the world. It imports by sea a large part of its petroleum, hard minerals, and raw materials. Its coastline is the fourth longest in the world, and the area of its continental margin is the fourth largest.[1] The creation of a universal 200-nautical-mile exclusive economic zone would give the United States the right to control resource exploitation in more than 2.2 million square nautical miles, which would be the largest such zone in the world and one rich in living and mineral materials.[2] The U.S. has a large coastal population and therefore would bear an important share of the cost of a decline in the quality of the ocean environment. Its effort in marine research probably surpasses that of any other country and its firms have led in the development of ocean technologies for petroleum recovery and deep-sea mining.

Thomas W. Fulton wrote in 1911 that "the United States more than any other Power has varied her principles and claims as to the extent of territorial waters, according to her policy at the time."[3] Throughout its history, the dominant ocean policy of the United States has been to maintain the freedom of the seas. Usually this policy has advanced U.S. security interests by ensuring the mobility of its navy and its economic interests by removing obstructions to maritime trade. In keeping with Fulton's observation, the United States has at two different times in its history—soon after becoming a nation and again in 1945—reversed its principles and made unprecedented claims to adjacent areas. In 1785, the United States and Morocco signed a treaty agreeing that each state would protect vessels of the other that were engaged with ships of a third party within "gunshot" range of the other state; in 1793, near the end of George Washington's first administration, Thomas Jefferson equated the gunshot rule with the three-mile limit to define a line of U.S. territorial neutrality when war broke out between Great Britain and France.[4] Although other countries had previously used the three-mile limit on an informal basis, the United States appears to have been the first to adopt it as a formal claim.[5] The second reversal was, of course, Truman's proclamation on the continental shelf.

Having made these declarations, the United States, perhaps again in keeping with Fulton's observation, has tried to hold other countries to a standard of conduct somewhat different from its own by opposing their enclosures whenever the resulting jurisdiction extended farther seaward or was more categorical than the self-imposed limits of U.S. claims. In more recent times, the United States has consistently opposed territorial sea claims that were broader than three miles[6] and has been adamant against the claims of various Latin American and African countries to territorial seas of 200 miles. And since Truman's time the U.S. has supported enclosures that were based on and limited by the geological extension of the submerged continental platform. But it has also opposed categorical claims that included the living resources of the water column superjacent to the continental shelf, especially the 200-mile Latin American proclamations which the U.S. believed were delimited arbitrarily without reference either to local geographical conditions or to existing international law.

At each of the three conferences on the law of the sea, the United States, like every other participating nation, has attempted to employ international law to advance its own national interests—to wit, maintaining freedom of the seas. Generally, the U.S. has seemed prepared to accept some limitation on navigational freedoms in return for a widely accepted treaty that would halt further territorial encroachments. At the First UNCLOS in 1958 it proposed that the territorial sea be limited to six miles plus a contiguous fishing zone of an additional six miles, but this proposal received only 45 of the 52 votes needed.[7] The same proposal lost by only one vote at the Second UNCLOS in 1960. The third attempt to limit territorial extensions came in the early years of the first Nixon administration when foreign policy and military planners feared that the accelerated enclosure movement of the 1950s and 1960s would progress to the point where no open seas would exist. They argued that U.S. security would be harmed not only by enclosures of territorial seas from the three-mile limit to the twelve-mile limit but also by the extension of resource jurisdiction out to 200 miles and beyond. These resource enclosures would gradually be transformed into extensions of sovereignty through what was believed to be a process of essentially arbitrary political calculations by coastal states, rather than, as I have argued, by an economic process that compared gains and costs. These beliefs became dominant as the U.S. ocean bureaucracy prepared policy options and negotiating tactics during 1969 and 1970 for the Third UNCLOS. This culminated in the announcement by the United States at Caracas in 1974 that it would agree to a universal twelve-mile territorial sea plus an additional 188-mile EEZ subject to guarantees of navigational, scientific research, and several other freedoms which it sought but had not fully negotiated through June 1978.

The approach of the U.S. government to the Third UNCLOS is striking in two respects compared with the previous conferences. First, the U.S. was prepared to acquiesce in territorial extensions and resource enclosures that were much broader than before. Second, it attempted to achieve its objectives this time by trading away resource rights of significant value. To facilitate these trade-offs, it encouraged a conference structure in which all issues would be negotiated at once within the same forum as a "package deal." Measured in diplomatic terms, this ocean policy has been only a mixed success, since the treaty that the conference is most likely to produce will contain certain important provisions that the United States originally sought very much to avoid as well as some provisions that it wanted. And in economic terms, the treaty negotiations have probably been a failure for the U.S. That is, the draft treaty terms for the structure and distribution of ocean property arrangements that were under debate during 1977 and 1978 will very likely offer less to the United States in economic rents than did either the package of military and resource rights which the U.S. had before the Third UNCLOS, or the package that would be implied or made express by the enclosure movement in its present state.

1. TRANSACTIONAL STRUCTURE OF OCEAN DECISION MAKING

Ocean authority within the U.S. Executive branch in 1976 was divided among eight cabinet departments, four administrative agencies, and four offices of the White House staff as listed in Table 48. The division of power among them, as shown in Table 49 by their shares of the total U.S. expenditure on ocean affairs, gives 87 percent of the budget to just four departments. Ocean policies result, Ann L. Hollick argues, from competition among these entities where the typical oceans bureaucrat advocates policies according to the particular gains that he (or his employer), rather than the public, can capture or the costs that he bears.[8] In some cases the gains and costs that individuals have taken into account in pursuing their self-interests appear to have diverged from the public's interest, that is, the total gains and costs that accrue to the nation as a whole. This occurs not because bureaucrats are inherently unthinking or vicious individuals but because, as Roland N. McKean suggests, the institutional incentives which impinge upon them usually make it relatively inexpensive to ignore certain consequences of their actions which turn out to be costs to others.[9] William A. Niskanen argues that bureaucrats are almost forced to ignore the broader impacts of their decisions:

> A bureaucrat . . . is neither omniscient nor sovereign. He cannot acquire all of the information on individual preferences and production opportunities that would be necessary to divine the public interest, and he does not have the authority to order

TABLE 48

DISTRIBUTION OF AUTHORITY FOR LAW OF THE SEA POLICY WITHIN THE
U.S. GOVERNMENT IN 1974—1975

Executive Branch
Membership of the Inter-Agency
Task Force on Law of the Sea[1]

Cabinet Departments	Other Agencies	Executive Offices
State	National Science Foundation	National Security Council
Treasury	Central Intelligency Agency	Office of Management and Budget
Defense	Environmental Protection	Council on Environmental
Justice	Agency	Quality
Interior	Federal Energy Administra-	Council on International
Commerce	tion	Economic Policy
Transportation		
U.S. Mission to the United Nations		

Committees of the Congress[2]

Senate	House
Appropriations	Appropriations
Armed Services	Armed Services
Foreign Relations	International Relations
Commerce	Merchant Marine and
Interior and Insular Affairs	Fisheries

SOURCES:

[1]Ann L. Hollick, "United States and Canadian Policy in Law of the Sea," *San Diego Law Review* 12 (1975):537; *National Ocean Policy*, Hearings before the Subcommittee on Oceanography and the Committee on Merchant Marine and Fisheries, U.S. House of Representatives, 94th Cong., 2d Sess., Serial No. 94—93, June and September 1976, p. 17.

[2]Don Walsh, "Some Thoughts on National Ocean Policy: The Critical Issue," *San Diego Law Review* 13 (1976):614.

an action that is contrary to either the personal interests or the different perceptions of the public interest by some other bureaucrats. . . . [I]n a bureaucratic environment, one person who serves his personal interests or a different perception of public interest is often sufficient to prevent others from serving their perception of the public interest. It is *impossible* for any one bureaucrat to act in the public interest, because of the limits on his information and the conflicting interests of others, regardless of his personal motivations.[10]

Interagency competition provides a mechanism for revealing to top decision makers a greater variety of policy options and their implied packages of gains and costs than a single bureau or a single bureaucrat would choose to supply. To some extent, competition in government is an antidote to the attempts by bureaucrats to

TABLE 49

U.S. EXECUTIVE BRANCH ORGANIZATIONS AND APPLICABLE SUBDIVISIONS HAVING SOME
JURISDICTION OVER OCEANIC AFFAIRS OR SCIENCE IN 1975
(figures in parenthesis indicate each organization's percentage
of total U.S. expenditures in this area)*

Department of Commerce (37%)	Maritime Administration National Oceanic and Atmospheric Administration
Department of Defense (12.5%)	Department of the Navy Defense Advanced Research Project Agency Defense Mapping Agency Army Corps of Engineers
Department of Health, Education, and Welfare (0.3%)	Federal Drug Administration National Institutes of Health
Department of Interior (6%)	Fish and Wildlife Service Geological Survey Office of Territorial Affairs
Department of State (0.7%)	
Department of Transportation (37%)	U.S. Coast Guard
Energy Research and Development Administration (0.8%)	
Environmental Protection Agency (1.5%)	
National Aeronautics and Space Administration (0.8%)	
National Science Foundation (3%)	

*Percentages do not add up to 100.
SOURCE: Don Walsh, "Some Thoughts on National Ocean Policy: The Critical Issue," *San Diego Law Review*
13 (1976):597.

monopolize ideas, information, or access to decision makers at higher levels. But competition among agencies is less likely to weaken monopoly positions in government than is competition among firms in weakening market monopoly, because the not-for-profit character of governmental services reduces the wealth incentives to attack the monopoly, and the entry of competitive bureaus is delayed by the transactional impediments of the congressional appropriations process. Shrewd bureaucrats will recognize the probable longevity of governmental monopoly and will, as Niskanen argues, attempt to

reduce the elasticity of [their] demands . . . by promotional activities which suggest that there is a public "need" or a military "requirement" that must be met at all costs. (Can you imagine a public discussion about collective programs being carried on without the use of these terms?) . . . [Also,] the present environment of bureaucracy—with severe constraints on the creation of new bureaus or new services by existing bureaus, and the passion of public administration reformers to consolidate bureaus with similar services—seems diabolically designed to reduce the competition among bureaus and to increase the inefficiency and, not incidentally, the budget of the bureaucracy.[11]

The Inter-Agency Task Force on the Law of the Sea was created in 1970 and has mostly been under the chairmanship of the State Department. Competition among the agencies listed in the upper half of Table 48 occurs within this group, and building a consensus involves almost continuous bargaining, logrolling, compromising, and an occasional power play.[12] When consensus cannot be reached within the Task Force, policy choices are referred through the National Security Council for presidential decisions. This occurs just before each session of UNCLOS and whenever actions in Congress, particularly unilateral enclosures, threaten to unravel the consensus. When the U.S. delegation goes to UNCLOS and takes along its retinue of advisers it is at least 100 strong—almost a mini-conference within UNCLOS.[13] The group is large not only because some members of the delegation are wary of having their interests represented by other agencies but also because the size helps to assure that "the instructions are not overstepped in the negotiating process."[14]

The transactional structure of the U.S. process of ocean policy making, like that of UNCLOS, is by no means a "neutral midwife," which brings forth a policy only after carefully comparing the full gains and costs of all the important options. Instead, it appears that the concentrated but narrow interests of one or two agencies have largely dominated the process. Moreover, the transactions costs within the government are so high that, Hollick argues, "once agreed upon, portions of U.S. policy are reopened or altered with utmost difficulty." Thus "the diversity of U.S. interests and of lines of influence makes the negotiation of a single national policy as difficult if not more difficult than negotiating the policy internationally."[15]

2. AMERICA'S INTERNAL *PACKAGE DEAL*: TYING MOBILITY TO RESOURCES

The progress of the enclosure movement during the 1950s and the 1960s, as viewed by American defense planners, posed serious security problems for the United States. A universal twelve-mile territorial sea would overlap a few confined international waterways of great importance and many lesser straits, through which submarines would be required by the rule of innocent passage to transit on the surface; the defense planners found the requirement unacceptable especially for submarines carrying ballistic missiles. Beyond territorial seas, the defense planners believed that resource enclosures and even single-purpose fisheries zones also were threatening since there was a tendency for economic claims to be converted by the fiats of coastal states into territorial claims, usually through a process that the planners called creeping jurisdiction. Thus, not only did the enclosure movement threaten the maximum mobility that the United States has traditionally sought for both its surface and submarine navies, but also it could produce international conflict if competition over economic resources should grow into conflicts over ocean territory. To halt this destabilizing process, it would be desirable to arrive in the near future at a widely accepted treaty which would ratify the status quo to some degree but at the same time put an end to the progress of the enclosure movement. In effect, the defense specialists were willing to trade limited restrictions on certain of their activities in coastal areas in return for simultaneous guarantees having the force of international law against further intrusions into the high seas by coastal states for any purpose.

One of the clearest statements of the theory of creeping jurisdiction was given in 1975 by Rear Admiral Max Morris, representing the Joint Chiefs of Staff on the Inter-Agency Task Force and testifying against a bill that would enclose U.S. fisheries out to 200 miles. Morris argued that ''Virtually all major conflicts in the past, both distant and recent, have had their roots in competing economic claims.'' Now that the continents are fully under sovereignty and sources of food and scarce minerals are becoming more difficult to develop on land, coastal nations are looking to the oceans:

The reason for pressing for a Law of the Sea Conference is to develop a uniform law . . . under which orderly development and usage can take place. Without such an agreed law, competing and overlapping claims will grow in breadth and in degree of control over all uses of the seas, not just over resources. From such unrestricted, uncontrolled claims come the conflicts we seek to avoid and the restrictions to navigation and overflight which we cannot accept.

. . . The reason such claims have been few thus far has been the adamant U.S. refusal to recognize them, whether they are to fishing zones, economic zones or full territorial seas. We have consistently and strongly stated that only in the context of a full treaty that protects all of our many oceans interests will we agree to any expansion of jurisdiction for resource purposes.

. . . [Although progress has been slow], a treaty will ensue—unless a flood of varied unilateral claims is stimulated by unilateral U.S. action; i.e. passage of [a 200-mile fisheries bill]. Once many claims are made, each different and each more expansive politically than that of neighbors, there will be little if any chance to persuade the 122 coastal states concerned to walk back their domestic laws in the context of a treaty. In such case, there will be no treaty, merely conflict because of competing and varying claims in the oceans.[16]

The creeping jurisdiction theory contains enough blemishes to raise serious questions of its validity. Its key hypothesis is that the nature, extent, and timing of all claims are determined by the arbitrary political calculations of coastal states, but it fails to give a logical explanation of certain of the most important features of their behavior. For example, what causes certain countries to make only resource claims but others to make territorial claims? What benefits do some countries derive from converting resource enclosures to territorial claims? Why has rivalry been more intense in certain regions of the globe, thus causing more enclosures there? Why has rivalry so far been limited mainly to coastal areas, rarely extending to the deep seas beyond 200 miles? Without a logical development of these issues,[17] the theory becomes little more than an unsupported assertion—what Senator Edmund S. Muskie (D.-Me.) has called "argument by horror story."[18] What is more, as Senator Henry M. Jackson has pointed out, the creeping jurisdiction argument is at odds with some important evidence:

> past international actions will show that nations do not always follow other nations' unilateral claims. In this regard, I would cite the Canadian decision to declare a 100 mile pollution zone in the Arctic Ocean, United States action to quarantine Cuba in 1962, and the requirement by our own Coast Guard [in 1966] to bar any vessels carrying liquified natural gas, U.S. flag or not, from entering U.S. ports unless they are constructed to Coast Guard standards. All of these actions have not been followed by automatic and identical actions by other nations.[19]

By the same token, the U.S.S.R.'s claim to a twelve-mile territorial sea dates back to 1909, and only one other country (Guatemala) extended its territorial sea to this limit prior to 1947 when Peru claimed a territorial sea of 200 nautical miles.[20] There were until 1975 only nine cases of territorial extensions out to 200 miles, and most of these claims have been mainly for resource purposes. This is not, I think, the vast degree of coastal state inroads into the high seas that Admiral Morris' statement implies, and all these claims have occurred in Latin American and African waters, which the Joint Chiefs of Staff admit are neither essential for nor capable of being enforced against U.S. naval operations in the vicinity, especially the operations of nuclear submarines.[21]

The data that the creeping jurisdiction argument attempts to explain can be explained equally well by the economic theory of enclosure that I outlined in Chapter 2, and this theory also explains events for which the political rivalry argument carries no implication. The areas that have been enclosed, especially those since 1945, were determined mainly by local geographic conditions and the most valuable resources to be found there. The extent of enclosure was limited by enforcement costs. The stronger claims of the nine Latin American and African nations to 200-mile territorial seas are probably related to their desire to establish exclusive rights to fisheries; long-distance fishing vessels (as distinct from prospectors for petroleum or hard minerals) could more easily justify their routings and operations by recourse to freedoms of navigation, which a territorial sea extension would limit. The timing of claims was determined generally by changes in demands and technologies. Although some enclosures appear to have been in response to the Truman Proclamation, this may have been due to the recognition by other countries that actions by the United States tended to indicate when new oceans activities were profitable. Also, as Senator Jackson suggested, not all U.S. claims brought responses from other countries. In some cases competing enclosures will affect wealth distribution in a zero-sum manner, but the creeping jurisdiction argument exaggerates such effects by its failure to recognize also the stability implications of more efficient property rights.

In the years 1968−70, the Inter-Agency Task Force of the Executive branch debated U.S. policy on the seaward boundary of coastal state jurisdiction and the nature and powers of the jurisdiction of the international regime in the area beyond this boundary.[22] The Defense Department strongly favored maximum mobility by limiting coastal states to narrow *legal* shelf jurisdictions, and in exchange was willing to sacrifice a strong seabed regime for the international area. The National Science Foundation, representing the marine scientists, also wanted narrow coastal state jurisdiction in order to expand research freedoms. But their proposal to reduce coastal controls over only civilian and open research aroused the opposition of the Defense Department. The Department of Interior, representing the petroleum industry, wanted broad legal shelves to minimize the area that would be subject either to revenue sharing or to international authority, and was willing to trade the strength of the international regime in exchange. The ocean miners had just the opposite position, wanting a weak regime and being willing to trade off extensive jurisdiction over coastal zones (in which comparatively few valuable nodules were likely to be found). In short, each lobby was willing to sacrifice the allegedly vital interests of its opponents to obtain a national policy that reflected its own limited conception of total gains and costs.

The clear winner was the Defense Department, which raised the security interest in maximum mobility to the level of a basic requirement which, in Niskanen's words, should be pursued "at all [resource] costs." As a result, these interests became the "No. 1 priority" of the U.S. at UNCLOS.[23] However, this victory inspired a strong counterattempt by Secretary of the Treasury George Shultz and his deputy, William E. Simon (both of whom had become deeply skeptical of the degree to which U.S. economic interests would be served by the prevailing U.S. policy toward UNCLOS), to force an Executive branch policy review in the summer of 1973. This review emphasized the advantages to the United States of unfettered exploitation of its own continental margin which would be associated with broad-shelf jurisdiction, the ability of its oil and mining firms to deal bilaterally with other countries for exploitation rights, the possibilities of generating economic rents in U.S. coastal fisheries by restricting entry, and the U.S. interest in avoiding a strong international regime which could monopolize the minerals that nodules contain and which the U.S. imports. Thus, in addition to looking after U.S. economic interests per se, Shultz's policy tended to favor more exclusive property rights for coastal states and thus lessen the degree of inefficiency in certain coastal resource uses.

Secretary Shultz's review was upsetting to both the Executive branch and the U.S. delegation, which at one time was left in the embarassing position of being seated at Geneva and ready to negotiate but without diplomatic instructions.[24] The review failed in its attempt to discredit the argument of creeping jurisdiction, but it brought the bureaucratic strengths of the security interests and the resource interests roughly into balance, and thereafter neither of them could overwhelm the policy apparatus.[25] It also brought the deep schism within the Executive branch into the "sunshine" of public discussion, as evidenced by Table 50. This study, formerly confidential, was prepared in 1975 and published in 1976 by Chairman John Murphy (D.-N.Y.) of the House Subcommittee on Oceanography. It indicates that the Treasury and White House economic staffs generally gave greater weight to the resource implications of the breadth of coastal state jurisdiction and other related law of the sea issues than did either the State Department or the Defense Department. Formerly it had been easy for this rift to be glossed over since the dissenting agencies were underrepresented when the Inter-Agency Task Force testified in behalf of the entire Executive branch before the interested congressional committees. As Congressman Paul N. McCloskey (R.-Calif.) observed, "we don't get an accurate and candid appraisal of the problem. No one dares contest the policy judgment as seen by the top of the delegation or the top of the Administration."[26]

Once maximum mobility had become dominant within the United States ocean bureaucracy, it could then perhaps be negotiated internationally. The young states that controlled the UNCLOS process cared less about navigation rights than they did about a seabed regime in the common heritage area and more cash for the purpose of economic development. Since the preferences of the United States were just the opposite, the U.S. could attempt to tie navigation rights to the negotiations on resource enclosures and the nature of the international regime. This tactic was explained in retrospect by John Norton Moore, chairman of the Inter-Agency Task Force, in testimony before Congress in 1974:

> [I]t is a mistake to try to take the [law of the sea] issues in isolation, to pick out one thing like the breadth of the territorial seas as we did at the conference in 1960. The difficulty is you cannot then functionally separate the kinds of resource jurisdiction that make sense in coastal States from the kinds of navigational and other freedoms that ought to be protected and remain in the international community, because you are taking them one at a time. States are free to pick and choose among one treaty that satisfies them on fish, and they do not sign the treaty on straits and

navigational freedom so that the only way we feel to satisfactorily resolve these problems, and the only way to get that oceans treaty really is an overall package.[27]

One side in a negotiation can establish an advantage, of course, if it is able to construct a package deal that is offered to its opponents on an all-or-nothing basis, thereby requiring that they accept more features that are undesirable from their point of view than if each provision were offered separately. However, the U.S. could gain this advantage only if it were in the position of being able to do the construction of the negotiating package. By 1974, when Moore testified in the wake of the Caracas session, it was more or less clear that U.S. influence in constructing the negotiating package would be very slight. The UNCLOS apparatus was overwhelmingly in the hands of the Group of 77, and to continue to push for the package-deal strategy at this time could only place the United States at a further disadvantage in the negotiations.

Perhaps the least desirable result of attempting to tie navigation rights to resource negotiations was that the younger countries might not be willing to make their resource enclosures conditional upon the transit rights that the U.S. sought. This was first emphasized by R. H. Coase in an unpublished paper written for the Treasury but circulated within the Executive branch:

> The difficulty with the [1970] United States position is that these extensions of sovereignty by the coastal states are probably inevitable. For the United States to tie the question of freedom of navigation to the question of jurisdiction for other purposes (so that such jurisdiction is assumed to imply the right to regulate shipping) means that freedom of navigation will be placed in jeopardy—and without any reason. The tying together of these two questions is unnecessary. Both clarity of thought and prudence in negotiation suggest that these two questions should be kept separate. It should be possible to maintain freedom for shipping (both on the high seas and in straits) without opposing the desire of coastal states to extend their jurisdiction over the exploitation of ocean resources. Indeed there is good reason to suppose that, in general, few countries would have any interest in regulating shipping: their concern is with fisheries, oil and gas, minerals and other ocean resources. Once jurisdiction over the exploitation of ocean resources is conceded, agreement on freedom of navigation (some special cases excepted) should not prove difficult. . . . My view is that the present association of the question of freedom of navigation with jurisdiction over the oceans for other purposes is completely unnecessary and makes more difficult the negotiating position of the United States.[28]

3. UNITED STATES' OFFERS

For U.S. navigation interests to be guaranteed in a treaty, the votes of the younger countries would be needed. Judging by the actions of the U.S.

TABLE 50

Positions of Various Agencies in the Executive Branch Concerning the Nature of an International Seabed Regime and Other Issues of the Law of the Sea in 1975

	State Department	Treasury Department	Defense Department	Interior Department	Commerce Department	OMB	Council on International Economic Policy
1. Seabed protection through voting system (unspecified).	Yes	Not acceptable, keep present instructions	Unrealistic to expect success	Yes	Needs more study	Washington must approve	Negotiability questionable
Protection through fundamental conditions	Yes	do	No comment	Yes	do	do	Inadequate
2. Extent of continental margin	Need flexibility	All	do	All	All the continental margin	All	All
3. Revenue sharing in economic zone	Yes	No	do	Comments ambiguous	Acceptable if limited	No	No
4. Tax credit	No	No	do	Yes	No	No	No
5. Ad referendum authority for negotiations	Yes	No	Very limited use	Yes	No	Washington must approve	No
6. Joint ventures with ISRA[1]	Yes	Must be limited		Limit on extent	Too general	Must be at arm's length	Must be at arm's length
7. ISRA exploits in parallel	Yes	No		Yes	No	Acceptable if not discriminatory	No
8. Decision-making protection (unspecified)	Yes	Nonnegotiable	Unrealistic to expect	Yes	Needs more study	Washington must approve	Nonnegotiable
9. Just fundamental conditions (unspecified)	Yes	Not good enough	do	Yes	do	do	Not good enough

10. Commission to help LDC[2] producers	Yes	Acceptable if advisory only	Limit actions	Has misgivings	No	Acceptable if advisory only
11. Reservation of mining sites	Yes	No	Yes	No		No
12. Training of LDC nationals	Yes	No comment	No	Reservations		Need safeguards
13. Joint ventures with LDCs	Yes	Less than 10 pct. participation	Less than 10 pct. participation		No	No
14. 3 pct. royalty or 50 pct. of profits	Somewhat limited	More study needed	Limited	Needs more study		
15. U.S. tax credits or moratorium	No	No	Yes	No	No	
16. ISRA[1] contracts with firms	Yes					
17. Abandonment of 1st-in-time rights	Yes	No	Ambiguous	No	Acceptable if not discriminatory	

[1]International Seabed Resource Authority
[2]Less developed countries

SOURCE: *Deep Seabed Mining*, Hearings before the Subcommittee on Oceanography of the U.S. House of Representatives Committee on Merchant Marine and Fisheries, 94th Cong., 2d Sess., Serial No. 94-27, May 16, 1975; February 23, 24, March 8, 9, 1976, pp. 83 and 86.

delegation, the only way to obtain these votes was to offer resources in exchange. James L. Johnston, once a member of the delegation, told the House Subcommittee on Oceanography in 1976 that "it is [the delegation's] view that any increased resource jurisdiction necessarily reduces navigational freedoms. They also believe as a corollary, that making economic concessions on resource jurisdictions will buy a larger set of navigational freedoms."[29] In other words, Johnston believed that the delegation viewed the UNCLOS negotiations as a zero-sum game and, by implication, rejected the argument made in Chapter 3 that most coastal states would not take it upon themselves to interfere with navigation without first considering the incidental negative impacts. If it were generally understood at UNCLOS that the United States was willing to pay for navigation rights, then the younger countries would not supply these rights at a zero price. They would logically attempt to extract from the United States the maximum value of cash, resources, or treaty principles that it would be willing to pay for navigation rights.

The leaders of the U.S. delegation denied that trade-offs of resources for transit rights had occurred or were even contemplated. This was stressed in the following exchange between Ambassador Stevenson and Senator Metcalf on September 17, 1974, just after the close of the Caracas session:

> Senator Metcalf.   In the Washington Post article of August 30, 1974, you were quoted as saying, "The No. 1 priority is the mobility of our naval and air forces and the importance of retaining our nuclear deterrent."
>
> If that is the No. 1 priority, then the economic area, minerals, fish, pollution control, all of these other matters are secondary issues, aren't they?
>
> *   *   *   *
>
> Ambassador Stevenson.   We have always stressed the critical importance to the United States of the mobility of our naval and air forces. There is absolutely no question about it.
>
> But the implication that we are not also interested in the U.S. economic, environmental and other interests, is just not correct. I think we have never talked simply in terms of a single interest, but always in terms of a complex series of interests. But clearly the question of mobility is a critical U.S. interest.
>
> Senator Metcalf.   I heartily agree. I just want you to assure us that you are not going to trade off some of the other important areas of national concern just for defense.
>
> Ambassador Stevenson.   Mr. Chairman, I think the only hope for a treaty that is generally acceptable, and which the Senate will consent to ratification of is a treaty that will substantially protect the various different U.S. interests involved.[30]

This exchange also reveals the delegation's dilemma. Failure to make navigation rights the number one priority in treaty negotiations would cause the Defense

Department to withdraw its support from the policy and force another round of transactions costs to build a fresh domestic consensus. But a failure to guarantee minimum U.S. access to resources could jeopardize ratification. How much of the economic interest could be sacrificed before the Senate balked?

Trade-offs between resources and navigation guarantees in United States' offers to the UN date back to the first comprehensive proposal submitted to the Seabed Committee in 1970. Evidently the American delegation assumed that a favorable treaty had to be concluded swiftly if the enclosure movement were to be halted. Otherwise, shrewd bargaining would have led the delegation to delay revealing its price offer for navigation guarantees until the final days of the last conference sessions when the hardest bargaining was likely to occur. In any case, the U.S. tipped its hand even before the UNCLOS agenda was set.

The United States Draft Convention on the International Seabed Area of 1970 was tabled as a U.S. working paper. It was not a document to which the U.S. government was bound, but it suggested the basic thrust of U.S. policy at the time—a policy that was dominated by the special interests of the Defense Department and the State Department. The three principal elements of the policy are illustrated in Figure 30. First, coastal states would have essentially exclusive rights to exploitation within the 200-meter isobath, subject to promises not to interfere with navigation and other uses. Second, the international authority would have full jurisdiction beyond the 200-meter boundary but could, at its discretion, permit the coastal state to exploit the living and nonliving resources between the 200-meter boundary and the edge of the continental margin as a trustee for all mankind. Between one-half and two-thirds of the tax revenues collected by the coastal state within this zone were to be shared with international institutions for the purpose of financing economic development, especially in landlocked and geographically disadvantaged countries.[31] Third, the international seabed regime would be a licensing authority with weighted voting for advanced technology countries, as described in Chapter 8. With this generous three-part proposal, it is little wonder that "the internationalists mark this period immediately following the May 23, 1970, presidential statement and the tabling of the U.S. Draft Treaty as the golden age of U.S. ocean policy."[32]

The U.S. negotiating strategy before 1971, according to Ann Hollick, was to divide the issues into two separate groupings: straits, the territorial sea, and fisheries in one group, and the continental shelf and the seabed regime in another. This way, "the Government thereby hoped to preserve its packages of tradeoffs— a narrow Continental Shelf for a generous seabed regime and freedom of transit through and over international straits in exchange for a twelve-mile territorial sea with preferential coastal state fishing rights in the area beyond."[33] The Draft Convention, however, lumped all these issues together in a single proposal along with revenue sharing and several others. This led the younger countries, which had the numerical majority to determine the agenda and thus the contents of the

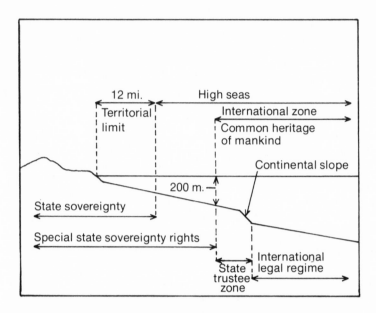

FIG. 30. Division of the seabed between coastal state and international
authority as proposed by the United States in 1970.

SOURCE: C. Richard Tinsley, "Mining of Manganese Nodules: An Intriguing
Legal Problem," *Engineering and Mining Journal*, October 1973, p. 87. Copyright 1973 McGraw-Hill, Inc., 1221 Avenue of the Americas, New York, N.Y.
10020.

package deal, to expect that even more concessions could be obtained within a
comprehensive conference that locked each of these items on the agenda. Four
months after the U.S. proposal, the UN voted to convene UNCLOS with the List
of Subjects and Issues (see Table 46) as its agenda.[34]

In 1973 Ambassador Stevenson told the UN Seabed Committee that "while
we have attempted to readjust our proposals to accommodate the views and
interests of others, we have thus far not seen sufficiently similar movement on the
part of some others. If this were to continue at [Caracas], we could approach the
point where the potential for achieving a widespread accommodation of major
points of view would be lost."[35] This was, of course, precisely what happened at
Caracas, and one year later the "potential" for achieving the "widespread
accommodation" in Committee I had vanished. The ocean mining provisions of
the Single Negotiating Text were quite "unacceptable" to the United States,
although the U.S. delegation was glad that, in Mr. Moore's words during a U.S.
Senate hearing, "we now for the first time have a focus in which these
negotiations really can proceed":

Senator Metcalf.   I would rather not have such a focus as you have on this single negotiating text.

Mr. Moore.   In Committee One it has hurt us, and in Committees Two and Three we have at least something that is a reasonable starting point.

Senator Metcalf.   It seems to me it would be harder to negotiate from an unacceptable text than it is from an acceptable one.

Mr. Moore.   I think that is probably true in Committee One, Senator. I think it has hurt us there, and it is going to be something we will have to overcome. But certainly we cannot meaningfully move toward a treaty in the absence of a single focus. We now have that focus.[36]

But instead of withdrawing from this negotiation or at least refusing to negotiate further without getting concessions on the portions that it found most objectionable, the United States offered more concessions of its own. Between 1975 and 1976, the United States had offered the younger countries (1) their Enterprise, (2) financial backing for it, (3) a reduced rate of U.S. exploitation until Enterprise was in operation, (4) a limited form of production controls for the first 25 years of mining and periodic review of this provision thereafter, and (5) an undetailed proposal to transfer U.S. technology to Enterprise. Secretary Kissinger's proposal for temporary production controls was later criticized in Congress as being flatly contrary to his earlier statement opposing permanent controls, but the debate actually was moot,[37] for the reason that the U.S., since 1970, had not opposed giving the proposed authority power to control production and thus prices *indirectly* through its right to establish work programs and determine general policies for the extent and timing of areas to be leased. This point, which was at the core of U.S. mineral interests, was probably lost, owing either to a failure to bargain deftly or to a willingness to exchange it for navigational guarantees.

4. INCAUTIOUS OPTIMISM

Beginning with President Nixon's Statement on Oceans Policy of 1970, the United States "has been foremost among those who have argued that a comprehensive and widely acceptable treaty is indispensable to this nation's interests in the oceans."[38] Since that statement, the U.S. delegation to UNCLOS has tended if anything to err on the side of optimism in their assessments as to whether a comprehensive treaty which also would protect vital U.S. interests could in fact be achieved. Cautious optimism has been the dominant point of view of American delegates even when cautious pessimism would have been realistic.

Ambassador Stevenson was "cautiously optimistic" about the 1974 Caracas session before it began, and his ranking colleague on the delegation, Mr. Moore, viewed the possible "failure" of UNCLOS as a "remote contingency, certainly the contingency that we hope will not occur."[39] This point of view prevailed after Caracas even though little had been accomplished there. In September 1974, Stevenson had a "firm conviction that a comprehensive treaty is obtainable by the end of 1975"; for such an outcome, however, he thought "governments must begin serious negotiation the first day [of the 1975 session] at Geneva. . . ."[40] Moore told the U.S. Senate Armed Services Committee the same year that "Fortunately, for the first time in the history of oceans law, it is realistic to expect such a broadly based agreement in the near future."[41] Nine months later, however, after the Geneva session had produced a negotiating text that was unacceptable to the U.S. in a number of ways, Moore was beginning to sound more cautious: "The difficulties of that negotiation are great. We should not minimize them. But, at the same time, I think we should not create undue expectations that it is an easy process, and we can easily get a treaty. I must admit that perhaps my testimony in the past has led to such overoptimistic expectations but I think the point is that we are on the right track. We are headed toward a Law of the Sea Treaty in my opinion; although there is still a good distance to go."[42] A year later, in 1976, Stevenson's successor, T. Vincent Learson, in testimony before Senator Metcalf's subcommittee, stated:

> Mr. Chairman, I do not want to underestimate the problems that still face the Conference and which must be resolved if we are to achieve a timely and satisfactory treaty. We are, however, much closer to such an agreement than we were at the start of the recent [spring 1976] session. It will take hard work and political will but the substantive negotiations can and should be completed at the August/September [1976] session. If we are successful, I would then expect the Drafting Committee of the Conference to do the technical work after that. In any case, the goal of the Conference is to have a treaty ready for signature in the first half of next year. I feel at this point that we have a better than even chance of achieving this scenario and obtaining an acceptable treaty. A better than even chance, sir, do you judge it to be optimistic? That is the way I place the odds.[43]

After two more years of unproductive debate, Ambassador Richardson considered recommending to President Carter that the U.S. "reevaluate" its participation in UNCLOS.[44] But a year later Richardson found that UNCLOS had "made sufficient progress to reinforce the conviction of the United States that it is still worthwhile to persist in the effort to construct a framework of international cooperation in the oceans."[45]

Parallel with its usual optimism for UNCLOS, the Executive branch has generally refused to support unilateral enclosures for the United States, even on the contingency that UNCLOS could fail. It opposed the 200-mile fisheries zone in 1976 and it opposed a variety of bills to regulate seabed exploitation by U.S. nationals. In each case it has been feared that U.S. enclosures would hamper the progress of UNCLOS. Although the State Department in 1973 stated that "prudence dictates that we begin at once to formulate a legislative approach on a contingency basis,"[46] it has never drafted such legislation. It promised that this work would begin in 1974, in 1975, and in 1976, but each time this effort was set aside after it "discovered a greater willingness on the part of some developing countries to explore reasonable solutions to the problems in Committee I."[47] This position was reversed in 1978 when the Carter administration declared that it would support a seabed mining bill of some kind, but the reversal was apparently intended to prod UNCLOS into writing a more reasonable Committee I text and did not reflect a shift in policy toward protecting U.S. interests through unilateral enclosures instead of through UNCLOS.[48]

The "overriding bias" at the State Department, Ann Hollick maintains, was "toward reaching an international agreement" of some kind.[49] If the State Department announced the provisions of a seabed mining bill that it deemed "acceptable," it could scarcely oppose such a bill if Congress seized the opportunity and enacted it. To express pessimism about UNCLOS would aid congressional skeptics, undermine the trade-offs that U.S. negotiators could offer in exchange for navigation guarantees, risk the possibility that the Defense Department would exercise its veto power, and thereby upset the delicate policy "consensus" within the Executive branch.

5. UNCLOS OR *CHAOS*

The only rational explanation behind United States ocean policy is the dominance given within the Executive branch to multilaterally negotiated military, and to a lesser extent commercial, navigation rights. If satisfactory navigation rights could neither be asserted unilaterally nor be negotiated bilaterally—premises which, I shall argue later, are difficult to support—then they had to be negotiated internationally. If the willingness of other countries to supply these rights depended upon the degree to which the U.S. offered concessions on other resource rights, then for the U.S. either to extend its coastal authority unilaterally or to mine the international area without the sanction of UNCLOS would reduce what the U.S. could offer in exchange for navigation in the package deal. For the U.S. to play both ends against the middle by pursuing fisheries or seabeds enclosures while negotiating at UNCLOS would jeopardize its number one priority, which the Defense Department could veto. There could be no "paella"—by which the maritime countries obtained navigational access and the younger countries obtained cash and their preferred seabed regime—if the U.S. made a grab for the very resources that the young countries wanted to have held in reserve for themselves. Not only could U.S. unilateral actions kill off any prospect for a treaty, but they would probably require a lengthy and time-consuming renegotiation of the domestic policy consensus within the Executive branch.

United States ocean policy has often been justified, at least in public, in drastically different terms—either fine-sounding generalities about the moral rightness of international negotiating processes or dire predictions of catastrophe should UNCLOS fail. Moreover, the defenders of the policy have never fixed their case on one justification only. Instead, the policy has been defended with two or three excuses at a time, as if to warn opponents that the debunking of any single argument would be unavailing since several others could be marshaled to take its place. Justification of this sort is either a façade or a gross exaggeration, or simply wrong.

Ever since Arvid Pardo proposed in 1968 that a new ocean conference be convened, the choice between UNCLOS and the enclosure movement has been cast generally as a choice between a treaty and chaos. Both Presidents Johnson and Nixon believed that without a treaty colonial competition or unrestrained exploitation would produce destabilization and finally anarchy. These themes have been taken up by the U.S. diplomats. Mr. Moore said in 1974 that without a treaty there would be "a crazy quilt of uncontrolled national claims . . . with its open ended invitation to conflicts."[50] In 1973 Ambassador Stevenson remarked that "it sounds incredible to say it, but today we have a completely lawless regime for 70 percent of the globe," which makes the "necessity to reach a [treaty] . . . overwhelming."[51] Mr. Stevenson was apparently equating "lawlessness" with the absence of a comprehensive ocean treaty, whereas in fact the enclosure movement of the oceans has effectively produced a body of customary international law that has responded economically to changing demands for ocean goods and changing technologies for producing them. Obviously, neither the enclosure movement nor UNCLOS is likely to function always with absolutely no amount of confusion or conflict: in choosing among competing institutional arrangements in a highly imperfect world, we are commonly faced with choices that have competing imperfections. Therefore the only relevant question, either for analysis or for policy, is: Which type of ocean institution appears to be the least flawed? In this case it is difficult to improve on the answer that R. H. Coase gave in 1974:

> By "unrestrained exploitation," I take President Nixon to mean that organizations engaged in the exploitation of ocean resources do so without regard to the future consequences of their actions. This implies either the absence of a law or an inappropriate law governing their actions. The reason why this state of affairs would inevitably come about if control is vested in the coastal state but not if it is vested in an international authority is hard to find. In fact, there is no such reason.

The laws of some coastal states would undoubtedly define more precisely the rights of exploiting organizations, would be more appropriate to the circumstances, and would be better enforced than would the regulations of an international authority. The view that there will be losses from "conflicting jurisdictional claims" is, of course, right but it is not evident why the period of "conflicting claims" would be longer or that those that existed would cause more serious harm if the general movement was towards recognition of the claims of coastal states than it would be if an attempt were made to establish an international regime to control the exploitation of ocean resources.[52]

What is more, UNCLOS would promote conflict if it created inefficient structures of property rights which encouraged nations to capture wealth by circumventing the treaty rules. For example, the structure of coastal property rights that UNCLOS contemplates is almost certain to be less efficient than the enclosure movement because of the division of certain fisheries and revenue sharing which raises the cost of offshore hydrocarbon production. In the deep seabeds, UNCLOS property arrangements would be almost rent minimizing as compared with the alternatives of no regulation at all or a registry. The enclosure movement is associated with the creation of greater rents as well as distribution of wealth in the direction of coastal states, both of which tend to produce more international stability than chaos.

As another justification for multilateral negotiations, the enclosure movement was equated with resurgent colonialism by President Johnson and with international conflict by Secretary Kissinger.[53] But surely there are important differences between subjugating entire populations in Africa and Asia during the nineteenth century and vacuuming pieces of rock on the bottom of the Pacific Ocean in the twentieth century. If my analysis in Chapter 8 is correct, there is no economic reason to believe that competition over these rocks would be destabilizing.

As still another justification, it has been argued that a thoroughly international approach to governing ocean uses is required because of the interdependencies or spillover impacts that various activities tend to cause.[54] The validity of this argument depends, however, upon the actual degree of interdependence that exists. Usually this degree is presumed to be very great. But the evidence that I have found suggests that the principal international spillover problems—as opposed to coastal or regional spillover problems—appear limited to scientific research, migratory fisheries, and vessel source pollution. UNCLOS would have little positive effect in internalizing the spillovers of either of the first two resources, and in the case of vessel pollution the approach that UNCLOS is most likely to select also appears to be the least economical. This indicates that an UNCLOS treaty to solve *most* problems of ocean interdependencies is neither necessary nor desirable.

6. THE *SUCCESS* OF
UNITED STATES POLICY

The effectiveness of the U.S. delegation in obtaining the consent of UNCLOS to U.S. policy goals must be distinguished from its effectiveness in promoting U.S. economic interests in the oceans. For example, although the inability of UNCLOS to produce a satisfactory compromise on the seabed regime is probably viewed as a failure of U.S. diplomacy, it is in fact a success in terms of U.S. economic interests in minerals. This section treats elements of U.S. policy for which diplomatic outcomes and economic interests appear to be at odds, and the discussion is summarized briefly in Table 51.

One of the most striking differences between diplomatic outcomes and economic interests is found in the case of navigation through straits. Both treaty texts guarantee the right of "transit passage," which prohibits straits states from interfering with the "continuous and expeditious" transit of ships in "their normal mode of operation" (see Chap. 9, p. 292). The U.S. delegation interprets this as permitting submerged passage of submarines since submerged operation is "their normal mode of operation."[55] The economic price of this diplomatic success in terms of economic rents forgone by the U.S., based on a simple hypothetical case, could be high. Assume that the U.S., to obtain its number one priority, had to share with developing countries only 10 percent of the economic rents it could capture from mineral exploitation on its continental margin and one-half of the rents it could capture from the deep seabeds.[56] Using the estimates for 1985 from Table 8, the sacrificed rents would be about $0.8 billion per year.[57] To my knowledge there are no detailed projections of the future rents to U.S. commercial use of straits. However, if the very rough estimates for 1972–74 (see Chap. 3, pp. 71–75) are used for illustrative purposes, then straits use would have to rise significantly by 1985 for this trade-off to be attractive from the perspective of U.S. economic interests.

Sacrificing a portion of the U.S. share of ocean rents as well as U.S. interests in economic efficiency might advance the overall national interest if it also produced national security gains, in the form of increased naval mobility through straits, that were more than offsetting. Indeed, it has been implicit in the position of the Defense Department and in the U.S. policy of pursuing "narrow shelves" at UNCLOS that tying transit rights to resource rights would produce more gains than costs. The impact of restricted transit through the 121 straits that would be overlapped by twelve-mile territorial seas on the vulnerability of the U.S. fleet of ballistic missile submarines was analyzed by Robert E. Osgood of the Johns Hopkins School of Advanced International Studies.[58] Osgood found that only sixteen of these straits had significance for submarine operations. Of the sixteen, however, four straits are controlled on at least one side either by the United States or by one of its military allies. Eight others—Gibraltar, two in the Indian Ocean,

TABLE 51

EFFECTIVENESS (+ OR −) OF U.S. DELEGATION TO UNCLOS ACCORDING TO DIPLOMATIC VS. ECONOMIC CRITERIA, BASED ON U.S. OCEAN POLICY THROUGH JUNE 1978

Category of U.S. Policy Goals	Diplomacy: Are UNCLOS Outcomes Similar to Goals of U.S. Ocean Policy?	Economics: Are Goals of U.S. Policy Consistent with U.S. Economic Interest?
Navigation in straits	+	−
Limitations on enclosure:		
1970 Trusteeship Zone proposal	−	−
1974 Full Continental Margin subject to five conditions:	+	+
Revenue sharing	+	−
Protect environment via international vessel construction standards	+	?
Maintain high-seas character of residual rights in EEZs	−	?
Integrity of investments	−	+
Compulsory dispute settlement	−	+
Fisheries:		
Full utilization principle	+	?
Anadromous species	+	−
Freedoms of scientific research	−	+
Seabed exploitation:		
Access of U.S. miners to international area	−	−
Weighted voting in regime	−	−
Avoid production controls	−	−
No control over non-mining activities	−	−

and five in the Caribbean—provide access to areas that appear to offer no targeting advantages over the North Atlantic. Of the remaining four straits, Osgood argued that Malacca and Sunda are too shallow for large submarines to transit while submerged, and two others, Lombok and Ombai-Wetar (which is east of Lombok and not shown in Fig. 9), lie in Indonesia's archipelagic waters which can be avoided, if necessary, by circumnavigating Australia. Thus, out of the 121 straits, only Lombok and Ombai-Wetar and perhaps Gibraltar appear to have much importance for submarine mobility, and protecting these interests boils down to maintaining satisfactory bilateral relations with Indonesia and perhaps Spain. Furthermore, even these relations will become less important for U.S. security purposes when the Trident class submarines with their ultra-long-range missiles (4,500−6,000 nautical miles) are introduced in the 1980s. This system, Osgood argues, "would virtually obviate the dependence of the U.S. underwater nuclear deterrent on transit of straits."[59] If Osgood's assessment is correct, it undermines the core of U.S. ocean policy—tying allegedly "vital" but in fact lower valued rights of mobility through straits to higher valued rights of resource exploitation.

Consistent with the dominance given by U.S. policy makers to questions of mobility, much of the U.S. effort at UNCLOS has been devoted to limiting the extent and nature of coastal state rights in EEZs even though the EEZ of the U.S. would be the world's largest and one of the richest. The Trusteeship Zone proposal of 1970 (Fig. 30) was an attempt to limit coastal resource enclosures to the 200-meter isobath, but it failed to gain support internationally or domestically. Internationally, many coastal states sought a broader EEZ with more exclusive resource rights than the U.S. proposed, and the landlocked and geographically disadvantaged states wanted a narrower EEZ with stronger international controls.[60] Domestically, the petroleum industry and a bipartisan group of U.S. senators pressed for the U.S. to adopt the "full continental margin" as the universal EEZ limit.[61]

The U.S. delegation adopted the 200-mile limit in 1973 and the full continental margin in 1974, but tied to this adoption five conditions, which have had mixed success both diplomatically and in protecting U.S. economic interests.[62] First, developed states would be required to share a portion of the revenues that they obtained from continental shelf exploitation beyond the 200-mile limit. Second, the marine environment would be protected from pollution by international ship construction standards. The first condition is probably contrary to U.S. economic interests since it would tax mineral production and thus raise prices by some extra amount. The second condition has a questionable impact on U.S. economic interests (see Table 47). The U.S. surely gains some amount by worldwide reductions in pollution, especially pollution that occurs near its coasts. But construction standards also raise U.S. shipping costs and the prices of materials shipped. Diplomatically, U.S. advocacy of these two conditions was successful since UNCLOS adopted them, but economically they have mixed impacts on the U.S.

The three other U.S. conditions have been rejected by UNCLOS thus far. The third condition was that all residual rights in the EEZ not expressly granted to coastal states should be held by the international community as high seas rights. This proposal was designed to protect U.S. mobility interests in that portion of the EEZ outside the territorial sea. It was rejected in both treaty texts with the definition of the EEZ as a zone *sui generis*—neither territorial seas nor high seas. As I argued in the previous chapter (p. 289), the concept of *sui generis* essentially protects U.S. interests in navigation although it represents weaker language than the U.S. delegation really wanted. Of course, more exclusive coastal state rights within the EEZ would have a mixed impact on U.S. economic interests: increasing the appropriability of economic rents by the U.S. from its own large EEZ but weakening automatic protections of its ships and fishermen in other EEZs.

The fourth condition required that coastal states guarantee the integrity of offshore investments in their EEZs made by foreign countries. Although this provision would probably advance U.S. economic interests, UNCLOS has shown almost no interest in it. This measure would be extremely difficult to enforce in any case because it would offer no protection against the uncompensated expropriation of onshore investments.[63]

The fifth condition was that the treaty should create institutions to settle disputes between countries over rights in EEZs, especially fisheries, and that procedures for such settlements should be compulsory for all parties. This proposal would probably advance both U.S. economic interests and economic efficiency generally by defining property rights more carefully, but it has been one of the most controversial issues at UNCLOS. The basic position of coastal states has been that no disputes related to their fisheries should be subject to any kind of compulsory procedure. However, the landlocked and geographically disadvantaged states along with the distant-water fishing states (particularly Japan and the U.S.S.R.) have argued that all disputes related to living resources of the EEZ should be settled by binding and compulsory arbitration. Coastal states have rejected even the concepts of compulsory fact finding, a moratorium on all disputes before the treaty comes into force, and selection by the state parties themselves of their preferred form of settlement (whether conciliation, arbitration, the International Court of Justice, or the Law of the Sea Tribunal).[64] Thus, the dispute settlement issue, along with scientific research and the deep seabeds, has proved through 1978 to be one of the least diplomatically successful elements of U.S. policy at UNCLOS.

U.S. proposals to give landlocked or geographically disadvantaged states fishing rights in EEZs unless the fisheries were "fully utilized" by the fleets of the cognizant coastal states were accepted by the conference.[65] But the effect of this proposal on U.S. economic interests is less certain owing to the divergence in U.S. fishing interests. The full-utilization clause gives some protection to U.S. distant-water fishing fleets. But it dilutes the exclusivity of U.S. resource rights to control fisheries in its own enormous EEZ, not only with respect to distant-water fishing countries but also with respect to the geographically disadvantaged countries of the Caribbean area. The U.S. proposal that anadromous stocks be protected "both within and beyond" the EEZ of the home country was no doubt consistent with U.S. economic interests but its acceptance by UNCLOS was limited to the portion of the stocks found within the EEZ.[66]

One of the most conspicuous diplomatic failures of the United States at UNCLOS has been the failure to obtain treaty articles permitting increased freedom of scientific research, an issue which the U.S. delegation has pressed at every UNCLOS session. Such freedom would be consistent with overall U.S. economic interests, but it is clear that it must be purchased individually from the various coastal states.

But the several aforementioned failures of the U.S. delegation either to negotiate U.S. objectives successfully at UNCLOS or to perceive U.S. economic interests accurately are minor as compared with the combined diplomatic and economic failures in the deep seabed negotiations. The seabed provisions of the Informal Composite Negotiating Text are so far removed either from the zero-regulation regime that would most advance U.S. economic interests and those of economic efficiency or from the quasi-contractual licensing authority which the U.S. proposed in 1970 that they were extremely unfortunate both in economic and diplomatic terms. Although the U.S. delegation since 1977 has perceived its main challenge as negotiating away from the Composite Text, the nature and results of this effort have been alarming. During the seventh session of UNCLOS in March, April, and May 1978, for example, the U.S. delegation appeared willing to leave most of the core seabed treaty articles intact. The principal exception was its unsuccessful attempt to negotiate weighted voting for the ocean mining countries in the council of the Authority. Apart from that, the major U.S. diplomatic effort was devoted to attempts to make slight changes in certain of the most discriminatory provisions of the treaty so that they would be somewhat less severe on U.S. mining firms, but more or less to give up on the rest of the articles. There were several clear examples of such behavior at the seventh session in 1978.

First, the Composite Text of 1977 made the transfer of technology from the ocean miner to the Authority a precondition of obtaining a license. Negotiations at the seventh session removed the precondition while still making technology transfer an obligation of the miner at "commercial terms" according to an arbitration procedure established by the Authority. Miners are required to provide the Authority with an up-to-date description of their technology (probably to enable the Authority to determine which technology is best) and under certain circumstances are obliged also to sell their technology to developing countries.[67] Thus, although certain clauses in the article on technology transfer were improved from the U.S. point of view, other provisions simultaneously were worsened. As a second example, the U.S. successfully obtained a revision of the article on the review conference (to be held twenty-five years after mining licenses are first granted) that would automatically have eliminated the "non-Enterprise" portion of the parallel system. However, the revision also permits the review conference to establish a moratorium on granting new mining licenses if the conference cannot reach agreement on amendments to the regime after five years of trying.[68] Third, concerning the power of the Authority to establish production controls, the U.S. obtained a new article that prevented such control over non-nodule minerals except by amendment to the treaty. But the U.S. appeared to be on the verge of accepting the principle of controls over the quantity of minerals produced from nodules and entered into negotiations with Canada, the largest terrestrial nickel producer. As the U.S. delegation report put it, "the U.S. and Canada concluded that their interests would be served by early agreement on a complete production control formula," although Ambassador Richardson said that such negotiations would inevitably require certain "painful decisions" for both parties.[69]

In short, the U.S. delegation seemed ready in 1978 to leave intact the essential structure of the Authority, the parallel system and the banking system, and the concept of production controls—treaty articles that were utterly inconsistent with United States economic interests—while attempting to negotiate slight improvements to relatively unimportant treaty articles which, even if they were accepted by the UNCLOS majority, would enhance the overall economic interests of the United States to an almost imperceptible degree.

7. UNILATERALISM IN CONGRESS

The United States Congress, because of certain lobbying pressures, has appeared more alert than the U.S. delegation to the impact of UNCLOS on U.S. economic interests. The burden of these lobbies and domestic industries has been the fear that the delegation would sacrifice their issue in exchange for the Defense Department's cherished navigation rights. Most successful were the coastal fishing interests who claimed that many species would be overcaught by the time an effective treaty was ratified. Also, as Senator Ted Stevens (R.-Alaska) said, "We feel there is every possibility that our fish may be traded off on those [other] issues."[70] The Executive branch argued that the U.S. 200-mile fisheries zone would prompt even more extravagant enclosures through creeping jurisdiction,[71] or could "precipitate a confrontation" in America's coastal waters.[72] In 1974, General George S. Brown, chairman of the Joint Chiefs of Staff, warned of serious consequences:

> It is highly unlikely that the major maritime powers who fish off our coast, especially Japan and the Soviet Union, would acknowledge the validity of a sweeping claim. . . . We must, therefore, assume that such vessels would not seek our permission to fish within 200 miles of our coasts and that they would continue to do so. Enforcement of the act would involve boarding, inspection, arrest, and seizure. I cannot predict with certainty how they would react to such enforcement measures by the United States.[73]

No serious incidents occurred, however, through 1978, in spite of several boardings, arrests, inspections, and seizures by the U.S., and both Japan and the U.S.S.R. obtained quotas for fishing in U.S. waters through diplomatic channels and negotiated similar agreements of their own.[74]

Environmental groups have pressed for unilateral extension of U.S. pollution controls out to 200 miles after concluding that "the international community is *not*, at this point in history, prepared to commit itself to taking measures adequate to protect the marine environment.''[75] The treaty articles were viewed as being so weak against all types of pollution sources that several environmental organizations recommended in 1975 that the U.S. Senate reject an ocean treaty containing them.[76] Unilateral measures were given more consideration after several serious tanker groundings, collisions, and explosions that occurred in 1976 to 1978. The several bills that were drafted would (1) tighten standards for tanker construction and operation beyond existing IMCO standards; (2) put more bite into U.S. enforcement and inspection procedures; (3) require tankers to carry electronic equipment to permit operation of an FAA-type traffic control system to reduce the possibility of collisions in harbors and congested coastal areas, and (4) extend jurisdiction for each of these activities, including controls on tanker ballast discharges, from the present limits of U.S. navigable waters and the three-mile territorial sea through a ''maritime safety zone'' of 200 miles in breadth.[77]

The U.S. ocean miners have been more fearful than perhaps any other domestic interest that the U.S. delegation would trade it off for other goals at UNCLOS. In each session of Congress since 1971, the industry has supported legislation that usually had four major provisions.[78] First, the legislation would regulate the seabed mining activities of U.S. citizens and firms, but it would not claim sovereign rights over the deep seabed or establish enforceable property rights of the kind found in EEZs. Second, a system of licensing would be administered by the Executive branch along the lines proposed by the U.S. in its 1970 Draft Convention (see Chap. 8, pp. 246−49). Once a treaty was signed and ratified, this system of regulation would be transferred to the Authority and anything inconsistent with the treaty would be repealed. Third, the licenses authorized by reciprocating states which enacted legislation similar to that of the U.S., would be accorded identical legal status as licenses granted by the U.S. Fourth, licensees would be given guarantees by the U.S. government to the extent that the value of their investment was impaired by the creation of an international regime binding on the U.S. These guarantees would be financed by premiums at usually less than one percent of investment value similar to those charged by the U.S. Overseas Private Investment Corporation designed to protect U.S. firms from losses owing to seizure or confiscation. (The limit of such insurance has usually been $350 million per licensee.) Most ocean miners believed that indemnification was necessary in order to reduce the political risk to which they were exposed by placing the expected cost of the risk on the single entity that could control for the risk, the U.S. government.[79]

The legislation has usually been opposed by the Executive branch on ''creeping jurisdiction'' grounds. Even a hint of ''carving up the common heritage,'' it was alleged, could produce a furious reaction by the younger countries at UNCLOS, perhaps in the form of another ''Moratorium Resolution.'' In the view of the U.S. delegation, this would make negotiations ''much more difficult," if that were possible.[80] Congressional committees have also had reservations about unprecedented investment guarantees that might amount to "blackmailing" the U.S. delegation. As Ambassador Richardson put it in 1977, "Legislation providing for a U.S. Government obligation to compensate for any losses caused by a treaty could force our negotiators to assure that the treaty would conform to U.S. legislation."[81] If the delegation brought back from UNCLOS a treaty that put the U.S. ocean miners out of business, the guarantee provisions could require that ratification of the treaty be accompanied by an additional appropriation of perhaps billions of dollars. Viewed positively, this would raise the cost to both the diplomats and the Senate of approving uneconomic treaty provisions. Viewed negatively, it could lead to a substantial "raid" on the Treasury. In 1978, the Carter administration decided to support legislation without the investment guarantees as "an interim measure" provided that it contained a provision for sharing revenues with developing countries in a fashion similar to the U.S. proposals at UNCLOS.[82] This action makes the likelihood of enactment greater than at any time since 1971. Ironically Executive branch support for the legislation comes at a time when it is less necessary politically because of the formation of multinational consortia,[83] since such arrangements provide tax advantages in addition to enabling the miners to be less dependent upon the protection of any single government. On the other hand, domestic legislation would still serve as something of a grandfather clause for whatever happens at UNCLOS, and this offers the U.S. government the political advantage of reducing objections that ocean miners might raise to an eventual treaty when it came time to ratify it in the Senate.

8. CONCLUSIONS FOR UNITED STATES POLICY

Since 1970 the Executive branch of the U.S. government has been committed to achieving treaty guarantees for naval and maritime mobility, particularly through international straits, by exchanging resource rights which by conservative calculations seem to be of much greater value. This policy has been unwise in both diplomatic and economic terms. Even if navigation were paramount to U.S. national interests, stronger navigation rights probably could be obtained by dealing bilaterally with the two or three straits countries involved than through a forum of 150 nations. In any case, future generations of U.S. ballistic missile submarines will carry weapons of extremely long range, sufficiently long as to eliminate the military demand for passage through straits. This will make the core element of present United States ocean policy about as obsolete as a battleship.

The late Senator Lee Metcalf (D.-Mont.), one of the most outspoken congressional skeptics of the UNCLOS process, remarked in 1975 that the seabed provisions of the first UNCLOS draft treaty text had been an "unmitigated disaster'' for U.S. interests and were ''a measure of sorts of the effectiveness of our negotiators in getting our point of view prominently displayed before the Conference.''[84] Mr. Metcalf's view in 1975 would be about as apt in describing the seabed articles of the Composite Text of 1977–78. Indeed, the defects of these articles make it extremely difficult to rationalize the continued participation of the United States in these negotiations—quite aside from its original decision to join UNCLOS and to promote it rather than the enclosure movement. Again, the analogy of the slot machine, an analogy suggested by the U.S. delegation itself in its report on the results of the sixth UNCLOS session in 1977, is appropriate: the odds at UNCLOS have essentially been rigged by the younger countries which dominate its agenda and voting. The more often players like the United States attend the conference, put their coins in the machines, and pull the handles, the more they will lose.

In addition, there is an overwhelming case not only for the United States Senate to refuse to ratify such a treaty but for the U.S. delegation even to refuse to sign such a document once it has been voted. Such a signature would, H. Gary Knight argues, impose upon the U.S. a ''good faith obligation'' (according to certain provisions of international law) to refrain from taking other actions that could frustrate the object of the treaty until the Senate has either ratified or rejected it.[85] The ratification process could, of course, take years, and in the meantime the U.S. could feel constrained to postpone unilateral actions that would otherwise be desirable. Not only could U.S. ocean mining be brought to a halt but the U.S. might be obliged to delay until after ratification hydrocarbon exploitation that did not share revenues with the Authority and marine research that had not been given approval by landlocked and geographically disadvantaged countries that were neighbors of the concerned coastal states.

As the cost to the United States of achieving its objectives at UNCLOS has increased, the attractions of the rival law-making process—the enclosure movement—have also increased. The brief history of U.S. ocean policy between 1969 and 1978 suggests that the policy-making process is not entirely monolithic. When U.S. economic interests were being given too little attention within the Executive branch during the period 1972–75, competition from agencies that had formerly had little to say on the subject (such as the U.S. Treasury) forced the dominant agencies (Defense and State) to change their positions somewhat. Congress has also intervened occasionally, usually by attempting to pressure the Executive branch into taking more account of U.S. economic interests but on one occasion by enacting a unilateral enclosure. Such actions, as I have argued, have relatively great potential for reducing economic inefficiencies in ocean uses. The U.S. 200-mile fisheries zone will promote efficient resource use if the same authority to restrict entry of foreign fishermen is used to limit domestic fishing effort as well. For pollution, there is less certainty of beneficial consequences of extended U.S. authority over oil tankers since there is so little information on the extent of oil pollution and the effectiveness of the seas in pollution transport. To the extent that the United States is affected along its heavily populated and long coastlines, it, like other coastal states, will face a structure of costs and rewards that will lead it to internalize many of these effects. For ocean mining, U.S. legislation (even with its imperfections) would probably cause fewer important distortions in resource allocation than the least inefficient treaty articles that UNCLOS has considered.[86] Moreover, to the extent that U.S. legislation would impel UNCLOS to abandon or at least to water down its attempt to control much of the seabeds, ocean mining would proceed and most countries would begin to reap benefits from increased supplies of metals.

Notes

1. U.S. Department of State, Bureau of Intelligence and Research, Office of the Geographer, *Theoretical Areal Allocations of Seabed to Coastal States*, International Boundary Study Series A., No. 46 (Washington, D.C., August 1972), p. 5.

2. Ibid., p. 32—not counting the area that would be enclosed if 200-mile zones were drawn around the Pacific Trust territories and the resources therein also were controlled by the United States.

3. T. W. Fulton, *The Sovereignty of the Sea*, p. 650.

4. Ibid., pp. 572–74. Jefferson's act in 1793 was a provisional wartime expedient, but the three-mile limit was enacted by Congress the following year, making the United States also the first country to incorporate the three-mile limit into domestic legislation. Thereafter, Great Britain championed the three-mile limit throughout her empire in legislation and in practice. See Sayre A. Swarztrauber, *The Three-Mile Limit of Territorial Seas* (Annapolis, Md.: Naval Institute Press, 1972), pp. 56–60, 64–71.

5. The chief precursors of the United States were the Scandinavian countries in the seventeenth and eighteenth centuries. See Fulton, pp. 537–75; H. S. K. Kent, "The Historical Origins of the Three-Mile Limit," *American Journal of International Law* 48 (1954):537–53.

6. Statements of Arthur H. Dean, U.S. representative to the First and Second UNCLOS, in *Conventions on the Law of the Sea*, pp. 5, 10, 13, 21, 85.

7. Ibid., pp. 4–6, 9–10.

8. Ann L. Hollick, "United States Oceans Politics," *San Diego Law Review* 10 (1973):470. The result is markedly different in Canada where decision making in ocean matters is centralized. See Hollick (1975).

9. See two articles by Roland N. McKean: "Divergences Between Individual and Total Costs Within Government," *American Economic Review Papers and Proceedings* 54 (1964):243–49; and "The Unseen Hand in Government," ibid. 55 (1965):496–506.

10. William A. Niskanen, Jr., *Bureaucracy and Representative Government* (Chicago: Aldine-Atherton, 1971), p. 39.

11. Ibid., p. 72.

12. For example, the model for forecasting voting at UNCLOS, developed by the Center for Naval Analyses and described at the end of the preceding chapter, had been sponsored for several years by the Department of Defense at a total cost of more than $400,000. When the Treasury Department took an interest in the law of the sea in 1973, it attempted to obtain access to the model and its results, but Defense allegedly refused to allow Treasury to purchase the data through contract. This unsavory episode, although perhaps an exception, suggests that the national interest was ignored at least once in the interagency competition. The event was publicized in 1975 by Congressman John M. Murphy (D-N.Y.), a skeptic of U.S. policy on the law of the sea and chairman of the Subcommittee on Oceanography of the House Committee on Merchant Marine and Fisheries. See *Deep Seabed Mining*, p. 85. The Defense Department, it should be added, says that it has no official record of Treasury having asked to purchase the information.

13. Barry Newman, "The Law of the Sea," *Wall Street Journal*, Aug. 27, 1974.

14. Hollick (1975), p. 542.

15. Ibid., pp. 536, 542.

16. Rear Adm. Max Morris, USN, "Why Unilateral U.S. Fisheries Legislation Harms Security Interests in the Oceans," *Emergency Marine Fisheries Protection Act of 1975*, Hearings before the U.S. Senate Committee on Armed Services, 94th Cong., 1st Sess., on S. 961, November 19, 1975, pp. 36–37.

17. An earlier and more complete statement by General George S. Brown, chairman of the Joint Chiefs of Staff, adds little to Admiral Morris' remarks. See *Extending Jurisdiction of the United States over Certain Ocean Areas*, Hearings before the U.S. Senate Committee on Armed Services on S. 1988, 93d Cong., 2d Sess., October 8–11, 1974, pp. 35–39 (hereafter cited as *Extending Jurisdiction*).

18. Ibid., p. 91.

19. Ibid., p. 89.

20. Prior to 1947, sixteen other countries claimed territorial seas of between four and nine nautical miles, five of which claims dated back to the nineteenth century. (Spain's six-mile claim dates back to 1760.) Of the dozen or so fishing claims before 1947 that extended beyond three miles, about half went to twelve miles and about half went to six miles. See U.S. Department of State, Bureau of Intelligence and Research, Office of the Geographer, *Limits in the Seas, No. 36: National Claims to Maritime Jurisdictions*.

21. See the exchange between General Brown and Senator Sam Nunn (D.-Ga.) in *Extending Jurisdiction*, pp. 56–59. The countries (and dates of claims) are: Argentina (1967), Brazil (1970), Chile (1953), Ecuador (1966), El Salvador (1950), Panama (1967), Peru (1947), Sierra Leone (1971), and Uruguay (1969). See *Limits in the Seas, No. 36*.

In a recent action that may be consistent with creeping jurisdiction, the government of North Korea announced the creation of a "military sea boundary" which extends approximately 50 miles beyond its territorial waters, and thus part of the way into its 200-mile EEZ. "South Korea Ship Safely Uses New North Korean Sea Zone," *Los Angeles Times*, Aug. 3, 1977.

22. See Hollick (1973) and (1975), and H. Gary Knight, "Special Domestic Interests and United States Oceans Policy," in Robert G. Wirsing, ed., *International Relations and the Future of Ocean Space*, pp. 10−43.

23. Remark of Ambassador Stevenson quoted in John Virtue, "Sea-Law Conference Closes in Deadlock," *Washington Post*, Aug. 30, 1974.

24. Ann L. Hollick, "The Clash of U.S. Interests: How U.S. Policy Evolved," *Marine Technology Society Journal*, July 1974, p. 25.

25. Ibid.

26. *Deep Seabed Mining*, p. 495.

27. *Extending Jurisdiction*, p. 54. Moore made approximately the same statement in "The Functional Approach and the Law of the Sea," in *Perspectives on Ocean Policy*, pp. 426−27.

28. Coase, "United States Policy Regarding the Law of the Seas," in *Mineral Resources of the Deep Seabed*, pt. 2, pp. 1163−64.

29. "The Likelihood of a Treaty Emerging from the Third United Nations Conference on the Law of the Sea," reprinted in *Deep Seabed Mining*, p. 499. The same argument has been made by H. Gary Knight, once an adviser at the U.S. delegation: "In its quest for free transit through international straits and high-seas navigational rights within 200-mile economic resource zones, [the Defense Department] is apparently willing to trade off any other interest of the American government or industry." Letter to the Editor, *New York Times*, Apr. 29, 1976.

30. *Status Report on Law of the Sea Conference*, pt. 2, pp. 970−71. Both Stevenson and Moore reiterated this position when Senator Metcalf raised the same question during the 1974 hearings one year later. Ibid., pt. 3, p. 1202.

31. Reply by Ambassador Stevenson to a question by Senator Metcalf in *Status Report on Law of the Sea Conference*, pt. 1, pp. 150−51.

32. Osgood, et al., *Toward a National Ocean Policy*, p. 153.

33. Hollick (1973), p. 490.

34. Ibid., p. 491n. cf. Chap. 2, n. 47.

35. *Status Report on Law of the Sea Conference*, pt. 1, p. 232.

36. Ibid., pt. 4, p. 1458.

37. See ibid., p. 1436. Kissinger's earlier opposition to production controls was reiterated by Under Secretary of State Carlyle E. Maw later in 1975 (ibid., pp. 1428, 1448−49). Ambassador Stevenson first stated U.S. opposition to such controls in 1974 (letter to the editor, *Wall Street Journal*, Jan. 7, 1974). Stevenson's successor, T. Vincent Learson, argued in 1976 that Kissinger's new proposal on temporary production controls was still consistent with his earlier position (*Status Report on Law of the Sea Conference*, pt. 5, pp. 1640−41).

38. See Richard M. Nixon, "Statement on United States Oceans Policy," *Weekly Compilation of Presidential Documents*, vol. 6, p. 677 (May 23, 1970), and Hollick (1976), p. 129.

39. See *Status Report on Law of the Sea Conference*, pt. 1, p. 88; also *Mineral Resources of the Deep Seabed*, pt. 1, p. 247.

40. *Status Report on Law of the Sea Conference*, pt. 2, p. 866.

41. *Extending Jurisdiction*, p. 40.

42. *Status Report on Law of the Sea Conference*, pt. 3, p. 1177.

43. Ibid., pt. 5, p. 1617.

44. Frank Del Olmo, "Richardson Warns on Law of Sea Talks," *Los Angeles Times*, Oct. 18, 1977.

45. Statement of Ambassador Richardson before the U.S. House of Representatives, Subcommittee on International Organizations, Committee on International Relations, May 22, 1978.

46. See *Status Report on Law of the Sea Conference*, pt. 1, p. 25; *Mineral Resources of the Deep Seabed*, pt. 1, p. 226.

47. *Mineral Resources of the Deep Seabed*, pt. 2, p. 930; ibid., pp. 935, 966; *Status Report on Law of the Sea Conference*, pt. 4, p. 1443; letter from Under Secretary of State Maw to Senator Metcalf, dated March 18, 1976, reprinted in ibid., pt. 5, p. 1954.

48. Statements of Ambassador Richardson in *Status Report on Law of the Sea Conference*, pt. 6, p. 1967; testimony before the U.S. House of Representatives, Committee on Ways and Means, April 13, 1978.

49. Hollick (1973), p. 478.

50. *Extending Jurisdiction*, p. 39.

51. Quoted by David Brand, "The Question of Who Owns Oceans Becomes Vital as Exploitation Grows," *Wall Street Journal*, Sept. 13, 1977.

52. Coase, "United States Policy Regarding the Law of the Seas," p. 1166.

53. See Chapter 2, p. 42, and Henry A. Kissinger, "International Law, World Order and Human Progress," in *Status Report on Law of the Sea Conference*, pt. 4, p. 1435.

54. This is emphasized in R. O. Keohane and J. S. Nye, *Power and Interdependence* (Boston: Little, Brown and Co., 1977), passim, but esp. chaps. 1–2; and by Brown et al., chaps. 1–8.

55. Testimony of Ambassador Learson and Bernard Oxman, in *National Ocean Policy*, pp. 184 and 192.

56. The second of the two assumptions is based on the treaty banking system whereby each firm that applies to the Authority for exploitation rights receives rights to only one tract out of every two that it has explored.

57. This calculation is based on the *lower* bound of the range of rents that Robert R. Nathan Associates calculated for 1985, the sacrificed rents being $.77 billion from coastal hydrocarbons and $0.03 billion from deep-sea nodules.

58. Robert E. Osgood, "U.S. Security Interests in Ocean Law," *Ocean Development and International Law* 2 (1974):1–36. The cost to an enemy of locating American

SSBNs would decline somewhat if the subs were required to transit straits on the surface; submerged, they are almost invulnerable.

59. Ibid., p. 17. H. Gary Knight reached essentially the same conclusions two years earlier in "The 1971 United States Proposals on the Breadth of the Territorial Sea and Passage through International Straits," *Oregon Law Review* 51 (1972): 780–81.

60. Hollick (1974), pp. 22–23.

61. Ibid., pp. 23–24. See letter to Secretary of State Henry A. Kissinger from Henry M. Jackson, Alan Bible, James Abourezk, Floyd K. Haskell, Paul Fannin, Clifford P. Hansen, James L. Buckley, James A. McClure, and Dewey F. Bartlett, June 7, 1974, reprinted in *Status Report on Law of the Sea Conference*, pt. 2, pp. 824–25.

62. United States of America, *Draft Articles on Economic Zone and Continental Shelf*, UN Doc.A/CONF.62/C.2/L.47 (August 8, 1974).

63. Kenneth Clarkson, "International Law, U.S. Seabeds Policy, and Ocean Resource Development," pp. 138–41.

64. Rev. Text, pt. IV, art. 18; Comp. Text, arts. 296(3) and (4), and 297; Amendments of May 1978, Results of the Work of the Negotiating Group on Item (5) of Doc. A/CONF.62/62, Annex A, NG5/10; U.S. Department of State, Delegation to UNCLOS, *Unclassified Report* on First New York Session, March 15–May 7, 1976, p. 18, reprinted in *Status Report on Law of the Sea Conference*, pt. 5, p. 1635; *Unclassified Report* on Second New York Session, August 2–September 17, 1976, p. 17; *Unclassified Report* on Sixth Session, May 23–July 15, 1977, pp. 19–21, reprinted in *Status Report*, pt. 6, pp. 1981–82; *Unclassified Report* on Seventh Session, March 28–May 19, 1978, pp. 27–31.

65. See *U.S. Draft Articles on Economic Zone and Continental Shelf*, arts. 13 and 15.

66. See ibid., art. 18.

67. Composite Text, Amendments of May 1978, art. 144; U.S. Delegation to UNCLOS, *Unclassified Report* on Seventh Session, pp. 11–12.

68. Comp. Text, Amendments of May 1978, art. 153; U.S. Delegation to UNCLOS, *Unclassified Report* on Seventh Session, p. 15.

69. U.S. Delegation to UNCLOS, *Unclassified Report* on Seventh Session, p. 14; testimony of Ambassador Richardson before the U.S. House of Representatives, Committee on International Relations, Subcommittee on International Organizations, May 22, 1978.

70. *Emergency Marine Fisheries Protection Act of 1975*, Serial No. 94-27 pt. 2, p. 100.

71. Statement of Secretary Kissinger, in *Legislative History of the Fishery Conservation and Management Act of 1976* (Washington, D.C., October 1976), p. 585.

72. John Norton Moore, "U.S. Policy on the Oceans: A Choice," *New York Times*, Sept. 17, 1974; "In Sea Law Talks, U.S. Misses the Boat," *Los Angeles Times*, Aug. 12, 1976; "Premature Action Would Ruin a High-Stakes Game," ibid., Nov. 2, 1975.

73. *Extending Jurisdiction*, p. 37.

74. Sam Jameson, "Japan and Soviet Union Initial Temporary Fishing Agreement," *Los Angeles Times*, May 25, 1977.

75. Statement of Richard A. Frank, representing the Environmental Defense Fund, Friends of the Earth, the National Audubon Society, the Natural Resources Defense Council, and the Sierra Club, in *Geneva Session of the Third United Nations Law of the Sea Conference*, Hearings before the National Ocean Policy Study of the U.S. Senate Committee on Commerce, 94th Cong., 1st Sess., Serial No. 94–30, June 3–4, 1975, p. 66.

76. Ibid., p. 58. This view contrasts sharply with their position in 1973 and 1974 that only a treaty could protect U.S. environmental interests. See the statements of Mr. Frank as a representative of the same five environmental groups in *Mineral Resources of the Deep Seabed*, pt. 1, pp. 319–30, and pt. 2, pp. 1070–79.

77. One such bill carefully avoided the imposition of overreaching burdens on navigation users by exempting from the provisions of the law any vessels passing through the U.S. maritime safety zone but not bound for a U.S. port, vessels passing through international straits that the U.S. may control, and vessels using the Panama Canal. See S.682, "Tanker Safety Act of 1977," an amendment to the Ports and Waterways Safety Act of 1972 by Senator Warren G. Magnuson, in *Congressional Record—Senate*, February 10, 1977, pp. S.2463–68; "Amendments to Ports and Waterways Safety Act of 1972," statements by members David F. Emery, Robert L. Leggett, and Norman F. Lent, in *Congressional Record—House*, February 2, 1977, pp. H.809–11.

78. See *Deep Seabed Hard Minerals Act*, Report of the U.S. Senate Committee on Interior and Insular Affairs to accompany S.713, 94th Cong., 2d Sess., Report No. 94-754 (April 14, 1976), and Report of House Committee on Merchant Marine and Fisheries to accompany H.R. 3350, 95th Cong., 1st Sess., Report No. 95-588, pt. 1 (August 9, 1977); *Deep Seabed Mining*, Hearings before the Subcommittee on Oceanography and the Committee on Merchant Marine and Fisheries, House of Representatives, 95th Cong., 1st Sess., on H.R. 3350 and H.R. 4582, Serial No. 95-4 (March, April, and May 1977), pp. 1–23.

79. Northcutt Ely, "Deep Seabed Minerals: Congress Steams to the Rescue," address to the American Oceanic Organization, Washington, D.C., March 23, 1976, reprinted in *Congressional Record—Senate*, vol. 122, no. 57 (April 14, 1976), pp. S.5799–80.

80. Statements of Ambassador Stevenson, in *Status Report on Law of the Sea Conference*, pt. 2, p. 161; pt. 3, p. 1211; statement of Mr. Moore, in *Mineral Resources of the Deep Seabed*, pt. 2, p. 963; James D. Mielke, *Ocean Manganese Nodules*, pp. 70, 72–74, 81.

81. Statement of Ambassador Richardson, in *Deep Seabed Mining*, Serial No. 95–4, p. 447.

82. Statement of Ambassador Richardson before the U.S. House of Representatives, Committee on Merchant Marine and Fisheries, June 1, 1978.

83. Mielke, p. 103.

84. *Status Report on Law of the Sea Conference*, pt. 3, p. 1162.

85. H. Gary Knight, letter to Ambassador Learson, May 12, 1976, reprinted in ibid., pt. 5, p. 1910.

86. U.S. legislation contains many of the defects of the 1970 Draft Convention's proposal for an international licensing authority, including work requirements, fractional relinquishment of blocks, and so forth. See Chapter 8, pp. 246–49.

CHAPTER 11

Conclusions

*[W]e are seeing the breakup of a universally
recognized law of the sea. This process will
go slowly and be diluted in time if a treaty
is signed: it will go very rapidly if a treaty
is not signed. In either case, states will rely
more and more on bilateral and multilateral
negotiations among members of compatible
groups in order to establish and sustain
their rights in the seas. This is inevitable,
unless present trends are reversed.*

> —Arvid Pardo
> *Perspectives on Ocean Policy* (1975)

The traditional law of the sea, which lasted for more than three centuries, is
breaking up because it was based on two principles that became contradictory by
the mid-twentieth century owing to economic and technological change. These
two principles were (1) that the oceans should be used to generate new wealth and
(2) that open access for this purpose should apply to all areas except for a narrow
three-mile band adjacent to coastlines. These principles were suitable to the old
era in which demands for most ocean uses were small relative to the supply of
ocean space. But rising world populations, increasing demands for ocean services
of varying types, and new technologies for exploiting these resources produced
scarcities in the valuable coastal areas where most activities occur. Unlimited
competition among users and sometimes among wholly incompatible uses in
these areas has tended to reduce the new wealth that the oceans are capable of
producing. The results have been congestion, the depletion of certain living
resources, and occasionally levels of pollution which appear to be uneconomically high. A more exclusive structure of ocean property arrangements would suit
the changed economic and technological conditions by eliminating the emerging
contradiction between open access and the creation of wealth.

The Enclosure Movement of the Oceans has provided an opportunity for resolving this contradiction by giving coastal countries the right to ration access to those areas having the greatest potential for producing new wealth. New technologies which have lowered the costs of monitoring and enforcement have made it economic for coastal nations to expand their areas of jurisdiction. Extensions of the territorial sea from three to twelve miles have increased the sovereignty of coastal states over directly adjacent resources, including navigation and other activities that are prone to pollution. Even more important has been the trend in recent years of many coastal states to extend their authority over resource exploitation (but usually not navigation) out to 200 miles, generally to enclose valuable fisheries and offshore minerals.

In one sense, the conversion to enclosure from the traditional freedom of the seas has been typical of the historical development of the law of the sea. As McDougal and Burke have described it, this body of customary international law changes when individual countries unilaterally assert claims to create property rights in certain ocean resources and the international community accepts (or rejects) these claims according to their reasonableness and other criteria.[1] What has been atypical of the enclosure movement in the development of customary international law is, as Lauterpacht noted in 1950 mainly in reference to continental shelf claims, that "seldom has an apparent major change in international law been accomplished by peaceful means more rapidly and amidst more general acquiescence and approval."[2]

The enclosure movement will produce different blends of distributional and efficiency gains for individual countries depending upon their geographical position, their demands for ocean goods and services, and their ability to supply these goods and services. Indeed, it is likely that the claims by coastal nations to expanded ocean resource jurisdiction have been motivated mainly by a concern for their own self-interests in capturing a larger *distributional* share of the economic pie that the oceans are capable of producing, and it is inevitable that coastal states that are adjacent to the most valuable living and nonliving resources will gain the most by this process. But competition among coastal states for these distributional gains, which has taken the form of enclosure, has led to the emergence of economically superior ocean institutions which will yield *efficiency* gains for coastal states and noncoastal states alike. The new structure of property rights resulting from the enclosure movement has created the opportunity for increasing the contribution of the oceans to the size of the world's economic pie by reducing the future inefficiencies that would have occurred if the principle of strictly open access had not been modified.

It is true that the widespread efficiency gains for the common good of all mankind that the enclosure movement is likely to usher in have been brought on by the actions of individual countries based on calculations of their own distributional self-interests. This may seem paradoxical to some—that the source of generalized benefits lies more in individual actions than in community actions—but it is a result that is typical of economic processes generally. Whether or not the enclosing coastal states as they each calculated their self-interests took these potential widespread efficiency gains into account is, as Demsetz indicated in a slightly different context, largely beside the point when it comes to evaluating the final improvements in institutions. What is more, these widespread benefits, which will be captured in varying degrees by many countries, appear to constitute a strong explanation for why the enclosure movement met with "acquiescence and approval" so quickly and peacefully. This result is, of course, quite the opposite of the "international instability" that was widely but erroneously expected to follow from a continuation of the enclosure movement, which was said to bear a resemblance to either a zero-sum game or a nineteenth-century "colonial scramble." This was an entirely superficial and groundless analogy. By promoting international stability through efficiency gains the enclosure movement has generated new institutions which are superior in political as well as economic terms.

Whether or not the enclosure movement continues will depend upon several economic factors which affect the net gains that coastal states can capture either by making broader claims or by enforcing existing claims more effectively. Net gains will continue to rise if there is a continuation of past trends of rising ocean resource values and improved technologies which lower enforcement costs. There is some probability that coastal states will find it in their economic interests to impose significant controls over navigation in areas beyond the territorial sea that are presently enclosed, but these actions are likely to be confined to a few special circumstances. Another important factor that will affect the future of the enclosure movement is the extent to which coastal nations continue to be motivated by opportunities to increase their wealth. My study and interpretation of the post-1945 history of the enclosure movement suggest that considerations of wealth have usually dominated these decisions—the extent of claims as well as their nature and timing—and therefore that the enclosure movement has brought forth new customary international law based more on careful economic calculations than on whimsical political ambitions. These three overriding factors— rising resource values, technological change, and at least a modicum of national regard for economic self-interest—suggest that the enclosure movement is probably here to stay, although the rates of change in ocean property arrangements in the future may not be as great as those of the past three decades.

The future of the enclosure movement also will depend upon what happens at UNCLOS, the alternative process for making new ocean law. UNCLOS was convened to resolve seven major controversies having the common element of dividing ocean resource jurisdiction between coastal states and the rest of the world usually represented in some way by an international institution.[3] But even as measured by its own criteria for success, it has so far in several instances met with failure.

First, UNCLOS was supposed to establish the typical seaward boundary between the area of exclusive coastal state jurisdiction and international jurisdiction. This it has more or less accomplished, but not by holding coastal state jurisdiction to the limits that were in effect in 1970 when UNCLOS began, (and certainly not by pushing back these boundaries to the limits that existed before the enclosure movement began). UNCLOS so far has adopted as the typical boundary the most extensive particular boundaries that any group of states has employed, and in a few circumstances has pushed the seaward boundary of internal waters (and therefore all jurisdictions that lie beyond these waters) even farther seaward than had previously codified international law.

Second, UNCLOS was supposed to find an accommodation between the rights of maritime states to utilize international straits for commercial and military purposes and the rights of straits states to protect these confined areas from dangerous pollution levels. This, in my view, UNCLOS has done although its decision continues to produce some controversy among the parties most keenly involved.

Third, UNCLOS was supposed to determine the extent to which the revenues collected by coastal states from offshore hydrocarbon exploitation would be shared with younger countries for the purpose of economic development. Although all the nations concerned, givers and receivers alike, have accepted the principle of sharing revenues for this purpose and have discussed the extent of sharing almost endlessly, the crux of the problem, the distribution itself, is still not settled.

Fourth, UNCLOS was supposed to resolve the general nature of coastal state duties to other countries within the exclusive economic zone, and in particular the division of fishing rights between the coastal states and other countries that have traditionally fished the area and also any adjacent landlocked countries that sought preferential fishing rights in the EEZs of their coastal state neighbors. This controversy appears to have diminished somewhat, but had not been resolved by mid-1978.

Fifth, UNCLOS was supposed to resolve pollution problems of several kinds. Land-based sources were of course entirely beyond its competence, but an agreement of sorts appears to have been reached on pollution from oil tankers. However, preliminary investigation suggests that this provision of the treaty would produce economic waste both by giving coastal states only limited rights to regulate serious pollution threats and by imposing drastic standards on the design and construction of tankers that are likely to cost more than the resulting reduction in pollution would be worth.

Sixth, UNCLOS was supposed to liberalize the rules that coastal states imposed against the activities of marine scientists in their EEZs. Almost nothing in the way of liberalized rules has been accomplished.

Seventh and probably most important to a majority of the participants, UNCLOS was supposed to write a charter for a new international authority to control mineral resource exploitation in the deep seabeds beyond the limits of national jurisdiction. From the very start this issue has been the most divisive of all and it twice nearly scuttled the conference. It had not been resolved by mid-1978 in spite of multiple concessions which the advanced technology countries that seek to mine have made to a coalition of ideologically motivated younger countries and self-interested land-mining countries which have united to try to control seabed mining.

What can UNCLOS do now? There are several possibilities.

First, it could adopt a treaty along the lines of what has already been more or less agreed. This would include the core of the texts from Committee II and Committee III along with, perhaps, some additional compromises in favor of the landlocked and geographically disadvantaged states. This approach, of course, would not yield a comprehensive treaty unless it accommodated to some extent the self-interests of the countries that want to halt seabed mining. One possible accommodation would be to establish a moratorium on seabed activities. Ostensibly this would provide more time for negotiations, but it is difficult to imagine how this by itself would break the deadlock.

Second, the ocean mining countries could concede more ground. This would be consistent with the trend of their concessions thus far. Alternatively, these countries might agree to create a "paper" regime without any funding as a means for getting the treaty adopted and ratified with somewhat less domestic opposition. Later on, the decision to fund the Authority, and the domestic quarrel that will accompany it, could be made within the context of the annual debates over the U.S. foreign assistance program.

Third, the U.S. and other ocean mining countries could adopt legislation, or perhaps a multilateral agreement, to proceed with seabed mining even in the absence of a treaty. This action might have wrecked UNCLOS in 1974–75, but its impact is less certain in 1979, and it might well serve to bring the conference around to a more balanced set of seabed treaty articles. Uncertainty over the final content of the treaty now appears to be the main roadblock to the commencement of ocean mining, and there would be very little that UNCLOS could do to stop mining if the mining countries were technically ready and had the political will to proceed with their plans. On the other hand, if ocean mining began in advance of a treaty and the conference disbanded as a result, the loss to the world would be small since the principal economic elements of the enclosure movement would still be intact.

Fourth, UNCLOS could attempt to sidestep some of its deepest disagreements by adopting a treaty containing highly contradictory language in its most important provisions. This could be the worst outcome of all. Ambiguous law produces ambiguous rules and possibly the support of international law to each side of a dispute. Such a treaty could foment disagreements and possibly even conflicts.[4]

One cannot know which of these possibilities will prove closest to what happens: the most likely outcome is perhaps not even on the list. What can be said with confidence is that the long-run structure of ocean property arrangements will resemble the property rights put in place by the enclosure movement more than anything else.

The ponderous movement of UNCLOS for six years through its Spring 1978 session has three explanations. The first of these is the transactional structure of the conference—the number and diversity of issues and participants, voting rules, and agenda. Success is impeded because bargaining is enormously expensive.

The second problem is a lack of urgency over oceans issues. There is little demand in the major capitals of the world for a comprehensive ocean agreement: there has been no recent event that compels an UNCLOS treaty and there is no foreseeable event that is likely to compel one. With the possible exception of vessel source pollution, there is no contemporary ocean problem that UNCLOS could settle that heads of state could not settle more reasonably or more quickly acting alone or in relatively small groups.[5] Many ocean problems will be resolved by way of the enclosure movement, especially after coastal states adopt effective municipal legislation to enforce enclosures and bring congestion down to economic proportions. Of course, some nations may act incompletely, inappropriately, or not at all, but as Coase has argued, there is no reason to believe that UNCLOS would yield an outcome that was generally superior according to economic criteria.[6] Indeed, there are several reasons for expecting the opposite. The enclosure movement, in general, has produced outcomes that are a triumph of rationality compared with the inefficiency, friction, and delay that are characteristic of UNCLOS. The one problem for which the UNCLOS process is probably superior to enclosure—vessel source pollution—is being attacked by UNCLOS in a manner that appears to be uneconomic and may be no better than what enclosure would have accomplished.

The third problem lies in the famous motto of UNCLOS—to organize ocean activities as "the common heritage of mankind." The concept of the common heritage has I think had much to do with shackling UNCLOS to inappropriate ocean outcomes in that the concept, or the usual interpretation of it, has been inconsistent with the new era of ocean economics and technology. For example, in coastal areas, where the creation of new wealth is associated with making property rights more exclusive and having fewer decision makers, the common heritage concept focuses on the communal elements of decision making—

property rights that are less exclusive and have more decision makers. Just the reverse has occurred in the deep-sea areas. Where efficient outcomes require avoiding regulations for the time being, the common heritage concept has been interpreted almost universally as requiring a vast and inefficient regulatory authority. It is easy, of course, to overemphasize the importance of a phrase, since meaningful watchwords do not guarantee success, but it is probably equally true that clearly inappropriate slogans do not enhance the prospects for success.

In addition, the division of the common heritage among the many participants at UNCLOS was almost certain to be thwarted to some degree by strenuous competition among groups of nations. I am not criticizing the trait of distributional self-interest which has motivated UNCLOS as well as the enclosure movement, but rather the way in which UNCLOS has channeled this sort of competition. With enclosure, individual coastal states having generally similar interests have competed for ocean resources in similar ways by creating property rights that are potentially exclusive, enforceable, and exchangeable. There has been no ganging up of one group of coastal states against another neighboring group in an attempt to take away their resource rights without compensation. At UNCLOS, which is more a political than an economic process, competition has been organized on the basis of voting and coalition-formation rather than on market-type exchanges. Nations that are young and numerous could use their tight majority control of the agenda to impose on the minority a treaty that is overwhelmingly favorable to their interests, and their numerical strength has already been evident in the process of drafting treaty articles. Competition in this form, which is probably intrinsic to dividing resources in a quasi-parliamentary setting, has contributed to the uneconomic nature of UNCLOS outcomes. The virtually incessant ideological bickering that has been associated with UNCLOS gives us a good idea how acrimonious any future seabed authority's decision making would be. If the most likely legacies of the enclosure movement would be a more carefully delineated structure of coastal property rights and market-type bargains among individual (usually coastal) states, then the most likely legacies of UNCLOS would be power plays and bitterness.

Hypocrisy is another legacy of the common heritage. Attempts by the majority faction of UNCLOS to write a treaty that would redistribute resources from the minority faction without the full compensation that is typical of market-type transactions have led each faction to employ the concept of the common heritage for its own pious self-justification. To the younger countries, common heritage has become the magic phrase whereby seabed resources can be said to belong to, and therefore are to be exploited by, any but the most developed countries, and especially not by the United States. To the developed countries, common heritage has usually been interpreted to mean that they too should have access to deep-sea resources, some of the proceeds of which would then be shared with the developing countries of the world through an international authority. As Coase argued, "there is a degree of hypocrisy in the present [United States] policy which reserves the least valuable part of the ocean floor 'for the benefit of mankind' and then puts it in the charge of the kind of organization least likely to use it productively."[7] The United States, for example, unwisely agreed in principle to the creation of a seabed regime, but then dug in its heels in the debate to determine either the precise extent of the common heritage or how extensively it can be controlled by a majority of nations. The debate over revenue sharing has been equally hypocritical. All countries have agreed, again in principle, to the concept of revenue sharing for continental shelf resources beyond some distance or depth, but the extent of revenue sharing has still to be determined after literally years of discussion. In this case, the haggling by the donor countries over the extent of the dollar transfer may be a self-serving tactic for trying belatedly to back out of the deal over the principle, acting as if they wish the deal had never been made. Hypocrisy also may have permeated even the most idealistic portions of UNCLOS literature, the UN resolutions that enshrined the concept of the common heritage and were justified in terms of universal morality and equity and the peaceful uses of the oceans. But if the ensuing treaty creates nonexclusive property rights and promotes uneconomic resource allocation, it may foment disharmony or even conflict—just the opposite of what was apparently intended when the whole UNCLOS process began.

In the future, the oceans will continue to contribute to mankind's actual heritage, but these widespread benefits will have been fashioned more by the enclosure movement than by UNCLOS. Part of this heritage will involve more carefully delimited rights and duties in the use of ocean resources and in the reduction of congestion where it reaches uneconomic proportions. Another of its elements will be the greater value of goods and services that will be produced from each of the major ocean resources. Yet another element will be a generally reduced level of conflict over the oceans as a result of more orderly processes for resolving disputes than have heretofore existed, which will, one hopes, be accompanied by a keener perception of the inherent weaknesses that lie in international decision-making mechanisms. This is a drastically different interpretation of the common heritage from that implied by the vernacular of most participants at UNCLOS, even the most developed countries among them, but it is an interpretation that mankind, over the long run, is likely to find the more accurate and the more useful.

Notes

1. McDougal and Burke, *The Public Order of the Oceans*, pp. viii–x, and 794.

2. H. Lauterpacht, "Sovereignty over Submarine Areas," p. 376.

3. The principal decisions facing UNCLOS were summarized in Chapter 1, pp. 16–17.

4. Coase, "United States Policy Regarding the Law of the Seas," p. 1167.

5. Clarkson, "International Law, U.S. Seabeds Policy, and Ocean Resource Development," pp. 123–24, gives several historical examples of the peaceful resolution of ocean conflicts by small groups of states.

6. "United States Policy Regarding the Law of the Seas," passim.

7. Ibid., p. 1174.

Appendix

TRUMAN PROCLAMATION ON THE CONTINENTAL SHELF
Proclamation 2667

*Policy of the United States with Respect to
the Natural Resources of the Subsoil and
Sea Bed of the Continental Shelf.* *

WHEREAS the Government of the United States of America, aware of the long range world-wide need for new sources of petroleum and other minerals, holds the view that efforts to discover and make available new supplies of these resources should be encouraged; and

WHEREAS its competent experts are of the opinion that such resources underlie many parts of the continental shelf off the coasts of the United States of America, and that with modern technological progress their utilization is already practicable or will become so at an early date; and

WHEREAS recognized jurisdiction over these resources is required in the interest of their conservation and prudent utilization when and as development is undertaken; and

WHEREAS it is the view of the Government of the United States that the exercise of jurisdiction over the natural resources of the subsoil and sea bed of the continental shelf by the contiguous nation is reasonable and just, since the effectiveness of measures to utilize or conserve these resources would be contingent upon cooperation and protection from the shore, since the continental shelf may be regarded as an extension of the land-mass of the coastal nation and thus naturally appurtenant to it, since these resources frequently form a seaward extension of a pool or deposit lying within the territory, and since self-protection compels the coastal nation to keep close watch over activities off its shores, which are of the nature necessary for utilization of these resources;

NOW, THEREFORE, I, HARRY S. TRUMAN, President of the United States of America, do hereby proclaim the following policy of the United States of America with respect to the natural resources of the subsoil and sea bed of the continental shelf.

Having concern for the urgency of conserving and prudently utilizing its natural resources, the Government of the United States regards the natural resources of the subsoil and sea bed of the continental shelf beneath the high seas but contiguous to the coasts of the United States as appertaining to the United States, subject to its jurisdiction and control. In cases where the continental shelf extends to the shores of another State, or is shared with an adjacent State, the boundary shall be determined by the United States and the State concerned in accordance with equitable principles. The character as high seas of the waters above the continental shelf and the right to their free and unimpeded navigation are in no way thus affected.

IN WITNESS WHEREOF, I have hereunto set my hand and caused the seal of the United States of America to be affixed.

DONE at the City of Washington this 28th day of September, in the year of our Lord nineteen hundred and forty-five, and of the Independence of the United States of America, the one hundred and seventieth.

HARRY S. TRUMAN

By the President:

DEAN ACHESON,
   Acting Secretary of State

---

*U.S. Department of State, Bulletin, vol. 13, no. 327 (September 30, 1945), p. 485.

Selected Bibliography

BOOKS, MONOGRAPHS, PAMPHLETS, AND REPORTS

Alchian, Armen A. *Some Economics of Property*. Santa Monica: Rand Corporation Report P-2316, May 26, 1971.

Allen, David W. et al. *Effects on Commercial Fishing of Petroleum Development off the Northeastern United States*. Woods Hole, Mass.: Woods Hole Oceanographic Institution, 1976.

Alexander, Lewis M., ed. *The Law of the Sea: The Future of the Sea's Resources*. Kingston, R.I.: Proceedings of the Second Annual Conference of the Law of the Sea Institute, University of Rhode Island, 1968.

―――, ed. *The Law of the Sea: National Policy Recommendations*. Kingston, R.I.: Proceedings of the Fourth Annual Conference of the Law of the Sea Institute, University of Rhode Island, 1970.

―――, ed. *The Law of the Sea: Needs and Interests of Developing Nations*. Kingston, R.I.: Proceedings of the Seventh Annual Conference of the Law of the Sea Institute, University of Rhode Island, 1973.

Amacher, Ryan C., and Sweeney, Richard James, eds. *The Law of the Sea: U.S. Interests and Alternatives*. Washington, D.C.: American Enterprise Institute for Public Policy Research, 1976.

Arrow, Kenneth J. *Social Choice and Individual Values*. 2d ed. New York: John Wiley & Sons, Inc. 1963.

Borgese, Elisabeth M., ed. *Pacem in Maribus*. New York: Dodd, Mead & Co., Inc., 1972.

Bradley, Harriet. *The Enclosures in England: An Economic Reconstruction*. New York: AMS Press, 1968.

Breckner, Norman V. et al. *The Navy and the Common Sea*. Washington, D.C.: U.S. Office of Naval Research, 1972.

Brown, Seyom; Cornell, Nina W.; Fabian, Larry L.; and Weiss, Edith Brown. *Regimes for the Ocean, Outer Space, and Weather*. Washington, D.C.: Brookings Institution, 1977.

Buchanan, James M., and Tullock, Gordon. *The Calculus of Consent*. Ann Arbor: University of Michigan Press, 1962.

Burke, William T. *Marine Science Research and International Law.* Kingston, R.I.: Law of the Sea Institute, Occasional Paper no. 8, University of Rhode Island, 1970.

Campbell, Blake A. *Limited Entry in the Salmon Fishery: The British Columbia Experience.* University of British Columbia Fisheries Programs, Pacific Sea Grant Advisory Program, PASGAP 6, May 1972.

Christy, Francis T., Jr., and Scott, Anthony. *The Common Wealth in Ocean Fisheries.* Baltimore: Johns Hopkins University Press for Resources for the Future, Inc., 1965.

Cox, Robert W., and Jacobson, Harold K., et al. *The Anatomy of Influence.* New Haven and London: Yale University Press, 1973.

Crutchfield, James, and Pontecorvo, Giulio. *The Pacific Salmon Fisheries: A Study of Irrational Conservation.* Baltimore: Johns Hopkins University Press for Resources for the Future, Inc., 1969.

Curtler, W. H. R. *The Enclosure and Redistribution of Our Land.* Oxford: The Clarendon Press, 1920.

Deepsea Ventures, Inc. *Notice of Discovery and Claim of Exclusive Mining Rights, and Request for Diplomatic Protection and Protection of Investment.* Gloucester Point, Va., November 14, 1974.

English, T. S., ed. *Ocean Resources and Public Policy.* Seattle: University of Washington Press, 1973.

Flipse, J. E.; Dubs, M. A.; and Greenwald, R. J. *Pre-Production Manganese Nodule Mining Activities and Requirements, Background Information to Describe Typical Phases and Activities of a Commercial Ocean Mining Development Program Including Equipment, Cost, Time, and Resource Requirements.* Mimeo, 94 pp. Deepsea Ventures, Inc., and Kennecott Copper Corp., March 15, 1973.

Friedheim, Robert L. *Parliamentary Diplomacy—A Survey.* Arlington, Va.: Center for Naval Analyses of the University of Rochester, CNA76-0046, January 8, 1976.

―――. *Understanding the Debate on Ocean Resources.* Denver: University of Denver Monograph Series in World Affairs, vol. 6, no. 3-1968–1969, 1969.

Fulton, Thomas Wemyss. *The Sovereignty of the Sea: An Historical Account of the Claims of England to the Dominion of the British Seas, and of the Evolution of the Territorial Waters: with Special Reference to the Rights of Fishing and the Naval Salute.* Edinburgh and London: William Blackwood and Sons, 1911.

Gonner, E. C. K. *Common Land and Inclosure.* London: Macmillan, 1912.

Heezen, Bruce C., and Hollister, Charles D. *The Face of the Deep.* New York: Oxford University Press, 1971.

Heezen, Bruce C.; Tharp, Marie; and Ewing, Maurice. *The Floors of the Oceans: I. The North Atlantic.* New York: Geological Society of America, Special Paper no. 65, 1959.

Hirshleifer, Jack; De Haven, James C.; and Milliman, Jerome W. *Water Supply: Economics, Technology, and Policy.* Chicago: University of Chicago Press, 1960.

Hodgson, Robert D., and Alexander, Lewis M. *Towards an Objective Analysis of Special Circumstances.* Kingston, R.I.: Law of the Sea Institute, Occasional Paper no. 13, University of Rhode Island, 1972.

Horn, David R., ed. *Ferromanganese Deposits on the Ocean Floor*. Papers from a Conference at Arden House, Harriman, N.Y., and Lamont-Doherty Geological Observatory, Columbia University, January 20–22, 1972. Washington, D.C.: National Science Foundation, International Decade of Ocean Exploration, 1972.

Horn, D. R.; Horn, B. M.; and Delach, M. N. *Metal Content of Ferromanganese Deposits of the Oceans*. National Science Foundation, International Decade of Ocean Exploration, Technical Report no. 3, NSF-GX-33616. Washington, D.C., 1973.

————. *Ocean Manganese Nodules, Metal Values and Mining Sites*. National Science Foundation, International Decade of Ocean Exploration, Technical Report no. 4, NSF-GX-33616. Washington, D.C., 1973.

International Petroleum Encyclopedia. Tulsa, Okla., 1976.

Johnston, Douglas M. *The International Law of Fisheries: A Framework for Policy-Oriented Inquiries*. New Haven: Yale University Press, 1965.

Kadane, Joseph B. *Analysis of the Voting Rule Adopted for Law of the Sea*. Arlington, Va.: Center for Naval Analyses of the University of Rochester, Memorandum CNA 1223-74, July 29, 1974.

Keohane, Robert O., and Nye, Joseph S. *Power and Interdependence*. Boston: Little, Brown and Co., 1977.

Leipziger, Danny M., and Mudge, James L. *Seabed Mineral Resources and the Economic Interests of Developing Countries*. Cambridge, Mass.: Ballinger Publishing Co., 1976.

McDougal, Myres S., and Burke, William T. *The Public Order of the Oceans*. New Haven and London: Yale University Press, 1962.

Mero, John L. *The Mineral Resources of the Sea*. Amsterdam, London, and New York: Elsevier Publishing Co., 1965.

National Academy of Sciences. Ocean Affairs Board of the Commission on Natural Resources, National Research Council. *Assessing Potential Ocean Pollutants*. Washington, D.C.: National Academy of Sciences, 1975.

————. Ocean Affairs Board of the Commission on Natural Resources, National Research Council. *Petroleum in the Marine Environment*. Proceedings of a Workshop on Inputs, Fates, and the Effects of Petroleum in the Marine Environment, May 21–25, 1973, Airlie, Va. Washington, D.C., 1975.

————. Ocean Science Committee of the NAS-NRC Ocean Affairs Board. *Marine Environmental Quality*. Washington, D.C., 1971.

Niskanen, William A. *Bureaucracy and Representative Government*. Chicago: Aldine-Atherton, 1971.

Organization for Economic Co-operation and Development. *Problems in Transfrontier Pollution*. Paris, 1974.

Osgood, Robert E.; Hollick, Ann L.; Pearson, Charles S.; and Orr, James C. *Toward a National Ocean Policy: 1976 and Beyond*. Prepared for National Science Foundation Research Applications Directorate under Grant no. GI 39643 by Ocean Policy Project, Johns Hopkins University. Washington, D.C.: National Science Foundation, NSF-RA-X-75-006, 1975.

Osgood, Robert E. et al. *Perspectives on Ocean Policy: Proceedings of a Conference on Conflict and Order in Ocean Relations*, October 21–24, 1974, Airlie, Va. Prepared for National Science Foundation under Grant no. GI 39643 by Ocean Policy Project, Johns Hopkins University. Washington, D.C.: National Science Foundation, NSF-75-17, 1975.

Pearson, Charles S. *International Marine Environment Policy: The Economic Dimension*. Baltimore and London: Johns Hopkins University Press, 1975.

Petrou, Basil N., and Ranson, R. David. *Resources from the World's Deep Seabeds: The Law and Economics of an Unborn Industry*. Mimeo draft, 102 pp. Washington, D.C., 1975.

Scoville, Warren C., and La Force, J. Clayburn, eds. *The Economic Development of Western Europe*, 5 vols. Lexington, Mass.: D. C. Heath and Co., 1969. Vol. 1: *The Middle Ages and the Renaissance*; vol. 3: *The Eighteenth and Early Nineteenth Centuries*.

Smith, Wayne J. *An Assessment of Deep-Sea Manganese Nodule Exploitation Technology*. Mimeo draft, 36 pp. Virginia Beach, Va., October 1972.

Swarztrauber, Sayre A. *The Three-Mile Limit of Territorial Seas*. Annapolis, Md.: Naval Institute Press, 1972.

Walford, Lionel A. *Living Resources of the Sea*. New York: Ronald Press, 1958.

Walter, Ingo. *International Economics of Pollution*. New York: John Wiley & Sons, Inc., 1975.

————, ed. *Studies in International Environmental Economics*. New York: John Wiley & Sons, Inc., 1976.

Wirsing, Robert G., ed. *International Relations and the Future of Ocean Space*. Columbia, S.C.: University of South Carolina Press, Studies in International Affairs no. 10, 1974.

Wooster, Warren S., ed. *Freedom of Oceanic Research*. New York: Crane, Russak, 1973.

ARTICLES

Alchian, Armen A., and Demsetz, Harold. "The Property Rights Paradigm." *Journal of Economic History* 33 (1973):16–27.

Alchian, Armen A., and Kessel, Reuben A. "Competition, Monopoly, and the Pursuit of Money," in *Aspects of Labor Economics*, pp. 156–75. Universities Committee–National Bureau of Economic Research. Princeton: Princeton University Press, 1962.

Agnello, Richard J., and Donnelley, Lawrence P. "Prices and Property Rights in the Fisheries." *Southern Economic Journal* 42 (1975):253–62.

————. "Property Rights and Efficiency in the Oyster Industry." *Journal of Law and Economics* 18 (1975):521–33.

Alexander, Lewis M., and Hodgson, Robert D. "The Impact of the 200-Mile Economic Zone on the Law of the Sea." *San Diego Law Review* 12 (1975):569–99.

————. "The Role of The Geographically-Disadvantaged States in the Law of the Sea." *San Diego Law Review* 13 (1976):558–82.

Amacher, Ryan C., and Sweeney, Richard James. "International Commodity Cartels and the Threat of New Entry: Implications of Ocean Mineral Resources." *Kyklos* 29 (1976):292–309.

Anderson, Terry L., and Hill, P. J. "The Evolution of Property Rights: A Study of the American West." *Journal of Law and Economics* 18 (1975):163–79.

Bascom, Willard. "Technology and the Ocean." *Scientific American*, September 1969, pp. 198–217.

Bentz, Alan P. "Oil Spill Identification." *Analytical Chemistry* 48 (1976):454A–472A.

Bergsten, C. Fred. "The Threat from the Third World." *Foreign Policy* 11 (1973): 102–24.

Bonatti, Enrico. "The Origin of Metal Deposits in the Oceanic Lithosphere." *Scientific American*, February 1978, pp. 54–61.

Bullard, Sir Edward. "The Origin of the Oceans." *Scientific American*, September 1969, pp. 66–75.

Burke, William T. "Aspects of Internal Decision-Making Processes in Intergovernmental Fishery Commissions." *Washington Law Review* 43 (1967):115–78.

Cheung, Steven N. S. "The Structure of a Contract and the Theory of a Non-Exclusive Resource." *Journal of Law and Economics* 13 (1970):49–70.

Christy, Francis T., Jr. "Economic Criteria for Deep Sea Minerals." *International Lawyer* 2 (1968):224–42.

————. "A Look at Fisheries Issues." *Marine Technology Society Journal*, July 1974, pp. 56–59.

————. "Marigenous Minerals: Wealth, Regimes, and Factors of Decision." *Symposium on the International Regime of the Sea-Bed: Proceedings*. Rome: Accademia Nazionale dei Lincei, 1970. Reprinted by Resources for the Future, Inc., Reprint no. 87. Washington, D.C., August, 1970.

Clarkson, Kenneth W. "Economic Effects of Work Requirements in Leases to Develop Seabed Resources." *Virginia Journal of International Law* 15 (1975):795–814.

————. "International Law, U.S. Seabeds Policy, and Ocean Resource Development." *Journal of Law and Economics* 17 (1974):117–42.

Coase, R. H. "The Federal Communications Commission." *Journal of Law and Economics* 2 (1959):1–40.

————. "The Lighthouse in Economics." *Journal of Law and Economics* 17 (1974): 357–76.

————. "The Problem of Social Cost." *Journal of Law and Economics* 3 (1960):1–44.

————. "United States Policy Regarding the Law of the Seas." In *Mineral Resources of the Deep Seabed*. U.S. Congress, Senate. Committee on Interior and Insular Affairs, Hearing before the Subcommittee on Minerals, Materials, and Fuels. 93rd Cong., 2d Sess., pt. 2, March 5, 6, 11, 1974, pp. 1160–74.

Coombs, L. F. E. "Right- and Left-hand Dominance in Navigation." *Journal of Navigation* 25 (1972):359–69.

Crutchfield, James. "The Marine Fisheries: A Problem in International Cooperation." *American Economic Review, Papers and Proceedings* 54 (1964):207–18.

Cummins, Philip A.; Logue, Dennis E.; Tollison, Robert D.; and Willett, Thomas D. "Oil Tanker Pollution Control: Design Criteria vs. Effective Liability Assessment." *Journal of Maritime Law and Commerce* 7 (1975):169–206.

Dam, Kenneth W. "The Evolution of North Sea Licensing Policy in Britain and Norway." *Journal of Law and Economics* 17 (1974):213–63.

––––––. "Oil and Gas Licensing and the North Sea." *Journal of Law and Economics* 8 (1965):51–75.

Demirali, Agim. "The Third United Nations Conference on the Law of the Sea and an Archipelagic Regime." *San Diego Law Review* 13 (1976):742–64.

Demsetz, Harold. "Some Aspects of Property Rights." *Journal of Law and Economics* 9 (1966):61–70.

––––––. "Toward a Theory of Property Rights." *American Economic Review, Papers and Proceedings* 57 (1967):347–59.

De Vany, A. S.; Eckert, R. D.; Meyers, C. J.; O'Hara, D. J.; and Scott, R. C. "A Property System for Market Allocation of the Electromagnetic Spectrum: A Legal-Economic-Engineering Study." *Stanford Law Review* 21 (1969):1499–1561.

Eckert, Ross. D. "Exploitation of Deep Ocean Minerals: Regulatory Mechanisms and United States Policy." *Journal of Law and Economics* 17 (1974):143–77.

––––––. "On the International Assignment of Property Rights in Ocean Resources." Paper presented at Annual Meeting of American Economic Association, San Francisco, December 28, 1974. Reprinted in *Congressional Record–Senate*, vol. 121, pt. 1, 94th Cong., 1st Sess. January 23, 1975, pp. 1093–1103.

Emery, K. O. "The Continental Shelves." *Scientific American*, September 1969, pp. 107–25.

Fawcett, J. E. S. "How Free Are the Seas?" *International Affairs* 49 (1973):14–22.

Friedheim, Robert L. "Enclosure Movement of the Oceans." Paper presented at the University of Southern California, Los Angeles, October 30, 1975.

Friedheim, Robert L., and Durch, William J. "The International Seabed Resources Agency Negotiations and the New International Economic Order." *International Organization* 31 (1977):343–84.

Friedheim, Robert L., and Kadane, Joseph B. "Ocean Science in the UN Political Arena." *Journal of Maritime Law and Commerce* 3 (1972):473–502.

Friedman, Alan E. "The Economics of the Common Pool: Property Rights in Exhaustible Resources." *U.C.L.A. Law Review* 18 (1971):855–87.

Froman, F. David. "The 200-Mile Exclusive Economic Zone: Death Knell for the American Tuna Industry." *San Diego Law Review* 13 (1976):707–41.

Furubotn, Eirik G., and Pejovich, Svetozar. "Property Rights and Economic Theory: A Survey of Recent Literature." *Journal of Economic Literature* 10 (1972):1137–62.

Gaskell, T. F. "Position Fixing for North Sea Oil." *Journal of Navigation* 27 (1974): 206–12.

Gordon, H. Scott. "The Economic Theory of a Common-Property Resource: The Fishery." *Journal of Political Economy* 62 (1954):124–42.

Gorham, Michael. "Dividing Up the Minerals of the Deep Seabed." *Federal Reserve Bank of San Francisco Economic Review*, Winter 1978:7–19.

Goria, Charles F. "Compensation for Oil Pollution at Sea: An Insurance Approach." *San Diego Law Review* 12 (1975):717–42.

Hammond, Allen L. "Manganese Nodules (I): Mineral Resources on the Deep Seabed." *Science* 183 (1974):502–3.

———. "Manganese Nodules (II): Prospects for Deep Sea Mining." *Science* 183 (1974):644–46.

Hardy, Michael. "International Control of Marine Pollution." *Natural Resources Journal* 11 (1971):296–348.

Hargreaves, E. R. "Safety of Navigation in the English Channel." *Journal of Navigation* 26 (1973):399–407.

Hedberg, Hollis D. "The National-International Jurisdictional Boundary on the Ocean Floor." *Ocean Management* 1 (1973):83–118.

Hirshleifer, Jack. "The Private and Social Value of Information and the Reward to Inventive Activity." *American Economic Review* 61 (1971):561–74.

Hollick, Ann L. "The Clash of U.S. Interests: How U.S. Policy Evolved." *Marine Technology Society Journal*, July 1974, pp. 15–28.

———. "The Origins of 200-Mile Offshore Zones." *American Journal of International Law* 71 (1977):494–500.

———. "United States and Canadian Policy Processes in Law of the Sea." *San Diego Law Review* 12 (1975):518–52.

———. "United States Oceans Politics." *San Diego Law Review* 10 (1973):467–501.

Holt, S. J. "The Food Resources of the Ocean." *Scientific American*, September 1969, pp. 178–94.

Hood, D. W.; Stevenson, B.; and Jeffrey, L. M. "The Deep Sea Disposal of Industrial Wastes." *Industrial and Engineering Chemistry* 50 (1958):885–88.

Hughart, David. "Informational Asymmetry, Bidding Strategies, and the Marketing of Offshore Petroleum Leases." *Journal of Political Economy* 83 (1975):969–85.

Isaacs, John D. "The Nature of Oceanic Life." *Scientific American*, September 1969, pp. 146–62.

Jannasch, H. W., and Wirsen, C. O. "Deep Sea Microorganisms: In situ Response to Nutrient Enrichment." *Science* 180 (1973):641–43.

Kent, H. S. K. "The Historical Origins of the Three-Mile Limit." *American Journal of International Law* 48 (1954):537–53.

Knight, H. Gary. "The 1971 United States Proposals on the Breadth of the Territorial Sea and Passage through International Straits." *Oregon Law Review* 51 (1972):759–87.

Krueger, Robert B. "The Background of the Doctrine of the Continental Shelf and the Outer Continental Shelf Lands Act." *Natural Resources Journal* 10 (1970):442–514.

Lauterpacht, H. "Sovereignty over Submarine Areas." *British Yearbook of International Law*: 1950, vol. 27, pp. 376−433. London: Oxford University Press, 1951.

Legault, L. H. J. "The Freedom of the Seas: A License to Pollute?" *University of Toronto Law Journal* 21 (1971):211−21.

Leifer, Michael, and Nelson, Dolliver. "Conflict of Interest in the Straits of Malacca." *International Affairs* 49 (1973):190−203.

Levine, Michael E. "Landing Fees and the Airport Congestion Problem." *Journal of Law and Economics* 12 (1969):79−108.

Levine, Michael E., and Plott, Charles, R. "Agenda Influence and Its Implications." *Virginia Law Review* 63 (1977):561−99.

Little, I. C. "The Problems of Operating Mammoth Tankers on the Cape Sea Route." *Navigation: The Journal of the Institute of Navigation* 22 (1975):81−85.

Lowe, A. V. "The Enforcement of Marine Pollution Regulations." *San Diego Law Review* 12 (1975):624−43.

————. "The International Seabed and the Single Negotiating Text." *San Diego Law Review* 13 (1976):489−532.

McGurren, Henry J. "The Externalities of a Torrey Canyon Situation: An Impetus for Change in Legislation." *Natural Resources Journal* 11 (1971):349−72.

McKean, Roland N. "Divergences Between Individual and Total Costs within Government." *American Economic Review Papers and Proceedings* 54 (1964):243−49.

————. "Products Liability: Trends and Implications." *University of Chicago Law Review* 38 (1970):3−63.

————. "The Unseen Hand in Government." *American Economic Review* 55 (1965): 496−506.

Marshall, John M. "Private Incentives and Public Information." *American Economic Review* 64 (1974):373−90.

Matthews, Gwenda. "Pollution of the Oceans: An International Problem?" *Ocean Management* 1 (1973):161−70.

Menard, H. W. "The Deep-Ocean Floor." *Scientific American*, September 1969, pp. 126−42.

Menard, H. W., and Frazer, J. Z. "Manganese Nodules on the Sea Floor: Inverse Correlation Between Grade and Abundance." *Science* 199 (1978):969−71.

Mero, John L. "A Legal Regime for Deep Sea Mining." *San Diego Law Review* 7 (1970):488−503.

Merz, A. W. "Optimal Evasive Maneuvers in Maritime Collision Avoidance." *Navigation: The Journal of the Institute of Navigation* 20 (1973):144−52.

Minasian, J. R. "Property Rights in Radiation: An Alternative Approach to Radio Frequency Allocation." *Journal of Law and Economics* 18 (1975):221−72.

Osgood, Robert E. "U.S. Security Interests in Ocean Law." *Ocean Development and International Law Journal* 2 (1974):1−36.

Oudet, L. "The Economics of Traffic Circulation." *Journal of Navigation* 25 (1972): 60−66.

Pearcy, G. Etzel. "Geographical Aspects of the Law of the Sea." *Annals of the Association of American Geographers* 49 (1959):1–23.

Plott, Charles R. "Axiomatic Social Choice Theory: An Overview and Interpretation." *American Journal of Political Science* 20 (1976):511–96.

Plott, Charles R., and Levine, Michael E. "A Model of Agenda Influence on Committee Decisions." *American Economic Review* 68 (1978):146–60.

Park, Choon-ho. "Fishing under Troubled Waters: The Northeast Asia Fisheries Controversy." *Ocean Development and International Law Journal* 2 (1974):93–135.

———. "The South China Sea Disputes: Who Owns the Islands and the Natural Resources?" *Ocean Development and International Law Journal* 5 (1978):27–59.

Peltzman, Sam. "The Effects of Automobile Safety Legislation." *Journal of Political Economy* 83 (1975):677–725.

Pontecorvo, Giulio. "Fishery Management and the General Welfare: Implications of the New Structure." *Washington Law Review* 52 (1977):641–56.

Ratiner, Leigh S. "United States Oceans Policy: An Analysis." *Journal of Maritime Law and Commerce* 2 (1971):225–66.

"Recent Developments in the Law of the Sea." *San Diego Law Review*, vols. 12–15 (1975–78).

Rona, P. A. "New Evidence for Seabed Resources from Global Tectonics." *Ocean Management* 1 (1973):145–59.

Ruff, Larry E. "The Economic Common Sense of Pollution." *The Public Interest* 19 (1970):69–85.

Schaefer, Milner B. "Freedom of Scientific Research and Exploration in the Sea." *Stanford Journal of International Studies* 4 (1969):46–70.

Scott, Anthony. "The Fishery: The Objectives of Sole Ownership." *Journal of Political Economy* 63 (1955):116–24.

Smith, Vernon L. "On Models of Commercial Fishing." *Journal of Political Economy* 77 (1969):181–98.

Smith, Wayne J. "International Control of Deep Sea Mineral Resources." *Naval War College Review*, June 1972, pp. 82–90.

Sohn, Louis B. "The Council of an International Sea-Bed Authority." *San Diego Law Review* 9 (1972):404–31.

Stang, David P. "Ocean Polemics." *India Quarterly* 29 (1973):138–50.

Stewart, R. W. "The Atmosphere and the Ocean." *Scientific American*, September 1969, pp. 76–86.

Stigler, George J. "A Theory of Oligopoly." *Journal of Political Economy* 72 (1964):44–61.

Swan, Peter N. "International and National Approaches to Oil Pollution Responsibility: An Emerging Regime for a Global Problem." *Oregon Law Review* 50 (1971):506–86.

Swing, John Temple. "Who Will Own the Oceans?" *Foreign Affairs* 54 (1976):527–46.

Thompson, Robert P. "Establishing Global Traffic Flows." *Journal of Navigation* 25 (1972):483–95.

Tinsley, C. Richard. "Mining of Manganese Nodules: An Intriguing Legal Problem." *Engineering and Mining Journal*, October 1973, pp. 84–87.

Umbeck, John C. "A Theory of Contract Choice and the California Gold Rush." *Journal of Law and Economics* 20 (1977):421–37.

Waldichuk, Michael. "Coastal Marine Pollution and Fish." *Ocean Management* 2 (1974):1–60.

Walsh, Don. "Some Thoughts on National Ocean Policy: The Critical Issue." *San Diego Law Review* 13 (1976):594–627.

Wenk, Edward Jr. "The Physical Resources of the Ocean." *Scientific American*, September 1969, pp. 166–76.

Wood, Lance D. "An Integrated International and Domestic Approach to Civil Liability for Vessel-Source Oil Pollution." *Journal of Maritime Law and Commerce* 7 (1975): 1–68.

Young, Elizabeth. "New Laws for Old Navies: Military Implications of the Law of the Sea." *Survival* 16 (1974):262–67.

Young, Richard. "The Continental Shelf in the Practice of American States." In *Inter-American Juridical Yearbook 1950–1951*, pp. 27–36. Washington, D.C.: Pan American Union, 1953.

———. "Further Claims to Areas Beneath the High Seas." *American Journal of International Law* 43 (1949):790–92.

GOVERNMENT PUBLICATIONS AND DOCUMENTS

Canada, Fisheries and Marine Service, Pacific Region. *License Limitation in the British Columbia Salmon Fishery*, by G. Alexander Fraser. Technical Report Series PAC/T-77-13. Vancouver, B.C., July 1977.

———. *Limited Entry and the Salmon Fishery of British Columbia*, by S. Fraser and W. McKay. Economics and Special Services Directorate Internal Report. Vancouver, B.C., June 18, 1976.

United Nations. *Draft United Nations Convention on the International Seabed Area*. United States Working Paper, August 3, 1970 (A/AC.138/25).

———. *Working Paper on the Regime for the Sea-Bed and Ocean Floor and Its Subsoil Beyond the Limits of National Jurisdiction, Submitted by Chile, Colombia, Ecuador, El Salvador, Guatemala, Guyana, Jamaica, Mexico, Panama, Peru, Trinidad and Tobago, Uruguay, and Venezuela*, August 4, 1971 (A/AC.138/49).

———. Food and Agriculture Organization. *Yearbook of Fishery Statistics*. Vol. 36, 1974.

United Nations. General Assembly, 22nd Session, August 18, 1967. *Request for Inclusion of a Supplementary Item in the Agenda of the Twenty-second Session: Declaration and Treaty Concerning the Reservation Exclusively for Peaceful Purposes of the*

Sea-Bed and of the Ocean Floor, Underlying the Seas Beyond the Limits of Present National Jurisdiction, and the Use of Their Resources in the Interests of Mankind, Note verbale dated August 17, 1967, from the Permanent Mission of Malta to the United Nations addressed to the Secretary General (A/6695).

————. General Assembly, 24th Session, Agenda Item 32, December 9, 1969. *Question of Reservation Exclusively for Peaceful Purposes of the Sea-Bed and the Ocean Floor, and the Subsoil Thereof, Underlying the High Seas Beyond the Limits of National Jurisdiction, and the Use of Their Resources in the Interests of Mankind: Report of the First Committee* (A/7834).

————. General Assembly, Committee on the Peaceful Uses of the Sea-Bed and the Ocean Floor Beyond the Limits of National Jurisdiction, August 16, 1972. *List of Subjects and Issues Relating to the Law of the Sea to be Submitted to the Conference on the Law of the Sea* (A/AC.138/66/Rev.1).

————. General Assembly Official Records, 22nd Session, First Committee, 1515th Meeting, November 1, 1967. *Examination of the Question of the Reservation Exclusively for Peaceful Purposes of the Sea-Bed and the Ocean Floor, and the Subsoil Thereof, Underlying the High Seas Beyond the Limits of Present National Jurisdiction, and the Use of Their Resources in the Interests of Mankind: General Debate on Agenda Item 92* (A/C.1/PV.1515).

————. General Assembly Official Records, 24th Session, 1833rd Plenary Meeting, December 15, 1969. *Question of the Reservation Exclusively for Peaceful Purposes of the Sea-Bed and the Ocean Floor, and the Subsoil Thereof, Underlying the High Seas Beyond the Limits of Present National Jurisdiction, and the Use of Their Resources in the Interests of Mankind: Report of the Committee on the Peaceful Uses of the Sea-Bed and the Ocean Floor Beyond the Limits of National Jurisdiction, Report of the First Committee, Agenda Item 32* (A/PV.1833).

————. General Assembly Official Records, 24th Session. *Resolutions Adopted during the 24th Session, 16 September—17 December 1969, Supplement No. 30,* Resolutions 2574A-D adopted at the 1833rd Plenary Meeting, December 15, 1969 (A/7630).

————. General Assembly Official Records, 24th Session. *Annexes,* vol. 1, September 16—December 17, 1969.

————. Inter-Governmental Maritime Consultative Organization. *Ships' Routeing,* 3d ed. London: 1973.

————. International Law Commission. *Yearbook of the International Law Commission.* 1950, vol. 1; 1951, vol. 1; 1953, vol. 1; 1956, vol. 1.

————. Second United Nations Conference on the Law of the Sea, February 8, 1960. *Synoptical Table Concerning the Breadth and Juridical Status of the Territorial Sea and Adjacent Zones: Notes by the Secretary General* (A/CONF.19/4).

United Nations, Third United Nations Conference on the Law of the Sea. May 22, 1974. *Economic Implications of Sea-Bed Mineral Development in the International Area: Report of the Secretary General* (A/CONF. 62/25).

————. Second Session, June 20, 1974. *Organization of the Second Session of the Conference and Allocation of Items: First Report of the General Committee* (A/CONF.62/28).

————. Second Session, July 2, 1974. *Organization of the Second Session of the Conference and Allocation of Items: Decisions Taken by the Conference at its 15th Meeting on 21 June 1974* (A/CONF.62/29).

————. Second Session, July 31, 1974. *United States: Working Paper on the Economic Effects of Deep Seabed Exploitation* (A/CONF.62/C.1/L.5).

————. Second Session, July 16, 1974. *Rules of Procedure (Adopted at its 20th meeting on 27 June 1974 and at its 40th meeting on 12 July 1974)* (A/CONF.62/30/Rev.1).

————. Second Session, August 8, 1974. *United States of America: Draft Articles on Economic Zone and Continental Shelf* (A/CONF.62/C.2/L.47).

————. February 8, 1975. *Economic Implications of Sea-Bed Mining in the International Area: Report by the Secretary General* (A/CONF.62/37).

————. Third Session, May 7, 1975. *Informal Single Negotiating Text* (A/CONF.62/WP.8).

————. Fourth Session, May 6, 1976. *Revised Single Negotiating Text* (A/CONF.62/WP.8/Rev.1).

————. Fifth Session, First Committee, August 20, 1976. *Weekly Report by the Co-chairmen on the Activities of the Workshop* (A/CONF.62/C.1/WR.2).

————. Fifth Session, First Committee, September 16, 1976. *Report by Mr. Paul Bamela Engo, Chairman of the First Committee on the Work of the Committee at the Fifth Session of the Conference* (A/CONF.62/L.16).

————. Sixth Session, July 15, 1977. *Informal Composite Negotiating Text* (A/CONF.62/WP.10).

————. Seventh Session, May 19, 1978. *Reports of the Committees and Negotiating Groups on Negotiations at the Seventh Session, Geneva* (A/CONF.62/62, Annex A).

United States. Commission on Materials Policy. *Toward a National Materials Policy: Basic Data and Issues.* Washington, D.C., 1972.

————. National Commission on Marine Science, Engineering, and Resources. *Our Nation and the Sea: A Plan for National Action.* Washington, D.C., 1969.

U.S. Congress, House. Ad Hoc Select Committee on the Outer Continental Shelf. *Outer Continental Shelf Lands Act Amendments of 1977,* H. Rept. No. 95-590 to Accompany H.R. 1614, 95th Cong., 1st Sess., August 29, 1977.

————. Committee on Merchant Marine and Fisheries. *Deep Seabed Hard Minerals Act,* H. Rept. No. 95-588 to Accompany H.R. 3350, pt. 1, 95th Cong., 1st Sess., August 9, 1977.

————. Committee on Merchant Marine and Fisheries. *Deep Seabed Mining, Hearings before the Subcommittee on Oceanography on H.R. 1270, H.R. 6017, and H.R. 11879,* 94th Cong., 2d Sess., Serial 94-27, May 16, 1975; February 23, 24, March 8, 9, 1976.

————. Committee on Merchant Marine and Fisheries. *Deep Seabed Mining, Hearings before the Subcommittee on Oceanography on H.R. 3350 and H.R. 4582,* 95th Cong., 1st Sess., Serial No. 95-4, March 17, 18, April 19, 26, 27, May 11 and 20, 1977.

————. Committee on Merchant Marine and Fisheries. *National Ocean Policy, Hearings before the Subcommittee on Oceanography, on Oversight to Examine General Ocean Policy for the United States and Law of the Sea Conference Briefing*, 94th Cong., 2d Sess., Serial No. 94-43, June 15, September 9, 16, 17, 1976.

U.S. Congress, Senate. Committee on Armed Services. *Emergency Marine Fisheries Protection Act of 1975, Hearing on S.961*, 94th Cong., 1st Sess., November 19, 1975.

————. Committee on Armed Services. *Extending Jurisdiction of the United States over Certain Ocean Areas, Hearings on S.1988*, 93rd Cong., 2d Sess., October 8–11, 1974.

————. Committee on Commerce. *Emergency Marine Fisheries Protection Act of 1975, Hearings on S.961*, 94th Cong., 1st Sess., Serial no. 94-27, pt. 1, June 6, 1975; pt. 2, September 19, 1975.

————. Committee on Commerce. *The Economic Value of Ocean Resources to the United States*. Prepared at the Request of Hon. Warren G. Magnuson [by Robert R. Nathan and Associates], Pursuant to S.Res. 222, National Ocean Policy Study, 1974.

————. Committee on Commerce and National Ocean Policy Study. *Geneva Session of the Third United Nations Law of the Sea Conference, Hearings*, 94th Cong., 1st Sess., Serial no. 94-30, June 3–4, 1975.

————. Committee on Commerce and National Ocean Policy Study. *A Legislative History of the Fishery Conservation and Management Act of 1976*. 94th Cong., 2d Sess., October 1976.

————. Committee on Commerce and National Ocean Policy Study. *The Third U.N. Law of the Sea Conference*. Prepared at the Request of Hon. Warren G. Magnuson and Hon. Ernest F. Hollings Pursuant to S.Res. 222, 94th Cong., 1st Sess., 1975.

————. Committee on Energy and Natural Resources. *Outer Continental Shelf Lands Act Amendments of 1977*. S. Rept. no. 95-284 to Accompany S.9, 95th Cong., 1st Sess., June 21, 1977.

————. Committee on Foreign Relations. *Conventions on the Law of the Sea, Hearings on Executives J, K, L, M, and N*, 86th Cong., 2d Sess., January 20, 1960.

————. Committee on Foreign Relations. *The Third U.N. Law of the Sea Conference: Report to the Senate* by Senators Claiborne Pell, Edmund Muskie, Clifford Case, and Ted Stevens. 94th Cong., 1st Sess., February 5, 1975.

————. Committee on Interior and Insular Affairs. *Current Developments in Deep Seabed Mining, Hearing before the Subcommittee on Minerals, Materials, and Fuels on Briefing by Ocean Mining Industry*, 94th Cong., 1st Sess., November 7, 1975.

————. Committee on Interior and Insular Affairs. *Deep Seabed Hard Minerals Act*. S. Rept. no. 94-754 to Accompany S.713, 94th Cong., 2d Sess., April 14, 1976.

————. Committee on Interior and Insular Affairs. *Development of Hard Mineral Resources of the Deep Seabed, Hearing before the Subcommittee on Minerals, Materials, and Fuels*, 92nd Cong., 2d Sess., June 2, 1972.

————. Committee on Interior and Insular Affairs. *Mineral Resources of the Deep Seabed, Hearings before the Subcommittee on Minerals, Materials, and Fuels on S. 1134*,

93d Cong., 1st Sess, May 17, June 14, 15, 18, and 19, 1973; pt. 2, 93d Cong., 2d Sess., March 5, 6, and 11, 1974.

————. Committee on Interior and Insular Affairs. *Ocean Manganese Nodules*. Prepared by James L. Mielke, Congressional Research Service, at the Request of Henry M. Jackson, chairman, 94th Cong., 1st Sess., June 1975.

————. Committee on Interior and Insular Affairs. *Outer Continental Shelf Oil and Gas Development, Hearings before the Subcommittee on Minerals, Materials, and Fuels on S.3221 and other bills*, 93d Cong., 2d Sess., May 6, 7, 8, and 10, 1974.

————. Committee on Interior and Insular Affairs, *Outer Continental Shelf Policy Issues, Hearings on Oversight on Outer Continental Shelf Lands Act*, 92d Cong., 2d Sess., Serial no. 92-27, pts. 1–3, March 23, 24, and April 11, 18, 1972.

————. Committee on Interior and Insular Affairs. *Status Report on Law of the Sea Conference, Hearings before the Subcommittee on Minerals, Materials, and Fuels*, 93d–95th Congresses, pts. 1–6, 1973–1977.

U.S. Department of Commerce. Maritime Administration, Office of Policy and Plans. *Potential Effects of Reopening and Expanding the Suez Canal on the Shipment Cost of Crude Oil*, by Joseph A. Gribbin. Mimeo, 34 pp. Washington, D.C., July 1974.

————. National Oceanic and Atmospheric Administration, National Marine Fisheries Service. *Ocean Fishery Management: Discussions and Research*, ed. by Adam A. Sokoloski. National Oceanic and Atmospheric Administration Technical Report NMFS CIRC-371. Seattle, April 1973.

U.S. Department of the Interior. Bureau of Mines. *Mineral Facts and Problems*, 1975 ed. Bureau of Mines Bulletin 667. Washington, D.C., 1976.

————. Fisheries and Wildlife Service. *The Groundfish Industries of New England*, by Edward Lynch et al. Washington, D.C., 1961.

————. Fisheries and Wildlife Service, Bureau of Commercial Fisheries. *An Economic Analysis of Policy Alternatives for Managing the Georges Bank Haddock Fishery*, by Lawrence Van Meir. Washington, D.C., 1969.

————. Geological Survey. *Geological Estimates of Undiscovered Recoverable Oil and Gas Resources in the United States*, by B. M. Miller et al. Geological Survey Circular 725 prepared for the Federal Energy Administration. Washington, D.C., 1975.

————. Geological Survey. *Summary of 1972 Oil and Gas Statistics for Onshore and Offshore Areas of 151 Countries*, by Sherwood E. Frezon. Geological Survey Professional Paper 885. Washington, D.C., 1974.

————. Geological Survey. *Summary Petroleum and Selected Mineral Statistics for 120 Countries, Including Offshore Areas*, by John P. Albers et al. Geological Survey Professional Paper 817. Washington, D.C., 1973.

————. Ocean Mining Administration. *Manganese Nodule Resources and Mine Site Availability*, by Alexander F. Holser. Washington, D.C., 1976.

————. Ocean Mining Administration. *Ocean Mining: An Economic Evaluation*, by Rebecca L. Wright. Washington, D.C., May 1976.

U.S. Department of State. Bureau of Intelligence and Research, Office of the Geographer. *Limits in the Seas, No. 36: National Claims to Maritime Jurisdictions*, 3d ed. Washington, D.C., December 23, 1975.

––––––. Bureau of Intelligence and Research, Office of the Geographer. *Limits in the Seas, No. 36: National Claims to Maritime Jurisdictions*, 3d ed., Supplement. Washington, D.C., 1977.

––––––. Bureau of Intelligence and Research, Office of the Geographer. *International Boundary Studies, Series A, No. 46: Theoretical Areal Allocations of Seabed to Coastal States*. Washington, D.C., August 1972.

––––––. Bureau of Public Affairs. *U.N. Law of the Sea Conference 1975*. Public Affairs Publication 8764. Washington, D.C., February 1975.

––––––. Delegation to the Third United Nations Conference on the Law of the Sea. Unclassified Delegation Report on the Caracas Session. Mimeo, 25 pp. September 9, 1974.

––––––. Delegation to the Third United Nations Conference on the Law of the Sea. Unclassified Delegation Report on Geneva Session, March 17–May 9, 1975. Mimeo, 29 pp. No date.

––––––. Delegation to the Third United Nations Conference on the Law of the Sea. Unclassified Delegation Report on First New York Session, March 15–May 7, 1976. Mimeo, 20 pp. No date.

––––––. Delegation to the Third United Nations Conference on the Law of the Sea. Unclassified Delegation Report on the Second New York Session, August 2–September 17, 1976. Mimeo, 20 pp. No date.

––––––. Delegation to the Third United Nations Conference on the Law of the Sea. Unclassified Delegation Report on the Sixth Session, New York, May 23–July 15, 1977. Mimeo, 21 pp. No date.

––––––. Delegation to the Third United Nations Conference on the Law of the Sea. Unclassified Delegation Report on the Seventh Session, Geneva, March 28–May 19, 1978. Mimeo, 36 pp. No date.

––––––. *Digest of International Law*, ed. by Marjorie M. Whiteman. Department of State Publication 7825. Washington, D.C., 1965.

U.S. Department of Transportation. Coast Guard, Research and Development Center. *Oil Spill Identification System*. Interim Report on Project no. CG-D-41-75. Springfield, Va.: National Technical Information Service, October 1974.

U.S. Department of the Treasury. *Comparative Costs for Oil Shipped by Alternative Routes from the Persian Gulf to the United States*, by David B. Johnson. Mimeo, 10 pp. Washington, D.C., May 24, 1974.

U.S. National Petroleum Council. *Ocean Petroleum Resources*. Washington, D.C., March 1975.

U.S. National Science Foundation, International Decade of Ocean Exploration, Seabed Assessment Program. *Inter-University Program of Research on Ferromanganese Deposits of the Ocean Floor, Phase I Report*. Washington, D.C., April 1973.

U.S. President. Proclamation No. 2667, Natural Resources of the Subsoil and Sea Bed of the Continental Shelf. *Federal Register*, vol. 10, p. 12303, September 28, 1945; Executive Order 9633, *C.F.R.*, vol. 3, 1943–1948.

———. Statement on Oceans Policy, May 23, 1970. In *Weekly Compilation of Presidential Documents*, vol. 6, p. 677.

———. Council on Environmental Quality. *Ocean Dumping: A National Policy.* Washington, D.C., October 1970.

TREATIES, CONVENTIONS, AND AGREEMENTS

Convention on the Continental Shelf. Done at Geneva, April 29, 1958 (effective for the U.S. June 10, 1964). *United Nations Treaty Series*, vol. 499, p. 311; U.S. Department of State, *United States Treaties and Other International Agreements*, vol. 15, pt. 1, p. 471, TIAS 5578.

Convention on Fishing and Conservation of the Living Resources of the High Seas. Done at Geneva, April 29, 1958 (effective for the U.S. March 20, 1966). *United Nations Treaty Series*, vol. 559, p. 285; U.S. Department of State, *United States Treaties and Other International Agreements*, vol. 17, pt. 1, p. 138, TIAS 5969.

Convention for the Prevention of Marine Pollution by Dumping from Ships and Aircraft. Done at Oslo, February 15, 1972. Reprinted in *International Legal Materials* 11 (1972):262–66.

Convention on the Prevention of Marine Pollution by Dumping of Wastes and Other Matter. Done at London, November 13, 1972. Reprinted in *International Legal Materials* 11 (1972):1291–1313.

Convention on the Territorial Sea and the Contiguous Zone. Done at Geneva, April 29, 1958 (effective for the U.S. September 10, 1964). *United Nations Treaty Series*, vol. 516, p. 205; U.S. Department of State, *United States Treaties and Other International Agreements*, vol. 15, pt. 2, p. 1606, TIAS 5639.

Final Act, Inter-American Specialized Conference on "Conservation of Natural Resources: The Continental Shelf and Marine Waters," Ciudad Trujillo, March 15–28, 1956. Washington, D.C.: Pan American Union, 1956. Reprinted in United Nations, International Law Commission, *Yearbook of the International Law Commission, 1956*, vol. 2, pp. 251–52.

International Convention for the Prevention of Pollution from Ships. Done at London, November 2, 1973. Reprinted in *International Legal Materials* 12 (1973):1319–87.

International Convention Relating to Intervention on the High Seas in Cases of Oil Pollution Casualties. Done at Brussels, November 29, 1969. Reprinted in *International Legal Materials* 9 (1970):25–44.

Index